HEALEY WILLAN: LIFE AND MUSIC

F.R.C. CLARKE

Healey Willan: Life and Music

UNIVERSITY OF TORONTO PRESS
Toronto Buffalo London

© University of Toronto Press 1983
Toronto   Buffalo   London
Printed in Canada
Reprinted 1984

ISBN 0-8020-5549-4

Canadian Cataloguing in Publication Data

Clarke, F. R. C. (Frederick Robert Charles), 1931–
Healey Willan: life and music

Bibliography: p.
Includes index.

ISBN 0-8020-5549-4

1. Willan, Healey, 1880–1968.   2. Composers –
Canada – Biography.   3. Willan, Healey, 1880–1968.
Works.   I. Title: Healey Willan : life and music

ML410.W54C52   780'.92'4   C81-094994-6

Photo credits: jacket illustration based on a 1951 photo by Tom Hyland (courtesy Tom
Hyland); St Paul's organ, David Reger; Willan ca 1950 (courtesy Ashley and Crippen); Gladys
Willan, Mary Mason (courtesy Mary Mason); Willan and MacMillan, C.A.G. Matthews
(courtesy C.A.G. Matthews); Willan outside St Mary Magdalene's, Donald McKay (courtesy
Mary Mason); St Mary Magdalene's, J. Fleetwood-Morrow, ARPS; Willan at McMaster, Tom
Bochsler; Willan in 'junk-room,' Don Newlands (courtesy Black Star). The illustration on
page 1 is of Willan at his piano in the Toronto conservatory in 1921. Page 89 shows a manuscript excerpt from an early attempt (ca 1903) at setting Thomas Hood's *Hymn to the Sun*
(courtesy National Library of Canada, Ottawa).

Contents

Foreword

The first time I met Healey Willan was in 1933. It really was not a meeting, rather it was an encounter. As a young music student, I was attending a class in musical history in the old Toronto Conservatory of Music on College Street. I had been sent by the instructor to the principal's office to fetch the key for the gramophone from the secretary. She wasn't there, but the vice-principal, Dr Willan himself, came out of his office at my knock and, after he had learned why I was there, promptly and with good-natured impatience ransacked Miss Hebden's desk until the key was found, accompanied by mutterings of repeated 'Let's see ...' and 'My dear boy!'

Of course I knew who he was. Often over many years, when I was home on holidays from boarding school, I had been taken to the Church of St Mary Magdalene where he appeared to rule over not only the music but also, apparently, the liturgy (and, for all I know, the theology)! Frequently I used to hear my older fellow students talk about Dr Willan, or Healey, or even 'Old Healey' (he was only in his fifties then), and the things he had done and said. In those years he was for me an awe-inspiring presence, more so when, after his dismissal from the conservatory, he scored that tremendous success (albeit a brief one) with the 1936 appearance of his first symphony at a Toronto promenade concert – we were all there cheering. We cheered again in 1937 when *Marche solennelle* (*Coronation March*) and *Coronation Te Deum* were performed, also at the prom concerts.

In the autumn of 1938 Norman Wilks, the executive assistant to the principal of the conservatory, called me in and told me that I had been given a bursary and that I was to study with Willan. 'O frabjous day! Callooh! Callay!' I chortled in my joy. My sessions with Willan were on

Fridays at two and were supposed to be for one hour. Ha! They lasted the whole afternoon. On at least one occasion we went on so long that he had to catch a brief bite at the local quick-and-dirty before rushing over to St Mary Magdalene's in time for choir practice. The first part of the lesson was given over to technique, going over what he had assigned me to do. Once, when I hadn't done enough, he said, 'Godfrey, I like you very much, but you're a lazy blighter!' True. Once he said that he would like his epitaph to be: 'He preachèd two-part counterpoint but nobody believèd him.'

The rest of the lesson he gave over to wide-ranging discussion. Once he said, 'The only two composers who irritate me are Berlioz and Sibelius!' Since both those masters were, at the time, particular enthusiasms of mine, it led to a spirited argument. During another lesson he got on to 'modern' music and showed that Berlioz and Sibelius, after all, were not the limits of his dislike: 'I can get the same effect by beating a garbage can with a metal basting spoon.' In fact he was generally unfamiliar with contemporary trends, and I didn't have the nerve to show him some of the things I was writing. (A few years later when his second symphony was first played my *Two Etudes for Strings* were on the same program. The études were not a new work but he had not heard them before. He said, sadly, 'You didn't show them to me.')

I cherished those sessions with him. He was warm, friendly, and often very funny. For the rest of his life he remained intensely loyal to and interested in his students. He always treated us as equals, and I am sure there were many occasions when he had to resist the temptation to put us down for our juvenile opinions. He never did put us down. He respected our strong points and would not hesitate to seek advice in those areas (my 'strong point' was orchestration and on two occasions he had me orchestrate for him). In important matters, however, he was his own master, turning to his friends and associates for help only in matters of detail in those rare moments of doubt.

I find from Fred Clarke's book that Healey did far more in his years in Britain than he cared to tell me. Since his reticence about that time was not caused by something he wished to conceal, I can only conclude that it was because he thought it not very interesting. But it is interesting. Only rarely did he say anything about the non-musical side of his life in England except for little yarns now and then. He recalled that once when his mother had recovered from an illness she established that fact by saying to Healey, 'Let's go out and knock over a policeman!'

Clarke mentions Willan's happy affiliation with the great London music publisher Novello and Co. The firm operated from a palatial establishment in Wardour Street, Soho, that 'most sumptuous and splendid music shop that London had ever seen – a cathedral to Victorian enterprise and Edwardian self-satisfaction' (Michael Hurd *Vincent Novello – and Company* London 1981). One of the methods of buying music was to go into the showroom, modelled on a Renaissance banqueting hall, examine the samples, and, after you had made up your mind what you wanted, write out your order (composer's name followed by title of the work) and give it to a rather deaf old man who would phone it up to the stockroom. Willan went in and wrote his order, 'R. Supwards: *She Floated down the River.*' The old man bellowed down the blower, 'Arse upwards, she floated down the river!' Immediately the joke spread through the offices and finally into the editorial office of the equally august *Musical Times*. Harvey Grace, the editor, said, 'Only Willan would do that – send him up!' Such is fame.

Although there has been an enormous amount of writing about Willan – Giles Bryant's *Healey Willan Catalogue* contains five pages of bibliography – Fred Clarke's is the first book, and what a book it is. I thought I knew quite a bit about Willan, but much of what Clarke tells us came to me as a revelation. Clarke is well qualified to write the first full-length book on Willan. He was a Willan pupil, so he saw his subject close up. His knowledge of organ and choral music has enabled him to trace Willan's models – it would never have occurred to me that Rheinberger's music was one of them! In writing about Healey's life and work he has left few stones unturned; those left unturned are because of the dictates of discretion or because nobody has found them.

Godfrey Ridout
Toronto, July 1982

Preface

From his arrival in 1913 till his death in 1968, Healey Willan occupied a leading position in Canadian musical life. His activities as composer, organist, choirmaster, teacher, examiner, and administrator enhanced the development of music in this country. Willan lived a long and productive life and ended his days full of years and honours as a grateful country recognized his accomplishments. He was looked upon as the dean of English-speaking composers in Canada and in 1967 was a member of that first small group of distinguished Canadians to be created companions of the Order of Canada.

By the time he left England out of financial necessity at the age of 33 his work was becoming known and highly regarded. His musical style – steeped in Edwardian England, plainsong, and Wagner – was largely settled and would undergo little change. Likewise his personality and outlook altered little; he remained essentially an Englishman to the end of his life.

Willan's reputation was not restricted to Canada. England honoured him with an invitation to compose an anthem for the coronation of Queen Elizabeth II. Some of his music was published in the United States; his work became well known and he acquired many musical friends and admirers there.

The centennial of Willan's birth was observed in Canada (and beyond) in 1980. The Canada Post Office issued a special Willan commemorative stamp, musicians gave special concerts of Willan's music, and universities offered special studies on Willan. A number of his works were rediscovered, performed, and published for the first time.

This book was also a centennial project and is the first full-length book on Willan and his music. The early chapters are mainly biographical; the rest examine, by genre, his enormous musical output – over 800 items, ranging from operas and symphonies to small church pieces. New light on the origins of some of these works is shed. Though Willan's reputation was greatest as a church musician and composer, he wrote much more non-sacred than sacred music. He had two quite distinct styles of writing, secular and sacred. It is my opinion that all of Willan's work merits attention and that concentration upon the church music would prevent an accurate or balanced view of his life's work.

Willan research owes a great debt to Giles Bryant and his *Healey Willan Catalogue*, published in 1972 by the National Library of Canada in Ottawa. The sorting out of Willan's many manuscripts and works – some apparently forgotten by Willan – was a monumental task, aided greatly by Willan's daughter, Mary Mason. Bryant developed the 'B' numbers to catalogue Willan's output. These numbers, which run by category rather than chronologically, are particularly useful for identifying untitled and unfinished compositions. I wish to thank Mr Bryant for his help and advice.

The bulk of Willan's musical estate is now, largely at the instigation of Mrs Roland Michener, a friend and former pupil, the property of the Music Division of the National Library. Dr Helmut Kallmann, chief of the Music Division and a personal friend of Willan, gave me much assistance, encouragement, and advice. Dr Stephen Willis, head of the Manuscript Collection of the Music Division, was very helpful, as were Drew Smith and Maria Calderisi of the library staff. At the National Library I had access to Willan's letters, musical manuscripts, tapes and transcriptions of interviews conducted with Willan by a number of people, and other materials.

My special thanks go to Healey Willan's sons, Michael, Bernard, and Patrick, and their wives, to his daughter, Mary, his cousin, Angela, and to many other people who knew and worked with Willan whose reminiscences did much to fill out the picture. My gratitude goes also to Hunter Bishop, archivist of the Arts and Letters Club, Toronto.

I would like to thank Keith Hamel for his careful and elegant drawing of the musical examples which form the extensive appendix to this book. I wish to acknowledge the kind assistance of Dr D.A. Jardine of Queen's University in the computer preparation of the index. My appreciation and thanks to John Parry for his extensive editorial assistance; indeed, the final shape of this book is largely the result of his expertise.

Acknowledgment is owed also to the many holders of copyright on the musical examples and photographs appearing in the book for their gracious permission to use these.

My wife, Martha, proof-read the manuscript. Her encouragement made the work more pleasant.

This book has been published with the help of grants from the Canadian Federation for the Humanities, using funds provided by the Social Sciences and Humanities Research Council of Canada, and from the Publications Fund of the University of Toronto Press, and assistance from the Canada Council and the Ontario Arts Council under their block grant programs. Funds for extensive editorial work on the manuscript were provided by the School of Graduate Studies and Research, Queen's University, Kingston. The Ontario Arts Council provided a grant for the preparation of the musical examples. To all of these my profound thanks.

PART ONE: THE LIFE

ABBREVIATIONS

CMJ *Canadian Music Journal*
HWC Giles Bryant *Healey Willan Catalogue* Ottawa 1972
'Matters Musical' a series of talks given by Willan on CBL radio, Toronto,
    in 1938

1

The years in England
1880–1913

The Willan family can be traced back for many generations and boasted merchants, clergymen, poets and authors, doctors, and schoolmasters. The Reverend Robert Willan, DD, was chaplain to Charles I. Leonard Willan, an Irish poet and playwright, flourished briefly after the mid-seventeenth century. Robert Willan, MD (the elder), and Robert Willan, MD (the younger), were both distinguished medical men of the eighteenth century; the classifications of the latter in dermatology are still used today.

In later life Healey Willan used to make much of his Irish extraction, especially when he was working on his opera *Deirdre*. Journalists wrote on occasion that Willan was Irish-born! It is difficult to trace any recent Irish input into the Willan family, though Willan's mother was a Healey, and the name Healy was common in Ireland (the name also has Yorkshire connections). Healey Willan claimed that Leonard Willan was 'somewhere back there, hanging on the family tree.'

According to another family story, the name Willan meant granite in old Celtic. An Irish chieftain, who did not bother to build fortifications around his land, was asked the reason by his neighbour. The chieftain answered, 'My archers are my fortifications.' Thereupon his neighbour said, 'If your archers are made of brick, you must be made of granite.' Later the Willan clan, having suffered defeat in Ireland, fled to Normandy. There they eventually joined Duke William and went over to England with him in 1066. This is supposedly why there are so many Willans in Kent.

The Willan family crest consists of three stars and a moon. Willan would say – with his typical humour and mock irreverence – that his ancestors were bootleggers of Hennessey's three-star! None of the Willans appears to have distinguished himself as a musician. Eleanor Healey was an amateur pianist who played the organ for church services before her marriage. Her husband was not musical, though he enjoyed music.

Healey Willan's parents, James Henry Burton Willan and Eleanor Healey, were cousins and had been married in 1879. At the time of their son's birth, they were living in Balham, Surrey, a suburb of London. Willan's father was a 'chemist' (druggist or pharmacist) and the path which had led him to that profession had been somewhat disappointing. He had attended medical school with his brother, George Thomas, and was nearly finished when a financial crisis forced the brothers from school. George found a patron, was able to return to school, and duly became a medical doctor. James had to give up his medical studies just a few months short of the goal. He was obliged to take up the profession of chemist. This position, though respectable, placed him on a lower social level than that of some other members of the Willan clan (notably George). This turn of events caused some resentment, which had some influence on James's son, Healey.

James and Eleanor's only son, James Healey, was born 12 October 1880, in Balham (12 October was also the birthdate of two famous musical figures who would later influence the boy: the conductor Arthur Nikisch and the composer Ralph Vaughan Williams). Some two years later the Willans moved from Balham to Beckenham. Beckenham was a pleasant town in Kent, and James Willan set up a pharmacist's business there. The Church of St George in Beckenham was to have a particular influence on their son. This church was 'Anglo-Catholic' (or 'high church') in its rite and, as a result of the Tractarian Movement, had abandoned Anglican chant and had restored plainchant (or Gregorian chant). Thus the glories of plainchant rang in Healey Willan's ears from a tender age. By the time he was four he would slip out the back door of his house whenever he could and go over to the church to hear the organist, G.J. Hall, practising the organ every day from noon to one o'clock. The rector encouraged the boy and told his father, 'Let him come in as much as he likes ... He's absorbing something that I can't give him ... Nobody else can.'

In June 1885 a daughter, Mary Helen, was born. The children's paternal grandmother lived with the family. The children had a St Bernard, Meg, who acted as a sort of watchdog for them and used to love to go to the railway bridge with them to watch the trains. Willan loved animals – particularly dogs – all his life.

By the age of five Healey was learning to play the piano, under the direction of his mother and a governess, Miss De Bruin. In later life he said, 'I could read music before I could read words,' and he seemed to know instinctively that a particular note written on a page of music corresponded to a particular note on the piano. He discovered the basic chords at the keyboard long before he knew their names. The organ also interested the child, and he used to sit at the window and pull the knobs on the blinds, imagining that he was pulling organ stops.

Home life seems to have been happy. The parents were good-tempered, loving, kind, and concerned. Healey and Mary had a strict and careful upbringing, but one filled with happiness and love. The bonds proved enduring, for Healey remained devoted to his mother after the death of his father in 1913, and Mary, who remained unmarried, lived with and cared for her mother until the latter's death in 1938.

By 1889 the family had moved to Eastbourne in Sussex (overlooking the English Channel). There was a fine choir school at Eastbourne, associated with St Saviour's Church. 'Anglican choir schools, after the Education Act of 1870, provided first class general schooling as well as strict and thorough training in music, especially church music. Entry into such schools became highly desirable because nowhere else was free schooling as good' (Godfrey Ridout *CMJ* 3, 1959, 5).

On 1 May 1889, his mother's birthday, Healey climbed the steps of the school 'feeling as if I were going to my execution.' He was given an audition by the organist, Walter Hay Sangster. Sangster first asked Willan to read five verses from a psalm and then gave him an unfamiliar hymn to look at. The tune of the hymn was printed on the left-hand side of the page, with the words on the opposite side. Willan had first to sight-sing the unfamiliar tune and then sing it again with the words. Sangster then played random notes on the piano ('dodged all over the countryside,' in Willan's words) and expected the boy to sing them. The singing of a few scales having determined the range of his voice as second soprano, the candidate was finally given the second soprano of the first dozen bars of the final chorus of S.S. Wesley's *The Wilderness* to sight-read. Willan passed all these tests easily and was admitted to the school as a second soprano probationer. On Advent Sunday he was made a full chorister, after six months as a probationer (rather than the usual twelve months) – a school record.

Willan had heard only plainchant at St George's, Beckenham, and when he heard his first Anglican chant at Eastbourne he thought it was very funny and that the boys were having a joke. 'I laughed and was promptly punished by the master. This may be one of the reasons for my lack of affection for Anglican chant.' There were some thirty to forty boys at the school. They received instruction in English, mathematics, history, and classics (Latin and Greek) and had to participate daily in choir rehearsal. Each day, also, they would sing evensong at five o'clock in St Saviour's Church. Some of the boys, Willan among them, also studied harmony, counterpoint, and organ with Dr Sangster. As in many English schools, sports were emphasized, particularly football and cricket. Willan, though not a gifted cricketer (he could bowl but not bat), was enthusiastic and remained interested in cricket scores and players all through his life. In 1938 he wrote: 'Singing is a very important factor in developing good breathing, and therefore good physical health ... The football teams of choirboys were often more than a match for many a team of older boys, due to the fact that they could last through a hard tussle and have sufficient energy in reserve for that all important last ten minutes of the game.'

Willan was a weekly boarder, going home on weekends. He was regarded as an excellent scholar, receiving good reports for both work and conduct. His musical studies progressed rapidly, and by the age of ten he had composed a march in A for piano (since lost) which he played at a school concert. Willan recalled that it was 'just like Mendelssohn ... I only went to three sharps in those days!'

By the age of eleven Willan had become sufficiently proficient on the organ to play for some of the evensongs. The organ at St Saviour's was a large one of four manuals built by Walker ('a lovely old four-decker') and was considered to have a particularly fine swell. Willan was a 'lanky lad' and thus had no difficulty in reaching the pedals or handling the large console. Willan was being entrusted also with some of the choir practices. Older boys, naturally, resented being corrected by a younger boy. Healey would often be set upon afterwards. The headmaster appointed Willan 'choir monitor' – a personal representative of the headmaster who must not be subject to any physical violence. ('Probably saved my life,' Willan often said.)

Willan soon became 'book boy' (setting out everything ready for choir practice), school librarian, and then assistant librarian at the church. Finally he reached the top post, that of 'Doctor's boy.' 'I had to be at church well ahead of whenever Dr Sangster was to play, find his places, dust the keys and prepare everything for him so that all he had to do was to sit down and doodle' (*Music* Dec 1967, 25). Another duty consisted of turning on the water, for the organ was a hydraulic instrument.

Discipline was strict. Willan never had cause to regret the disclipline he learned in his youth. He told of an experience while a choir boy. The boys were on an outing by the cliffs at Eastbourne and young Willan had gone to the edge. Suddenly the master shouted, 'Willan, lie down!' and the boy obeyed immediately. A strong wind was blowing and there had been stories of people being blown over the edge of the cliffs. The master crawled out to the edge and pulled the boy back. Willan considered that this decisive action by the master and his own disciplined response may well have saved his life.

At Christmas 1893 Willan received for Form IV the first English prize and the Memoriter prize. Both were books of poetry, one *The Poetical Works of Thomas Hood*. Willan's first five songs, which he composed in 1899, were to poems by Hood. At Easter 1894 Willan received a holiday task prize – a book on Handel. Despite a slight stutter (traces survived to old age), Willan took part in theatricals and, according to one account, was outstandingly good in a 'dude' part.

Willan's voice broke when he was fourteen or fifteen but he had become so useful to Dr Sangster that he was kept on for an additional year. When Willan left the school Dr Sangster said, 'Well, Willan, I'm sorry you're going. I'll miss you. You never had a great voice, but you never missed a lead.' Willan never ceased to delight in quoting this remark.

Willan thought he had received the finest training possible and that a choir school education was the best. He wrote: 'Statistics taken over a period of twenty years in one of the Oxford colleges ... showed that twenty-five percent of the students studied music, and that these twenty-five percent won seventy-five percent of the prizes ... offered by the college.'

After leaving school Willan spent a year at home in self-study. He was not healthy and 'had to take it easy for some months' while he gained strength. He worked on strict counterpoint and the solving of contrapuntal puzzles. 'Writing counterpoint lost its terrors for me, and I have always enjoyed it.'

Willan's father had some thoughts about his son becoming a schoolmaster. His headmaster thought he could become a successful lawyer or parson. But there was now no question in his own mind – and had not been for some time – that music would be his profession. His parents gave him what help and encouragement they could.

The family had moved to St Albans, Hertfordshire, a cathedral town northeast of London. Willan continued his organ studies and in 1897, at the age of sixteen, became an Associate of the Royal College of Organists (ARCO). He had actually tried the examination six months earlier but had failed because his feet had skidded on the slippery organ pedals during his playing of Schumann's *Fugue in B Flat*. Six months later he went back to try again, this time carrying a piece of billiard chalk in his pocket. Just before he went in to play he chalked the soles of his feet carefully and had no problem (though he did leave white footprints across the carpet).

In January 1898 he was appointed organist of the small mission church of St Saviour's in St Albans. Though this was a fairly 'high' church, nothing very ambitious musically had been attempted. The congregation did sing the creed and the gloria, however, and knew four settings of them (Merbecke, missa quinta toni, Dumont, and missa de angelis). The choirmaster was a Mr Scroggs. The organ was poor. A new one was dedicated the following September, but it was quite small, with twenty-two stops spread over three manuals and pedal (seven on the great, eight on the swell, four on the choir, and three on the pedal). There were no mixtures, mutations, or super-octave couplers, and only two of the stops were at two-foot pitch. Nevertheless the designer, a Mr Speers (Mus B), managed to get through Wagner's *Prelude to Parsifal* at the morning dedication, and Willan managed Bach's '*St Anne*' *Fugue* as well as Lemare's *Romance in D Flat* at the evening service.

Soon after, the St Cecilia Choir was formed at the church. This choir, consisting entirely of women, sang choral Eucharist on all holy days occurring upon weekdays. For this group Willan wrote his *Sanctus, Benedictus and Agnus Dei in E flat* for SSA and organ. This work was published ca 1900 (similar efforts by Speers and Scroggs remained in manuscript) and was Willan's second publication; the eucharistic anthem *All Hail! All Hail!* was printed ca 1898.

In June 1899 Willan became choirmaster as well as organist. In June 1900 he resigned in order to take a better-paid position at Wanstead in northeast London. He was presented with a gold watch at his leaving. He returned to St Saviour's at least once, for the dedication of the nave by the bishop of Colchester on All Saint's Day 1902. In St Albans Willan had lived with his parents. He had had a room on the ground floor of the house to use as a music and work room; it had a door leading to the garden and another leading to the back stairs. When he was composing both doors would be closed.

On 14 July 1899, Willan became a Fellow of the Royal College of Organists (FRCO). The marking standard was and is very high; most people do not succeed the first time. Sir Hubert Parry, when presenting the diploma to the eighteen-year-old Willan, asked if he were there on behalf of his father! Willan was the youngest candidate to have gained the diploma. Among the examiners was Willan's teacher, Dr William

Stevenson Hoyte, organist of All Saints', Margaret Street, London, and a renowned instructor. (Among Hoyte's other pupils were Gustav Holst and Leopold Stokowski, then organist of St James, Piccadilly.) Of Hoyte Willan later said, 'It was his idea to be at old Margaret Street ... I know he was offered two or three of the biggest jobs in England ... He wasn't interested ... He was where he wanted to be ... He stayed there till he died, in all forty-nine years.' It was the leading Anglo-Catholic church in London.

Willan gave his first organ recital at Christ Church, Wanstead, on 10 December 1900 and followed it with six more during 1901 and 1902. He served also as choirmaster and gave lessons in piano, organ, harmony, and counterpoint. He lived at 43 Gordon Road. In 1901 he gave recitals in St Peter-upon-Cornhill and St John the Baptist, Upping, and three recitals at St Andrew's, Leytonstone, and in 1902 two further recitals in St Peter-upon-Cornhill. Between 1900 and 1912 he gave some thirty recitals in more than a dozen churches. Many were in aid of the organ funds of the churches; they probably provided little income for Willan.

Willan was now studying piano at an advanced level with Evlyn Howard-Jones, a noted expert on the piano music of Brahms. He wanted to specialize in Brahms, but his aspirations were circumscribed by an old injury to his right elbow. Nevertheless the sessions were valuable and Willan became a fine, sensitive pianist.

Willan liked to describe his marathon piano lesson with Howard-Jones. He arrived at 10 am and went on till lunch break. Howard-Jones invited him to lunch. Then the two men did a run-through of Beethoven's *Emperor Concerto*, with two pianos, which took them to tea time at 4 pm, when Arthur Schnabel arrived. Schnabel had lost his copy of Brahms's *Piano Concerto No. 2*, a work he was supposed to perform the following week. Another concerto run-through on two pianos resulted, with Schnabel playing the solo and Howard-Jones and Willan the second part. All three went to dinner at 7 pm, returning to Howard-Jones's house at 9. Thereupon Schnabel and Howard-Jones engaged in musical antics all evening during which Willan acted as time-keeper to see who could play Chopin's *Minute Waltz* faster. Drinks followed, and Willan eventually left at 2 am.

Willan attended many London concerts. His first experience with orchestral music was in 1901, when he heard Schumann's *Symphony No. 2* at one of the Crystal Palace Saturday concerts under August Manns, 'with his large shock of white hair and his white kid gloves.' He first heard Dvořák's *Symphony No. 8* in 1903, played by the London Philharmonic Society, and Bach's *B Minor Mass* in 1905, sung by the Bach Choir in Queen's Hall under Walford Davies. The Promenade Concerts in Queen's Hall under Henry Wood were another important resource for Willan in those days before recordings.

Willan first heard Beethoven's *Symphony No. 9* in 1901: 'I had just enough money to take the train from the suburbs to Liverpool St. Station. From there it was a four-mile walk to Queen's Hall, where I bought a bun, a glass of milk and my ticket. After the performance there was the walk back to Liverpool St. Station, train to Stratford (London suburb), then on foot the rest of the six miles home.'

Throughout his life Willan maintained that Arthur Nikisch, who specialized in Tschaikowsky and Wagner, was the greatest of all conductors. Willan heard most of Wagner's music dramas conducted by Nikisch, and these works had a profound effect on his style of composition, particularly in his secular works. Willan's love of Tschaikowsky doubtless began with Nikisch. One of Willan's most cherished experiences was being introduced to Nikisch, who invited him to lunch.

In St Albans Willan had become acquainted with the Toulmin family. One of the family, Mary, Lady Carberry, became Willan's sponsor at the Royal Academy of Music in London. Her sister, Lilian Toulmin, became a pupil of Willan, and in 1901 he wrote one of his best early songs, *To Electra*, for her; it was his fifteenth art-song.

In the winter of 1902 Willan was busy preparing his choir at Christ Church, Wanstead, for a performance with orchestra of Mendelssohn's *Lobgesang*. The concert (on 13 March) was probably Willan's début as an orchestral-choral conductor. The following year he continued his activities in this direction, conducting three performances of *The Pirates of Penzance* in February in the county hall in St Albans, and a performance of an abridged version of Mendelssohn's *St Paul*, with orchestra, by his church choir at Wanstead on 8 March. For the latter performance Gladys Hall (later Willan's wife) was at the piano. At Wanstead Willan made his only appearance as soloist with orchestra, performing Josef Rheinberger's *Concerto No. 1 in F* for organ and orchestra.

After Willan left Christ Church in 1903 he still served as conductor of the Wanstead Choral Society (active 1904 to 1906), which had probably grown out of Willan's choral-orchestral productions at the church. Willan's first concert with the choral society, on 21 January 1904, featured Elgar's *Banner of St George* and W.H. Bell's *Hawke* (with Gladys Hall again at the piano). On 3 November Willan conducted the same group in a performance of Coleridge-Taylor's *Song of Hiawatha*, with 'chorus and orchestra of 130 performers.' Willan conducted also Stanford's *The Revenge*, Elgar's *Caractacus*, and Handel's *Messiah*. At the Stanford concert Willan's own 1904 song cycle, *In Praise of Music* (on poems by Robert Herrick), was sung.

In mid-1903 Willan became organist-choirmaster at St John the Baptist, Holland Road, Kensington (London). He had been rejected as too young in 1900, but now was the successful one among 130 candidates. At his trial choir practice he had been able to subdue the rather unruly boys and make them work for him. He controlled the boys effectively and won their loyalty and affection.

St John the Baptist was Anglo-Catholic and one of the more prestigious church positions in London. The organ had four manuals and thirty-three speaking stops and was situated in an organ gallery about forty feet above the ground floor of the church in the north transept. Sometimes, according to Willan, the London fog would get into the church; up in the organ gallery he could not see his choir but only hear the voices coming out of the fog.

In November 1904 Willan was elected an associate of the Philharmonic Society. His diploma was signed by Parry, Sir Edward German, and Francesco Berger (secretary of the society and Gladys Hall's teacher). This diploma allowed Willan to attend rehearsals of the London Philharmonic Orchestra, and he always tried to attend if Nikisch was conducting.

On 29 November 1905, Willan married Gladys Ellen Hall, a well-trained musician who had studied at the Royal Academy of Music. The marriage was to last almost sixty years, until Gladys's death in 1964.

In 1906 Willan became conductor of the Thalian Operatic Society, which specialized in Gilbert and Sullivan operettas. Its stage director, Geoffrey Snelson, had learned his craft under William Gilbert and Arthur Sullivan. In 1906 and 1907 Willan conducted *The Pirates of Penzance*, *Patience*, and *Iolanthe*.

Willan's first important publications were beginning to appear. In 1906 came *There Were Shepherds* (a Christmas anthem), *The Office of Holy Communion in G* (dedicated to the choir of Christ Church, Wanstead), *Magnificat and Nunc dimittis in B Flat* (dedicated to the choir of St John the Baptist, Kensington), *Fantasia on 'Ad Coenam Agni'* for organ, and *Romance in E Flat* for violin and piano. In 1907 there followed *While All Things* (a Christmas anthem), *I Looked, and Behold, a White Cloud* (a harvest anthem), and six songs (of the fifty he had composed by then!). Some other works (eg, the *Te Deum in B Flat*) had been composed but were not published till later.

When Willan first came to St John the Baptist in 1903, he went to live with the Woods family at 12 Minford Gardens, West Kensington. After his marriage, he and Gladys moved to a flat at 34 Avonmore Road, Kensington. Their first son, Michael Healey, was born 20 February 1907. Edward Bernard arrived 14 February 1909, and Patrick Kingston on 21 February 1911. The family needed larger quarters and took up residence at 5 Sydney Road, Ealing.

In addition to playing at St John the Baptist, Willan would often play evensong at All Saints, Margaret Street (Hoyte's church). He was also organist for two other organizations: the Guild of All Souls and the English Church Union. 'They had one or two big festivals during the year and I used to organize those festivals and conduct the music, and I trained the choir for them.'

Willan was fond of rowing and during the summer would hire a boat from Mitcham's Boathouse, Twickenham, and go out on the river three or four nights a week. (On weekends the boats were more expensive to hire.) Throughout his life he remained fond of the sea and made many transatlantic voyages. Upon being told once that he looked like a naval commander, Willan replied that but for his poor eyesight he would have wished a naval career!

In 1908 Willan took part in the St Albans Pageant. For it he wrote one of his finest organ pieces, *Epilogue in D Minor* (published 1909). The pageant was held on a very hot day and Willan, dressed as a monk, had to walk one and a quarter miles in procession wearing a heavy serge robe. On 7 September 1909, Willan's song *The Tourney* was sung, with piano accompaniment, at a Promenade Concert in Queen's Hall, London.

During Willan's period in London, Sir Richard Terry was director of music at Westminster Cathedral, and his services attracted musicians from far and wide to hear the then seldom-sung Renaissance polyphony. His performances of works by Palestrina, Victoria, and by the composers of the Tudor school had a great effect on Willan and influenced his interpretation of this music in performance and his own liturgical compositions. Willan attended some of the Thursday evening parties in Terry's house, at which this music was discussed.

For some years Willan had been associating with Francis Burgess. Burgess's writings, lectures, and demonstrations were a major factor in the revival of plainsong and its re-establishment in a number of churches. Willan's love of plainsong went back to his childhood days at St George's, Beckenham, and Burgess served to fan the flames. Willan gained a reputation as an authority on vernacular plainsong (ie with English rather than Latin texts). Burgess was musical director of the London Gregorian Association, which he founded in 1870 for the 'promotion of the study and practice of plainsong within the framework of the English Rite.' He arranged annual festival services of Gregorian music at St Paul's Cathedral, London, in which choirs of more than 600 voices took part. Willan became a member of the association in 1910 and at the 1911 festival was a sub-conductor for a choir of some 800 voices. Realizing that he had to gain some height in order to be seen, Willan commandeered a chair on which was sitting a priest – Father Hiscocks (later rector of Willan's church in Toronto!).

In 1912 Willan contributed a faux-bourdon for the processional hymn for the Gregorian festival. It was praised by C.W. Pearce as 'worthy of the best 16th century traditions.' The hymn-tune was a Rouen church melody. Also in 1912 Willan illustrated the accompaniment of plainsong for a lecture Burgess gave at the Royal College of Organists.

While at St John the Baptist Willan began his association with the publishing firm of Novello and Co. Henry Brooke, son-in-law of the owner and a financial director of the firm, was a sidesman at St John the Baptist. His son Harold (a pianist who had studied in Germany) and Willan became close friends. Another good friend was Jack Littleton, son of the owner. Willan referred to himself and his two friends as 'the three musketeers.' Willan knew John E. West, musical editor at Novello, and Elliott Button, also on the staff.

Willan was given occasional employment as proof-reader at Novello. He proof-read Elgar's *Symphony No. 2, The Music Makers,* and *Violin Concerto.* While reading a proof of the latter Willan observed a C sharp in the oboe part against a C natural in the violin part. Thinking that this could not be correct, Willan noted it and sent it to Elgar. The score came back with the following notation: 'C sharp in both parts. Thank you. E.E.' An impromptu first performance was given in John West's office. The proofs of the solo part had just come in and, as the ink was not quite dry, the single sheets of music were tacked up around the walls. A violinist happened to be present. While Willan and Brooke at the piano played the orchestral score, the violinist walked around from sheet to sheet, sight-reading the solo part! Willan actually met Elgar briefly on two or three occasions and knew Stanford a little.

Willan did not make much money in London. His church paid a salary of £100 per annum, which was not sufficient to cope with the demands of his growing family. He never had more than six or eight private pupils at a time, either at Christ Church or at St John the Baptist, and the sums he earned proof-reading for Novello were small. Willan had some expensive tastes. All through his life he insisted on being well dressed and was noted for this even in these London days; as a young man he always carried a cane. (Willan's father had had to accept a lower professional and social status than he had hoped for; perhaps Willan wanted to appear a 'somebody' regardless of his background and modest profession.) After his father's death in early 1913, Willan had to contribute to the upkeep of his widowed mother and his sister.

Willan suffered from stomach troubles, probably aggravated, if not brought on, by financial worries. He went to see a Harley Street specialist and was told not to eat pastry, fried foods, or twice-cooked meats. These things thus became outlawed in Willan's family thereafter, and items such as pies and carbonated drinks were never allowed in the household.

In 1909 Willan's *Ave verum corpus* for choir and organ had appeared. This work made its way to Canada, where it made a great impression on Richard Tattersall, organist of St Thomas' Church, Toronto, and Dr Alexander Davies, an enthusiastic and influential music amateur. Two important figures at the Toronto Conservatory of Music had recently died: Dr Edward Fisher, the principal, and Dr Humfrey Anger, the head of the theory department. Dr Augustus Stephen Vogt succeeded to the principalship in 1912, and one of his first tasks was to find a replacement for Anger. Davies mentioned Willan to Vogt. Davies went to London during the summer of 1912 and, at Vogt's request, looked Willan up and sounded him out. They became good friends. After Davies's return to Canada, Vogt invited Willan to become head of the theory department. Beset with financial problems, Willan accepted. Even though he loved his church and London dearly, he could no longer afford to remain. Willan set sail for Canada in 1913, leaving his family to follow later. His leave-taking from his church was painful: 'I nearly wept whan I played my last service there – I did – I was very happy there.'

By 1913 Willan had written seventy-six songs, nine partsongs, six canticle settings, four communion settings, a number of organ pieces (including *Prelude and Fugue in C Minor* and *Prelude and Fugue in B Minor*), some piano pieces, the dramatic cantata *Cleopatra*, a choral-orchestral setting of Browning's *Prospice*, and a symphonic poem, *Through Darkness into Light*. He made beginnings on three or four string quartets, a piano quartet, a piano trio, several sonatas, and some small chamber pieces. There are unfinished fragments of three works for piano and orchestra and of several symphonic poems and other pieces for orchestra; some of the symphonic fragments are in full orchestral score and some exist only in condensed score. At this time Willan did not consider himself primarily a church composer. He was anxious to attempt all forms of composition and absorbed many influences, including the piano and chamber music of Brahms; the symphonic idioms of Wagner, Strauss, Tschaikowsky, and Elgar; and the songs and church music of Parry and Stanford. Had Willan's career not been steered increasingly into the sphere of the church, by both material circumstances and personal inclination, and had he had independent means, he might well have composed a great deal more chamber and symphonic music. Certainly the interest was there and, judging from the fragments, the imagination.

In a 1912 article in *Organist and Choirmaster* (15 April, 308–10) the theorist C.W. Pearce states, 'Mr. Healey Willan ... we have known for some time past, not only as a gifted organ player possessing keen ecclesiastical instincts, but also as a writer of some merit both for the instrument of his choice and for the choir which he knows so exceedingly well how to accompany. But we were not prepared to find him – as we undoubtedly do – a composer of what may conveniently be termed 'all round' proclivities ... The perusal of this parcel of music has given us much real pleasure. It shows that Mr. Willan is a composer of high artistic aims and ideals. Evidently he is content to write for *art* rather than the *mart* ... He deserves every encouragement to go on.' (Pearce was not acquainted with the additional promise shown in the many unpublished songs and the unfinished chamber and symphonic works.)

Willan had been successful in England; by 1913 his career was well under way. He would doubtless have received in due course the knighthood and other honours which that country bestows upon its leading musicians. But he did not have a private income (as many of his cathedral organist colleagues had); he could not survive in relatively low-paying positions, however prestigious. The move to Canada was a necessity.

2

The conservatory years
1913–1936

Musical Opinion had high hopes for Willan's success in his new land: 'We are confident that he will prove himself a worthy inheritor of the fine traditions of the Toronto Conservatoire. To foster the growing sense of Canadian nationality in music is no light thing to undertake, but the placing of such a task in the hands of a fertile and versatile Irishman[!] is a wise move on the part of the Toronto authorities and a high compliment to us on this side.' At the end of his long life Willan would be affectionately termed the 'dean of Canadian composers'; many Canadian composers and musicians would learn from him. But Willan's musical idiom had already been largely set in England and would undergo little change. His arrangements of French-Canadian chansons aside, there would be nothing particularly Canadian about his music; during all his years in Canada he would continue to think and live as an Englishman.

Willan arrived in Canada on 25 August 1913. His position as head of the theory department at the Toronto Conservatory of Music carried an annual salary of $3,000, a sizable sum. Three weeks after his arrival in Toronto he was offered the position of organist and choirmaster at St Paul's Anglican Church, Bloor Street. The gigantic building, of cathedral proportions, was just under construction. Willan was offered $1,200 per annum (he had been receiving £100 per annum at St John the Baptist). An annual income of $4,200 (plus extras) could be considered a fairly comfortable situation in 1913. Willan's financial woes were alleviated, even though he had a wife and three sons – and a mother and sister – to support.

On the morning of 18 September Willan gave his first public lecture in Canada to a large audience in the lecture hall of the Toronto Conservatory of Music. He spoke on musical form, with piano illustrations taken largely from the Beethoven sonatas. At the end of the lecture a complete sonata was played by Viggo Kihl, a Danish pianist who had just arrived in Canada and who had lived near Willan in London. A newspaper account referred to Willan's 'remarkably good presence and carrying voice.'

For the first few weeks Willan played the services in the old St Paul's Church (the present parish hall). During the service of dedication for the new building, on 30 November, Willan's *Te Deum in B Flat* was sung. The new organ was not ready, and for five months Willan played the services on a large Steinway grand piano, sometimes assisted by the Blachford String Quartet. The new organ was opened on 29 April 1914. Willan was assisted by Miles Farrow, organist of the Cathedral of St John the Divine, New York. Farrow's organ at St John The Divine had 106 stops; the new Casavant at St Paul's had 107! The magnificent instrument – perhaps the finest in Canada at the time – inspired Willan to write his greatest organ work, *Introduction, Passacaglia and Fugue in E Flat Minor*.

Having such an instrument at his disposal spurred Willan to a flurry of recital giving. By the end of 1917 he had played nearly thirty organ recitals at St Paul's. After 1917 his recitals at St Paul's virtually ceased, though he remained at the church till 1921. He did continue to give recitals in other locations, however. He played some forty recitals in fourteen locations (the University of Toronto, the Toronto Conservatory of Music, and twelve churches). Some recitals were out of town, in Ottawa, London, Stratford, Galt, and Orillia, and often involved the opening of a new organ.

Willan's recitals doubtless helped to enliven the meagre Toronto musical scene. The contrast to London must have been striking. Willan wrote:

Yonge Street then was about as interesting as an English village street. It seemed like the last place in the world for the development of music. There was an orchestra of a sort (a few musicians from the Toronto Conservatory Orchestra which disbanded at the beginning of the First World War). There were also a few visiting artists, but the only annual event of musical interest was the Toronto Mendelssohn Choir Festival – about three days of it at Massey Hall, usually in February. Even with the Mendelssohn Choir, in those days one felt a dearth of music. Sir Robert Falconer told me when I arrived: 'You'll find a great difference here; it's a young country; the errand boy has not yet learned to whistle.'

In November 1914 Gladys and the three boys arrived. War had broken out: they had already seen the Zeppelins over London, and they had to travel on a troop ship, the SS *Grampian*. Willan had an apartment in the Wellsborough on Jarvis Street and for a while the family lived there. The boys attended the old Havergal College downtown. It was a girls' school, but it took small boys at the time. Soon the family moved to a more spacious apartment at 26 Park Road, and the boys were sent to Rosedale Public School.

However, Willan would soon be less than pleased with the language and habits his boys were picking up at public school. As a result in 1917 he sent his eldest son, Michael, to Ridley College, a private boarding school in St Catharines, for two years on a Leonard Scholarship (arranged by the rector at St Paul's, Canon Cody). After the two years, Willan was presented by mistake with a bill for $2,000. Willan pulled his son out of Ridley and sent him to Upper Canada College, a private school in Toronto, as a day boy. Eventually all three boys would be sent to Upper Canada College.

Their education doubtless caused Willan some financial hardship. His English background and class-consciousness probably influenced his decision. The English school system was much different from that in North America, and he perhaps overestimated the advantages of a private school in Canada. At least one of Willan's sons later questioned the advantage and said that he and his brothers tended to be treated as second-class citizens by their wealthy fellows.

In 1914 Willan began his long association with the University of Toronto when he was appointed an examiner for the faculty of music. The position was part-time, since the faculty offered only a bachelor of music degree (extramurally) and conducted examinations for it. Willan had to give only four lectures per annum. Dr Vogt was dean of the faculty (as well as the principal of the conservatory). Among Willan's colleagues as faculty examiners were Dr Albert Ham, organist of the Anglican cathedral in Toronto, and Dr F.A. Mouré, the university organist.

In 1915 Willan became a member of the Arts and Letters Club in Toronto. Willan would come to love his club very much; it was almost his 'home away from home.' Here he got to know his fellows in all fields of the arts and found the exchange of ideas stimulating. He also made contacts which were of assistance to his own career. The Arts and Letters Club had its premises over the police station on Court Street; in the spring of 1920 it moved to its present location on Elm Street. Willan's portrait, painted by Adrian Dingle in the 1930s, later hung in the club.

Late in 1915 Willan's new *Trio in B Minor* for piano, violin, and cello – the composer's largest chamber work – was premiered. He had begun it in England and had completed it in Canada. Willan played the difficult piano part himself for this performance. The violin and cello parts were played by two of Willan's colleagues, Frank Blachford and Leo Smith. According to a newspaper report, 'It was the opinion of many competent critics present that this trio is the most important contribution of its kind to British music during the past decade.'

In April 1916 a complete program of Willan's music was performed in the conservatory's concert hall under the auspices of the Toronto Clef Club. The concert consisted of the great *Prelude and Fugue in C Minor* for organ, played by Richard Tattersall, nine of Willan's songs, his new *Sonata in E Minor* for violin and piano (probably its first performance), and *Trio in B Minor*.

In Toronto Willan's fame as a composer was spreading beyond the little *Ave verum corpus* of 1909! In 1914 he had written two works for chorus and orchestra: *England, My England* and *Dirge for Two Veterans* (the orchestration was completed for the former but not the latter). In 1915 he had completed his piano trio and his major piano work, *Variations and Epilogue on an Original Theme* for two pianos. The year 1916 saw the appearance of two of his greatest works: *Sonata No. 1 in E Minor* for violin and piano, and *Introduction, Passacaglia and Fugue* for organ. All these works are secular, large-scale, and predominantly instrumental.

In 1917 Willan returned to sacred works, with the *Benedictus and Jubilate Deo in B Flat Major* for choir and organ, the anthem *In the Name of God We Will Set up Our Banners* (also for choir and organ), and the unaccompanied eight-part motet *The Dead* ('How They So Softly Rest'). The latter, Willan's first motet, was written for the Toronto Mendelssohn Choir in memory of its members killed in the war. *In the Name of God* had been composed for the depositing of the colours of the 169th Battalion, Canadian Expeditionary Force, by the 109th Regiment, in St Paul's.

Willan was beginning to get job offers from big churches in the United States. Ca 1918 the Church of the Advent in Boston tried unsuccessfully to get Willan to go there. In 1919 Dr Vogt was in poor health and was ordered by his doctors to take a six-month rest. The conservatory's board of governors, after granting Vogt a leave of absence, appointed a 'committee of four' to undertake the musical part of his duties. Willan was chairman; the other members were Ernest Seitz, Viggo Kihl, and Paul Wells. Vogt did not recover as much as had been hoped and when he returned to his duties he could only undertake part-time office hours. To provide assistance for Vogt, the board appointed Willan assistant musical director (ie vice-principal). Willan would remain in that position for sixteen years.

Willan's interest in the theatre found an outlet in 1919 with the Hart House Theatre. Hart House, built by the Massey Foundation and presented to the University of Toronto in 1919, had in its sub-basement a theatre seating 450 to 500 people. This theatre became the home of the University Players Club, whose first resident director was Roy Mitchell. In 1921 Mitchell was succeeded as director by Bertram Forsyth, who held the post till 1925. From 1919 to 1925 Willan acted as musical director for the theatre, composing incidental scores for fourteen productions, ranging from Greek dramas, through Shakespeare, to a new play by Forsyth himself. Willan's first incidental score for Hart House was *The Chester Mysteries*.

Willan's rent at Park Road had been $60 a month, but was suddenly doubled. The time was ripe to buy a house, and Willan purchased one, at 139 Inglewood Drive. Originally a farmhouse, it stood in 1920 in comparative isolation. At the time of Willan's death, in 1968, it was virtually in downtown Toronto! (The address of 139 Inglewood fell in with Willan's contention that his life had been to some extent guided by 3s and 13s. He had received his letter of appointment from Dr Vogt on the third day of the third month of 1913 in his thirty-third year. Three weeks after his arrival in Canada he had been invited to be organist at St Paul's. He had lived at 26 Park Road – which is twice 13 – and then at 139 Inglewood Drive – which is 13, and 3 squared.) With a new house and three boys attending Upper Canada College, Willan had to trade in his fine grand piano for an upright. (Later Mason & Risch would lend him a small grand piano which he would keep all his life.)

In June 1920 Willan was granted the degree doctor of music (honoris causa) by the University of Toronto, and on 11 July his wife gave birth to their fourth child, and only daughter, Mary. In the summer of 1921 he wrote his choral masterpiece, *An Apostrophe to the Heavenly Hosts*. Father Hiscocks and Dixon Wagner provided the lovely mystical text. This unaccompanied work for eight-part double chorus and mystic choir was commissioned for the Toronto Mendelssohn Choir by its conductor, Dr Herbert Fricker.

St Paul's Church was in the evangelical or low church Anglican tradition. In his early days at St Paul's Willan's high church sympathies did not seem to worry him unduly, possibly because he did not wish to rock the boat while establishing himself in his new country. He also loved the magnificent organ at St Paul's for his organ recitals.

After 1917 Willan's recitals at St Paul's virtually ceased. Correspondence ca 1920 between Willan and his mother hints that Willan was looking for an opportunity to move back to England. In the summer of 1921, Willan recalled, 'I said to my wife, "I'm getting fed up with St Paul's," and she said, "I know you are." "Well," I said, "I've drawn a line and I shall tell nobody what that line is, but if anybody puts their little toe half an inch over that line, I'm going." She said, "Well, if you say so, I expect you will." I said, "You're darn right I will." And on October 10th they did just that – put their toe over the line. I wrote my resignation right away, but waited to the twelfth to mail it to give myself a birthday treat' (Parker tapes).

Willan's relationship with Canon Cody had always been friendly, even in disagreement. This friendship would continue for many years after Willan left St Paul's.

Stories abound regarding Willan's tenure at St Paul's. There is a story of Willan extemporizing a chorale prelude on *How Dry I am* just after prohibition had been declared; or playing *The Robber's March* while the collection was being brought forward. Willan's son Bernard remembers sitting, as a small boy, on the organ bench beside his father with various admirers standing around. One of the admirers asked what one of the pistons was for. 'For the beer!' replied Willan. Another story concerned a rather poor tenor singing an equally poor piece of music at a wedding for which Willan was playing. During the tenor's final long note Willan muttered 'Oh shut up!' and pressed the full organ button, thereby 'obliterating the blighter.'

One factor in the timing of Willan's resignation from St Paul's may have been that he had his eye on another position. Father Hiscocks had earlier approached Willan for help in finding an organist for his church, St Mary Magdalene's, Toronto. Hiscocks wished to make his church Anglo-Catholic, but had had little luck in finding a suitable organist. Willan had assisted Dr C.T. Rogers at some choir practices at St Mary Magdalene's during January and February 1920 and had given a lecture to the congregation on plainsong in the late spring.

When Willan resigned from St Paul's he telephoned Father Hiscocks to find out if he had found an organist. He hadn't. Willan said he thought he had someone who would be all right and would bring him round for dinner. When Willan arrived at Hiscocks' house, the latter said, 'Come in, old man. Where's your friend?' Willan answered, 'What friend?' Hiscocks said he thought Willan was bringing an organist with him. Willan said, 'Dammit, you're getting snooty, aren't you? I've come to apply for the job.' Willan and Hiscocks sat up till the small hours planning. Willan was to be not only organist and choirmaster, but also precentor. (A precentor in an English church or cathedral had absolute charge over the music and was often a member of the clergy. The term is not much used in Canada.) Willan began his duties on Advent Sunday 1921.

The Church of St Mary Magdalene had only a chancel choir, including boys, but Willan wanted a gallery choir as well. After some structural alterations, access for the choir to the back gallery was made. Some years later the organ console was moved up there also. Willan now had two choirs at St Mary's and eventually divided up the musical portions of the high mass in the following manner.

1 The ritual choir, a male choir in the chancel of the church, sang all the propers of the mass in plainsong (introit, gradual, alleluia, offertory, and communion). The plainsong was accompanied by the organ (the pipes located directly behind the ritual choir, even though the console was put up in the gallery).

2 The gallery choir was a choir of mixed voices which sang the Kyrie, sanctus, benedictus, and Agnus Dei of the ordinary of the mass (ie the missa brevis) as well as the motet. The gallery choir always sang unaccompanied.

3 The congregation sang the hymns, and the credo and the gloria from the ordinary. Willan by this time felt that the gloria and credo, being long texts, must be congregational, sung in plainsong to a small number of settings which the congregation would know well. ('I think nothing is more dismal than to hear a highly trained choir warbling away at an interminable credo.') Willan would have five settings of the gloria and four of the credo ('The people know them backwards'), following the pattern he had found at St Saviour's, St Albans, in 1898.

These changes were not accomplished all at once, or without opposition. It took Willan several years to remove the boys from the chancel choir. He still had boys in the fall of 1924. In January 1922, the church and its vicar were the subjects of harsh and bitter attacks in the local press. Ontario was very much under the influence of the Orange Lodge in those days, and thus the ritual, ceremonial, vestments, and services were vigorously condemned as smacking of popery. Within the Church of England in Canada the cleavage between high and low elements was much more severe than it is now.

Despite the criticism and the opposition, Hiscocks and Willan carried on according to plan. Within his first year there Willan had put St Mary Magdalene's on the musical map. The Montreal *Standard* reported on 30 December 1922: 'The gallery choir ... gave exquisite and expressive renderings of a number of motets and carols ... Plainsong as sung at St Mary

Magdalene's is an inspiration, an uplift and a delight ... The responsorial and antiphonal chants were exceedlingly well rendered ... The organ accompaniments were magnificent ... The people of Toronto are fortunate indeed in having in their midst an organist and a choir so capable of making plainsong attractive and inspiring.'

Willan had gone to St Mary Magdalene's at considerable financial loss. His salary at St Paul's had been $1,500 per annum in 1921; his honorarium at St Mary's would be next to nothing. Despite its fame, the parish would remain a poor one. However, as vice-principal of the Toronto conservatory, Willan did not depend upon the church for a livelihood and could thus afford to be there, doing what he really wanted to. He found there a 'sense of home – absolute completion.'

In 1922 Willan was elected president of both the Canadian College of Organists and the Arts and Letters Club. He was the first musician to hold the latter office, and he set the club constitution to music: 'I sat up most of the night with a small group of dear old chums, moderately stimulated by a bottle of gin, and with their help and encouragement I put together a potpourri of themes for the entire constitution. We even included *Nobody Knows the Trouble I've Seen* to represent members behind in their dues ... Eventually we had the high honour of having the whole thing sung for us, and sung superbly, by the touring members of the Savoy Opera Company.'

Another work Willan wrote for the club that year, *Choral March* for male choir and small orchestra, became the processional march for the club's Christmas festivities. In 1960 Sir Ernest MacMillan reported: 'The *Choral March* is still almost invariably a feature of the Christmas Dinner festivities, and Healey Willan's setting of the constitution always appears on the agenda of the annual meetings.'

Willan's compositions were becoming more widely known. MacMillan had played *Introduction, Passacaglia and Fugue* at Timothy Eaton Memorial Church in 1922, and the great Canadian-born virtuoso Lynnwood Farnam had played the work in 1923 at Westminster Cathedral, London. On 13 February 1923 the Toronto Mendelssohn Choir gave another performance of *An Apostrophe to the Heavenly Hosts*, after which, according to the newspaper report, Willan received a 'salvo of applause.'

In 1923 the Christmas cantata *The Mystery of Bethlehem* was published and had a highly favourable reception. As a result Willan received a request from Ann Arbor, Michigan, to compose a large (one-hour) choral work for its 1925 May Festival. H.W. Gray had agreed to publish such a work. Willan did not comply with the request. His unfinished work for several choirs and organ, *In the Heavenly Kingdom*, has a title page dated June 1924. Perhaps it is the beginning of the piece for Ann Arbor. Willan gave his first organ recitals in the United States, in Albany and Rochester, in 1923. At the end of the Albany recital he improvised a complete sonata in three movements on themes submitted by the audience!

Willan's church music had consisted of anthems, canticles, and communion settings for choir and organ. Now, since he was not using the organ, except to accompany hymns and plainsong, his interest shifted to the writing of unaccompanied church pieces, and in 1924 six motets he had written for his gallery choir were published. He composed many more such works for his church.

On 6 April 1924, Willan made one of his rare appearances as an orchestral conductor, directing a string orchestra at Hart House in a performance of several of Bach's double and triple concerti (Viggo Kihl was one of the solo pianists). The works by Bach were billed as 'new to Toronto audiences!' Other performances later that year included his playing of his *Trio in B Minor* in the Hart House Theatre, an organ recital in Winnipeg, and the accompanying of a song recital in Ottawa. In Winnipeg he gave a lecture on plagiarism in music at the convention of the Manitoba Music Teachers' Association. The program included a performance of Willan's *Sonata No. 2 in E Major* for violin and piano (1923).

From time to time throughout his career Willan was approached by authors – of varying degrees of competence – to set their words to music. A number of typed and hand-written texts exist among the composer's papers; pencilled comments indicate that he may have considered them for musical settings at one time or another. They include a preliminary sketch for an opera libretto entitled *La Longue Traverse*; an untitled libretto of what appears to be an operetta set in the country of Cockaigne; a play called *Poems Should Be Read Aloud*, suggesting 'recurring soft music ... throughout the play'; and the text of a ballet, with three solo voices and orchestra, called *The Miracle of the Valley of Dry Bones*. Also among the papers are a number of poems, some of which were doubtless sent to Willan in the hope that he would set them to music. In 1924 he was asked to write an operetta (or song cycle!) on a text called *Loranya*, or *The Spell of a Hindu God*. Willan considered the text 'too short for an operetta and too long for a song cycle.' At least that was his diplomatic reply!

In 1926 Dr Vogt, who had brought Willan to Canada, died. It might have seemed logical for Willan to succeed him as principal of the conservatory. But the position was given to Ernest MacMillan. MacMillan was a good administrator, but many people felt that the job should have gone to Willan. The latter continued as vice-principal for ten years.

On 10 February 1926, a recital of Willan's works was held in Montreal, at the Church of St Andrew and St Paul. The program included *Introduction, Passacaglia and Fugue* for organ, *Trio in B Minor*, and *An Apostrophe to the Heavenly Hosts* (sung by the Montreal Elgar Choir). Some songs, motets, and *Sonata No. 2* rounded out the concert. The program was well received by the critics: Lawrence Mason of the Toronto *Globe* wrote, 'Until the advent of Dr Willan, Canada did not possess a creative genius of Dr Willan's art standard, and today he stands in the front rank among living composers.'

On 23 February 1925, Willan played an organ recital in Buffalo, and on 28 July 1926, in Philadelpia. The latter was part of the Sesquicentennial International Exposition celebrating 150 years of American independence. At this recital Willan played his new chorale prelude *Puer nobis nascitur* (the first of nearly one hundred chorale and hymn preludes he wrote).

In April 1927 Willan was vocal and choral adjuducator in Port Arthur and Fort William for the first Northwestern Ontario Musical Competition Festival. Adjudicating music festivals, as well as examining for such bodies as the Toronto conservatory and the Canadian College of Organists, became part of his career. The extra money was doubtless welcome!

Concerts devoted to Willan's works continued to be arranged from time to time. One was put on 10 November 1927 by the Women's Musical Club of Toronto. At this event Mme Dusseau sang eleven of Willan's songs, and Harry Adaskin played both of Willan's violin sonatas.

Willan wrote his last incidental score for the Hart House Theatre in 1925, and his association with that group apparently ended at that time. However he arranged several ballad operas between 1927 and 1930, including an arrangement of *The Beggar's Opera* for voices, flute, clarinet, and strings. For his ballad opera *L'Ordre de Bon Temps*, set in Champlain's Port Royal of 1606, Willan arranged twelve French-Canadian folksongs for voices and small instrumental ensemble. *L'Ordre* was written for a Canadian folksong festival at Quebec in May 1928. The première took place on 25 May with Willan conducting the production from the harpsichord. Some of the melodies had been collected by the Canadian folksong pioneer Marius Barbeau. J. Murray Gibbon did the English translations. (The following year there appeared two volumes of Willan's arrangements for voice and piano of chansons canadiennes collected by Barbeau.)

Later in 1928 Willan composed his *Missa brevis No. 1*, the first of fourteen for St Mary Magdalene's.

At the end of August 1929, Willan was in Banff, Alberta, to attend the performance of his third ballad opera, *Prince Charlie and Flora*, at the Highland Gathering and Scottish Music Festival. For this work he had arranged a number of traditional Scottish melodies. The words were written by J. Murray Gibbon, who also organized the festival. *Prince Charlie and Flora* was repeated at the 1931 festival.

In late 1929 Willan's *Sonata No. 1* was getting an airing again, in Winnipeg and in Toronto. On 29 December an 'Evening with Healey Willan' was held at the Royal York Hotel in Toronto. Willan led his choir in his own and other choral works, performed his *Sonata No. 2* (with Donald Heins, violin), and Harvey Robb played several of Willan's organ pieces and transcriptions on the big Royal York organ. This charity concert raised $105.77 for the Hospital for Sick Children.

In 1930 Willan worked on his fourth ballad opera, *The Ayrshire Ploughman*, from traditional Scottish melodies. It was intended for performance at the Scottish Music Festival at Banff that year. He also gave organ recitals in Winnipeg and Chicago.

Willan had stated that he could write music anywhere, any time, regardless of noise or disturbance. His friends at the Arts and Letters Club decided to put him to the test. Willan was placed on a stage, with Ernest MacMillan playing the piano, Elie Spivak practising a Bach violin concerto, and a gramophone blaring some jazz. Willan was handed a poem by J.E. Middleton to set to music. He set the words to a vocal line supported by a figured bass. Later he went home and reworked the piece, which was eventually published as a part song for SA and piano, *When Belinda Plays*.

Willan's family had been growing up. The three boys were now all out of school. None went on to university. Each had gone into the stockbroking business. The great crash of 1931 cut their careers short, however, and they were out of jobs. Their father had to help them all.

In March 1931 there was a second Montreal concert of Willan's works, at Tudor Hall. On the program were *Trio in B Minor* and *Sonata No. 1*, along with some anthems and songs. Willan was not merely a 'Toronto' composer. Later that year the Feast of the Dedication at St Mary Magdalene's (15 October) was a special occasion for Willan, for he opened the restored organ. The console had been moved up into the gallery and its action, which had been pneumatic, was now electric. Willan gave three further recitals on the instrument during Advent.

Willan's good friend Lynnwood Farnam had died the year previous at the age of 45. Willan and Farnam had both been students of Hoyte in London. At one time Farnam had been organist of Christ Church Cathedral, Montreal. The cathedral was having a service, on 23 November 1931, at which a memorial bust would be dedicated. Willan was invited to give the oration at the service. He composed his fine funeral motet, *O King to Whom All Things Do Live*, for the occasion, and it was sung by the choir.

In 1932 Willan played no less than six organ recitals on the restored organ at St Mary Magdalene's. Though the organ was only a smallish three-manual instrument of thirty-one stops, Willan managed to play his *Introduction, Passacaglia and Fugue* on it as well as *Sonata on the 94th Psalm* by Reubke. The organ's sound was sweet and mellow, but it was basically a liturgical instrument. It lacked the resources of the St Paul's organ, yet Willan loved it dearly.

Willan was appointed University of Toronto organist in 1932. The four-manual Casavant organ of seventy-six stops was located in Convocation Hall and was used for university ceremonies and organ recitals. Dr Mouré, university organist since 1912, had retired. The position was a purely honorary one, but it did give Willan charge and use of a fine recital instrument. He was to play many recitals and convocations on it over the next thirty-two years. Willan was appointed by Dr Cody, by this time president of the university. In Willan's own words, 'There had been all sorts of silly stories about animosity between Dr Cody and myself, which were untrue. We were always very good friends.' Cody was a strong supporter of Willan in the years ahead.

Willan's madrigal choir, the Tudor Singers, was founded in 1933. The group started with about twenty voices, but by 1935 there were close to thirty. It was decided to cut the numbers to ten (three sopranos, two altos, two tenors, and three basses) in order to have a more professional standard and to perform the music more authentically. The singers often sat around a table when they sang, as they would have done in a manor house of the period. The ladies wore Tudor-style dresses. Willan, seated at a spinet, on which he would give notes and sometimes play introductions, would direct the group from the end of the table. The repertoire was not entirely secular, as motets were also included. The singing of the ensemble was much praised by the critics. Perhaps the high point of critical acclaim came in 1936, when the Tudor Singers were chosen to perform illustrations for a lecture in Toronto on Tudor music given by E.H. Fellows. After the lecture Dr Fellows paid high tribute to the group for the correctness of its interpretations. The Tudor Singers were active until the outbreak of war in 1939, when the male singers joined the armed forces and the group disbanded.

Willan's church choir also sang some outside engagements (eg a Hart House concert in 1932 and a Christmas concert for the Lyceum Club in 1934). The rehearsals for these groups kept Willan busy. The Tudor Singers rehearsed twice a week; the church choir once. Then there was Sunday evening service at St Mary's, after which there was usually a short rehearsal.

Willan was busy at least four evenings a week. He was rarely home in the evenings except on Saturdays. His typical day during this period would begin with his coming down to breakfast at 8 am in his dressing gown. After breakfast he would read the comics, the cricket scores, and concert reviews. He would then bathe, dress, and leave the house about 10 am. When Willan left the house all the family would wave. They became known as the 'waving Willans of Inglewood Drive.' Willan never owned a car and always took the St Clair Avenue streetcar to work; he knew all the streetcar drivers and liked to chat with them. He would often not return home till 10 pm.

From 1933 to 1935 Willan, in addition to performing his regular examining duties, set the examinations in all the courses for the bachelor of music and doctor of music degrees for Bishop's University in Lennoxville, Quebec. During this time he was also president of the Canadian College of Organists again.

In 1935 Willan first met three women who would be close friends for the rest of his life: Margaret Harmer and Margaret Gillespie joined St Mary's choir, and Margaret 'Peggy' Brown (later Drynan) joined the Tudor Singers (and the St Mary's choir the following year).

In the summer of 1935 Willan sailed to England. On board ship he wrote his *Mass of St Hugh*, which had been requested by Sir Sydney Nicholson for the Royal School of Church Music. It seems he could indeed write music anywhere and any time! On 31 July he addressed an organists' conference at the Royal College of Music in London. He took the opportunity to note his displeasure at the state of Anglican church music in Canada, declaring 'The Anglican Church in Canada is at least thirty years behind the mother church in ceremonial music. The main idea of the cathedral service is to induce contemplation, but the young and vital Canadian mind does not approach religion from a contemplative angle. Canadian congregations regard with jealous interest the size of the organ, the number of pipes and the mileage of its intestines, and hanker to possess organs with chimes.'

The Toronto Conservatory of Music had been experiencing financial difficulties during the Depression, but had continued with the help of Col Gooderham and others. When Col Gooderham died, the conservatory's board of governors decided that drastic action had to be taken. In a letter to conservatory faculty and graduates, the president, Col F.H. Deacon, stated, 'Economies have been forced upon us, and included some unavoidable measures, taken only with keenest regret. One of the moves that was dictated by circumstances was the abolition of the post of vice-principal.' Willan's duties as vice-principal would cease on 31 August 1936, but the office would exist for another year. Willan would have a year's leave of absence on full salary.' This arrangement made it possible for Dr Willan, if he wished, to retain his office, telephone, secretarial assistance and all the conveniences afforded him as vice-principal, while entirely free to pursue his own work. It was always the hope of the governors that Dr Willan should remain a valued member of the staff as a teacher and lecturer.'

Willan reacted angrily and bitterly: 'I have never received any official communication from the board of governors regarding the points so eloquently enumerated by Deacon in his statement.' Col Deacon countered by saying that Willan had been acquainted fully with the plan.

The office of vice-principal was replaced by that of executive assistant to the principal. The man appointed was Capt Norman Wilks, teacher and pianist, and holder of a distinguished war record. He had recently run unsuccessfully as a Liberal candidate in two provincial elections. It was reported that Wilks's salary would be $4,000; Willan's had been $3,600.

There was a great outcry in musical circles at Willan's treatment, and many letters were written to the newspapers, including some from outside the country. Some correspondents saw politics behind it all: 'Is Hepburn Party Politics even entering the realm of music in Toronto?' 'Is it possible that Norman Wilks is being offered this job as a plum for his defeat in the past elections?' 'The Toronto Conservatory Board is appointed by the Toronto University Board which is appointed by the Ontario Government!' 'It appears that Dr Willan is another victim of the Hepburn Government.' Many letters extolled Willan's virtues, indicating that it added lustre to the conservatory just to have his name associated with it. Several suggested an endowment or the equivalent to a research fellowship, so that Willan could devote his time to composition.

Concerning the appointment of Wilks, Deacon had said that the board had 'wanted a man who has equal capacity in music and executive work to take over – not the vice-principalship, but a more effective job, as assistant to the president and virtual controller of the Conservatory business.' In a letter announcing Willan's retirement, Deacon had said, 'It is unfortunate that it is not possible for the Conservatory to provide places on its salaried staff for outstanding musicians whose genius may not run to administrative and business routine.'

The board, consisting of successful businessmen and given the task of putting the conservatory back on its financial feet, was attempting to make music a business; 'Music is merchandise' was a phrase heard at the time. Such people expected conservatory officials to 'keep business hours' and be at their desks by nine o'clock each morning. Obviously a man such as Willan did not fit into this pattern.

The Toronto Conservatory of Music Residence Alumnae severed its association with the conservatory, renaming itself the Vogt Society, and terminated its $200 annual scholarship to the conservatory. These actions were taken in loyalty to Willan and to Miss Marion Ferguson, who had been 'retired' as registrar of the conservatory. Those who were upset at Willan's treatment did not blame the principal, Sir Ernest MacMillan. Indeed, Sir Ernest had told the board that he was willing to have his own salary reduced if it would help to save Willan's position. These unpleasant events tended to overshadow the special jubilee concerts and other celebrations for the 1936 fiftieth anniversary of the conservatory.

Willan would not consider continuing with the conservatory after his leave of absence. 'My return would be as a private teacher, and of course I could not do that.' So Willan left the conservatory and set up a studio a short distance away at 68 Grenville Street, near Malloney's art gallery.

As the year 1936 saw a rift in one place, it also saw some healing in another. In July Willan played a wedding service in St Paul's, the first time he had touched the organ there since 1921. 'I was startled to find that every part of that marvellous mechanism was as familiar to me as it was in 1920. I've played many organs ... never one that has quite the gripping magic of St Paul's.'

Also in July Willan was quoted in the newspapers as saying that he expected to have time now to complete *Pageant of Our Lady*, on which he had been working for some time. It was referred to then as a 'sacred opera.' In fact, he never did finish it. Willan said, 'People are turning more and more to what they can see while they listen. That is why ritualistic pageantry has such a tremendous hold on the imagination.' He also expressed some intentions of producing Bach's *St John Passion* at St Mary Magdalene's using 'restrained pageantry' that would help 'to give that work the character that Bach intended.'

The première performance of Willan's *Symphony No. 1 in D Minor* was given on 8 October 1936 at a promenade symphony concert conducted by Reginald Stewart in Varsity Arena, Toronto. Material in its two outer movements appears in sketches and works dating back to at least 1909. The work was enthusiastically received and the audience of 7,000 gave Willan a standing ovation which lasted at least fifteen minutes. One critic referred to the ovation as 'the like of which has not been given an artist in Toronto within easy memory.' The ovation could perhaps be accounted for in part by the sympathy felt over Willan's recent dismissal from the conservatory. Nevertheless, the symphony was a landmark for Willan as a composer. (It was, however, neither the first symphony to be composed in Canada, as is sometimes claimed, nor the first one to be performed. Calixa Lavallée and Clarence Lucas had both written symphonies which have since been lost. Percival Price's *St Lawrence Symphony* received two performances in Toronto in 1934.)

Later in the month Willan was invited to arrange and direct incidental music for the Toronto première at Massey Hall of T.S. Eliot's *Murder in the Cathedral*. For this Willan used two choirs, one male and one mixed, following his pattern at St Mary Magdalene's.

In 1936 Willan had heard his first symphony performed. His reputation as composer, organist, church musician, and teacher had become firmly established in Canada. Canada now looked upon him as one of her own. Willan was fifty-six years old. He was finished with the conservatory, but he was not finished with himself or his work.

3

The university years
1937–1950

Willan's years as vice-principal of the Toronto Conservatory of Music had ended in August 1936, but he remained on salary with a leave of absence until the summer of 1937 when, as we shall see, he joined the Faculty of Music of the University of Toronto. But in the mean time he was free to work on several projects close to his heart. The coronation of King George VI and Queen Elizabeth was to take place in 1937 and inspired him to compose several works, including *Marche solennelle* (*Coronation March*) for orchestra and *Coronation Te Deum* for chorus and orchestra. They would not receive their premières till summer and Willan was free to travel and perform.

On 14 February 1937 Willan's *Symphony No. 1* was played by the Montreal Symphony Orchestra, conducted by Douglas Clarke. Willan went to Montreal not only to hear his symphony played but also to see and hear his old friend and teacher Evlyn Howard-Jones, who was playing Brahms's *Piano Concerto No. 2* on the same program. It must have afforded Willan considerable satisfaction to have Howard-Jones present at the second performance of his new symphony. Brahms's piano concerto must have reminded them both of the days in London with Schnabel. Immediately after the Montreal event, Willan took the train to Regina, where he was to give an organ recital. As Willan stepped off the train at Regina, a newspaper boy tried to sell him a paper. When Willan refused, the boy said, 'You'd better buy it, mister, your picture is in it.' Willan bought the paper and found a two-column picture of himself in it. The following month Willan gave three organ recitals in Toronto, one in Convocation Hall and two at St Mary Magdalene's.

Since the première of Willan's *Symphony No. 1* there had been a feeling in Toronto musical circles that the work should be repeated. In

March the Toronto Symphony Orchestra conducted a poll of its patrons regarding what works should be played on a future 'request' program. In the category of symphonies – and there were quite a number of these – Willan's took second position, immediately behind that of César Franck! The repeat performance took place on 1 July in a Dominion Day Promenade Symphony Concert conducted by Reginald Stewart. On the same program was premièred Willan's *Marche solennelle*, probably his most frequently performed orchestral piece during his lifetime; between the coronations of 1937 and 1953 it was played fifteen times in Canada alone.

Coronation Te Deum was premièred on 10 June 1937 by the Promenade Symphony Orchestra under Reginald Stewart, assisted by the Bach Choir. The performance was in Varsity Arena, Toronto, before an estimated audience of 7,000. The response was so enthusiastic that a repeat performance had to be scheduled for the following week's concert on 17 June. At that performance, the applause was so vigorous that the whole work had to be encored!

Shortly afterwards, Hector Charlesworth wrote in *Saturday Night*: 'It is obvious that the circumstances which have enabled Dr. Willan to devote more time to composition than in the past have had important results for the musical public and have unquestionably enriched Canadian music. His high place as a composer of choral and organ works was already established; but his recent compositions of larger scope definitely place him not merely as the foremost of Canadian composers, but in the first rank of the composers of North America.'

However, Willan's year's leave of absence at full salary would run out at the end of August 1937. There were still his wife and daughter at home (Mary was attending Havergal College). Willan's salary at St Mary Magdalene's had risen only to $90 a month, still considerably less than his salary at St Paul's in 1921. Dr Cody had been working toward the expansion of the University of Toronto's faculty of music into a teaching as well as an examining body. This change would give it the resources to offer intramural degrees. Cody proposed appointing Willan as professor of music in the university. The faculty would use the premises of the conservatory, and there was a close connection between conservatory and university. Willan refused to have anything further to do with the conservatory. Cody asked Willan if he would mind having conservatory students attend some of his lectures, and Willan said he would not mind as long as the standards were the same. Then Cody asked: 'Bearing in mind the conditions of your leaving the Conservatory, would you mind

giving your lectures in the Conservatory?' Willan replied, 'No ... if I, as a
University Professor, give a lecture in a room in the Conservatory, that is
University ground for the time being.' On 28 June 1937, the conserva-
tory's board of governors gave Willan 'permission to take the position of
Professorship of Music so long as the appointment in no way interferes
with the close and harmonious relations between the University and the
Conservatory.' Willan was not to think that he could 'rock the boat' of
the new régime.

From September 1937 to June 1938 Willan received no steady income
outside that from the church. Fortunately he was invited to be guest
professor of composition at the University of Michigan summer school
in 1937. In the spring of 1938 he gave a series of ten talks entitled 'Matters Musical' on radio station CBL in Toronto. He was already sketching a
second symphony. According to the *Toronto Star* of 25 January 1938, he
hoped to have his *Symphony No. 2* ready for performance by Reginald
Stewart and the Promenade Orchestra by that summer. The article was
accompanied by a picture of Willan playing some of his new symphony
on the piano for Margaret Gillespie. However Reginald Stewart resigned
as conductor of the Proms not long after, and the symphony was not
finished as planned. Work on two operas and a piano concerto delayed
its completion till 1948. On 27 March *Marche solennelle* was played by
the Montreal Symphony Orchestra. The Englishness of the music was
not lost on the local critics, the Montreal *Gazette* observing: 'It has a most
impressive opening, and an alternate theme that could hardly have been
written by anyone except an Englishman born and bred.'

Willan's professorship began officially on 1 July 1938. His stipend of
$4,000 per annum was made up of equal contributions of $2,000 each
from the conservatory and the university, the entire amount paid to Willan through the university as his official salary. This latter point was
probably a concession to Willan's sensitivities regarding the conservatory – he could not have tolerated being paid directly by that institution.
He did not allow his name to appear on any official conservatory publication, even though part of his new duties consisted of '7 hours tuition
and lecturing weekly for 40 weeks, setting of papers and sight reading
tests, examination work, etc.,' for it. Willan did have a few 'powerful
friends at court' during the negotiations, including Sir Frederick Banting
with whom he would often have lunch in a little tea room beside the
Banting Institute on College Street.

During the summer of 1938 Willan was again visiting professor of
composition at the University of Michigan summer school. His teaching

for the University of Toronto would commence in the fall and would be primarily concerned with counterpoint and fugue. His colleague from the early days, Leo Smith – also appointed professor of music in 1938 – looked after harmony. The dean of the faculty, Sir Ernest MacMillan, taught some orchestration. The bachelor of music degree requirements at that time were modelled closely on the English bachelor of music. Classes were often small, with the students enjoying close personal contact with their professors.

In 1938 Willan's mother, eighty-seven years old and nearly blind, died. Willan had remained devoted to his mother all his life, and the two had a very close relationship. When he was studying in London, his visits home were irregular and unannounced, yet the night before he would arrive his mother would hear his footsteps, his key being placed in the lock, his cane being hung upon its customary peg, his tread going up the stairs to his room, and the door being opened and closed as though someone had gone in. The next morning she would announce: 'Healey's coming home today – I'd better get his room ready.' She never visited Canada, but Willan would always visit her when he was in England. His *Missa brevis No. 8* (Missa ss Philippi et Jacobi) had been recently composed for her birthday.

On 8 February 1939, *Marche solennelle* was played at Massey Hall by the Toronto Symphony Orchestra conducted by Sir Ernest MacMillan. This was the first time the Toronto Symphony, in its regular season and with its regular conductor, had played a work by Willan. Reginald Stewart, who had conducted earlier performances of Willan's music, would soon leave Toronto; but MacMillan and, more particularly, Ettore Mazzoleni would take up Willan's music. Sir Ernest had stationed three extra trumpets in the balcony of Massey Hall for *Marche solennelle*. The performance was perhaps not entirely to Willan's satisfaction – one critic observed: 'When the conductor looked to the balcony for the composer to rise, Willan was unseen.'

The early summer of 1939 saw the royal visit to Canada of King George VI and Queen Elizabeth, the first time a reigning monarch had visited the country. On 18 May there was a Promenade Symphony Concert in Toronto, 'under Royal Patronage,' in honour of the visit; Willan's *Coronation Te Deum* received its third performance, before an audience of 5,000 people. Unfortunately the concert was held several days before the royal couple's visit to Toronto. On 6 August, while in Vancouver lecturing at the University of British Columbia, Willan conducted the Vancouver Symphony Orchestra in a performance of *Marche solennelle* at an open-air concert in the Malkin Bowl of Stanley Park.

When war broke out in the autumn of 1939, Willan's male choristers began joining the armed services. The Tudor Singers had to be disbanded as a result. Willan was discontented when he wrote to a friend on 24 January 1940: 'I have given up music altogether, and find crossword puzzles and foreign stamps much more interesting. I do my lectures, etc., but outside that music is a revolting thing and I haven't been to a concert for two years.'

Yet Willan kept busy. In the autumn of 1939 his church choir gave three liturgical recitals in its own church and one at St Matthew's Church, Kitchener. In addition, it sang a Christmas concert at Hart House. (With the demise of the Tudor Singers, Willan's choir at St Mary Magdalene's would do more 'outside' work than previously. The remnants of the Tudor Singers were gradually absorbed into the church choir and, in 1945, the two merged groups became the St Mary Magdalene Singers for giving secular concerts.) During the summer of 1940, Willan was back at the University of British Columbia, teaching a music appreciation course at the summer school.

Probably the most spectacular musical event in Toronto in 1940 was the Coliseum Chorus Festival held in Maple Leaf Gardens on 18 October and repeated the next day. The chorus numbered 2,000 (including 250 from Hamilton) and was accompanied by symphony orchestra. The conductors were MacMillan and Charles Peaker. Willan's *Marche solennelle* was played by orchestra alone and his *A Song of Canada* and *Agincourt Song* were sung by the great chorus with orchestra. This great patriotic musical orgy included also Parry's *Jerusalem* and Elgar's *Britons Alert*; at the end a life-sized photograph of the king and queen and Winston Churchill was unveiled under spotlights.

The Coliseum Chorus staged another 'spectacular' on 21 April 1941, a 'Salute to Britain' concert in Massey Hall. For this Willan wrote a short work for chorus and orchestra, *The Trumpet Call*, to words especially written by Alfred Noyes. Most of the piece was sung by the 300-voice 'inner choir,' with the full 2,000 voices joining in only at the climax.

By the summer of 1941, Willan was in a crisis concerning his music. The successful performances of his recent large-scale works doubtless caused him to reconsider his compositional priorities. He found himself limited by church music. The old dreams had come flooding back: of being an all-round composer. He realized, however, that he was 'out of the swim' of things musically. His style had been largely formulated just after 1900 in England and had been reasonably contemporary by English standards (always on the conservative side). By 1940 music had moved on, however, and Willan, by and large, had not. He seriously considered leaving Toronto and moving to Hollywood to write music for films. Arthur Bliss was doing precisely that. Willan's style would probably have been quite suited to the writing of film scores; he would probably have made money and have been able to get away from the petty annoyances of Toronto the Good.

Willan's crisis of the summer of 1941 was also more personal. Willan's warm, almost hypnotic personality had always been attractive to women. Throughout his career in Canada there had been a number of women with whom he had formed relationships. Now he was sixty years old and very much in love with a young woman. He was probably going through what other men often experience earlier – doubts about many aspects of their lives. Willan's church told him he must give up either his affair or his church. This was a difficult decision; St Mary Magdalene's had been a focal point of his life for twenty years. At the end of August 1941, he sent in his resignation.

On 6 and 20 November 1941, two concerts of Willan's compositions took place at the Malloney gallery in Toronto, strangely enough 'under the auspices of The Friends of St. Mary Magdalene.' The first concert included both sonatas for violin and piano, nine songs, and four partsongs. The second included the 1915 *Variations and Epilogue on an Original Theme* for two pianos (probably its first performance), three songs on texts by Heine, three pieces for string quartet,[1] four chansons canadiennes arrangements, and *Trio in B Minor*.

December 1941 saw the beginning of Willan's radio opera *Transit through Fire*. Commissioned by the Canadian Broadcasting Corporation, it was Canada's first radio opera. The libretto was written by the Irish playwright John Coulter, who had been living in Canada since 1936 and knew Willan through the Arts and Letters Club. Although the CBC had hoped for a short ballad opera, *Transit through Fire* turned out to be an hour-long stinging denunciation of the plight of the jobless young people of the 1930s.

While Coulter was writing the libretto, the CBC was apprehensive. Willan was not worried, however; in John Coulter's words, 'nothing scared Healey. With glee and seriousness he abetted me in lambasting the more

---

1 *Three Pieces for String Quartet* (prelude, scherzo, and poem) does not appear as such in the catalogue of Willan's works. The prelude and scherzo were possibly arrangements of two of the six short pieces for organ published in 1910 (later to become *Miniature Suite*). The poem was an original piece for string quartet, completed in 1930 from an unfinished quartet movement of ca 1905.

predatory of the ticker-tape tycoons of Bay Street and exposing the frustrations and miseries of young people looking for jobs in that anti-social community of the Depression years. He said the woes of Sergeant William Thompson, hero of the opera, were so like those that assailed his son, Bunny, that he was writing out of an experienced and bitter truth.' Perhaps Willan's glee was also fired by the memory of his own treatment by 'tycoons' in 1936, when he was dismissed as vice-principal of the conservatory!

When Coulter had written the text of the prologue, he met Willan for dinner at the Arts and Letters Club. After scanning the text, Willan asked Coulter to read it aloud. When Coulter asked why, Willan replied, 'I want to get the cadences and stresses exactly as you naturally speak them.' Dinner was ordered, and by the time it was served Willan had already sketched the music for the prologue. He wrote the entire score in less than eight weeks, between 23 December 1941 and 14 February 1942. His absence from his church may well have made possible the short time of composition. Lucio Agostini took on the time-consuming task of orchestration. The work received its première on 8 March 1942, over CBC radio, with MacMillan conducting.

Willan's successor at St Mary Magdalene's eventually ended up in trouble with the police and was no longer available. Willan's young lady had called a halt to their relationship and thereby earned several years of his displeasure. By June 1942 the church approached Willan to be its organist again, and he returned in September. He would stay there till his death. On 14 December Willan gave the first liturgical recital with his choirs since his return. The church had undergone considerable redecoration and, according to a newspaper account, 'Willan and his two choirs presented this recital in order to make sure that all the costs of this restoration work were covered.' The many liturgical recitals which Willan gave with his choirs during his long years at St Mary Magdalene's had the double purpose of presenting fine liturgical music well and authentically performed and raising money for the meagre finances of the church. It was a matter of pride with Willan that his choirs were self-supporting, purchasing all their music and supplies with their own funds.

Transit through Fire received its first public performance on 18 February 1943, in Convocation Hall, University of Toronto, by the Toronto Conservatory Symphony Orchestra and chorus. The large crowd reacted favourably. The work touched the temper of the times and the audience, deeply moved, gave Willan an ovation. Some critics were touched by the opera's 'message'; however, Neil MacDonald, in the *Toronto News*, acutely observed, 'The libretto is the weakest part of the whole, in fact it is only Dr Willan's exceptional ability that has given the opera its undeniable importance.' Some critics commented on Willan's fine orchestration, apparently unaware of Agostini's contribution! The conservatory's new principal, Norman Wilks (MacMillan's executive assistant after Willan's departure in 1936), asked Ettore Mazzoleni to conduct this concert. This began a long association: for more than twenty years Mazzoleni would conduct the première and later performances of Willan's major works.

On 20 February 1943 Willan's daughter, Mary, was married. Dr Cody conducted the service, and MacMillan played the organ. Sir Ernest later recalled: 'During the signing of the register, when the wedding party was in the vestry, I found my fingers leading me into a portion of Healey's *Passacaglia*. Presently a door near the console opened and the father of the bride slid over on the bench beside me. "I say, old man" said he, "what is that? Sounds familiar, but I can't place it."' MacMillan added: 'Healey Willan's compositions are so numerous that he must find it difficult to keep track of them.'

Two incidental scores by Willan appeared that year. *Hymn for Those in the Air* was first performed over the CBC on 23 April. It was of four minutes' duration, a rambling piece of background music for small orchestra to accompany the reading of Duncan Campbell Scott's famous words. The CBC commissioned Willan to write the music for a radio version of his friend E.J. Pratt's narrative poem, *Brébeuf and His Brethren*. Willan completed the music on 15 July. The first radio performance took place on 26 September; Mazzoleni conducted.

In 1943 the Canadian College of Organists was anxious, in Willan's words, 'to do something in a practical way to assist our fellow-musicians in England, who, in an appalling time of devastation hitherto unimagined, had suffered privation and losses of which we in Canada had little or no conception. The Cathedral of Coventry was selected as the epitome of bombing outrages and as the appropriate point of concentration.' The college started the British Organ Restoration Fund Committee, with Willan as chairman, to raise money towards a new organ in a rebuilt Coventry Cathedral. In 1946 the objective was set at $50,000, to be raised largely through organ recitals and other performances by members of the college. In 1950 the objective was changed to £10,000 ($30,000). The required sum was realized by 1952. This project was close to Willan's heart, and he remained chairman of the committee till its task was completed.

On 18 January 1944, the Toronto Symphony Orchestra and Mendelssohn Choir under MacMillan presented a public performance of

Brébeuf in Massey Hall. Willan's services as a guest organ recitalist were still in demand. On 27 January 1944 he inaugurated the restored organ in Brant Avenue United Church, Brantford, with his choir from St Mary Magdalene's assisting. On 5 June he opened the new organ at St Matthew's Lutheran Church, Kitchener, with a performance of his *Introduction, Passacaglia and Fugue*.

Willan had written his *Piano Concerto in C Minor* for the Canadian pianist Agnes Butcher, a close friend. She had been a scholarship student at the Toronto conservatory in the mid-1930s, went to Budapest to study with Béla Bartók in 1938, returned to Canada in 1940, and taught at the conservatory. On 24 August 1944, she performed the concerto's radio première with a CBC symphony orchestra, conducted by Jean Beaudet. She played the work in Massey Hall with the Toronto Symphony Orchestra under Mazzoleni on 28 November. The concerto, full of lovely tunes and romantic in style, was well received by the audience. Willan received his customary ovation.

Piano Concerto in C Minor would be Willan's first and only completed concerto and his only completed work for piano and orchestra. He had started three works for piano and orchestra in London (including a piano concerto in D minor and a ballade for piano and orchestra) but had left them unfinished. The concerto was Willan's first major symphonic work to be recorded and available commercially. On 29 March 1945, one of the earliest record albums of Canadian music was recorded in the CBC Montreal studios (under the auspices of the International Service of the Department of External Affairs). The album included *Suite canadienne* by Claude Champagne and Willan's *Piano Concerto in C Minor*. The performers were Agnes Butcher and a CBC Symphony, conducted by Jean Beaudet. In 1948, RCA Victor issued the recording of Willan's *Concerto* separately, for commercial distribution.

Willan took his St Mary Magdalene Singers to Town Hall, New York, to give two concerts on 24 and 25 September 1944. The group, consisting of nine women and seven men, was well received by large and enthusiastic audiences. At one performance the choir had to sing two encores, and even then the audience was reluctant to leave. The programs included works by Willan, Palestrina, the Elizabethans, Tschaikowsky, Rachmaninoff, and one of Willan's pupils, the Canadian composer Robert Fleming. For these concerts Willan made his SATB unaccompanied arrangement of *The Star Spangled Banner*, a gesture well appreciated by his American audiences. On 2 December, the St Mary Magdalene Singers gave a Christmas concert in the Great Hall at Hart House. This event would continue annually until 1963, except for 1957, when flu ravaged the ranks of the singers.

Following the success of *Transit through Fire*, the CBC had commissioned Coulter and Willan to write a full-length opera for radio. Willan worked on this gigantic score, *Deirdre of the Sorrows*, for several years, from September 1943, and it was to be his largest and most ambitious work. It had its première on 20 April 1946. The three-hour broadcast was heard from coast to coast; a New York station also carried part of it. One on the CBC transmitters went out of commission part-way through. Willan's own account is rather amusing: 'The day arrived. John Coulter and I found ourselves seated in front of a mike, with a Grand Inquisitor on the other side of the table who asked us pertinent questions as to how, why and when we wrote the work, until at last, thoroughly non-plussed and confused, I felt disposed to admit my guilt and accept whatever sentence might be forthcoming. But I learned afterwards that the power had gone off during one of my answers and that I finished with a wail which would have done credit to Conochar [one of the opera's characters] in the last act.'

Critical reaction was generally favourable, with many calling the work a triumph and praising the performers. Some wondered about the length, however, and indicated that it could profit by some pruning. (Some cutting was done for the stage versions produced in 1965 and 1966.) The radio première was an important Canadian musical event – the first time in Canada that a full-length opera had been commissioned and performed.

On 13 May 1946 Willan's *Piano Concerto* was performed at the Prague Music Festival by the Czech Philharmonic Orchestra. Willan's symphonic work was beginning to get international exposure.

Willan took his choir to sing on 14 January 1947 in Buffalo, New York, at a 'know your composer' concert sponsored by the Buffalo chapter of the American Guild of Organists. The composer to be known was, of course, Willan himself, and the program was devoted to his works.

Willan had always been fit and in good health, aside from 'growing pains' in the mid-1890s, stomach trouble in the early 1900s, and some problems with kidney stones in the 1920s. He looked and acted much younger than his actual years and had tended to live life to the full. He had been working especially hard during the previous decade composing large-scale works – two symphonies, two operas, and a concerto. He had not eased up on any of his other fields of musical endeavour. All this activity finally caught up with him. He had been playing several recitals a year at Convocation Hall, University of Toronto. On 24 February 1947, he played another recital, and shortly afterwards he suffered a heart attack. He spent five weeks in Wellesley Hospital and convalesced till the end of May. Charles Peaker took over Willan's class at the university for the remainder of the term, and Margaret Harmer assumed the duties of organist and choirmaster at St Mary Magdalene's.

In June 1947 Willan was well enough to resume his church duties. By the fall things were back to normal, Willan giving liturgical recitals with his choir on 6 October and 1 December. The St Mary Magdalene Singers gave Christmas concerts in Hart House on 7 December and at the Art Gallery of Toronto on 21 December. Willan found time to play continuo for a performance of Bach's *St Matthew Passion* on 12 November in Metropolitan United Church. (He had played piano continuo for McMillan's early presentations of the *Passion* in Toronto. MacMillan often spoke of the beauty of Willan's realizations.)

Prior to Willan's radio commission for *Brébeuf* (1943) there had been a plan to stage a pageant at the Martyrs' Shrine at Midland, Ontario. This idea was now revived. Pratt's poem was to be the basis of the script, and Willan was to expand his score. Willan produced a second version, but the project floundered because the money necessary to mount the pageant was not found. The second version had to wait till 1967 for a performance!

All Willan's children had left the family nest. In the years immediately following the war, housing for university students was very scarce in Toronto. Gladys Willan took in a couple of students who became part of her family (one was a relative).

On 27 January 1948 MacMillan conducted Willan's *Symphony No. 1* with the Toronto Symphony Orchestra at a special concert of music by Canadian composers. Also on the program was *Festal Overture* by one of Willan's former composition students, Godfrey Ridout.

Willan's love of the water was indulged in the early summer when he took a Great Lakes' cruise, accompanied by his student, the organist George Maybee. From 2 August to 11 September, he gave courses in choir and church music at the University of California (Los Angeles campus). He was paid $840 and given a travel allowance of $275. He met Patton McNaughton, conductor of the UCLA Concert Band, and soon composed for him his major work for wind ensemble, *Royce Hall Suite*.

On 8 November, Willan played at the dedication of the new organ in Wycliffe College, Toronto. The instrument was installed in memory of an old friend and colleague, the singer James Campbell-McInnes. The organ was a small two-manual one, not capable of handling large recital repertoire. Willan played chorale preludes and his own *Prelude and Fugue in B Minor*. Wycliffe had spearheaded the Anglican 'low church' element; clearly a 'thaw' was beginning to take place between the two factions!

In December 1948, RCA Victor issued commercially the CBC recording (Agnes Butcher, pianist; Jean Beaudet, conductor) of Willan's *Piano Concerto in C Minor*, under its own label, which would permit wide distribution in Canada and the United States. The album was one of the last 78 rpm records. The same year saw also the completion of the revised score of *Symphony No. 2 in C Minor*, bringing to an end a dozen years of feverish creative activity by Willan in the realm of symphonic and operatic music.

In 1949 Willan was asked to provide a fanfare and faux-bourdons for the enthronement of the archbishop in Kingston, Ontario, and a setting of the evening canticles (magnificat and nunc dimittis) for an Episcopalian church congress in Boston. In May a CBC symphony orchestra, under Geoffrey Waddington, played *Symphony No. 1*, and the UCLA Concert Band, under Patton McNaughton, gave the première of *Royce Hall Suite*. The latter was the first and largest of his three works for concert band, which included also *Élégie héroïque* (1960) and *Ceremonial March* (1967); Willan had others score all three. Willan returned to Los Angeles to teach in his last summer appointment at the university level. During the fall he played several organ recitals, including one at the dedication of Islington United Church, Toronto, and another in the United States.

Willan's association with Concordia Publishing house began about this time. In early 1950 he wrote the first set of his Concordia chorale preludes for organ. Willan took the manuscripts of several of these freshly composed pieces to counterpoint class one day in March of that year and went through them, playing the manual parts on the piano while we (his students) supplied the pedal part, an octave lower, underneath.

On 16 May 1950 Willan played a pre-service organ recital and accompanied a massed choir of 500 voices in St George's Cathedral, Kingston. For this choir festival he had written his great Ascension-tide anthem, *Sing We Triumphant Songs*. The first section was intended to be sung by all voices together, the middle section by the cathedral choir alone, and the final section antiphonally by the cathedral choir as one unit and the remaining choirs as the other. Over the vocal line to be sung by the other choirs in the final section Willan had written the direction 'V.F.' Musicians are accustomed to abbreviations but the organist, George Maybee, was mystified by this one. Willan explained that it simply meant 'visiting fireman.' Maybee, in turn, played the same joke on Archbishop Lyons (to whom the anthem is dedicated), and there was much amusement. It is doubtful if the visiting choirs were aware of their special appellation!

News of the impending première of Willan's new symphony had spread as far as Vancouver; on 13 May, the Vancouver *Province* reported the story and carried a large picture of the composer. On 18 May the long-awaited performance of *Symphony No. 2 in C Minor* took place in Massey Hall; the (recently retitled) Royal Conservatory Symphony Orchestra was conducted by Mazzoleni. On the same program were *Etudes for Strings* by Willan's pupil Godfrey Ridout and Beethoven's *Piano Concerto No. 4*, played by seventeen-year-old Glenn Gould! *Symphony No. 2* received an enthusiastic response from the audience, one critic reporting that the symphony 'got such an ovation Dr. Willan had to make his way from the balcony to the stage to take repeated bows.' The news of Willan's impending retirement as professor of music was in the air and doubtless added intensity to the applause. One critic was somewhat less enthusiastic, dryly remarking, 'There was a fugue in it, of course.' *Symphony No. 2*, however, has all but eclipsed *Symphony No. 1*.

Symphony No. 2 was repeated six days later by a CBC symphony orchestra under Geoffrey Waddington. The program included Willan's *Coronation March*, which was played again shortly afterwards at the opening concert of that season's proms.

At the end of June 1950, three months before his seventieth birthday, Willan retired as professor of music. Retirement age was sixty-five, but it was possible for a professor to be reappointed annually up to the age of seventy by mutual consent. Willan recalled his visit to the president: 'When I went to express my final goodbye to him (Sidney Smith), he said "Now look here, you are Organist to the University and that has nothing whatever to do with the Faculty of Music; that's my affair, and as long as you can dodder over to the organ, you can be the organist."' An annual honorarium of $1,000 was attached to the position, which had previously been unpaid. Willan continued as university organist for another fourteen years and remained an honorary member of the Trinity College Senior Common Room.

Canon Cody wrote to him, 'I am sorry that you are retiring from the University. The Music Faculty will be greatly crippled. Thank you for all you did for it. I never forget your expressed good will in days when it was specially cheering.' Cody had been responsible for Willan's appointment as organist of St Paul's in 1913, as university organist in 1932, and as professor of music in 1938.

During his years as professor Willan wrote most of his symphonic and operatic works. His activities as church musician and organ recitalist had continued unabated, save for the exceptional events of 1941–42 and his illness in 1947. Had he retired completely in 1950 his reputation would have been secure. However 'retirement' for Willan would mean merely less activity in some areas balanced by more in others.

4

Retirement
1950–1968

At the time of his retirement Willan wrote to a friend, 'I have never been so busy.' Many things demanded his attention, including a number of requests for compositions. In contrast to the symphonic and operatic emphasis of the late 1930s and the 1940s, the major thrust now would be in church anthems and organ pieces. (There were exceptions of course: notably revisions to *Deirdre* and some orchestral marches.) This would be a period of 'music to order'; Willan was now 'on pension' and in need of all the extra money he could earn.

Willan had an 'order' from Concordia Publishing for six motets, six hymn anthems, and six more chorale preludes for organ (as a result of the success of the first set of six). Then there were the five plainsong preludes for organ requested by Oxford University Press. All these works were written and published during 1950 and 1951. The summer of 1950 saw the composition of one of Willan's greatest choral works, the large motet *Gloria Deo per immensa saecula*, commissioned by the Community Centre of the Village of Forest Hill in Toronto.

An early and longstanding interest of Willan's now blossomed again. The Gregorian Association of London (England) had been founded in 1870; Willan became a member in 1910. In 1950, four members of the Gregorian Association of London happened to come together in Toronto and founded the Gregorian Association of Toronto with Willan as musical director (a post held until 1964). From his early days with Francis Burgess, Willan had been an enthusiastic promoter of Gregorian chant (ie plainsong), particularly within the English rite. For many years at St Mary Magdalene's he had carried the fight nearly single-handed. Now there was the opportunity for an association to reinforce and add new vigour to the campaign. Unfortunately the new association was short-lived and of limited influence. Perhaps it was modelled too closely on its English counterpart; in Canada a musical association restricted to male Anglican communicants is bound to operate within a comparatively small circle. Women and non-Anglicans were allowed to be non-voting 'associate' members.

During the summer of 1950 Willan spent some time teaching at the Put-in-Bay Choir School in Ohio. This new type of summer activity for Willan would come to fruition during his decade as director of the Toronto Diocesan Summer Choir School (1954–63).

To celebrate Willan's seventieth birthday, a concert was held in St Paul's, Toronto, on 14 October 1950 before an audience of 2,000. The program, selected from Willan's anthems, motets, and organ works, was presented by the St Paul's choir (in the chancel) and the St Mary Magdalene choir (in the gallery), with Charles Peaker playing the magnificent organ. The music ranged from one of Willan's earliest anthems, *I Looked, and Behold, a White Cloud*, to his latest organ composition, *Five Preludes on Plainsong Melodies*, being given a première performance by Peaker, who played from manuscript. Proceeds from the concert were given to Willan's beloved British Organ Restoration Fund.

There were other events connected with his seventieth birthday. The CBC gave over a Wednesday night program to performances of Willan's works. On 7 and 8 November Sir Ernest MacMillan included Willan's *Symphony No. 2* in the Toronto Symphony Orchestra concerts in Massey Hall. The work had been premièred 18 May and broadcast on CBC radio 24 May; the November concerts were its third and fourth public performances that year, exceptional for a major new Canadian symphonic work.

At least two organ works were written by Willan's colleagues in honour of his seventieth birthday: *Prelude and Fugue in E Minor* by George Coutts, an old friend of Willan's, and *Festival Fanfare* by Drummond Wolff, one of Willan's colleagues at the university. Both pieces were subsequently published.

Willan's health was remarkably good. Looking more like a man of fifty than one of seventy, he had recovered very well from his heart attack of 1947. When he went for a medical examination on 1 November, the report was quite favourable: 'At the present moment he has no complaints whatever ... He has only very mild occasional angina if he exerts himself extremely, however he knows enough to restrict himself along this line.' The only problem was a lesion on the left lip due to the constant use of a pipe; the doctor warned him of possible cancer at a later date and suggested that he move his pipe to the other side of his mouth.

In 1951 occurred the thirtieth anniversary of Willan's taking up duties at the Church of St Mary Magdalene. The rector, Father Brain, asked Willan to write a letter on the subject 'What St Mary Magdalene's means to me.' The following are extracts from Willan's letter:

From the age of 4 I realized that music was the only thing to which I could devote my life's work, and, with gratitude to my dear father and mother, my regular attendance at St George's, Beckenham, started me off with the idea that the music of the Liturgy was the logical expression of everything that was beautiful. Financial necessities led me through many vicissitudes and, after many years of change (I had almost added 'and decay'), I found my home in St Mary Magdalene's, where ... I was able to embark upon a work which I have since felt more and more strongly as the years have passed was my special job in this life.

The beautifying of the Liturgy is the main part of my work at St Mary Magdalene, and that, in my opinion, is only possible through the use of the Church's own music, so that plainsong has been the essential backbone of my work.

When I was very much younger I used to have a romantic idea that, in my old age, it would be rather nice to work in an old and dusty organ-loft. My youthful visions have now materialized – sometimes with an over-emphasis on the dusty side of things!

On 15 August, Willan received a National Award of Merit (an inscribed medallion) from the University of Alberta, Banff School of Fine Arts, the first of many honours he would receive late in his life.

The St Mary Magdalene Singers had prepared a special program at the request of the British Broadcasting Corporation. It was broadcast from England on 22 November by the overseas service as part of a series, 'British and Dominion Cathedral Music.' The broadcast was yet another indication of the growing international regard for Willan and his choir. Earlier that year, on Dominion Day, the BBC had broadcast a recording of Willan's *Piano Concerto*.

The Arts and Letters Club was the scene of a meeting on 8 March 1952 of the Canadian Branch of the Royal School of Church Music. The meeting had been called to consider the present status and future of the RSCM in Canada; there was not much activity outside Toronto, Kingston, and Montreal. Willan was in the chair. The guest of honour was Dr William McKie, organist of Westminster Abbey and director of the RSCM. He and Willan became good friends.

Willan had been commissioned to write works for the centenaries of Trinity College, University of Toronto (1951), and of the synod of the

Anglican diocese of Toronto (1952). For Trinity Willan wrote one of his finest large-scale anthems, *Blessed Art Thou, O Lord*, and for the diocese he wrote one of his best later motets, *Great Is the Lord*. The diocesan centenary was celebrated 1 June 1952 with a service in Maple Leaf Gardens; Willan rehearsed and conducted the massed choir.

Later in June 1952 Willan was awarded the degree doctor of laws by Queen's University, Kingston. Willan had two well-known admirers in Kingston: Dr Graham George, professor of music at Queen's, and Dr George Maybee, cathedral organist. On 20 June Willan gave his final report as chairman of the British Organ Restoration Fund Committee. Largely because of Willan's hard work, the £10,000 objective had finally been reached (and oversubscribed by £350).

During the summer of 1952 Willan received notification that his *An Apostrophe to the Heavenly Hosts* (1921) had been chosen to be part of the royal concert to be held on St Cecilia's Day (22 November) in the Royal Festival Hall, London. St Cecilia's Day festivals in England had a long history, going back to 1683, and had been revived in 1946 in aid of the Musicians' Benevolent Fund. The festival would start with a church service in the morning, attended by the lord mayor. In the afternoon there would be a public luncheon followed by the royal concert in the evening. Willan was invited to be present for this occasion, since it would be the first time that a work by a 'Dominion' composer had been included. The invitation read in part, 'Not only will it give London musicians very great pleasure that you should be present, but also we feel that the whole musical life of Canada would wish you to be here.' Such a journey would be expensive. However, the congregation of St Mary Magdalene's came to the rescue and presented its beloved precentor with his airplane ticket for the occasion. So off to London Willan went, staying at the Savage Club (the London affiliate of his Arts and Letters Club).

Queen Elizabeth and Prince Philip were indeed present on 24 November in the Royal Festival Hall to hear, along with its composer, *Apostrophe* sung by the Alexandra Choir of nearly 300 voices, conducted by Charles Proctor. Willan was pleased with the performance as, apparently, was the press. *The Times* called it 'a surprise from Canada.' His old friend Harold Brooke wrote 'I was thrilled with the *Apostrophe* last night – it was a splendid performance of a fine work, and you fully deserved the ovation you got.' After the performance Willan was presented to the queen.

In addition to giving Willan's reputation in England a considerable boost, this royal concert led to two immediate results. Willan was approached by Sir George Dyson and other members of the St Cecilia Festival Committee to write something for the 1953 festival; he would oblige with his anthem *A Prayer of Rejoicing*. He also received an invitation from Sir William McKie to compose one of the homage anthems for the coronation service scheduled for June 1953. McKie had to have Willan's choice of words immediately to present to the archbishop of Canterbury for approval, and Willan was leaving London in a day or two. So Willan 'dashed up to the library of the Savage Club' and discovered there an old prayerbook of Queen Victoria's time. In this he found a service of thanksgiving for the reign of Queen Victoria and compiled a text from extracts of psalms which it contained. He sent the selection to McKie and, the same evening, received word of the archbishop's approval.

Willan travelled to Coventry to present officially the British Organ Restoration Fund Committee's contribution to the new cathedral's organ. The four-manual Harrison and Harrison with seventy-three stops, completed ten years later, cost £25,000; the Canadian contribution covered two-fifths. The provost gave Willan one of the twenty-four crosses made from the nails of the roof of the bombed-out cathedral; it now hangs on a pillar at St Mary Magdalene's. There was some discussion of Willan writing something for the new cathedral, but he became very busy and nothing materialized. On the same trip to England Willan also took time out to visit his sister, Mary.

On 28 November, four days after the royal concert, the BBC presented a live broadcast of Willan's music from York Minster, sung by the Radshaw Singers and played by York Minster's organist, Francis Jackson. *Gloria Deo per immensa saecula* received its English première. Jackson would do much through his recitals to acquaint English audiences with Willan's organ works. About this time, Willan, as musical director of the Toronto Gregorian Association, was appointed a vice-president of the London association, and A.W. Clarke, musical director of the London group, was made a vice-president of the Toronto association.

After his return from England, Willan got right to work on his coronation anthem, and by 9 December was able to send the manuscript to Dr McKie. It is remarkable how quickly he could compose; some of his greatest pieces (eg *Apostrophe*) were written in a few days.

Willan was fired with coronation projects for 1953. Chief of these were the homage anthem *O Lord, Our Governour* for the coronation service, and *Coronation Suite* for chorus and orchestra commissioned by the CBC. There is also some evidence that Willan considered a third work, *A Masque of Aurora* ('Divertissement in Two Acts, with Ballet, in Honour of

H.M. the Queen'), but he did not proceed further. The pressure of his coronation commissions prevented him from accepting an invitation from the choir of Appleby College in Oakville, Ontario, to write a new motet for it to sing at a special service in St Alban's Abbey during its tour of the United Kingdom.

Willan was in London for the coronation, staying at the Tavistock Hotel. It was the first time a non-resident composer had been asked to write special music for a coronation. It was a great honour for Willan and a recognition of the high musical standards of Canada. Willan had a special pass to the final rehearsal in the abbey on 29 May and another for the service itself on 2 June. He also received a commemorative coronation medal.

The music of the coronation service was splendid. Sir Adrian Boult directed the choir and orchestra, and Willan's *O Lord, Our Governour* received a fine performance. Unfortunately, the homage of the peers was taking place during its performance and Willan's music was not always clearly audible. Francis Jackson wrote to him: 'I very much enjoyed your Coronation anthem. It was too bad of them to talk over it – we could have done with much less talk all the time, and certainly there is no excuse for spoiling the music ... It is a fine piece, I thought, and particularly apt for the occasion.' Willan's piece certainly held its own with the other short anthems written by his eminent British colleagues. At the same time that *O Lord, Our Governour* was being performed in London, Willan's *Coronation Suite* was being broadcast over the CBC.

Willan could look forward to three important performances of his music later that year. On 21 September the Republican Guard Band of Paris played his *Royce Hall Suite* during a program given in Maple Leaf Gardens, Toronto. Unfortunately, the audience for this concert was very small. On 16 October Leopold Stokowski conducted *Coronation Suite* at Carnegie Hall, New York, in an all-Canadian concert. Both Willan and Stokowski had been organ pupils of Hoyte. On 16 November Willan's new anthem, *A Prayer of Rejoicing*, was performed at the St Cecilia's Day Festival Service at St Sepulchre's Church, Holborn, London. Willan donated the proceeds from his *Coronation Anthem* and *A Prayer of Rejoicing* to the Musicians' Benevolent Fund. He was not well off, yet this act of charity was not untypical.

Willan had continued to give his regular liturgical recitals at St Mary Magdalene's and organ recitals in Convocation Hall. He was still playing 'outside' recitals also; during the fall of 1953 he gave two recitals in Holy Trinity Church, Toronto, in aid of that church's organ repair fund, and one in St James' Cathedral, Toronto.

In a 1953 list compiled from thirty-seven leading choirs in the United States and Canada, Willan ranked second only to Bach in the frequency of use of his music; see Leonard Ellinwood *The History of American Church Music* (New York 1953) page 138. The results give a strong indication of Willan's leading position in North America as a church composer in the mid-twentieth century.

On 14 December 1953 the BBC Symphony and Chorus under Sir Adrian Boult performed two movements of *Coronation Suite* in a broadcast concert of Commonwealth music commemorating the twenty-first anniversary of overseas broadcasting by the BBC. *Coronation Suite* received performances in Massey Hall on 13 and 14 April 1954 by the Toronto Symphony Orchestra and Mendelssohn Choir, conducted by Sir Ernest MacMillan. It received acclaim from all the Toronto critics and enthusiastic applause from the audience.

In May 1954 Willan was in Winnipeg to receive a doctor of letters degree from the University of Manitoba. While there he played an organ recital of his own works in St Luke's Church. The program was rather curious, consisting of the 1909 *Prelude and Fugue in B Minor*, followed by nine chorale preludes taken from the three sets he published in 1950–51. This would be one of the last of Willan's 'outside' recitals.

Throughout his life Willan had always been a firm believer in choir schools and constantly lamented Canada's lack of them. Traditions in Canada were different from Britain, of course; there is no established church, boys mature more quickly and their voices break sooner, and educational practices and facilities vary. Nevertheless there were a number of people who thought as Willan did, and in 1952 an Anglican priest, Father Pugh, left a summer property to the diocese of Toronto for a choir school. The property was not suitable for the purpose and was sold. The interest on the proceeds was enough to allow a short summer choir school to begin.

Willan was appointed director, and the locale was Trinity College School in Port Hope, Ontario. For two weeks during the summer of 1954, the Toronto Diocesan Choir School was held for the first time. From a registration of 49 boys from eighteen churches in 1954, the school grew to 120 boys from thirty-three churches by 1960. Willan's good friend Francis Jackson was on staff that first summer. Willan would continue as choir school director for ten summers, eventually retiring after the 1963 session. During this time he had the enthusiastic support of Philip Ketchum, headmaster of Trinity College School. Ketchum was a great admirer of plainsong and fondly dreamed of all the 290 boys at his school singing Gregorian music!

Willan was much beloved by both staff and boys alike, and the work afforded him great personal satisfaction. His mind must have gone back many times to his own days at Eastbourne. The days were full, starting with the rising bell at 7:30 am and continuing till lights out at 9 pm. The staff had even longer days! Rehearsals, music classes, sports activities, and daily evensong filled the timetable. In spite of his advanced age and periodic ailments, Willan coped with his work and responsibilities at the choir school with remarkable vigour and good humour. At the last night of the session he would dress up in shorts, cap, and Eton collar and entertain the boys by singing in his cracked voice songs he had composed for the occasion. The songs were usually take-offs on the boys and staff present, and all would be reduced to near hysteria.

In the summer of 1954 Willan heard that the BBC was planning to broadcast a performance of his large work of 1915, *Variations and Epilogue on an Original Theme*, to be played by the Canadian two-piano team, Margaret and Harry Heap. The Heaps had performed *Variations* at a Wigmore Hall recital a short time earlier and had favourably impressed such people as the English pianist and composer York Bowen. Willan had always felt that *Variations* was one of his finest works and regretted that it was never published and hardly ever played.

On 9 July 1955 Willan's *Song of Welcome* for chorus and orchestra was premièred at Stratford, Ontario, by the Hart House Orchestra (conductor, Boyd Neel) and the Festival Chorus (conductor, former Willan chorister Elmer Iseler). The work had been commissioned for the opening of the inaugural season of music at the Shakespearean Festival.

Willan's seventy-fifth birthday on 12 October was the occasion for a number of special programs. The CBC mounted a two-and-a-half-hour radio broadcast devoted to Willan and his music. It consisted of forty-five minutes of Willan's organ and choral music, sung by the St Mary Magdalene's choir and played by Gerald Bales; forty-five minutes of recollections and tributes by Willan's pupils, colleagues, and friends; and an hour of Willan's music played by the CBC Symphony Orchestra under Geoffrey Waddington. The latter was chiefly devoted to a performance of *Symphony No. 2*, though *O Lord, Our Governour* and part of *Coronation Suite* were also included. At seventy-five Willan did not appear an old man: Louis Applebaum, a former student, observed during the CBC tributes, 'He is probably one of the youngest seventy-five-year-olds we have around today.'

There was also a concert of his music performed before 2,000 people in St Paul's. This time, however, there was something extra. At the reception following the concert, Willan was given an award of merit by the mayor of Toronto. The medallion was inscribed 'Award to Healey Willan, MusD, LLD, FRCO, in recognition of his outstanding contributions to the musical and cultural life of this city as distinguished composer, organist, and choirmaster.' The mayor kept referring to Willan as 'Mr Williams'; in his correspondence with Dalton Baker, Willan hereafter became 'Williams' and Baker became 'Barker'!

Willan received forty-five telegrams and more than 100 letters on his seventy-fifth birthday. Perhaps his greatest birthday present came in a letter:

Lambeth Palace, S.E.1

24th October, 1955.

Dear Dr. Willan,

The suggestion has come to me from people in Canada that I should offer you a Lambeth Degree of Doctor of Music. Of course you already have such Doctorates, and it might appear like bringing coals to Newcastle, but a Lambeth Doctorate has a special flavour of its own: it is given by the Archbishop of Canterbury in the name of the Church and does confer honour upon some who have devotedly served the Church. Amongst them you stand extremely high as a musician of the highest possible reputation, and one who has so gloriously served the Church in Canada and beyond. I do not forget that at the Coronation we were privileged to have a work contributed by you.

The suggestion came, as I have said, from Canada, but I have consulted those who are most able to advise me in England and they all enthusiastically encourage me to make this offer. Accordingly I do so and I very much hope that you will find it possible to accept. If you were able to be in England any time in the near future I could then present you with the Degree in person: if that is not possible then I should choose some suitable person in Canada to confer it on my behalf.

Yours sincerely,

Geoffrey Cantuar.

Willan replied that he expected to be in London the following February, and the ceremony was tentatively set for the twenty-first. Then, on 21 December Willan had to write to report that his doctor had advised against a trip in February owing to 'disturbing symptoms of late' regarding his heart condition and to suggest a postponement till the summer. A new date was set for 9 July 1956. For his trip to England Willan received $800 from the diocese of Toronto and the University of Toronto. In addition to his travel and hotel expenses (he stayed again at the Tavistock Hotel), Willan also had to pay a £31 fee for the degree and to supply himself with an Oxford doctor of music gown and hood.

The degree was conferred in the chapel of Lambeth Palace before a congregation of some thirty distinguished men of music. Sir William McKie played several of Willan's chorale preludes and the choir sang his motet *O Trinity, Most Blessed Light* and one of his plainsong magnificats with faux-bourdon. The degree was conferred by the archbishop of Canterbury assisted by the dean of York. One disappointment was the inability of Vaughan Williams to attend the ceremony. On 3 July he wrote to Willan, 'I had fully intended to be present, both for the pleasure of meeting you and to show appreciation of the esteem in which your name is held by musicians in this country. Unfortunately I am down with an attack of phlebitis, and my doctor insists.' The two men never did meet; Vaughan Williams died two years later. Willan travelled also to Lincoln to play an organ recital in the cathedral. The cathedral organist was an old friend, Gordon Slater.

Willan did not neglect his other duties. In 1955 he had been a co-judge for the Saskatchewan Jubilee Music Composition Competition and caused quite a bit of correspondence when he would not accept any submission as worthy of performance! For several years he served as examinations committee chairman for the Royal Canadian College of Organists until he retired from the position in December 1956. In November 1956 he was asked by Prince Clemente Rospigliosi to be a member of an international 'Comité d'honneur' sponsoring a new Ur-text edition of seventeenth- and eighteenth-century Italian music. Willan accepted.

Willan's beloved little dog, Trixie, died in 1956 at age seventeen. She has been variously described as a fox terrier and as 'a bitch of almost indeterminate ancestry.' She had a firm hold on her master's affections. She was Willan's alarm clock and judge of composition. Willan used to tell the story that whenever he played over a new composition, Trixie would come from any part of the house to hear and approve. She loved to sit on his knee and get her chest rubbed. Willan maintained that she liked Haydn and Mozart in particular, but that she did not like 'this modern music' and would walk away in disgust when she heard any of it. Willan once stated: 'I have always said there are two things you can't buy, one is contentment, and the other is a dog's affection.' He was also quoted as saying 'Anyone who doesn't like a dog can hardly be trusted.' The Willans did not get another dog – 'We didn't have the heart to.'

Another sad event was the sudden death of Willan's old friend from Novello, Harold Brooke, on 20 September. Willan wrote an elegy for organ 'in memoriam' and this was subsequently published as the middle movement of *Rondino, Elegy and Chaconne* for organ.

Willan composed another organ piece earlier that year, *Epithalamium* (Sortie), for the wedding, late in life, of his good friend and supporter Sir William McKie. *Epithalamium* was first performed by Henry Ley at the wedding in Westminster Abbey on 5 April.

Willan continued as busy as ever with his organ and choir compositions, chiefly of the 'music-to-order' variety. In 1957 he was in the middle of composing thirty organ chorale preludes for C.F. Peters Corp. His health was becoming more of a problem, and his heart acted up again during April and May. In July his honorarium as university organist was raised from $1,000 to $1,200 per annum. Willan was unable to play all the university recitals himself and had to invite other organists to share the work and, presumably, the honorarium! The McGill Chamber Orchestra approached Willan to write a work for it, but nothing came of this.

In 1957 evensong was halted at St Mary Magdalene's. Willan had been experiencing difficulties with choir attendance at evening services (a situation by no means unique) and eventually he had to bow to the inevitable. For St Mary Magdalene's, however, the short choir rehearsals which usually followed evensong were now lost as well. As a result – though Willan's increasing age was doubtless a factor – the appearances of the St Mary Magdalene's Singers outside the church became increasingly rare; they ceased altogether in the final years of Willan's life.

A music column appeared in the *Toronto Star* in October 1957 entitled 'T.S.O. Consistently Ignores Willan's Second Symphony.' The columnist argued that Willan's symphony ought to replace yet another performance of Tschaikowsky's fifth. A flood of letters of support ensued, and a special concert, sponsored by the *Star*, was arranged for 5 March 1958. Sir Ernest MacMillan's successor as conductor, Walter Susskind, took a lot of time and trouble learning Willan's work. Susskind became very impressed with Willan's symphony, and the result was a first-rate and fresh reading of the work. Willan received a standing ovation.

The following summer at the Lambeth Conference in London, Willan's setting of Psalm 43 in plainsong with faux-bourdons was used during the closing communion service. Its use at such an important event was another example of Willan's prestige as a church composer.

In September 1958 Willan was elected a Fellow of the Ancient Monuments Society of England, his only non-musical fellowship. Another honour came on 8 December when the Canadian Club of Toronto held a testimonial dinner to honour Willan, E.J. Pratt, and A.Y. Jackson. Leonard Brockington was guest speaker. The printed program contained the first nine bars of the vocal score of *O Lord, Our Governour*, a poem by Pratt, and a painting by Jackson. But perhaps the most appreciated compliment in 1958 came from Alexander MacMillan (a noted hymnologist and Sir Ernest's father), then over ninety. He told Willan (who was a mere seventy-eight) that he was 'a very promising laddie.'

Willan's health was beginning to reflect the effects of advancing age. During 1957 there had been further heart trouble. In 1958 he was complaining of arthritis, and the following year he was warned of the possibility of cataracts (which did eventually come).

He had kept up a lively interest in cricket and rugger all his life and early in 1958 had been invited by the Ontario Rugger Union to a reception held for the touring Australian team. In October, he attended a rugger match 'to relive the thrills of my youth.'

The National Film Board of Canada had decided to make a short film on Willan. Robert Fleming, composer and former Willan student, was the music director of the NFB. Unable to leave his duties in Montreal, Fleming delegated Louis Applebaum, another former student, to be music supervisor. Filming began in early 1959. For ten days Willan was 'on deck' from early morning till late at night. The film crew marvelled at his stamina. Robert Blais, producer of the film, later wrote, 'The crew was amazed to see Healey Willan stay up sometimes till four o'clock in the morning. He never wanted to leave as long as any member of his choir or any students of the University were still at work. He stayed around, telling jokes, playing the piano, clowning while the crew were fixing the set. The next day he would return as fresh and neat as usual.' To Willan himself Blais had earlier written, 'What surprised me most was your immense capacity for working, understanding of another's job, and your astonishing sense of humour which made our work so easy.'

Man of Music runs some seventeen minutes and shows various aspects of the composer's life, including choir practice and evensong at St Mary Magdalene's. It also shows him dropping in on a class at the faculty of music (where he extemporizes a fugue on the piano for the students) and composing in his studio at home. The script had suggested a scene in the

Arts and Letters Club, where he still lunched once a week, but this did not materialize. He had not lost the natural acting ability which had been noted when he was a student at Eastbourne. *Man of Music* played as a 'short' in commercial theatres for some time and doubtless helped to spread Willan's fame. Now in the NFB library and available to any organization, it provides an appealing portrait of a great man.

On 23 March 1959, Willan's 'Cinderella,' *Variations and Epilogue* for two pianos, received another of its rare performances, this time in Oshawa, at a concert given by Margaret and Harry Heap. On 17 June his *Royal Salute*, commissioned for the visit of the queen and Prince Philip to Canada, was premièred by the CBC Symphony Orchestra. In July, his *Three Fanfares* for brass and percussion was played before the queen in Winnipeg at the presentation of tribute by the Hudson's Bay Company.

The same year, his *Passacaglia and Fugue No. 2* for organ was first performed, by Charles Peaker at Convocation Hall, University of Toronto, during the golden jubilee convention of the Royal Canadian College of Organists. In the audience was the eminent French organist André Marchal, the successor at St Eustache, Paris, of Joseph Bonnet, who had proclaimed Willan's *Introduction, Passacaglia and Fugue* of 1916 as 'the greatest since Bach's.' Opinions are divided on the 1959 work, but there can be no question that it is one of Willan's most important organ works, and all the more remarkable given that the composer was nearly eighty when he wrote it!

The church compositions continued to sell well. In 1959 the motet *Hodie Christus natus est* sold 14,279 copies and was the publisher's (Carl Fischer) bestseller of the year. Fischer's number two seller, at 10,103 copies, was Willan's anthem *Before the Ending of the Day*. Substantial sales of anthems do not translate into large royalties however; Willan received for all his Carl Fisher publications only $358.52 for 1959. By 1959 Willan's salary at St Mary Magdalene's had risen to $1,500 per annum, exactly the sum he had been earning before he left St Paul's in 1921!

Willan was made honorary president of the Canadian Federation of Music Teachers Associations in 1959. In 1960 the Royal Canadian College of Organists set up the Healey Willan Scholarship Fund to provide capital for an annual Willan Prize to be awarded in connection with the college examinations. The newly formed private Anglican boys' school in Toronto, St George's College, made Willan its honorary warden (he found the title chancellor a bit pretentious and suggested the office be called 'warden').

Willan's eightieth birthday party was hosted by the Toronto office of Oxford University Press, at the urging of its music division manager, Freda Ferguson. Oxford had published much of Willan's music and Willan had for many years acted as a manuscript reader for it. A large number of dignitaries from the musical world were in attendance. Letters of congratulations came in from all over, including one from a leading English church composer, Herbert Howells: 'It cannot surprise you that those of us who, over many years, have had at heart the well-being of organ music and of the musical part of the services of the church look to you as an outstanding figure in both domains. The 12th October has been always a blessed day in our English Calendar of Musicians. Annually it was the day on which we affectionately greeted Ralph Vaughan Williams as now we greet you.' Official greetings also came from the Royal College of Organists in England. The *American Organist* printed a two-page tribute.

Despite his spry appearance, the years were catching up with Willan. In the 1960s he would experience increasing difficulty with both seeing and hearing. Mrs Willan wanted him to wear a hearing aid, but he refused. His endurance shortened, and though he attacked his choir practices with his usual vigour, they increasingly exhausted him. 'During choir practices I feel like a man of thirty, but afterwards I soon realize that I am eighty.'

Willan started in 1960 on one of his last large projects, *The Canadian Psalter, Plainsong Edition*, based on the Revised Prayer Book and the new translation of the psalms. This gigantic task would occupy him for three years but was close to his heart, and he undertook it gladly.

Willan was suffering from lumbago during 1961 and had to cancel many engagements upon doctor's orders. He kept working on his composition, however, particularly on a second volume of anthems for junior choir, following the success of his first volume in 1953. He wrote other anthems and organ pieces, as well as continuing work on *The Canadian Psalter*. He and his sometime collaborators E.J. Pratt and Marius Barbeau were among the first recipients, in 1961, of the Canada Council Medal and $2,000 cash.

Willan had always hoped that his radio opera *Deirdre* would be staged. The Royal Conservatory Opera School agreed to mount a production; this required many revisions to the musical score and occupied Willan through much of 1962. More revisions were required in 1964, and the performances did not take place until 1965. In 1962 Willan gave his last 'out-of-town' organ recital. He had acted as a consultant for the enlarging of the organ at Erskine Presbyterian Church in Ottawa, and now he was asked to give a recital on the completed instrument. Willan was reluctant; he was concerned about his 'nerves' and whether there would be 'any good organists present.' However, on 20 May he gave his recital before an audience of 600 to 700. Afterwards the church presented Willan with a clock.

Willan was becoming aware of his own mortality and that of his friends. In July he wrote to John Coulter, 'I suppose you saw the account of Quentin MacLean's death. He was one of my old London friends and the fifth to die since the middle of May! It is really rather frightening.' His work at St Mary Magdalene's, the prospects of a stage performance of *Deirdre*, and his church composition would keep him going for a few years yet, however. He knew he was appreciated: with his royalty cheque from Concordia came a letter from his friend Ed Klammer: 'We are always happy to send your royalty cheque to you because we realize that the music you have written for Concordia has filled a very great need.' In 1963, Willan gave permission for his Concordia chorale preludes for organ to be set in Braille type, without royalties.

In the spring of 1963 Willan had another of his 'disagreements with his heart' and had to be hospitalized. Margaret Drynan one night had a dream in which Willan appeared doubled up in pain, saying, 'It hurts so much, Peggy.' The next morning she called friends to report her dream and was told that Willan had just suffered a heart attack. On 15 April he wrote me: 'I returned from hospital on the 11th, and although recovering, I do not expect to take any further part in the activities of the present season.' Margaret Harmer took over his duties with the choir and organ at St Mary Magdalene's, as she had done in 1947. Margaret Gillespie, the choir secretary, helped with Willan's correspondence.

At the end of the summer Willan was ill again, this time with a bad case of influenza. However by early October he was able to write to a relative in England that he was now 'quite fit and ready to scrap with all and sundry,' and that he had told his doctor – an old rugger fan – that he always played his best game when the odds were against him.

In May 1963 Willan had been made a Fellow of the Royal School of Church Music (FRSCM). He and his friend George Maybee at Kingston were among the three 'overseas' musicians so honoured in this, the year of the fellowship's creation. On 13 August, at the opening service in Maple Leaf Gardens, Toronto, of the Anglican World Congress, combined choirs of nearly 1,000 voices sang the anthem *O Praise the Lord* that

Willan had written for the occasion. Three days later, at a festival of Anglican church music in St Paul's, his famous motet, *Behold, the Tabernacle of God*, was sung; Willan occupied a seat of honour as 'honorary director of the Music Council of the Anglican Congress.'

Willan's almost legendary gift for speedy composition had not left him. On 21 October Walter Hinrichsen of C.F. Peters had written asking for more SS and/or SSA hymn anthems. Willan sent off the manuscripts of *Jesu, Good above All Other* (for SS and organ) and *Let All the World* (for SSA and organ) on the twenty-fourth!

Between June and September, the interior of St Mary Magdalene's underwent restoration and redecoration. This altered the acoustics of the church somewhat, producing a shorter and sharper reverberation. Some careless painters had covered up two bas reliefs of St Cecilia of which Willan had been very fond. The old man was quite upset by these changes in the church he had served and loved for more than forty years. Loyalty and devotion won out over anger, however, and he remained. By this time Willan had resigned as director of the Toronto Diocesan Choir School and had been created director emeritus.

Late in the autumn Willan learned that two of his motets, *Fair in Face* and *I Beheld Her*, had been sung at the White House before President Kennedy. He also had the satisfaction of knowing that *The Canadian Psalter* was now completed and published.

Willan was sick again in the spring of 1964. Overtired – perhaps from his work on *Deirdre* – he contracted influenza, which subsequently turned into pneumonia. As a result he was in hospital for six weeks over the Easter season. He was asked to lecture on plainchant at the University of Toronto summer school but declined. He had a 'pet peeve' that summer: 'The proposed new [Canadian] flag, which is nothing more than a very anaemic piece of bunting, could only have been designed by either an idiot or a political buffoon. The red Maple leaves have a very significant prophesy, for when they become red they are ready to rot and fall!' Willan did not appreciate this erosion of Canada's British heritage.

In October Willan resigned as university organist, after thirty-two years of service. He calculated that he had played 250 convocations! His last act was to play for the installation of Douglas Le Pan, the son of an old university friend, as principal of University College.

In November Willan resigned as music director of the Toronto Gregorian Association, the group he had helped found in 1950 and of which he had been musical director ever since. Though enthusiastic about the association and working hard on its behalf, he was disappointed at the small impact it had had on church music in Canada. In 1960, it had only fifty members and a choir of thirty to thirty-five. In the summer of 1964 he had written: 'I am very dubious about the future. The G.A. has gone down steadily for the last 5 or 6 years, and I fear that it is nearing the time when we can add R.I.P.' He and his colleagues were unable to comprehend that 'male Anglican communicants' were an insufficient base to effect a movement towards plainsong in Canada (whatever the situation might be in England). The failure of this project must be counted as one of the major disappointments of his life.

On 8 December Willan's wife died suddenly. Gladys had had some blood pressure problems and a fall downstairs earlier in the year, yet her death was quite unexpected. During the night she had gone into the bathroom, suffered a heart attack and died. The bathroom door was locked, and when he realized something was wrong Willan had to get the police to break the door open. The night after her mother died, Mary Mason heard her father extemporize on the piano: 'It was very beautiful music – it was his leave taking.'

The relationship had had its ups and downs. Nevertheless Willan and his wife had grown close together in old age, and the loss of his wife was a severe blow. From that time onwards his own physical decline seemed to accelerate. Some attribute this to the fact that Gladys was no longer there to look after him as she had done in the past.

Plans for a stage version of *Deirdre* had begun in 1961; on 2 and 3 April 1965 the University of Toronto Opera School presented the opera in the MacMillan Theatre. Ettore Mazzoleni conducted. The production was so successful that an extra performance had to be arranged for 5 April. In the next year or so, Toronto audiences would have an opportunity to attend three further performances. This success resulted in talk of a revival of *Transit through Fire*, but none took place.

In July Waterloo Music Company approached Willan about republishing ten of the art-songs he had composed between 1901 and 1905. These had been published shortly afterwards, but by 1965 had long been out of print. Songwriting had been Willan's first major area of creative activity and he felt – quite correctly so – that some of his best work lay there. He was anxious to have these early songs in circulation again.

During the summer Willan returned, after a year's retirement, as music director for the Toronto Diocesan Summer Choir School. It was reported that the boys were very glad to have 'the old Doc' back!

Life at 139 Inglewood Drive was not easy for Willan after the death of his wife. He was lonely and was having difficulty obtaining housekeepers. He was even toying with thoughts of moving to Victoria, British Columbia, where he had a cousin and some other acquaintances. However it would take much to remove him from St Mary Magdalene's and there was a possibility of further stage performances of *Deirdre*. Willan did not move after all, but two of his sons retired to British Columbia within a few years.

There were some ruffled feathers – Willan's – at St Mary Magdalene's at the end of the summer. On 1 July a dozen members of the church's choirs got together to make a tape, and 100 record discs were subsequently cut from the tape. Willan was furious when he found out. He was angry about the use of the choir library without his permission and the use of the title 'St Mary's Singers'; he complained about a usurping of his authority and stated that 'enthusiasm may become a menace.' Plans for making a second record were subsequently squelched. There seemed to be a general misunderstanding all round, and apologies were sent to Willan. Clearly the old man's fuse was short and his sensibilities easily singed, but he was labouring under considerable difficulties with his sight, hearing, and other infirmities.

Willan's eighty-fifth birthday went by with somewhat less fanfare than that which had accompanied his seventieth, seventy-fifth, and eightieth. When the CBC approached him in November about a television program, he declined; it was 'too much strain.' (He did, however, agree to a similar proposal the following year.) In November he was made a Fellow of the Royal Hamilton College of Music.

A pleasant surprise awaited Willan on 3 May 1966 when he appeared as – so he thought – a guest at a luncheon at the Park Plaza Hotel in Toronto. It was only after his arrival that he realized he was the guest of honour! The luncheon was sponsored by Columbia Records to coincide with the release in Canada of *Selected Organ Works by Healey Willan*, recorded at York Minster by Francis Jackson. This was the first commercial LP devoted entirely to Willan's organ works and included *Prelude and Fugue in C Minor* and *Passacaglia and Fugue No. 2*. At the luncheon Willan spoke of his philosophy of keeping occupied: 'I do like to keep busy. I'm like an old London cab-horse: keep him in harness and he'll go on for ever, put him out to pasture and he'll drop dead in a few days.' He also remarked: 'If I can leave behind me some music which is good, and if I can be held in memory for a while by a few kind friends, I shall turn up my toes happily and willingly when the time comes.'

Life at home was a little more settled. Willan was still sometimes lonely and missed his wife very much. However at least he now had a man coming in twice a week 'to help tidy up,' and he was very busy. His many friends frequently dropped in.

In June Willan was asked by George Maybee to compose an anthem for the celebrations in Kingston of the birthday of Sir John A. Macdonald. Nothing came of this, however. Willan was already busy on several things for Canada's coming centennial, the new productions of *Deirdre*, and some revisions to the *Deirdre* score.

Deirdre was included in the Canadian Opera Company's 1966 season and received three professional performances at the O'Keefe Centre in Toronto on 24 and 29 September and 4 October. Mazzoleni again conducted; the director of the Canadian Opera Company, Herman Geiger-Torel, supervised the stage production, and the sets were designed by Lawrence Schafer (fresh from some experience with the Bayreuth Wagner festivals). Willan and John Coulter received standing ovations. For Willan this was the climax of his career. He considered – probably correctly – that *Deirdre* was his greatest work. Critics were quite complimentary, though some complained of the Wagnerian influence.

Things were unsettled at St Mary Magdalene's. Earlier in the year the rector, Father Crummer, had become a Roman Catholic, and Willan's friend Father Fairweather of Trinity College, had taken temporary charge. Willan wrote to a friend on 11 June: 'The defection of Crummer was an unfortunate thing, but S.M.M. is used to upsets and such like, and our motto is "Business as usual." ... The choir is going strong, but we need more men in the Ritual Choir. Motor-cars and weekends have played the devil with choirs all over the place.'

Throughout his retirement years, Willan was bombarded with requests for information about himself. In October he replied to one such request: 'As regards your "research" into my murky past, I must definitely say NO. I have been asked for this sort of information during the past ten years at the rate of about 5 per annum and I have said NO to all – for the simple reason that I want them to say what *they* think about me, not what I think about myself!' Just before Christmas, the CBC presented *Portrait of Healey Willan*. He had been persuaded to change his mind.

Willan's *Centennial Anthem* was performed on Parliament Hill, Ottawa, on 31 December 1966. It had occasioned much correspondence between Willan, Robert Choquette, the author of the French text, and John Glassco, who made the English translation. All this effort did not produce a memorable piece of music; perhaps inspiration was somewhat stifled by too much care. Possibly the idea of a Canadian centennial did not stir Willan very much. He wrote to a friend: 'I have been invited to go to Ottawa to take part in the Lighting the Candle on December 31. If it were a barrel of gunpowder I might give it serious consideration.' He did not attend.

Through much of 1967 Willan was engaged in proofreading the 580-page orchestral score of the final version of *Deirdre*, which was being printed by BMI Canada Ltd. This proved a great strain on his already failing eyesight. He had grown very fond of *Deirdre*, and it would be his last great musical legacy. Perhaps he could sense that the preparation of this large score for printing was a race against time. In April he wrote to his old pupil Robert Fleming, 'Since Gladys died I have grown old.' The previous year he had written to John Coulter: 'Oh John, I have come to the sad conclusion that I am not getting old – I've got!'

In May Willan received from Waterloo Music the proposed artwork for the cover of *Ten Songs*, the album first discussed in July 1965. Frank Daley wrote: 'It is unusual for us to consult an author or composer concerning any art work. My pleasure in having these works for our catalogue and my respect for you is the reason that this is sent for your comment.' This beautiful album, containing reprints of songs Willan composed between 1901 and 1905, appeared later in the year.

Later in May there was a special centennial salute concert of Willan's music held in St Paul's. An estimated 3,000 people attended; hundreds had to stand and many were turned away at the door (including one of the local critics!). The Toronto Mendelssohn Choir performed *An Apostrophe to the Heavenly Hosts*, and the Festival Singers sang *Missa brevis No. 10*, three motets to the Blessed Virgin Mary, and *Gloria Deo per immensa saecula*. The hymn anthem *O quanta qualia* was also performed. Willan's former chorister and pupil Elmer Iseler conducted; this concert was Iseler's idea. Francis Jackson played three of Willan's finest organ works: the chorale prelude on *Vulpius*, *Prelude and Fugue in C Minor*, and the legendary *Introduction, Passacaglia and Fugue*, originally composed for the St Paul's organ. The program was a distillation of the finest of Willan's choral and organ compositions. At the end of the concert the whole audience stood; Willan was deeply moved. St Paul's had been the site of Willan's first church activities in Canada in 1913; and now, more than half a century later, it was the scene of this great tribute.

In June the Healey Willan Chapter of the Imperial Order of the Daughters of the Empire established an annual scholarship for composition valued at $200, in Willan's honour. Dominion Day, 1 July, was the occasion for a gala concert for Canada's centennial at the Place des Arts, Montreal; the Toronto Mendelssohn Choir gave another performance of

Apostrophe. In August Willan's last orchestral work, *Centennial March*, commissioned by BMI Canada, received its first performance (in a band arrangement by Capt C.A.W. Adams), at the Centennial Centre, Ottawa, by the Grenadier Guards Band.

In September came the long-awaited première – twenty years late – of the second version of *Brébeuf*. It took place in Timothy Eaton Memorial Church, Toronto, with the church's organist, Dr David Ouchterlony, skilfully playing the orchestral score on the large organ. (Ouchterlony used to drive Willan to St Mary Magdalene's each Sunday morning before proceeding on to his own church.) Willan conducted the choir – the last time he would conduct in public. The performance was broadcast by the CBC to mark the feast of St Jean de Brébeuf. A tribute to Willan followed the broadcast and centennial medallions were given to him and each member of the choir.

Among the many birthday wishes Willan received on 12 October 1967 was one from Walter Hinrichsen, who had encouraged him to write his *Passacaglia and Fugue No. 2*. Hinrichsen asked him to consider writing an organ sonata, since there was none by a contemporary composer in the C.F. Peters catalogue. Unfortunately, nothing came of this proposal.

In centennial year the Order of Canada was created. Willan was made one of the first companions in a ceremony held by Governor-General Roland Michener in Ottawa on 24 November. Mrs Michener had been a pupil and chorister of Willan, as had her daughter Wendy. Willan had intended to be present but had asked that his daughter be allowed to accompany him because of his eyesight. By 9 November, however, he had to write that he was awaiting eye surgery any day. His son Patrick went to Ottawa to stand in for him. Canada had abolished knighthoods many years earlier; but it now conferred on Willan its highest honour, Companion of the Order of Canada.

Willan had been warned in 1959 of the possibility of cataracts, and in his final years both eyes were afflicted. In November 1967 he underwent an operation to remove a cataract from one eye. Unfortunately his recovery proved slower than he expected, though the operation was relatively successful. Willan could not return home without a nurse or housekeeper; his son Bernard returned from a stay abroad and he and his wife moved into 139 Inglewood to look after his father.

On Christmas Eve 1967, Willan, by an almost superhuman effort, made his way to St Mary Magdalene's to play midnight mass. He had not been at the church since before his operation in November; Margaret Harmer had assumed his work with the choir and organ in his absence.

When it became known that Willan was present, a 'bodyguard' from his choir guided him, fore and aft, up the narrow and steep steps to the gallery. These he ascended weakly and with difficulty. Since he could not really see, he played the whole service from memory. Margaret Harmer stood beside him, helping him with his music and telling him the key signature and mode to use (she also conducted some of the unaccompanied choir works so that Willan would not have to leave the organ console). At the end he patted the console of his beloved organ and said goodbye to the 'old girl.' His bodyguard then eased him down the steep stairs for the last time.

On 27 December Willan was back in hospital, this time for a prostate operation. Malignancy was discovered, necessitating further major surgery. Three operations within a few weeks left Willan very weak, and progress was slow. Many thought he would never leave hospital, and the doctor warned the family to expect the end. Suddenly, toward the end of January, Willan confounded his doctor and rallied. He was allowed to return on 10 February to his beloved 'junk-room' (workshop-studio), into which his bed was moved. A nurse stayed with him at night, and members of the family helped during the day.

For several weeks Willan was happy and cheerful, chatting with friends who dropped in. He did not know about the cancer which had spread, but which was not as yet painful. He spoke of how he was going to 'fight his way back.' However his heart, with which he had been having 'disagreements' for some twenty years, was to have the last word. After a succession of seizures, he died quietly in his sleep on Friday, 16 February 1968. He died at home, in his 'room,' as he would have wished.

High mass on Sunday morning, 18 February, at St Mary Magdalene's had been scheduled to be televised, and this could not be postponed. Willan's choir carried on, though under great duress. An even more severe strain would come the next day at the requiem high mass (though the family had suggested there be no music). There was no eulogy and the organ was silent, but the choir sang Cascilioni's *Requiem*, Willan's funeral motet, *O King, under Whom All Things Do Live*, and the Russian *Contakion of the Departed*. Many had to stand in the church, which was overflowing with people. Sir William McKie flew from England to attend and was joined by distinguished mourners from the United States and Canada. Willan's honours were arranged on top of his coffin, and a floral tribute from the family of the governor-general was placed nearby.

Willan had prepared Cascilioni's *Requiem* with his choir for the Mass of All Souls on 2 November 1967 and had added: 'Now you have it all practised up for my funeral and I hope you sing it as well. If you don't, I will sit up in my coffin and conduct you.' Some in the church may have remembered also the words with which Willan concluded a parish letter in 1951: 'When my work at S.M.M. is finished I think I shall feel like Don Camillo, and say "Well, Lord, I've tried to make your worship beautiful, and I've done it for your glory, not for mine: but You know that, so I needn't say anything more about it." And perhaps He'll smile. I hope so.'

Of the many tributes written, perhaps the most eloquent came from John Coulter, in his *Lament for Healey Willan*:

> ... he made music,
> cared chiefly for music,
> reality and meaning for him were music.

> As a master-craftsman contemptuous of the meretricious,
> he was repelled by the strident new, the bright facetious,
> Likewise in person: in taste and habit fastidious,
> debonair. He burnished his fingernails, wore spats.
> Yet behind the defensive stockade
> his nature was gentle, warm, responsive;
> an intuitive creature of quick perception
> and touching childlike suspicions
> and trust and a chuckling mischievous
> sense of humour. His mind was a rich
> compendium of hilarious bawdy tales.
> There was a sort of laughter round him.
> ... he being a man of faith
> for whom faith (to which I never heard him allude)
> presumably was a luminous assurance transcending reason.
> I shall remember him with affection ...
> tinged only with some regret
> for his incurious satisfaction
> with the already-achieved, the language formulated ...

Willan with his mother, sister, and Grandmother Healey ca 1890

Willan ca 1900

En route to Canada 1913

Willan at the St Paul's organ ca 1918

The Willan family at Lake Simcoe 1917

Willan with conservatory students ca 1925

Willan with the cast of *L'Ordre de Bon Temps* 1928

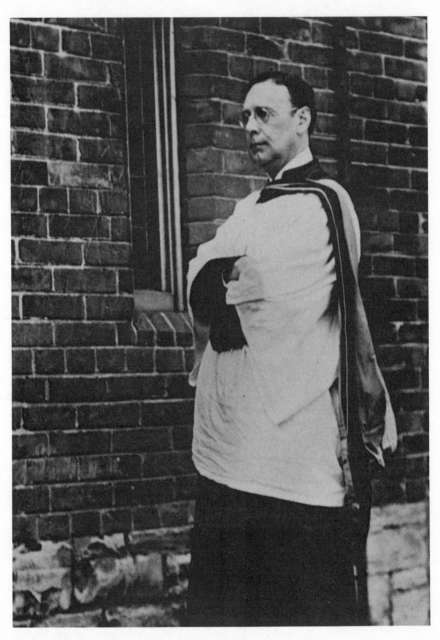

Willan outside St Mary Magdalene's mid-1920s

St Mary Magdalene's ca 1950

Willan ca 1950

Willan ca 1940   Gladys Willan 1962

Willan and Sir Ernest MacMillan at the Arts and Letters Club 1962

Eightieth birthday party at Amen House 1960

Willan with Francis Jackson 1967

Willan receiving honorary degree at McMaster University 1962

Willan in his 'junk-room' 1967

5

Musician and teacher

Willan started his study of the organ at St Saviour's Choir School, East-bourne, with Walter Hay Sangster, in 1889. Within a year or two he had progressed sufficiently to play services for the school, though he was only eleven years of age. When sixteen he became an associate of the Royal College of Organists and at eighteen he became a fellow – the highest professional diploma an organist could attain. About this time Willan began advanced studies with William Stevenson Hoyte, organist of All Saints', Margaret Street, London. Throughout his life Willan held both his organ teachers in high regard. He admired Sangster's 'noble' playing of Bach, and received from him a solid grounding in service playing. Hoyte was generous with his time at lessons and in particular encouraged – and strove for – musicality in his students' playing.

Willan's training as an organist was thus in the late-nineteenth-century English tradition. German and English music accounted for most of the repertoire, with less attention being given to the French and virtually none to other countries. Bach, Mendelssohn, and Rheinberger were perhaps the most important. Comparatively little was played or known of the music of Bach's predecessors and contemporaries. Before the days of radios, recordings, and the expansion of symphonic concerts, the organ transcription was an important means of making a repertoire known and thus appeared frequently in recitals.

The following list of Willan's repertoire between 1900 and 1912 is a summary of the main items: J.S. Bach: preludes and fugues in G minor, A minor, and B minor, *Passacaglia and Fugue in C Minor*, *Toccata and Fugue in D Minor*, and *'St Anne' Fugue*; Guilmant: a number of short pieces; Handel: transcriptions of the overtures to *Semele* and *Occasional Oratorio;* Harwood: *Sonata in C Sharp Minor;* Hollins: *Overture in C Minor;* Humperdinck: transcription of the 'angel scene' from *Hansel and Gretel;* Karg-Elert: *Claire de lune* (copy autographed by the composer) and several choral improvisations; Liszt: *Fugue on the Name of BACH;* Mendelssohn: sonatas 1, 2, and 3; Rachmaninoff: transcription of *Prelude in C Sharp Minor;* Reubke: *Sonata in C Minor* (on Psalm 94); Rheinberger: sonatas 2, 7, and 9 and *Abendrühe;* Sangster: preludes and fugues in D minor and G minor; Schumann: *Fugue No. 1 in B Flat* on BACH; Wagner: transcriptions of Trauermarsch (*Götterdämmerung*), prelude to act I (*Lohengrin*), prelude to act I (*Parsifal*), Good Friday music (*Parsifal*), *Huldigungsmarsch;* S.S. Wesley: *Choral Song and Fugue;* John West: *Song of Triumph;* Widor: finales only of symphonies 2 and 5; Willan: preludes and fugues in C minor and B minor, *Epilogue,* and *Scherzo.*

Willan performed two ensemble works, Merkel's *Duet Sonata in D Minor* and Rheinberger's *Organ Concerto No. 1 in F,* at least once. There were none of the organ works of César Franck or of Handel's organ concertos (even in transcription). Most of the transcriptions were of works by Wagner, but there were some of works by Tschaikowsky and others.

Willan is known to have played organ recitals in at least twelve churches in London and environs: Christ Church, Wanstead; St Peter-upon-Cornhill; St Andrew's, Leytonstone; St John the Baptist, Epping; St John the Baptist, Kensington; St Lawrence Jewry, Gresham St; St Peter's Church, Ealing; St Mary-le-Bow, Cheapside; Dartford Parish Church; Holy Trinity, St Marylebone; St John's Church, St John's Wood Road; and All Saints', Margaret Street.

During his first ten years in Canada, 1913–23, Willan played nearly fifty recitals, more than half of them on the magnificent new organ at St Paul's Church, Toronto. He added a number of items to his repertoire, of which the following are the most notable: J.S. Bach: preludes and fugues in C major, A major, and G major and *Prelude and Fugue in D Minor;* Borowski: *Sonata in A Minor;* Elgar: transcriptions of 'Prelude' and 'Angel's Farewell' (*Gerontius*), 'Triumphal March' (*Caractacus*), and 'Meditation' (*Lux Christi*); Franck: *Cantabile* and *Finale in B Flat;* Guilmant: *Sonata No. 1 in D Minor;* Handel: transcriptions of *Overture to Richard I* and *Organ Concerto No. 2;* Mozart: *Fantasy in F Minor;* C.W. Pearce: symphonic poem on *Corde natus;* Rheinberger: *Sonata No. 6;* Saint-Saens: *Rhapsody No. 3 in A Minor;* John West: *Finale Jubilante;* Widor: *Symphony No. 6* and additional movements from symphonies 2 and 5; and Willan:

Introduction, Passacaglia and Fugue. Many transcriptions of pieces by various composers (including quite a few more by Tschaikowsky) were added. Willan himself made about two dozen organ transcriptions of works by other composers.

In the list of repertoire in England all the Bach pieces, except 'St Anne' *Fugue*, were in minor keys. The list in Canada contains pieces mostly in major keys, as if to rectify an imbalance. Willan also played various Bach chorale preludes. He does not appear to have played the trio sonatas, at least in recital.

Willan made few major additions to his repertory after this time – indeed, after he left St Paul's. Except for a few smaller pieces and his own new works as they came along, the only major additions after 1923 were Karg-Elert's *Sonatina in A Minor*, Mendelssohn's *Sonata No. 4*, and Rheinberger's *Sonata No. 4*.

Willan used Rheinberger's *Sonata No. 4* as part of a special program based on the Tonus Peregrinus for performance at one of his Convocation Hall recitals at the University of Toronto in 1932. The first and last movements of the sonata make reference to the Tonus Peregrinus. Willan used the first movement as a prelude to start the recital and the last movement as a postlude. In between he used all the small pieces based on the Tonus Peregrinus, by various composers, which he could find. This was a particularly interesting example of Willan's programming, and he performed it a number of times.

Again an almost complete absence of Franck is notable, and there is no Vierne. Few, if any, post-First World War compositions were added by Willan to his repertoire, save for his own works. For weddings, convocations, Sunday church services, and so on, he had a large repertoire of small pieces. For example he owned many well-worn transcriptions of choruses, arias, and marches by Handel – pieces which would make good 'occasional music.'

In his prime as a recitalist Willan had considerable facility. Fine technique (enhanced by piano study with Howard-Jones), long experience, natural precocity, and great ability as a composer and improviser all played a role in his skill as an organist. Between the world wars Willan was in considerable demand as a recitalist in Canada and in the United States. In 1923 the *Albany Evening Journal* wrote: 'No one who has ever heard Dr Willan will confuse his playing with that of any other great recitalist ... [He is] like Dickinson of New York in his refinement of essentially poetic nature ... There is an austerity and high mysticism that is quite his own ... He is the least vulgar of organists.' Concerning a recital in Rochester the same year, the *Diapason* wrote: 'Dr Willan is like no other player familiar to American audiences. He does not regard the organ as an orchestra ... While you are listening to him you are not thinking of his registration, you are feeling a compelling emotion which only a great artist can achieve ... He is a haunting player, a fine musician.'

By the late 1940s some of the flair was gone. Willan's Convocation Hall recitals tended to be rather casual. He would shuffle on to the stage before the opening recital of the season and announce, 'Ladies and gentlemen, these recitals will start promptly – five minutes late!' He would ease himself on to the organ bench, slowly open up his music, pull out a few stops, and start. The programming and playing were sometimes dull and monotonous – at one recital he played no less than *nine* Advent and Christmas chorale preludes in a row – at other times they were quite interesting. Willan particularly loved Rheinberger's sonatas and played them magnificently. He was also fond of Karg-Elert's works and gave them sensitive interpretations.

In the 1950s, Willan's organ playing still commanded respect. In 1955 one of Canada's leading recitalists, Charles Peaker, said of Willan: 'His organ playing is very sound. I don't know how he does it, because he gets very little time to practice. He knows the value of silence. The instrument does not intrude where it should not, and when it does come in, it comes with a colossal sound.' In 1958 the *Toronto Star* reviewed a recital of 27 January: 'Dr Willan is 77 now, and some of the sheer facility has gone out of his playing ... but depth of perception and feeling were very much present.' Willan liked to make statements such as 'As an instrument the organ bores me – I play it just out of habit.' Perhaps he was getting tired of the repertoire he had been playing for fifty years.

He had received all his organ instruction and had acquired his repertoire and playing style before the Baroque revival in organ building and performance style. These new developments had no influence on him – he loved his Bach dearly and was quite content to play Bach as he had been taught in 1900. He disliked what he considered to be the strident dissonances of 'modern' music and did not care for what he considered the shrill and ugly sounds produced by the new Baroque-style organs that were being built. He was particularly upset by the changes made to the big St Paul's organ that he had known so well. In a letter to me (15 April 1963) he unburdened himself:

There was a very beautiful organ, but which has been spoiled by adherents of the so-called Baroque system. These evil people apparently leave behind them a trail of sheer ugliness and negation of beauty. Such organs have been described by Vaughan-Williams as 'nasty bubble-and-squeak contraptions' and by Bishop Wilkinson of Toronto as 'pseudo-sanctimonious calliopes' – two lamentably fitting descriptions! ... From time to time the term 'organist' has possessed (unfortunately with some justification) a derogatory connotation in the minds of many musicians, and it is difficult to see how those who favour such ugly and unbeautiful sounds can possibly expect to rise in the estimation of those interested in the art of music.

Willan in his later years viewed the organ as primarily a church instrument rather than a recital one; in a postscript he added: 'They apparently overlook the fact that Lady Susi Jeans has said, "they [ie Baroque-style organs] are of very little use for accompanimental purposes." What is the main use of a church organ?'

Willan had an extraordinarily sensitive and subtle style of plainsong accompaniment. It was the product of a lifetime of experience. But plainsong accompaniment was also instinctive with him: he maintained that, beyond a point, it could not be taught; one either had a natural feeling for it, or one did not.

His style of hymn-playing was unique. The most obvious feature was the massive rolling (arpeggiation) of the chords, which, combined with the peculiar tone qualities of the old Breckell and Matthews organ and the acoustics of St Mary Magdalene's, produced a most impressive effect. Willan's treatment of one of the Rouen church melodies (eg *Iste confessor*) in this manner was quite unforgettable.

He had other tricks as well: 'When pitch shows signs of dropping, it is a mistake to attempt to pull the singers up by "turning the organ on them" ... By playing the left hand on the Swell or Choir ... [and] the right hand ... on the Great playing the treble and alto parts inverted, the singers can generally be pulled up to pitch in a very short time.' He also noted that: 'Dragging ... is another common fault. If a soft verse is being sung, the melody played on the open diapason in the tenor is a useful help. Should the dragging take place during a hymn of robust character, the left hand and pedals played legato and the right hand strongly emphasizing the rhythm will generally cope with the situation' (Conservatory *Quarterly* 1926).

Finally there were his improvisations, some of which scaled glorious heights. The combination of a fluent technique with an imaginative and highly skilled creative mind allowed him to improvise at a level attainable by few. I noted earlier such feats as the improvisation of a full sonata in three movements on themes submitted by the audience following an organ recital in Albany, and the extemporization of a fugue on a subject comprised of notes suggested by a class of students during the film *Man of Music*. Willan's extemporizations of interludes between the verses of a processional hymn, such as *The First Nowell* at midnight mass on Christmas Eve, were masterful and always perfectly timed.

But perhaps most memorable of all were the postludes he improvised at the ends of services. These have been described by Thomas Hyland: 'He usually "lets loose" with the organ in his improvised postlude at the conclusion of High Mass. Starting quite often with a snatch of melody from the last hymn sung, he gradually builds up the organ into a gigantic mountain of sound, ascends it with one or two majestic modulations, and crowns it with a cadence of such colossal stature that the very walls do tremble.'

CHOIRMASTER

Willan was conducting choir practices by the age of eleven at St Saviour's Choir School. He was an active choirmaster for seventy-five years. Of his work in England little is known, except that he obtained the position at St John the Baptist, Holland Road, at least partly because he was able to handle an unruly group of boys – he was a good disciplinarian and attuned to the psychology of the boy chorister. Likewise little is known of his work as conductor of the Wanstead Choral Society (1904–6) or the Thalian Operatic Society (1906 and 1907), save for the actual works that he performed (see chapter 1). Willan's sister stated: 'Healey was in great demand as a conductor of orchestras for classical works and of performances of sacred music and choral works.'

Much more, of course, is known about Willan's years as a choirmaster in Toronto, at St Mary Magdalene's and with his Tudor Singers in the 1930s. He expected his choristers to be able to read English, read music, read and sing with pure vowels and what he called 'refined' consonants, sing softly, and not 'wobble.' He did not want 'soloists' in his choir. He could be scathing when a sound was produced which he did not like: 'A tenor is not a voice, it is an affliction'; 'A file is a useful tool, but not in a choir'; and 'There are singers who are musicians and there are those who make noises with their necks.' He wrote in 1962, 'I always feel that girls who really dress well and look well have the aesthetic qualities which make for good singing.'

Willan has been described as a disciplinarian, a taskmaster, and a perfectionist in his handling of his choirs. He was probably all of these.

Walter MacNutt, a former pupil, writes, 'We were all in fear that we might commit some musical offence. If one of us did, first there was a shattering silence, then a glare, sometimes a roar, or at other times the prettiest, most apt comment that just hit the nail on the head.' He stood for no fooling at choir practice and demanded the most from his singers. He would labour long for perfection of phrase and words. He was, however, ready to acknowledge and compliment good results and always had a supply of anecdotes and personal reminiscences to ease the tension or to illustrate some aspect of the music being rehearsed. He was strict about attendance and became angry if a rehearsal or a service were missed. He deliberately kept his choir small and every member was important. Choir practices were usually unaccompanied: 'If you can't sing without the organ, how on earth do you expect to sing with it?' His expressive face was an important factor in his choral directing. He always looked choir members in the eye when conducting and had a power of communication with his choir which transcended speech. A glance, a quick look of anticipation, a 'hooded' listening expression, a flittering of satisfaction or annoyance worked wonders.

The words were crucial to Willan: 'Sing words, sing words – any fool can sing notes – takes brains to sing words' was his frequent advice to his choristers. He wrote: 'One of the weaknesses in the best of modern choirs stems from the fact that the conductors have not learned the importance of language. They do not realize that if a choir is aware of the importance of a single word or phrase the entire work can become a new and exciting experience.' On another occasion he wrote: '[It is] a real delight to get a small body of really sensitive people – everything sounds different, and the words colour the voices ever so much better than all the silly marks of expression added by editors who put music first and words nowhere.'

Two long-time members of Willan's choir, George and Margaret Drynan, wrote in *Diapason* in 1960: 'Dr Willan does not train his singers, they train themselves; he exhorts by precept, anecdote, joke, explanation, and all the devices of a born teacher. He will explain why, and his singers will discover the "how".'

Willan inspired a fierce loyalty in his choristers. His warm personality, his humility and humanity, and his satisfaction in great music well performed drew his choir members to him. His choir was, in many ways, his 'family,' especially in the later years. He had also a way with choirs other than his own. For the première in 1937 of his *Coronation Te Deum* by the Toronto Bach Choir, he came to some of the rehearsals. The conductor,

Reginald Stewart, wrote about him: 'He also played the piano at some of the rehearsals, completely captivating everyone with his ability and his hypnotic charm.'

Willan held firm views on the function of a church choir. In *Cap and Gown* in 1959, he said: 'The choir should realise that the main reason for their existence is to sing the choral parts of the service in such a way that the incomparable words of the liturgy are enhanced and not obscured, for they are neither exhibitionists nor entertainers. The anthem, which is too often an excrescence, is not their chief job, and a choir which regards the anthem as the all-important part of their work may be at times not only a hindrance, but even a menace.' Willan always planned the music (including hymns) for the service very carefully, so that all the texts fitted in with the liturgical theme of the day: 'I do that every Sunday, and it takes me very often hours to pick them out and get them right.'

The sound of the gallery choir at St Mary Magdalene's was distinctive. Beautiful tone was one of Willan's main objectives. He kept his singers at mezzo-piano or mezzo-forte level during rehearsal and even in performance he rarely allowed his voices to 'let loose.' The result was a beautiful blend of a small number of amateur voices, and even when there were only one or two voices on a part, these rarely protruded. The fine acoustics of the church assisted. One could always hear the altos; indeed, Willan seemed to discourage brilliant soprano sound. There was, however, a somewhat limited range of dynamics and colour. Perhaps he felt changes of colour and dynamics more subtly than most and was not aware that these were not always conveyed to his hearers.

Willan had a high sense of drama when performing the liturgy and indeed considered opera, drama, and church ritual to be closely linked. He looked for musicality in other choirs and found one famous group 'rather tedious' because he felt that they strove for technical perfection at the expense of the music. (He liked to quote 'an old Czech friend' in saying, 'Yah! Notes – notes – notes! Yah! but music – Nottings!')

In 1945 Willan took his St Mary Magdalene Singers to New York for two recitals in Town Hall. The group consisted of nine women and seven men and was well received by its audiences. There was much comment on the group's clear enunciation. The *Journal-American* wrote: 'The singers performed their task with sincerity and reverence, revealing meticulous preparation, ably capturing the spirit of the music with an appropriate value of mood, accurate in intonation, and attractive in the blending and the balance of the voices.' The *Herald Tribune* praised the high artistic standard of the program, the well-unified performance, the choir's responsiveness to Willan's interpretive wishes, the rhythmic flexibility, the clarity of detail, the good balance, and the finesse of dynamic shading (especially in the softer passages). It criticized the limited range of colour and dynamics and complained that the concert lacked the expressive variety and differentiation of style which the program warranted and that the emotional differences between joyous and penitential works were not fully conveyed.

The reviews during the 1930s of the Tudor Singers introduce a further dimension. A number comment on the lack of 'exhibitionism' and the avoidance of 'platform capers.' Willan is described as 'a self-effacing sort of musician.' Restraint, control, good taste, and absence of histrionics characterized his performances.

Willan had many different choristers singing under him through the years. Many members of his gallery choir were music students from the conservatory or the university. He would invariably 'suggest' to any of his own students who were interested in church music that they should enter his choir. There were a continual change of personnel in the choir as the students moved on and a constant training of new choristers. Many people world go out from St Mary Magdalene's to all parts of the country enriched by their exposure to the great music of the church and Willan's direction. Many became active proponents of a richer church music and its proper performance as a result of their years with Willan. His work as music director of the Toronto Diocesan Choir School and the Toronto Gregorian Association had a similar impact.

TEACHER

On Willan's effectiveness as a teacher there is some division of opinion. Some think he was a great teacher; others think it was an inspiring experience to study with him, but that one did not necessarily learn from him what was set down in the curriculum; yet others think that he had little time for – or interest in – teaching; and some think he was a rather poor teacher. His time for and interest in teaching perhaps varied according to the subject being taught and to whom it was being taught. The current demands of his compositional and other activities also influenced his teaching. In one of his 'Matters Musical' talks of 1938 he said regarding education, 'The meaning of the word, from the Latin *educo* (I lead out), should be illuminating, and too often in these days of rush and hurry and taking a course of this, and a course of that, and a course of something else, education is regarded as a system of cramming in instead of a means of drawing out – the very antithesis of its real meaning.'

Willan was not basically a scholar, as his lecture notes (in the National Library of Canada) reveal. He was known as an authority on plainchant, which had been a lifelong interest; yet even here his experience and knowledge were mainly concerned with plainchant in the Church of England, and his knowledge was derived more from long performing experience than from academic study. He never studied for a degree from a university. However, the written examinations which he took at eighteen for the FRCO diploma required a fluency and standard of musical writing which few of today's bachelors of music on this continent could meet.

Much of what Willan accomplished was instinctive. In later life he felt that certain things could not be taught. Some considered him a born teacher and thought the evidence could be seen in the choir rehearsal room as well as the classroom. His activity as a composer and practical musician afforded him little time for 'ivory tower' study; in fact, it is remarkable that he had time for any teaching at all.

Willan's teaching activities were largely the result of financial necessity. Yet he was very interested in his students. As an old man, he stated in a speech: 'In political circles the term "elder statesman" has a noble ring: but in art the terms "old fogey" ... "venerable has-been" ... are more prevalent – and perhaps more suitable. However, into whichever of the latter categories my old students place me, no one is happier to hear of their success than their one-time teacher and their very interested friend.'

Willan's legacy as a teacher rests mainly in his composition students. Of those who achieved distinction, none followed his manner of writing, and all developed separate styles. This, of course, is what he encouraged; after the basic technique had been secured, his students were expected to find their own way (as he himself had done).

In his faith in the importance of a thorough grounding in traditional fundamentals he never wavered. During his retirement he was disturbed by the tendency to stop teaching strict counterpoint and to skimp generally on traditional training in composition. 'I don't think these contemporary methods will produce anything of lasting value. It is rather like erecting a building without a foundation – one big storm and it is all gone' (*Globe Magazine*, 24 Dec 1966).

Music appreciation (or 'musical perception,' as he preferred to call it) was for Willan the basis of musical study. In another of his 'Matters Musical' talks, he observed:

The understanding of the language and the style of any period is the first step in appreciation. This is of far greater importance than knowing that the second subject enters at the thirty-second bar in the key of the dominant, or that in the development the principal subject is combined with the second subject upsidedown. This is all very well from an analytical point of view ... but so far as any perception of the aesthetic value of the music is concerned it is of very secondary importance ... It is through sound, not through text books, that the first approach to music must of necessity be made ... The wise student will do well to realise that music is first and last sound, and that without a perception and a hearing of sound, appreciation is a meaningless term.

'Music is sound' was one of Willan's mottos as a teacher of composition. He would say to his students, 'If your writing sounds rotten, then chances are it is rotten, no matter how cleverly it is contrived; if it sounds lovely, then chances are it is a worthwhile piece of work.' He insisted that his students acquire a fluent technique in traditional harmony and counterpoint. He believed that good technique was built upon a mastery of fluent two-part counterpoint; he often stated his own epitaph should read: 'He preached two-part counterpoint, but no-one believed him.'

Though his music was looked upon as academic and 'typical British organist' in style by some younger Canadian composers, especially following the Second World War, he was remarkably unacademic in his teaching and always gave good sound precedence over some obscure academic rule. He said that textbooks on harmony and counterpoint 'undoubtedly have their value during the spelling process, but once having accomplished that, they are of no more value to a composer than a spelling book is to a normally well-educated person.' When asked his opinion of an eminent theorist whose books were then in wide use, he replied: 'Delightful chap he was – excellent books too, but he was one of those men who couldn't admire a beautiful woman unless he had her on the operating-table dissecting her.' 'Never be ashamed of being vulgar, old man ... be as vulgar as you like,' was his advice to one of his students, Godfrey Ridout.

Of Willan's teaching in England little is known, except that he usually had only six or eight private students. Ca 1910 one of his students was a

lad of fifteen named Cecil Gray. Years later, a well-known and provoca-
tive member of the English musical scene, Gray wrote, 'My parents
allowed me to take up the study of music seriously, and by a remarkable
stroke of good fortune engaged for that purpose the services of a first-
rate musician who was also a sympathetic personality, and seemed to
take an interest in me – Healey Willan ... Under his able tuition I learnt
the rudiments of musical technique, and he is the only teacher from
whom I ever succeeded in learning anything at all' (*Musical Chairs*, London 1948, 85).

Of Willan's teaching in Canada accounts vary regarding both the work
he put into it and the work he expected from his students. Godfrey
Ridout has written, 'He encouraged us, but he could also lash us terrible
for sloppy work or laziness ... He made me work harder than I ever did
before, or after, for that matter' (*CMJ* 3, 1959, and *RCMT Bulletin* mid-
winter 1968). Another pupil, Geoffrey Waddington, said in an interview
in 1953, 'As a teacher I don't think he would be considered a great
taskmaster ... I don't think teaching was his forte.' In 1956 John Beckwith
compared Healey Willan and his colleague Leo Smith as professors of
music: 'In fact Willan, warm and lovable personality that he was and is,
had little interest, one felt, in teaching: his energies went mostly into his
choir work and his prolific writing. On the other hand, Smith seemed
born for the academic life' (*Letters in Canada* 1956, 329).

If a student were bright, or even just conscientious and hard-working,
he could acquire a great deal merely by his association with the great
man. One did not learn that much from formal studies with Willan, but
one was inspired to teach oneself what was necessary in that regard.
Listening to him talk about 'matters musical' in general, even when their
connection with the curriculum was remote, was an enriching experience. But students not highly motivated towards self-study, who expected 'the teacher' to feed them the required material, probably did not
learn a great amount from Willan.

Willan was generous with his time in private lessons with promising
students. It was here, in a one-to-one relationship, that a student could
derive the most from him. His classes in counterpoint at the university
often consisted of only four or five students at a time; he sat in his arm-
chair with his students sitting around him, a situation permitting individual exchanges between professor and student. It was here that he
shone.

As a lecturer in music history, to a large class, Willan was less successful. Many remember him coming in to history class with textbook in

hand, sitting down at the grand piano, opening up the text, and commencing to read aloud from it. The only thing that enlivened the proceedings was his seemingly inexhaustible supply of musical anecdotes and reminiscences. He was obviously not too interested in music history as such and probably resented the time this lecturing took away from his composition.

A number of Willan's students later distinguished themselves in one or more fields of musical activity: Louis Applebaum, John Beckwith, Patricia Blomfield, Francean Campbell, Margaret Drynan, Jean Fraser, Robert Fleming, James Gayfer, Reginald Godden, Phyllis Gummer, Daniel and Margaret Harmer, Margaret Heap, Eugene Hill, Kelsey Jones, Weldon Kilburn, Horace Lapp, Walter MacNutt, George Maybee, William McCauley, Oskar Morawetz, Kenneth Peacock, Eldon Rathburn, Godfrey Ridout, Geoffrey Waddington, John Weinzweig, and Ernest White. Students who distinguished themselves in the non-musical world include Bishop Wilkinson of Toronto and Norah Michener.

6

The man's character

Willan displayed even as a child those warm and attractive qualities of personality that were to distinguish him in later life. His sister, Mary, described him: 'He was always an even-tempered, contented boy, popular with his friends and acquaintances ... His was a tolerant and kind nature, full of generosity for the members of his family and for his friends.' She added: 'Healey was a very quiet, modest and perhaps even a shy boy ... He hated being pushed to the fore.'

In his days at the conservatory and the university in Toronto he was known to be genuinely interested in struggling students and to be always ready to discuss students' problems with them, no matter how busy he was. His gentleness as an examiner is gratefully remembered by all who appeared before him. 'A strange vocal defect which seems to prevent this candidate from uttering any musical sound' was Willan's kind way of dealing with my own inability to sing and to perform some ear tests for an organ diploma examination!

Genial in company, especially among his friends, he was socially the perfect English gentleman. Upon meeting Willan, one would often be asked, 'I say, old man, have you heard this one?' He had a seemingly endless supply of stories and jokes upon which to draw. Though courteous and good natured, he could not abide 'humbugs and toadies' (John Cook's phrase) and had no use for flattery. Possessing dignity, he also possessed humility and disliked being fussed over. Yet his was not a false modesty.

Willan could be gruff and brusque with strangers (perhaps because of shyness) and, on occasion, even with friends, and with flatterers and other people who annoyed him. He did not appreciate people telling him how to do his job, especially if he felt them unqualified. There is a story about a radio engineer who was trying to tell him how to play the organ for a broadcast. Pointing to the engineer's equipment, Willan exclaimed,

'That's your instrument and I don't know a dashed thing about it – well, that organ is my instrument and you don't know a dashed thing about it. You look after your part, and I'll do mine!'

Willan never owned a car. In Toronto he walked or travelled by street-car. Out-of-town journeys would be by train. But most of all Willan loved sea travel – he would have liked a naval career had his eyesight permitted. He really enjoyed his ocean trips back and forth to England. He generally took these trips alone. Despite his geniality and gregarious-ness, there were times when he liked to be on his own; he once wrote to a friend that he preferred living in hotels to being 'put up.'

Willan possessed a great sense of fun. In some respects he was an over-grown school boy, always ready for a prank of some sort. One day, when he was organist at St John's, Holland Road, a beautiful cope, belonging to the vicar, was lying on the vestment chest. Willan just 'happened to have' an empty ink bottle and an imitation ink blot at hand and placed both side by side on the cope and withdrew to watch the fireworks as the vicar approached!

Willan's natural acting ability made him a natural for any skit. He could laugh at himself; on a program for a song recital given in 1914, which he was accompanying, he wrote 'Can't sing for nuts' after the singer's name and 'Can't play for biscuits' after his own. He would often say, 'I must go and get my hair cut – I don't want to go around looking like a musician.' His description of his ancestry – 'English by birth, Irish by extraction, Canadian by adoption, and Scotch by absorption' – has often been quoted.

At St Paul's Church a special service was planned during which five windows were to be dedicated in memory of distinguished parishioners. The rector would have to move to various parts of the building to dedi-cate the windows and he asked Willan to suggest a suitable piece of music. 'Here We Go Round the Mulberry Bush' was the reply!

Willan loved musical spoofs. He wrote several of these for his friend Father Carmino de Catanzaro, in which he lampooned the airs, mys-tiques, and jargon of a certain type of musicologist (Willan could not stand pretension of any sort). One of these musical jokes was a piece based on the phrase 'Imprimatur nihil obstat.' Under it Willan wrote: 'Transcribed from a Ms in Lincoln Cathedral. Its Tudor origin is clearly shown by the cadence in the alto on the last bar but one, and, realizing the meticulous care Byrd employed, the obvious erasure and correction in the alto in bar 8 suggests that he might have been the composer.' According to de Catanzaro, 'Imprimatur nihil obstat' are 'portentous words occasionally found at the beginning of such works of church

music as the *Liber Usualis*.' Willan developed a unique musical signature
for his compositions, in which the final double bar of the piece would
serve as part of the H for his initials, H.W.

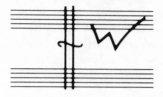

Willan had a slight speech impediment, more pronounced when he
was young but still noticeable in his later years, which made his stories
seem even funnier when he told them. The effect was further enhanced
by his 'appearance of owlish innocence' (Walter Bowles's phrase) when
telling a story or quoting a limerick. He was a skilled writer of limericks,

A soprano there was named Yvette
And she really was rather a pet,
   When she sang Christmas carols
   The clergy wept barrels,
And passed out when she sang a motet.

There was a young lady from Wantage
Of whom the Town Clerk took advantage.
   'Of course you must pay her,'
   Said the District Surveyor,
'You've altered the line of her frontage!'

Willan's Rabelaisian sense of humour was tempered with a strict sense
of propriety and decorum, however. Stories he would enjoy hearing in
secular surroundings, such as the Arts and Letters Club, he would not
appreciate hearing inside a church. One colleague found himself the
object of Willan's wrath for just that reason. Willan was not priggish, or
even pious, but he was devout; he thought there were a time and a place
for everything.

Willan had a strong belief in the supernatural. He was quite convinced
of the existence of ghosts and used to tell ghost stories in absolute seriousness. 'Ghosts are quite common. We have one at St Mary's – old girl
who used to be the charlady ... I've seen her frequently in the church
when I have gone in to practice at night. She doesn't bother me, so I

don't bother her. As a matter of fact, I'm rather fond of her, you know – I believe she likes plainchant.' Others have claimed to have seen the 'little gray lady.'

Likewise Willan was certain at one time that there was a ghost on the third floor of his house at Inglewood Drive. Other members of his family were aware of it too; it sounded like a woman combing her hair. Willan's rector subsequently came to the house to exorcise the ghost, and it was not heard from again.

On one occasion Willan referred to music as 'my chief delight, my chosen profession, my relaxation and my hobby.' He had other hobbies, of which the chief one was stamp collecting. He collected stamps to satisfy his love of collecting and saving beautiful things rather than for monetary gain. His stamp hobby was spasmodic; for a day or two he would sort and classify the stamps, from which he had carefully removed the paper in water, and then he would put them aside. Crossword puzzles served to keep his mind sharp. Willan was also interested, on occasion, in framing pictures and polishing brass. He read a good deal of poetry. He was fond of 'gadgets' and liked to make things ('inventions' he would call them). In his last years he sometimes watched television in the evening or played double patience, which he said he could make come out 'once in nine or ten shots.' He had compassion for all animals and a great affection for his dog, Trixie.

Willan spent much of his life in his 'junk-room' at 139 Inglewood. It was a long room, though somewhat narrow, having been formed by knocking down a wall separating two smaller rooms. In one part of it were his library, a writing desk, and an old chair that had belonged to Dr Vogt. The other part contained Willan's grand piano, a large desk for writing music scores, a settee, some chairs, a small table, and a fireplace. The piano was usually littered with music, while the fireplace bore the marks of many thousands of matches having been struck. Willan had more than twenty pipes in his room; these pipes were all named and had usually been presented to him. The room was filled with photographs of friends and other bric-à-brac which he had collected over a lifetime. In later years the room took on a somewhat faded appearance, its furnishings and other objects seeming to stand up to age less well than their owner. Cardboard boxes filled with papers gave a feeling of clutter, yet it was an orderly clutter, and everything was filed away systematically and methodically.

Willan was aware of his duties and obligations as the 'provider' for his family. His main reason for moving to Canada had been because he could not support his family on what he was able to earn in England. Financial pressures probably accounted for his remaining for eight years as organist of St Paul's in Toronto, even though its outlook was sharply at variance with his own.

Because of his many activities, Willan had to be out most evenings during the time his family was growing up. He was usually home on Saturday evenings, however, and was always available to the family then. His daughter, Mary, recalls that he indeed 'listened,' rather than just 'heard,' when his children wanted to talk to him. He did not force his children to take music lessons and none of his sons became musicians. His son Bernard did sing in the choir at St Mary Magdalene's for some years.

Willan advised his boys on a number of matters – including how to drink like gentlemen – while they were growing up. But after they were finished school he let them find their own way, with little guidance. He had never gone to university and had had to fend for himself. He probably felt his sons should be able to do the same.

Gladys Willan has been described by a friend of the family as 'long suffering.' Willan would not have been the easiest person to live with when one of his creative moods was upon him. The problems that her sons encountered in gaining employment during the 1930s must have been a worry to her as well. Willan's liaisons could scarcely have gone unnoticed and unfelt. Yet their marriage lasted, and many think that it was largely because of Gladys's care (including a proper diet) that Willan remained so well-preserved and active in old age. Certainly after her death his health declined quite rapidly.

Willan's appearance changed comparatively little during the last half of his life. He wore glasses from quite an early age, being very short-sighted. During his years in England he was comparatively thin. A few years in Canada, in relative prosperity, filled him out a bit. A picture of him sitting at St Paul's organ, ca 1918, shows a fuller face, with the beginnings of the sagging jowl and double chin that became standard features later. A certain pudginess had set in by the 1930s. After that the black hair gradually turned to grey, but there was comparatively little change otherwise. Godfrey Ridout states: 'In the whole time I knew him [ca 1930–68] he changed less than any other person I know.' In 1962 he was described by Kildare Dobbs as 'a somewhat portly figure of 5 foot 10 [who] has weighed 174 pounds for 35 years.'

In dress he had always been debonair. People who knew him in his London days remembered him as 'a very well dressed young man.' He always had a cane. In Canada he continued to be particular about his attire. Reginald Godden recalls his appearance in 1926: 'He was ... wearing shoes of such gleaming blackness I'd never seen – they tapered to a fine graceful point and I recall thinking they must have been made especially for articulation on a pedal keyboard – the black hair was tight to the scalp and flowed back in a perfect sequence of tiny waves.' Blue blazer, grey flannels, bow-tie, spats (only in winter), and cane became one of his standard ensembles. The bow-tie was always hand-tied. Willan characteristically would never use ready-tied or clip-on types; to him that was cheating. In later years he experienced difficulty obtaining bowties. At Christmas 1968 his old friend Edward Klammer, of Concordia Publishing, sent him a black and white polka-dot bow-tie from St Louis; Willan had said earlier how much he liked them but that they were difficult to find. He also had a fondness for British tweeds.

Willan remained essentially an Englishman. In his later years he could appear quite aristocratic, with his elegant dress, dignified walk, cultivated manners, and British accent. Some people have compared Willan's appearance – in his more solemn moments – to that of Winston Churchill. His accent was, as John Cook expressed it, 'High Table, or R.C.M. corridor.' His standard forms of greeting were 'old man,' 'old chap,' or 'my dear fellow.' His demeanour may have reflected his English consciousness of class and his father's disappointment at not becoming a doctor. His concern about dress and appearance was perhaps compensation for his own low-paid profession. The ritual of breakfast in housecoat, followed by the reading of the paper, followed by the daily bath, followed by dressing is also part of the picture, as is the sending of all four children to private school.

At school Willan had played cricket and English rugger enthusiastically, if none too successfully, and as a young man did quite a bit of rowing. After his move to Canada he still followed the cricket and rugger scores avidly, as well as the Oxford-Cambridge boat races. Christopher Woods once observed that Willan was 'a vigorous figure, walking as if a Rugby ball were under his arm.' His sports interests remained English; he disliked baseball (which he referred to as 'rounders') and never warmed to Canadian football.

Willan always looked to England as the mother country and considered Canada part of the empire. In 1953 he wrote to a friend, 'I was very pleased when I was invited to write a work for the Coronation, but I was really glad that it shows a *recognition of work in the Empire.*' In his later years he seemed to be under the delusion that he was quite Irish, but in reality he was typically English by birth, training, and inclination.

Willan wore his honours and accolades lightly. Near the end of his life he said 'there are very few things in life worth taking seriously – and even fewer people. The crowning mistake is to take yourself seriously.' He was, however, very appreciative of the love and affection shown him by his friends and colleagues; in 1959 he wrote to a friend, 'I feel that no small delight in music lies in doing things for others, and although the reward is too often very small – the real reward comes in after years in the form of affection on the part of members of the community who have been helped by your labours. And when all is said and done, affection is the one thing which, in this mad money-making and money-worshipping world, we cannot buy.'

Willan was generous in his praise of the work of others that he admired. I remember attending in 1951 a score-study lecture he gave on *Deirdre*: he spent most of the time illustrating the beauties of John Coulter's words, saying very little about his own music.

Willan enjoyed life to the full. To the end of his days his reactions to good food, good drink, good pipe tobacco, good conversation, good fun, good companionship, good clothes, good sport, good music, and attractive women remained enthusiastic.

Willan's character was perhaps best described by three of his close friends at the time of his eightieth birthday. Arthur Gough called him 'a very devout man who leavened his profound devotion with unrestrained merriment, – a man who was "too big" to be grandiose.' Rev R.T.F. Brain said: 'Healey's approach to church music is best summed up in the phrase "the holiness of beauty". As he sees it, the liturgical worship of God is the consecration of beauty, and the spirit of the liturgy speaks to us of the holiness of beauty as well as the beauty of holiness.' Sir William McKie observed: 'He will never feel the loneliness which is commonly said to be the penalty of greatness, for he is held in respect, admiration and affection such as come to very few men in their lifetime.'

The final word must come from Willan himself – an oft-quoted statement first made in an address to the Canadian Club: 'Music has been my chief delight, and if at any time I have been able to share this delight with others, I am content.'

7

Symphonies and concerto

In this chapter I shall examine Willan's *Symphony No. 1 in D Minor* (1936), his *Symphony No. 2 in C Minor* (1948), and his *Piano Concerto in C Minor* (1944).

SYMPHONY NO. 1

In some works, such as *Piano Concerto in C Minor* and *Poem* for string orchestra, Willan's borrowing of early material turned out well. With *Symphony No. 1 in D Minor* (1936), however, this procedure has been less successful, particularly in the finale, where the Mendelssohn-like second subject, borrowed from his 1909 *Epilogue* for organ and orchestra, sits uncomfortably in its Straussian surroundings. Willan took a considerable quantity of material from his early (ca 1910) unfinished sketches of orchestral works (B85, B87, and B91a) for the two outer movements of the symphony[1]; the slow middle movement, apparently not based on previous material, is perhaps more successful. Willan later regarded the symphony as 'an uneven work' (letter to F.R.C. Clarke, 1961).

The first movement has a slow introduction (largo) followed by an allegro feroce in sonata-allegro form. The main theme of the allegro feroce is almost identical – for the first six bars – to the opening of the allegro feroce section of the unfinished orchestral rhapsody of 1911, *From the Highlands* (B85), and further resemblances in the treatment of the mate-

---

1 In England (ca 1910) Willan started at least two works for piano and orchestra: *Piano Concerto in D Minor*, B90 (of which only 127 bars of the finale survive), and the unfinished *Ballade*, B86.

rial occur. A full-score sketch (ca 1910) opens with the same eight bars of largo as does the D minor symphony, only in B flat minor. Further on the sketch material is more like *From the Highlands* and ends after only some thirty bars of allegro. Both the rhapsody and the symphony are in D minor; probably the B flat minor version came first.

The slow introduction begins as in Example 1. Willan develops the melodic pattern contained in bars 2 and 3. This material has no direct thematic connection with the following allegro, though passages based on it do appear in the development and coda sections of the latter. The introduction finishes with a succession of chords (Example 2), of which considerable use is made in the following allegro.

The allegro feroce is written in sonata form, and the opening paragraph of its exposition (in D minor and in 6/8 time) is largely developed from the theme in Example 3. Two subsidiary motifs appear in due course (Example 4). The ensuing bridge section is well constructed, initially carrying on in the style of the opening paragraph and then gradually preparing us for the very different music of the second tonal area (Example 5). The style of the latter is different (andante cantabile as opposed to allegro feroce) as are the metre (3/4 rather than 6/8) and the tonality (an unusual E major). This lovely E major music does not appear to have been taken from earlier sources. It evokes an atmosphere similar to some of Ravel's *Mother Goose* or Vierne's *Berceuse*, showing perhaps a certain French influence. After about two dozen bars the E major tonality gives way to chromatic wanderings, though E major does return briefly at the end of this section.

A quiet passage, starting (Example 6) with a motif derived from the opening of the slow introduction, and followed by oboe and flute solos, ushers in the development section proper at the resumption of the allegro tempo and the 6/8 metre. This section starts off promisingly in C minor with material derived from the main theme. The music soon slips into B minor, where it stays for some time, reaching a climax at bar 207. The second part of the development section, starting mezzoforte at bar 208, mainly treats the two subsidiary motifs of the first tonal area of the exposition. Tonality in this section can best be described as fluid. The development reaches its second climax, fff, between bars 257 and 270, over a dominant pedal, presumably for the eventual return to D minor.

To this point the development section has been well written and exciting, but now Willan introduces a largo third section based upon motifs derived from the introduction. It starts impressively with an unexpected crash in C minor; yet the excitement so carefully and skilfully built up in the previous parts of the development has largely been lost by the time the recapitulation begins at bar 294. In his notes for a radio interview, Willan observed: 'The first part of a movement in sonata form generally ends with a codetta ... but in this case it might be more correct to say that the codetta *follows* the development section and that we are now at the codetta.' The logic is less than compelling! The recapitulation is quite regular, with the opening paragraph of the exposition repeated in toto. The second part of the bridge is modified to allow the andante cantabile subject to return in the tonic key (D major).

We now come to the second disappointment of the first movement, the coda. The composer repeats his mistake of interpolating a largo section based on the introduction, and the coda is much too brief in proportion to the other main sections of the movement. Despite these two problems, there is much fine work in this first movement.

The second movement, a lovely piece of music, wends its rhapsodic way through many tonalities and shifting chromaticisms. It concludes as it begins in B flat major. The term rhapsodic describes not only the mood of the piece but also its form. There are, however, several discernible motifs which reappear from time to time (see Example 7). The movement works up through 100 bars to an impressive fff climax, at which point the B flat tonality of the opening is finally re-established after many and far-reaching tonal excursions. The remaining 30 bars of the piece return to a mood of quiet repose.

This slow middle movement is probably the most satisfactory and has been performed successfully as a separate piece. It exhibits greater unity than the outer movements, perhaps because the musical material fits the rhapsodic form. It appears to have been newly composed, with the exception of the horn theme quoted at the end of Example 7, which comes from Willan's song *Dreams*, of 1912.

The third and final movement, allegro jubilante, is in D major and is cast – like the first movement – in sonata form. Its energetic and impressive opening paragraph commences with a scalic rush of semiquavers on strings and winds almost identical to the beginning of the early unfinished overture *Know'st Thou the Excellent Joys of Youth* (B91a). After this the music is built around three main motifs, of which the first is shown in Example 8. The second full bar (y) seems to be derived from part of the main theme of the first movement. This first motif also bears a kinship to the opening bars of Willan's early unfinished symphonic poem *The Call of the Sea* (B88) (material he had also used for the orchestral ritornellos in his *Hymn to the Sun* for choir and orchestra of 1930). The second motif (Example 9), which appears at bar 11, is identical to the horn-call in the *Excellent Joys of Youth* overture (from bar 9). The third motif (Example 10) is treated in various forms. Willan would use it again in *Piano Concerto in C Minor* and *Symphony No. 2*, and I have dubbed it the 'Willan motto.'

Unfortunately the expectations raised by this opening section of fifty-two bars are not sustained. The bridge section begins with a surprise appearance of the second motif in C major, but this is followed by a mere four bars to lead into the second main tonal area (andante cantible). This second tonal area involves a change of style (from allegro jubilante to andante cantabile), metre (4/4 to 3/4), and key (D major to A major), and the join is too brief and abrupt to accommodate this. The theme of the second tonal area (Example 11) is taken from an early work, *Epilogue* for organ and orchestra (completed 1909), where this Mendelssohn-like passage fits reasonably well; here it seems incongruous.

It is not clear just where the development section begins, though the tonality has started to wander by letter E (bar 94). The development is certainly under way by letter F (bar 111, marked 'poco animato' in pencil in the score), where fragments of the horn-call motif start to appear. Strangely enough, phrases and fragments derived from the Mendelssohn-like theme prove effective in development, and the first big climax of this section is reached at bar 145. At bar 148 the music, which has been in 3/4 since the beginning of the andante cantabile, now reverts to 4/4 time and, over a dominant pedal in D, starts to build once more with material derived from the second movement (introducing a cyclic element into the work). Passages based on developments of motifs 1 and 3 follow, rushing headlong to the recapitulation section, which begins at bar 205.

This time Willan does not repeat his mistake of the first movement in letting the climax flag; he maintains the momentum. He does not recapitulate the whole exposition, but starts at bar 21, with the horn-call motif blazing out in an unexpected B major. The effect is electrifying. The music is also somewhat different from the exposition because the composer treats the section based on the Willan motto in different tonalities. The bridge section to the andante cantabile theme does not seem as abrupt this time, probably because the reference to the horn-call motif is omitted. The andante cantabile is not in the expected tonic key of D major, but rather in B flat major. D major is eventually re-established at the coda (marked allegro) at bar 308. This coda is sixty bars long and makes a much more satisfactory and exciting ending than did the rather disappointing coda of the first movement. Beginning with a treatment of material derived from the short bridge section, the coda builds to a 'largamente' appearance in augmentation of a form of the Willan motto. The last nine bars contain some hints of the semiquaver figure which opened the movement.

As a sonata form structure the finale is more successful than the first movement, though the stylistic incongruity of the andante cantabile theme with the rest of the movement tends to weaken the total effect.

SYMPHONY NO. 2

Willan shared Brahms's awe of the symphonic form and the composer's responsibility in regard to it, and he did not want to rush the composition of his symphonies without adequate reflection. He was organist, conductor, teacher, and administrator, as well as composer; he was also writing large quantities of music for other media. His music for the church was much in demand and readily published, while the incentive to spend the large amounts of time and energy required to write symphonic works was small. The wonder is not that Willan wrote only two symphonies, but rather that he wrote any at all! His first symphony was approximately twenty-six years in gestation; his second took twelve.

Willan started sketches for *Symphony No. 2 in C Minor* in May 1936, four months before completing his first symphony. He finished the short score in August 1941 and wrote at the end of the manuscript 'Commenced May, 1936. Various parts written and sketched up to 1938. Put aside till the summer of 1941, and then completed.' Then, presumably, the work was put aside once more, for the final full-score version did not appear till 1948. It received its first performance in May 1950. Between then and 1970 it received performances under six conductors; one only hopes its well-deserved success will not force its predecessor into complete oblivion.

The second symphony marks a considerable advance over the first. In the second the composer works with a surer hand; there do not appear to be any structural miscalculations. The first symphony was sometimes marred by borrowings from his early works; in the second symphony there is virtually no borrowing (save for two bars of the main theme of the slow movement), and the material is better integrated. The organic

connections and developments of motifs in the first movement reveal a
mastery of symphonic style.

As with the first movement of *Symphony No. 1*, that of *Symphony No. 2*
consists of a slow introduction (lento) followed by an allegro in sonata
form, both in C minor. The introduction consists largely of slow-moving
mystical harmonies of the type that Willan wrote so well. The opening
five bars (Example 12) of the introduction illustrate this. The motif
marked 'x' provides the germ for the main subject of the ensuing allegro,
while motif 'y' is heard again in the fugue subject used in the recapitulation. The imitative opening might also be noted. The final bars (Example
13) of the introduction consist of a harmonic progression which is used
again in the second and fourth movements in an almost cyclic manner.

The opening paragraph of the exposition of the sonata-allegro movement is nearly seventy bars in length, and though it begins and ends in C
minor it ranges as far afield tonally as F sharp minor. There are five main
motifs, all of which seem to grow out of parts of previous motifs. The
first motif (Ia, see Example 14) grows from the x motif of the introduction. The interpolation of one bar in 5/4 metre adds some extra interest.
The second motif (Ib; Example 15) appears to be an extension of the x
figure, going with itself in inversion. The third motif (Ic; Example 16)
grows out of Ia. The fourth motif (Id; Example 17) in turn grows out of
Ic. The fifth motif (Ie; Example 18) contains the ♫ rhythm of Ia and Ic, as
well as the ascending scale pattern of Ib. There is a fair amount of 5/4
metre. From bar 68 to bar 71 Willan has successive measures of 3/2, 4/4,
5/4, and 3/4 time; this frequent mixing of metres is unusual in Willan's
instrumental music. The bridge section of four bars is based on a rhyth-
mical variation and partial inversion of Id.

A further similarity to the first movement of *Symphony No. 1* occurs at
the appearance of the second tonal area. In *No. 1* the opening tonality of
D minor was followed by an unusual second tonality of E major; here C
minor is followed by an equally unusual E minor. In both cases the
tempo becomes slower. This lyrical second tonal area is built on two
main motifs, the first of which (IIa; see Example 19) bears some resemblance to the opening of the slow movement of *Symphony No. 1*. The
dropping semitone also allies it with Id. The second motif (IIb; Example 20)
is obviously connected with Ic. These two motifs are then developed and
extended for about twenty-five bars and pass through many tonalities.

The development section commences at bar 146 with a resumption of
the allegro tempo and a treatment of Ie starting in E minor. This is fol-

lowed by a passage beginning in F major and minor based on the rhythm which had been prominent in Ia, b, and d and IIb. The tempo then slows again, and a solo oboe passage leads into the 'big tune' (Example 21) which unfolds splendidly in E flat major. This tune is made up of elements of practically all the previous motifs. Placed just after the half-way point in the movement, it becomes not only the climax of the development section but also the apex of the movement. (Sibelius used a similar structure in the first movement of his second symphony.) During the final part of the development section the tempo increases as the music prepares for the recapitulation. The material is derived from Ia. Instead of the expected dominant pedal (on G), the pedal point is on F sharp (the leading note of the key of the dominant, or the 'leading note once removed' of the tonic!) – a rather uncommon procedure for Willan.

The recapitulation is also somewhat irregular. It commences with the expected return of the home tonality of C minor and presents Ia and b. During Ib it strays from home tonality through E flat minor and C flat major and finally arrives in D minor. This D minor section is a partial fugue on the subject in Example 22 which commences with the opening rhythm of Ie and continues by using figure y from the introduction and a melodic shape taken from IIa. The partial fugue is followed by a free development of the subject, building constantly toward a climax and reintroducing elements of Ia. The main tonality for this is F sharp minor. At bar 267 the big tune bursts out in B major in full tutti as the climax of the movement. The home tonality, C minor, is re-established at bar 300 – the beginning of the coda. The coda is in the nature of a 'final wind up,' allegro molto, based on extensions and inversions of Ia.

Thus this first movement is indeed a well-knit, well-integrated piece, perhaps Willan's finest symphonic writing. Tonally it is among his most adventurous, with its prominent use of F sharp minor in both exposition and recapitulation, its use of E minor as the second main tonal area, and the big climax in B major just before the end of the movement. The key of the dominant (G) is rarely used, while the relative major (E flat) is saved for one great occasion: the first appearance of the big tune in the middle of the movement. This is certainly no mere textbook sonata-form structure!

The second movement of *Symphony No. 2* is an adagio of great tenderness and lyric beauty. The condensed score was completed 1 August 1941, during Willan's 'summer of '41.' This is very much love music – not the impetuous and forceful love of youth, but the mellow love of age. Some critics might consider this music sentimental, and they would be correct.

The expressiveness of this movement came from the experience of its composer. In form this adagio is a large three-part structure, with the middle part accounting for half the total length of the movement and performing something of the function of a development section.

The piece commences with a short introduction consisting of solemn chords derived from the last four bars of the introduction to the first movement. Part I proper begins at bar 5 with the appearance of a lovely melody in E major (Example 23), first played as a horn solo. (The origins of this tune can be found in the fragments of incidental music B39 and B40.) A short link of eight bars' duration leads to part II, marked 'animato.' Part II consists of two main sections. The first, starting in F sharp minor, is a development of a short motif (Example 24) through constantly shifting harmonies. All this builds to the first climax, which occurs at bar 97 when the Willan motto blazes forth in B major (Example 25).

The second section of part II moves to C major, and a new motif (Example 26) appears. This new motif, along with fragments of the previous ones, is developed for some 30 bars till the arrival of the next climax at bar 138. Here the Willan motto is heard again, triumphantly in B flat major. A retransition section, based on the Willan motto and the chords of the introduction, and making prominent use of a solo violin, leads back to the home tonality of E major and the beginning of part III, a shortened repetition of part I. The concluding coda is based on fragments of the first two motifs, with some reference to the chords of the introduction. It is largely built over a tonic pedal, and the solo violin of the retransition section returns. The music finally fades into a mist of loveliness.

The third movement, Willan's only symphonic scherzo, might be considered his 'musical joke.' (His few other scherzos, ie the two little ones for organ and the third movement of the piano trio, are not composed on the same scale and are not particularly joke-like.) A first hearing might give one an impression of naïvety and lack of substance, but the score reveals a structure that is relatively complex, certainly more so than that of the classical scherzo and trio. The composer seems to bandy about his themes in a carefree and whimsical fashion, but there is a carefully controlled ordering of material which follows a somewhat stretched sonata-form structure. Some structural similarities with the scherzo in Mendelssohn's *Octet* for strings may indicate that Mendelssohn provided an initial model.

The exposition begins in G minor with a four-voice quasi-fugal exposition on a staccato subject (Example 27). This subject is a transposed version of the opening bars of the introduction to the first movement!

Willan begins his series of 'jokes' right here, for we find that the 'answers' to the subject are inverted (ie upside down), which might lead us to expect a learned 'fugue by inversion.' This we do not get, for the counterpoints are sporadic, fading in and out in a delightfully 'unlearned' fashion, and for the codetta (or link) between the pairs of leads we have a surprise (Example 28). This quasi-fugal section serves as the first subject (or tonal area) of the exposition of this sonata-form movement. The second subject group and tonal area begins at bar 34 in B flat major with a carefree theme (Example 29), followed closely by a cheerful passage (Example 30). The bass part accompanying the new theme is none other than the initial fugue-subject, transposed into the relative major.

A transitional passage, commencing with an appearance of the fugue-subject in its original G minor form, leads the music to the third tonal area of the exposition, D major, with a syncopated theme (Example 31) appearing at bar 63. Mendelssohn had used the same three tonal areas in the exposition of his scherzo (G minor, B flat major, D major). Willan suddenly jumps back into B flat major with the syncopated motif, only to surprise us further with a completely unexpected open-fifth chord on E natural after a bar's silence. E is the dominant of A, and this unexpected chord ushers in the closing section of the exposition at bar 84, beginning with a three-voice fugato based on the first four bars of the initial fugue-subject in A minor, D minor, and G minor respectively. The effect of this fugato, scored for two bassoons and low clarinet, is comical, with its mock seriousness and instrumental colour; perhaps Willan is having a spoof here at the expense of *The Sorcerer's Apprentice*! The music moves back into B flat major with a passage derived from the syncopated motif, and Willan now starts a new, lyrical theme in E flat major (Example 32). This he suddenly breaks off in mid-stream with a double bar repeat sign (indicating both the end of the exposition and that it is to be repeated). The whole exposition is not repeated, however, and the composer has his joke once again – this time by having the exposition repeat only from bar 32, the beginning of the second subject group!

The development section picks up the new theme from where it was abruptly cut off at the end of the exposition and carries it on through A major and C major, leading to a section derived from the third motif at bar 129. A passage based on the syncopated theme (Example 31) starts at bar 145 in B major and then moves into D major. At bar 168 the next Willan joke slips into the musical fabric almost imperceptibly – a parody of the Willan motto in F major, followed by E major (Example 33).

The next point of interest is the appearance of the 'carefree' third motif in D major, followed by rapid peregrinations, through D major, F major,

A flat major, E major, G major, B flat major, D flat major, and E major, of a figure derived from the 'cheerful' motif, accompanying itself in mirror (Example 34). Might this be another parody, this time of a 'learned' device? Next, at bar 212, comes further treatment in C major and E flat major of the syncopated motif over pedal points, giving the listener the impression that the final build-up (or dominant preparation) for the recapitulation is under way. But Willan suddenly stops proceedings with a totally unexpected open-fifth chord on A (bar 233) and, as he had done in the exposition after a similar jolt, starts up a four-voice fugato on the opening subject. Tonality ranges through D minor, G minor, C minor, and F minor, moving finally into E flat major with a passage based on the syncopated motif.

The recapitulation slips in suddenly at bar 270 with the appearance of the second subject group in E flat major. The first subject is omitted altogether, possibly because the composer felt that it had had sufficient exposure already. Willan returns to the home tonality (G minor) via a passage in B major (= C flat major) and B flat major on material based on the syncopated motif. G minor is finally re-established in a coda built on fragmentations of the first subject. The movement ends very abruptly with a sudden shift to G major and a final appearance of the syncopated motif. The listener is left still travelling after the music has stopped. At the end of his condensed-score sketch Willan wrote 'a! ha!'

A word is needed here concerning the Mendelssohn scherzo mentioned above. The tonal schemes employed by Mendelssohn and Willan are remarkably similar, and Mendelssohn gives a precedent for the large amount of E flat tonality in Willan's recapitulation:

MENDELSSOHN		WILLAN	
Exposition	*Recapitulation*	*Exposition*	*Recapitulation*
G minor	G minor	G minor	(omitted)
B flat major	E flat major	B flat major	E flat major
D major	G major (coda)	D major	(omitted)
		B flat major	B major, B flat major, G minor and major (coda)

Willan's scherzo uses fifteen keys, a much wider range than Mendelssohn's.

Considerable changes took place in the movement between the condensed score and the final full score. The most interesting is the beginning of the recapitulation. The original starts with an appearance of the first subject. Though Willan begins the theme on the note G as expected, he puts it in upside down (inverted) and then harmonizes it in E flat major rather than G minor! In the final version he goes directly into subject II, omitting subject I altogether.

Ettore Mazzoleni, to whom *Symphony No. 2* is dedicated, compared this scherzo movement 'with the famous picture of Healey Willan, sitting with a pipe in his left hand, a "pint of bitters" in his right hand, and wearing a mischievous grin.'

The fourth and final movement is cast in a similar mould to the first movement: a slow introduction (adagio) followed by a fast sonata-form (allegro feroce) movement. With its sombre and mystical chord progressions, the introduction – twenty-seven bars in C minor over a tonic pedal – is similar in style and mood to the orchestral introduction (also in C minor) to act III of the final version of *Deirdre*.

The opening section of the exposition of the sonata-allegro is built upon two main motifs, Ia and Ib. The bracketed part in the third bar of Ia (Example 35) is similar to the odyssey motif from *Transit through Fire*. After its initial appearance in C minor, the theme is repeated in the unlikely key of G sharp minor. The second motif, Ib (Example 36), is presented in G minor and repeated and developed at various pitches and through various transitory tonalities, eventually settling on D. Here the 'four chords' from the end of the introduction to the first movement are produced again. A bridge passage, starting at bar 83, continues the Ib idea initially and then introduces hints of the second subject. This makes a very good and smooth link.

The tempo slows to a moderato for the appearance of the second main subject (II) and tonal area (Example 37). A long musical paragraph grows out of developments of II, starting in E flat major and proceeding through B major and D major. This builds to a majestic climax at bar 152, where the Willan motto again appears, in D flat major.

The development section as such is quite short (only twenty bars) and consists of treatments of Ia in F sharp minor and D minor. A continuous build-up of tempo and volume climaxes at the appearance of the recapitulation and the return to the home tonality of C minor.

The recapitulation commences with material from the introduction, changed into triple meter. Subjects Ia and Ib are omitted, Ia doubtless because it was the sole basis of the development section. But why is Ib, the basis of some thirty bars in the exposition, not referred to again? A bridge passage, consisting of the second half of the corresponding section in the exposition, transposed, follows. At bar 202 II appears, producing a lengthy paragraph of moderato like its counterpart in the exposition. It starts and finishes in E major, progressing through C major on the way. E major might seem a rather unusual key to use here, but the composer thereby touches on the home tonality of C by the same means as he had used in the exposition to move the same distance of a major third:

Exposition: E flat major to B major (equals C flat major) to E flat major
Recapitulation: E major to C major to E major

As in the exposition, the second musical paragraph builds to a climactic appearance of the Willan motto. Here it is fashioned into a majestic coda: it has appeared in some form in the second and the third movements and now becomes the climax of the whole symphony. At bar 272 Willan re-establishes C major with the introduction of a major-mode version in slow tempo of the main theme of the third movement (itself a version of the introduction to the first movement) and subject Ib of the first movement, thus further tying together the whole.

There is not the degree of integration of material in this fourth movement that there is in the first movement. Similarly, the development section is less substantial. We wonder what became of subject Ib. These turn out to be minor considerations, however; the music does work, the composer having found a way to handle his material.

In the short-score manuscript for this finale the composer has several times written arithmetical calculations (eg 304 minus 180 equals 124) concerning the number of bars – an interesting glimpse of his creative process in large-scale forms. Like Bruckner, who was known to calculate the number of bars, Willan was concerned with the relative proportions of his sections.

PIANO CONCERTO IN C MINOR

The overall structure of *Piano Concerto in C Minor* (1944) is as follows:

First movement	Introduction and free sonata-allegro	C minor structure
Connecting interlude I		
Second movement	Ternary form	D flat major structure
Connecting interlude II		
Third movement	Three-refrain modulating-rondo	E flat major to C major structure

The composer envisaged the work as one continuous whole beginning and ending in C, with the three movements connected by interludes. In such a context the seemingly strange tonal scheme of the rondo finale becomes much less strange. The joining together of three movements of a concerto to make one continuous work was not new in itself; Liszt had done it in his *Piano Concerto No. 1* in E flat. However Liszt began his finale in the home key; Willan did not reintroduce the home tonality till the end of his finale, thereby giving his work a greater degree of indivisibility.

The first movement might be considered to be an introduction and allegro, with the allegro a very free adaptation of sonata form. The introduction is marked 'allegro energico,' though in fact the music here is more of a rhapsodic moderato in style and tempo, and at bar 22 a metronome mark of $\downarrow = 72$ appears over the piano part. Following two bars of tonic pedal in the orchestra, the piano enters with an impressive unison passage in octaves (Example 38). From this passage most of the material of the introduction is developed (see Example 39). The three descending semitones at the beginning of Examples 38 and 39 also form the chief characteristic of a motif which first appears at the end of the introduction, but which turns up again in the second and third movements as a sort of motto (Example 40). Three descending semitones form the basis of the motto theme also in Liszt's *Piano Concerto No. 1* (Example 41).

The exposition of the sonata-allergro commences at bar 80. Its main theme (Example 42) is obviously derived from the material of the introduction. The opening section in C minor is quite short, moving quickly into a much longer second tonal area in E major and C sharp minor. Two new motifs appear here, the first (Example 43) given out antiphonally between trumpet and woodwinds against a background of sustained strings and passage-work in the piano part. The second motif (Example 44) is the Willan motto. This second tonal area of the exposition also includes some development of the theme from the opening section between the appearances of the two new motifs.

The development section, commencing at bar 148, uses no key signature and wanders through C major, E minor, C minor, D flat major, E major, C major, and C sharp minor. It is based on motifs presented in the exposition, during which a new theme (Example 45) seems to emerge naturally. The solo cadenza for the piano occurs toward the end of the development section and is based on the new theme and the motto first heard at the end of the introduction.

The structural return to the tonic, C minor, appears at bar 219. This section is no mere repetition of the exposition; the material of the entire second tonal area is omitted. At bar 250 the music leads directly into the first connecting interlude, based on a melodic fragment which had first appeared in the introduction (Example 46). Reference is made also to the motto and its three descending semitones.

The second movement is a beautiful and lyrical adagio, built on a simple ternary structure in D flat major. Part I consists of an expressive theme (Example 47) played by the cor anglais against a sustained background of strings and a gentle chord figuration in the piano. This is followed by an episode for solo piano, labelled 'cadenza,' which leads to the key of B flat major. Part II begins in B flat with a new subject (Example 48). This is immediately displaced by a passage based on the motto theme of the concerto. The new theme wins out, however, with a triumphal reappearance in D flat major that sets the stage for part III. Part III is a varied treatment of the theme of part I and is followed by the second of the connecting interludes in the concerto, a trio for solo cello, piano, and flute, based on the semitonal motto and concluding in E major with a reference to the second part of the main theme of the finale. The interlude ends with a half-cadence in E major, immediately followed by the main theme of the finale in the totally unexpected key of E flat major!

The structure of the third movement is most interesting – a three-refrain, 'modulating' sonata-rondo, with each refrain in a different key! The refrain theme itself appears to be the only portion of this work which Willan derived from his earlier works – in this case the unfinished finale of a piano concerto in D minor (ca 1910). Willan reshaped this theme (in the finale of *Symphony No. 1* he had essentially merely borrowed earlier material). A comparison of the two versions of this refrain theme is interesting. The early version is of fifteen bars' duration; it quickly ranges far afield harmonically and exhibits an interesting structure of progressively lengthening phrases (four bars plus five bars plus six bars). Nevertheless the endings of the second and third phrases are weak. The later version (sixteen bars: appearing on the surface to be a regular 4 + 4 + 4 + 4) has subtle inner phrasing and elision of phrases. It is more finely wrought, displaying the results of thirty-five additional years of experience. (The first nine bars of the early version appear in Example 49; the first nine of the later in Example 50.)

The opening refrain is presented three times: in E flat by orchestra alone, in D by piano alone, and in E flat again by piano and orchestra. A bridge passage extends this material until the second tonal area of the movement is reached. No fewer than six subsidiary motifs are presented in this second section, the first two (Examples 51 and 52) in B major and the remaining four (53–6) in D major. The first is an extension of the Willan motto, while the fourth appeared in the first movement of *Symphony No. 2*. After the six motifs are presented, the last four are developed at some length through B major, F sharp minor, and E major. A modulating passage follows, based on the second motif and the semitonal motto from the first movement, ending up on a dominant $\frac{4}{2}$ pedal in the key of C. This leads one to expect a return of the refrain in that key, but Willan now surprises us and introduces the refrain not in C major but in B major – a stroke of genius.

The music moves into the development section proper. Prominent use is made here of extensions of the refrain theme and antiphonal passages based on the second of the subsidiary motifs. Tonality ranges widely, commencing in B major and moving through such keys as D flat major, F major, A flat major. At the end of the development section, during the preparation for the final return of the refrain, reference is made to the opening motif of the first movement, thereby introducing a further cylical element into the work. The third and final appearance of the refrain theme follows, swelling forth 'nobilmente' in C major. This is the first time that the home tonality of C has been re-established since the end of the first movement!

The finale exists with two different endings. The 1944 version bore some minor resemblance to the ending of Elgar's *Violin Concerto* (though surely not enough to worry anyone). Perhaps for this reason, or perhaps because he was advised that the concerto needed a more expanded ending, Willan wrote a new ending for the 1949 revision. Having heard both many times, I believe Willan's first inspirations were sound; the second ending is a mistake.

An examination of the tonal relationships between the three movements reveals a C structure which contains within itself an E structure and a D flat structure. In fact the D flat structure is the only one common to all three movements (see the chart on page 106).

Complaints have been raised about the concerto being derivative. While short passages may recall Elgar or Rachmaninoff, I consider the concerto a highly original piece of work. It certainly contains some of Willan's most adverturous structural experiments. Willan's originality, like that of Sibelius and Nielsen, lay in finding new ways of handling traditional

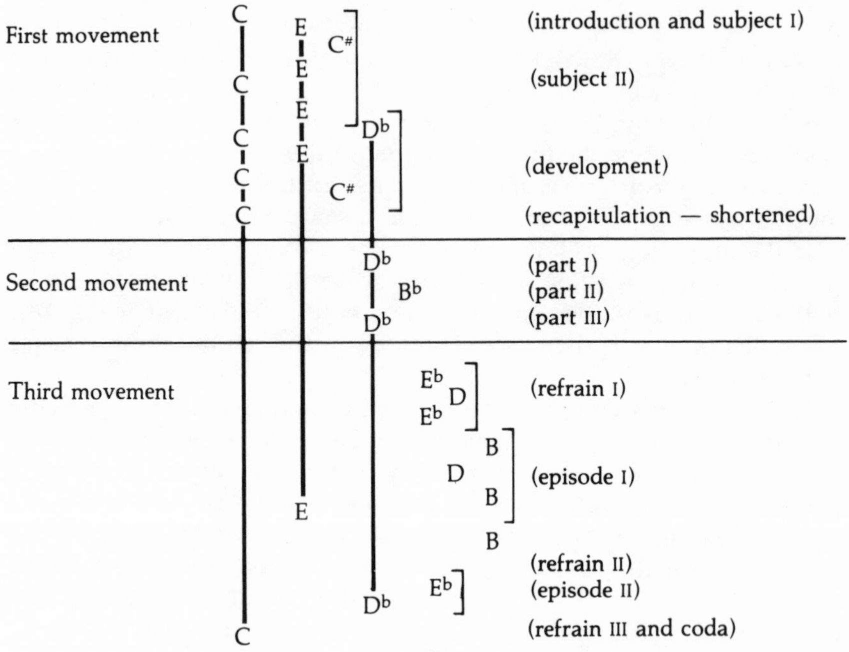

First movement

C	E	C# ⌉ (introduction and subject I)
C	E	(subject II)
C	E	Db ⌉
C	E	(development)
C	C#	
C		(recapitulation — shortened)

Second movement

Db — (part I)
Bb — (part II)
Db — (part III)

Third movement

Eb D ⌉ (refrain I)
Eb

D B ⌉ (episode I)
E B

B
(refrain II)
Db Eb ⌉ (episode II)
C (refrain III and coda)

material. He once said about this concerto that he had deliberately 'filled it full of tunes' (score-study lecture at the RCMT ca 1950). It follows the Liszt-Rachmaninoff tradition rather than the more classically structured concertos of the Brahms-Dvořák school. Willan had studied piano extensively as a young man, and the piano writing in this concerto is idiomatic for the instrument and often unlike anyone else's. The concerto is not purely for soloist with perfunctory orchestral accompaniment; Willan's orchestral score is full of colour and interest, producing a good balance between soloist and orchestra. Rachmaninoff's concertos have survived because they are well-written and attractive works. I can see no reason why Willan's concerto should not occupy a similar place of honour.

8

Other works for
orchestra and band

In the first decade of this century Willan was much occupied with ideas
of orchestral composition and left a number of unfinished symphonic
poems, rhapsodies, overtures, and so on. Three works were completed,
though he orchestrated only two of them. The first, *Allegro marcato*, was
composed in 1904 and scored for small orchestra. Though only nine bars
long the piece is complete and is Willan's first surviving orchestral effort.
It is a rather ingenious 12-in-1 canon in C minor, the tune being four
bars of 3/4 time and the entries being separated by only one beat. Willan
sketched the theme of Strauss's *Till Eulenspiegel* on the back page – evidence that he was familiar with at least one of the Strauss tone poems.

Through Darkness into Light was Willan's first and only completed orchestral tone poem. The music was not orchestrated by Willan, though there
are a few directions for orchestration in his condensed score. (An orchestration was done by Godfrey Ridout in 1980.) Completed on 10 March
1908 'in memoriam Dennis O'Sullivan,' the work divides itself into six
main sections.

Section I is twenty-seven bars of 'Lento e solenne' in B minor, 4/4 time.
The music is in the nature of an introductory solemn dirge, and moves
over a constantly repeating rhythmic ostinato in the drums: ♩♪♪♫. Section II, twenty-three bars long, 'Molto espressione,' is in D major, 3/4
time. Here the cor anglais plays a very beautiful, sad, and tender melody
which is in fact the ancient Irish song, *Jimmy mo mhíle stór* (Jimmy, my
thousand treasures). It is quoted in toto, though Willan gives no clue as
to its origin in his score (Example 57); Hamilton Harty (1871–1941)
made extensive use of the tune in his *Irish Symphony* of 1904, and perhaps Willan had heard this. Section III consists of thirty-seven bars, 'Agi-

tato e poco piu mosso' in B minor, 3/4 time. The material for this section is developed from its initial motif (Example 58). These developments, accompanied by a throbbing, syncopated rhythm, lead to such splendid passages as that in Example 59.

Section IV, sixty-four bars of 'allegro feroce,' is written in 3/4 time. There is no key signature. Development continues of the motif from the previous section. Willan also introduces passages of some length based on the theme of the prelude of his great 1908 *Prelude and Fugue in C Minor* for organ. Section V, eighty-seven bars of 'largo' in 3/4 time, starts in B major (Example 60). This is obviously the 'Light' section referred to in the title. There is prominent use of the rhythm ♫♩ in sections III, IV, and V. After sixteen bars the metre of section V shifts to 4/4, and the rhythm of the 'Light' motif becomes ♩♫|♩♫|♫♩|○, ♫♩|♩♫ , and so on. Tonality in this section shifts constantly, though C major seems to be rather favoured (perhaps influenced by Haydn's C major 'Light' in *The Creation*).

Section VI, sixty-one bars in length, 'molto maestoso' in B major, is set in 3/4 time. This final section begins with a long noble theme (Example 61) introduced by horns, cellos, and bassoons and repeated by full orchestra. The theme does not appear to have much connection with its surroundings save for a certain 'Irish' flavour. Its two-octave range would seem to preclude the possibility of its being a true folksong like *Jimmy mo mhíle stór*. This section is followed by a build-up over a dominant pedal which leads to a triumphal fff presentation of the Irish melody from section II. The brief coda which concludes the work makes reference to the 'Light' motif again.

In all, in spite of its rather sectional appearance, this is a well put-together piece. Tuneful melodic writing, colourful harmony, and skilful counterpoint – all trademarks of the mature Willan – are present in this remarkable early work. The main influences seem to be Wagner (especially in sections III and IV), Franck (especially III), Rheinberger (V), and the Irish-English school of Stanford (II and VI).

The only other orchestral piece Willan completed in England was *Epilogue* for orchestra and organ, which he finished on 19 May 1909. It exists in full orchestral score. Willan appears to have prepared a full set of orchestral parts, but these seem not to have been used and the work was probably never performed. The organ is not used in a solo capacity but as a member of the orchestra. This orchestral *Epilogue* does not come close to the fine *Epilogue in D Minor* for organ solo, published in the same year. It begins with a quotation from the plainsong hymn-tune *Urbs beata Hierusalem* (which would figure prominently in the organ prelude on the tune composed in 1950 and the big anthem *Blessed Art Thou* of 1952). Here, however, the quotation does not reappear in the piece and none of the subsequent material is related to it. The thematic material is not very interesting, save perhaps for the 'Andante maestoso' theme which Willan used later as the second main subject for the finale of *Symphony No. 1*. Willan scored this piece and yet left *Through Darkness into Light* unscored. Perhaps he thought there was a chance for a performance of *Epilogue*.

During the 1920s Willan was busy writing incidental music for plays, and for these he sometimes employed a small orchestra. A piece such as the little *Overture to the Alchemist* (1920) could count as a purely orchestral piece. In 1931 Willan composed *Three Dances* for small orchestra, but the score has been lost. All that remains is the oboe part.

During 1936 and 1937 Willan composed his *Marche solennelle* (*Coronation March*) as a tribute to the coronation of King George VI. It was the first of several orchestral marches and march-like works Willan was to compose in his later years. In structure it follows the usual ceremonial march form as employed by Elgar and Walton, a three-part structure consisting of march (tonic key, and usually vigorous in style), trio (contrasting key, and lyrical in style), march (return to tonic key and opening material), and coda (in which the lyric tune of the trio returns, transformed into a triumphant 'nobilmente,' 'grandioso,' or 'maestoso;' the end of the coda usually makes reference to the opening march material).

Marche solennelle commences with a lengthy introduction of some thirty bars, the first part a fanfare which uses consecutive root position triads, giving 'consecutive fifths' (Example 62 shows bars 10 to 12). The fanfare material is the basis for effective links between the three main sections and for the ending to the coda. This device would be used again in *Brébeuf*, *Royal Salute*, *Élégie héroïque*, and *Fanfare* for organ.

The march movement proper begins at bar 31 and is based on the theme shown in Example 63. Then a brief secondary motif containing a Scottish snap (Example 64) appears after a short episode. A longer episode follows, leading back to a repetition of the main theme. The fanfare motif now reappears to form the basis of a linking passage to the next main section, the lyric trio.

The trio, in D major, is marked 'cantabile e nobilmente' and consists of a broad, hymn-like theme (Example 65). When the D major section is concluded, the fanfare (along with other material from the introduction) serves as a retransition back to the tonic key of B flat major for a somewhat shortened repetition of the march section. This in turn ends on a dominant pedal over which peals of bells are introduced, building up to the 'grandioso' restatement by full orchestra of the trio theme, this time in B flat. The phrase endings of the theme are effectively punctuated with combinations of trumpet fanfares and peals of bells, and the music ends triumphantly with a final flourish of trumpets, bells, and full orchestra.

Marche solennelle was probably Willan's most frequently played orchestral piece, receiving fifteen performances in Canada between 1937 and 1953.

Suite for Rhythm Band, published in 1938, consists of three short movements: march, intermezzo (in waltz time), and jig. Scored for piano four-hands, triangle, tambourine, cymbals, and drums (no particular type of drum specified), this little suite could perhaps more properly be considered chamber music. The percussion parts are quite easy and the music is very traditional, indicating that Willan had young children in mind here. Musically, *Suite for Rhythm Band* is of little importance.

Willan's next orchestral march, *A Marching Tune*, was composed during 1941 and 1942. It was dedicated 'To all loyal gentlemen, with a special thought for the Queen's Own Rifles of Canada'; the composer's son Bernard was serving in the Queen's Own Rifles. The wording of the dedication had its origins in Elgar's dedication for his *Spirit of England* in 1916: 'I dedicate to the memory of our glorious men, with a special thought for the Worcesters.'

Much of the orchestration is by Godfrey Ridout. Willan, pushed for time, enlisted his aid in this project. Ridout used Willan's pen for the occasion and even tried to imitate Willan's manuscript writing. The manuscript score certainly does not betray its secret to the unsuspecting! Ridout was familiar with Willan's style; according to him their only disagreement concerned the height of the trombone parts (Willan liked low trombones and he liked high ones!)

A Marching Tune is a ternary-structured piece (ABA plus coda) and is rather attractive in spite of a pronounced difference of musical styles between the two main sections. The 'A' section is based on a long modal-type tune (Example 66) which gives the impression of origins in English folksong.

Willan's first work for concert band, *Royce Hall Suite*, was composed in 1949. Like *Sonata No. 2* for violin and piano (1921) it imitates Handel, though it tends to stray into other styles. Willan wrote the music in short score only; he left it to William Teague to score it for band. The published band score differs in tonality from Willan's original quite radically. Willan had used the key of B flat major for the first and third movements and G minor for the middle movement. Teague changed these to F major and A minor respectively. Willan's keys of B flat major and G minor are good 'band' keys; here the arranger has changed not only the keys but also the tonal relationships between the movements, with the middle movement up a major third in relation to the outer movements instead of down a minor third (ie to the relative minor).

The first movement, prelude and fugue, is the most Handelian. It is cast in the mould of a French overture, commencing with a slow, majestic introduction (the prelude) based on dotted and double-dotted rhythms, followed by a vigorous fugue (Willan's original manuscript had suggested ♩ = 66 for the fugue; the published score has ♩ = 80). Except for a somewhat uncharacteristic French sixth in the fourth bar, the prelude is, quite successfully, Handelian; so is the fugue, based on the subject in Example 67. The only exception is a very chromatic passage (Example 68) near the end which does not co-exist very comfortably with its neighbours. The fugue, an academic 'tour de force' for five real voices in vigorous counterpoint, is more complex than one would normally find in Handel or even (with a few exceptions) Bach. As a result the texture tends to be dense, and Willan's original tempo of ♩ = 66 is more suitable than the ♩ = 80 in the published version. This movement can indeed sound thick and obscure in performance, and choice of tempo is therefore crucial. The scoring itself may also be to blame. Willan sent the band score to his colleague Capt Charles O'Neill, a well-known Canadian bandmaster. O'Neill wrote about the scoring of the prelude and fugue: '[He] does not seem to mind important parts sounding within basses in octaves. Also seems to like the basses doubled in the octave above rather than below ... There seems to be a general lack of knowledge of how to handle individual voice parts.' Concerning the suite as a whole, O'Neill wrote, 'The scoring is about average – perhaps a little better than average – turned out by American band men' (note attached to original manuscript in the National Library of Canada).

The second movement, the minuet, is a charming little piece, again à la Handel, though in the middle section the composer allows the style to stray somewhat (Example 69).

The third and final movement, the rondo (Example 70), is really a quick march and is so subtitled (Alla Marcia, ♩ = 120). Here Willan forsakes Handel and adopts a more recent style (Stanford, MacKenzie, German). The piece is a three-refrain rondo. In the second episode (separating refrains 2 and 3), in the subdominant key of B flat, Willan allows himself to be almost Schubertian (Example 71).

The suite, dedicated to Patton McNaughton, conductor of the band of the University of California at Los Angeles (UCLA), was first performed by that band in May 1949 and has been repeated frequently since then. It was a welcome addition to the small amount of first-rate material for concert band, which in 1949 included only the suites of Holst and Vaughan Williams and Schoenberg's 1943 *Variations*.

One of the most attractive of Willan's short orchestral works is *Overture to an Unwritten Comedy*, which appeared in 1951. It was dedicated 'To my old friend, John Adaskin, with whom I have often exchanged the merry quip and prank.' The wording gives the clue to this music: some years previous Napier Moore and Willan had intended to write a comic opera, but Moore died before the project got under way; however Willan had already composed this overture for the 'unwritten' comedy. Scored for comparatively small orchestra and of only four minutes' duration, this piece is of the sort popular with many amateur and semi-professional orchestras which like to include 'Canadian content' provided it is short, easy to play, and easy to listen to. Willan is deliberately conventional in style, eschewing the complex chromatics that are a feature of his more ambitious and serious works and writing music which simply 'aims to please.' As such the piece is very successful.

The overall structure is a simple ternary one. The first section, in D major, is made up of three musical ideas (Examples 72–4). The first is a bustling passage of an almost introductory nature; the second is a broad tune (taken from the last few bars of the unfinished orchestral rhapsody of 1911, *From the Highlands*); the third is a short rhythmic figure. There follows a brief transitional passage which leads to the second section, in B flat major. This transition refers to the final motif of the first section and also to the triplet eighths which will be part of the second section.

The second section proper begins at bar 50, and has two main motifs (Example 75 and 76). There are some hints of material from the introductory motif of the first section. Another short bridge passage, starting as an extension of Example 75 and concluding with a reference to material from near the beginning of the piece, leads to the third and final section. Here the tonality returns to D major and the music of Examples 72 and 73 is recapitulated. The first transitional passage now reappears, shortened and transposed, this time leading to the coda. The coda is based on the opening motifs of both sections, transformed into triple time.

In June 1959 Queen Elizabeth II paid a visit to Canada, and the CBC commissioned Willan to compose a royal salute. Willan wrote the work (a march in E flat for orchestra) during April and May. Perhaps pressed by time, he took over for the first section the whole of the orchestral opening section of his *Choral March* of 1922. (This had been transposed from his 1921 march music for *Cymbeline*, in turn from an unfinished 1912 march in E.) The music of *Royal Salute* is cast in the same form as the 1937 *Marche solennelle* (*Coronation March*).

Another early work occupied Willan's attention during 1959. *Poem* for string quartet of 1930 had initially appeared as an unfinished slow movement of a projected string quartet ca 1903–5. Now Willan rewrote the piece as *Poem for String Orchestra*. This arrangement is no mere reproduction of the string quartet parts with double bass added. In many places Willan amplifies the texture by the use of divisi in the violin and viola parts, and this often results in the rewriting of other parts. The double basses do not always double the cello line, and there are some very effective places where the basses 'shadow' the cellos in pizzicato. In structure *Poem* is in arc form (ABCBA).

Section A is a musical paragraph of some thirty bars in E major. The music develops rhapsodically from the opening bars (Example 77). Note the octave leap with the note of anticipation at the beginning, a characteristic of the composer's style (via Elgar and others). Section B begins with a question-answer dialogue between orchestral sections, mainly in G sharp minor. The music then settles into B major for a long winding melody over an undulating accompaniment in triplet eighths. For the beginning see Example 78. In section C the tempo changes from adagio to allegretto scherzando, and the metre from 3/4 to 2/4. The section is developed out of a playful theme (Example 79). In the middle of this section there is a reference to the G sharp minor figure of section B, after which the scherzando theme is repeated a tone higher. It is difficult to assign a tonality for section C, as there is much shifting about: the music appears to start in B minor and come to rest in C sharp major. Section B reappears with the original tempo and metre. There is only a partial repetition, with the music starting off in D flat major. Section A is then repeated, with some variation. The tonic key of E major is re-established with the return of the opening material, and the movement ends with a short coda.

Poem is a remarkable example of the combination of youthful imagination and expression with mature craftsmanship. It is one of Willan's most beautiful pieces and, given its 1903–5 origins, is not really old-fashioned.

The next of Willan's orchestral marches, *Élégie héroïque*, was composed in 1960 for the centennial of the Queen's Own Rifles of Canada. Strictly speaking the piece is not really an 'orchestral' march, since it is scored only for band. Willan wrote the music on four pages of short score and then left it to be arranged for band by someone else. Interestingly, the first 60 per cent is in D flat major while the remainder is in B flat major.

Willan's last completed orchestral piece is *Centennial March*, composed in 1967. If there is nothing particularly original about this march, it is nevertheless tuneful and well-written. Willan thought it had 'a couple of very pretty tunes.'

9

Dramatic cantata
and operas

Willan completed a dramatic cantata, *Cleopatra* (1907), and two radio operas, *Transit through Fire* (1942) and *Deirdre of the Sorrows* (1944; later staged as *Deirdre* in 1965 and, revised again, in 1966).

CLEOPATRA

Willan's cantata *Cleopatra* for SSAB soli, mixed choir, and large orchestra (2333/4331/percussion, harp/strings), written in 1907, was his first completed large-scale work in any genre.[1] Willan had already mastered the complex chromatic Wagnerian and post-Wagner harmonic style which remained the basis for his large dramatic and symphonic works up to the final revisions of *Deirdre* in 1965. Opposite the opening page of music in the piano-vocal score the composer wrote out the work's leitmotifs: night (Example 80), Cleopatra's longing (81), bliss (82), Antony (83), battle (84), and bars 4 and 5 of Example 81, which are to represent the mutual longing of Antony and Cleopatra. In subsequent works employing the leitmotif technique (such as *Pantaloon*, *Transit through Fire*, *Brébeuf*, and *Deirdre*) Willan would use about the same number of motifs as here; he preferred to use a small handful of leitmotifs than to clutter the score with many. This had been Elgar's approach in works such as *The Dream of Gerontius*.

1 *King Ragnar*, an unfinished work of which only 206 bars of rather sketchy condensed score remain, appears, from the manuscript and style (very Wagnerian), to date from about the same time. Willan was perhaps inspired by Elgar's *King Olaf* (1896) which treated a similar type of Norse saga; Willan conducted Elgar's *Caractacus* in 1905 with the Wanstead Choral Society. Some stage directions written over the music on the first page of *King Ragnar* might indicate that Willan intended it to be an opera! *Cleopatra*, clearly a dramatic cantata, has no such stage directions.

Cleopatra remains unorchestrated, save for some thirty-five bars of the first scene. Perhaps there was no performance in view and Willan, trying desperately to make ends meet, simply could not afford the necessary time. His name does not appear on the completed piano-vocal score or on the orchestral fragment, but the former does have 'music by "FAC ET SPERA,"' perhaps a nom de plume for a competition? The authorship of the text remains a mystery: it is possible that Willan (like Wagner for many of his own works) wrote it himself. It deals with Cleopatra's relationship with Mark Antony.

Cleopatra, lasting just over half an hour, is divided into six movements (or scenes) with the first three proceeding on into the next without break. In the opening scene, two of Cleopatra's ladies-in-waiting, Iris (a soprano) and Charmion (an alto), discuss the signs they have observed of their queen's excitement over Antony's expected return. A distant chorus seems to foretell that this will be their last night together. In order to enhance the effect of distance Willan keeps the tessitura for the voice parts very low; the voices seem to come from the floor of the desert and the pyramids (behind which the sun had now fallen) – an imaginative touch indeed. The choruses are short and homophonic, with no repetitions of text. The music for this scene uses the first four of the leitmotifs shown earlier.

The twenty-bar orchestral introduction commences with an expansion of the night motif down the full length of a chromatic scale, giving a mystic 'long ago and far away' effect (Example 85). (One is reminded of a similar musical procedure in the magic ban music in Wagner's *Die Walküre* where, as here, a succession of colourful chromatic chords bearing little or no relation to one another is held together by a descending chromatic scale in the upper part.) The remainder of the orchestral introduction is based upon the motif of Cleopatra's longing.

After the entry of the voices the bliss and the Antony motifs appear with some frequency. They are used in suggestive as well as more obvious ways: when Iris sings of the appearance of her queen that day, 'her lips ... parted with the expectation of proud assault,' the Antony motif appears in the orchestra even though Antony's name is not mentioned till the end of the scene. In this section the Antony and bliss motifs are joined (Example 86). The leitmotifs are confined to the orchestral part and do not appear in either the chorus parts or in the arioso of the solo singers.

Scene II sees the first appearance of the battle motif as Antony appears, returned from combat. The orchestral introduction, commencing with a passage based on the battle motif alone, proceeds to show an ingenious, simultaneous combination of the battle motif with that of Antony (Example 87). The scene is a love duet between Antony (a baritone) and Cleopatra (a soprano), and, although through most of it they sing separately, they join together at the end for a rapturous climax (Example 88).

Scene III is for soprano solo and might be called Cleopatra's soliloquy. Antony is gone again but still on her mind, and at the words 'and I would through darkness peer, leaving the couch you slept upon,' another interesting combination of leitmotifs appears – this time night and Antony (Example 89).

Scene IV is for chorus and orchestra, without solo voices. Unlike the first scene, in which the chorus sang only short fragments, this is a complete choral movement on a meditative text which begins 'Great silence is o'er everything, the sweet tired silence of Spring.' Willan had had considerable success with writing for choir, and his skill is evident here. The choral part is through-composed with no repetition, and the writing is largely homophonic, interspersed with a few imitative passages (but not enough to obscure the words). The structure is held together by the orchestral accompaniment, based mostly on the bliss motif and a new figure of descending sixths (which Willan used again in the 1908 song *Rest*).

Scene V is Cleopatra's poignant lament on the death of Antony. Here Willan transforms the Antony motif into a majestic dirge played first by orchestra alone and later used as the accompaniment to Cleopatra's vocal line (Example 90). Rarely has the composer written anything more moving. The musical structure of this movement is basically three parts with coda, though there is no corresponding repetition of any of the text.

The sixth and last scene is, like the fourth, completely choral. The text is a continuation of what the chorus was singing in the first movement, but about what has happened rather than what was about to happen. The short orchestral introduction (Example 91) consists of an unaccompanied unison cello–double bass passage (like those Willan favoured in his later works) derived from Cleopatra's motif. The opening words of the chorus, 'The sun has gone away to sleep,' are accompanied by the night motif, and material from this motif and that of Cleopatra forms the basis of much of the subsequent accompaniment. The final seven bars of chorus (Example 92) make, in their simple but direct way, a moving conclusion. The completely satisfying effect of this ending is difficult to express in words – one simply 'feels' it.

The cantata is in B flat minor, and the keys of the various scenes (or movements) are, in order: B flat minor, E flat major, B major, E major, C minor, and B flat minor. A certain parallelism of tonal relationships emerges between scenes I and II and scenes III and IV which might correspond to that of the moods of the various scenes: I, expectation, leads to II, fulfilment; and III, after-glow, leads to IV, reflection. In addition there is a fair amount of C major in I, II, and IV which might account for the choice of C minor as the key of the great lament in V. Willan appears to have considered B major Cleopatra's key (at least when she wasn't lamenting!) and E flat major Antony's key. However in an idiom as chromatic as that of *Cleopatra*, with its constantly shifting tonalities and implied tonal changes, one must be wary of attaching particular significance to a fleeting tonality.

TRANSIT THROUGH FIRE

Transit through Fire (An Odyssey of 1942) was Willan's first opera and the first opera in Canada commissioned for radio. It is about fifty-five minutes long, to fit into a one-hour broadcast. The work requires six soloists, a mixed chorus, and a medium-sized orchestra (1121/2320/timp, perc, harp/strings). The libretto was by John Coulter. *Transit* was premiered over the air in 1942 and on 18 February 1943 received a public performance at Convocation Hall, University of Toronto. It was repeated by the CBC that year. Willan wrote the opera in less than two months, between 23 December 1941 and 14 February 1942. The orchestration was done by Lucio Agostini.

The work is dated. The text is so directed to 1942 that it would prove an embarrassment if performed now. Phrases such as 'living democracy,' 'Christian democracy,' 'brotherhood,' 'Christian theory of life in community,' and 'marching ... for a future' abound. Its message was sincere, however, and made a deep impression on its wartime audiences.

The printed synopsis of the story in *Transit through Fire* (Toronto 1942) is as follows: 'In a remote skiing cabin a young soldier, Sergeant William Thompson, is spending a brief leave with his wife, Joan. In reverie they recall scenes in their lives since they graduated from Varsity [University of Toronto] in 1937. The dances, the trivial disputes, the serious questionings of end and purpose, the cocktail parties, the degradation of having to wangle "influence" with possible employers, the criminal maiming of pride and spirit as it becomes clear to William and Joan that in the economy of the community there is no necessary place for them. At the end of these scenes the idealism of youth is shattered, and it is only by a supreme individual effort that the clue to the good life in community is discovered.'

Perhaps the text should have become a play rather than an opera. Many lines have deep meaning, but are lost in the music.

Coulter wrote in his introduction: 'I may have written a texture of words too closely wrought to be easily followed in the surge of the music.' In his introduction to the printed libretto for *Deirdre of the Sorrows* (Toronto 1944) Coulter observed: 'Sometimes I have suspected that words for music should be no more than clues for music, that it may be mistaken to attempt the full articulation of a theme in literary terms, since what then should be the need for music? In short, I have often wondered whether the idiotic empty jingles which have so often served as words for music and which clutter the bottom of the literary garbage can, are not ideal for libretto-writing after all.'

Transit appears more a philosophical meditation than a drama or action piece. Is it really an opera? Perhaps it is a new sub-species, radio opera – a type not requiring staging. With its narrator (not in the score, but used in the broadcast), its extensive use of chorus, and its non-use of staging, it is perhaps closer to certain types of oratorio and cantata. The general form of this score differs little from that of *Cleopatra*. Indeed Hector Charlesworth, writing in *Saturday Night* after the February 1943 staging of *Transit*, referred to it as a dramatic cantata.

Willan set the text carefully to allow the words to be intelligible. The music for the solo voices is written in a continuous arioso style with great attention to proper speech rhythm. There is only one metrical song, and it occurs where the text moves into poetic lines of trimetre and is therefore quite appropriate. The chorus parts are written almost entirely in homophonic or unison style, so that there is only one set of words at once. The sung words are readily perceived by any listener with the printed text in front of him. However, the nature of music and singing being what it is, it is unlikely that more than a fraction of the text would be understood by someone hearing the opera without the libretto to follow. In most operas this situation does not matter a great deal, but in a work such as *Transit*, where so much depends upon comprehension of the words, it is a different thing.

Willan's score consists of four scenes, preceded by a short prologue. Coulter's libretto has six scenes, but the last three are quite short and Willan has treated them together as scene IV. As he had done in *Cleopatra* (1907) and for the incidental music to *Pantaloon* (1921), Willan builds his musical score around a number of leitmotifs. His use of these is not concentrated; there are many fairly lengthy passages which make no reference to them.

The prologue commences with a motif (Example 93) in the orchestra. Subsequently it undergoes various transformations, such as Example 94. This motif, with its prominent use of the ♫ rhythm in stepwise melodic motion, bears an affinity with the opening of Elgar's *Piano Quintet* and might be labelled the odyssey, after the sub-title. The prologue is sung by the baritone lead, Thompson, and is one of the clearest and most effective passages of declamation in the opera. Thompson announces his story, summing it up as follows: 'This is our Odyssey, our transit through fire out of the futile 1930's into the fighting 1940's.'

Scene I finds Thompson and his wife sitting in a ski shack in front of a fire, recalling their days at university, particularly their graduation day. It opens with an orchestral motif which seems to denote reminiscence and the cabin in the snow. The reminiscence motif and some of its transformations are given in Example 95.

The first part of the scene, marked adagio, is given over to a leisurely 'Do you remember?' dialogue. In the second part the tempo picks up and the style changes ('Allegro in jazz time and rhythm') to that of the popular music of the 1930s. In their imaginations William and Joan are now back at Varsity and, assisted by the chorus, they go through one of their university songs, complete with rah-rah-rah's. They recall their graduation day and the message of the president: 'Each man must find his individual good in seeking first the general good of the community.' Towards the end of the scene Willan skilfully combines these elements: the chorus sings the university song, the president drones his message, and the orchestra beats out its dance-band accompaniment (Example 96). This untypical Willan music fits beautifully. Agostini's scoring doubtless assisted greatly. The scene ends with the odyssey motif.

Scene II opens with a passage derived from the odyssey motif, but much changed to set the mood for William's lines 'Out of the universities like rudderless ships upon uncharted seas we sailed' (Example 97). This gloomy mood soon gives way to the music of *The Lambeth Walk* (Example 98) as William and Joan recall their first dance. They recall their ensuing quarrel, which resulted in Joan's going around with another fellow in order to make William jealous. During all this Willan treats the *Lambeth Walk* material almost as a leitmotif and skilfully keeps it developing in the orchestra under the conversation of the principals and the comments of the chorus. Thus scene II ends as scene I did: on a light, popular-music-influenced musical note. Willan's imaginative, fragmented treatment of the chorus during the dancing lesson and the quarrel deserves mention: short scraps of chorus are skilfully woven into the action. One must marvel at Willan's success in working with a popular music idiom that lay outside his usual fields of endeavour.

Scenes I and II, though they have their serious moments, are generally light-hearted. With scene III a mood of gloom and frustration sets in. This is foreshadowed by the orchestral opening, which is built upon minor-mode inversions (Example 99) of the reminiscence motif. After some preliminary dialogue on the triviality of their squabble, William sings a 'rueful song' with which, he says, he consoled himself at the time. This is the one aria (if one can call it such) in the opera, though it is just a little song of some thirty bars rather in the style of some of the more serious airs found in Gilbert and Sullivan. The next section is given over to women gossiping about the 'break-up'; a chattering little figure (Example 100) in the orchestra is derived from part of the odyssey motif.

The dialogue resumes and touches upon their discovery after graduation of what the 'cynical and obscene world' was really like. They are interrupted by the 'stockbrokers' chorus' (my title) 'high, low, buying, selling, profit taking, money making.' One is reminded of the patter choruses of Gilbert and Sullivan, though Willan's music here is more modern; it also resembles the demon's chorus from *The Dream of Gerontius*. The dialogue continues, this time concerning William's lack of success in obtaining a 'position,' and cynicism reigns for several pages of score. There is a particularly realistic touch with the sound of a typewriter when William visits an office for a job interview. The chorus is used effectively in this section, and toward the end there is an impressive treatment of a text which begins:

And songs were sung and hymns were sung
And comics played their antics at the fair
And business men stung business men
And parsons prayed long prayers into the air.

At the end of scene III William has decided to go to the ski-cottage 'to find by merciless flagellation of my most secret mind my individual salvation,' and the music concludes with a motif which might be labelled 'quest for individual salvation' (Example 101). One wonders whether the resemblance to the yeomen's theme in *Yeomen of the Guard* (Example 102) was intentional.

Scene IV begins with another appearance of the quest motif. William goes through his soul-searching in the wilderness and is counselled by two voices: 'the Syrian Mystic who died two thousand years ago' (accompanied by a Parsifal-like theme; Example 103) and the beast (a tempter in bowler hat!), who has no leitmotif. There is an interesting short chorus, on the text 'This mystery the saints and sages of all the ages do faithfully declare,' in Willan's motet style. It occurs at the only place in the libretto where such a choral style would be appropriate.

William, having 'passed through transforming fire,' finds peace, and the dialogue between him and Joan resumes. They find meaning in, and derive strength from, their relationship and they sing a beautiful duet, 'A future where love has begun.' This is the only place where they sing together rather than consecutively (as in the dialogues); the style is quite Elgarian here and reminds one of some of the duet passages between Gerontius and the Angel. The duet finishes with a triumphal statement of the mystic's motif.

The music moves without break into scene V. William and Joan recall their marriage and William's joining the army (his first job!) to fight for democracy, brotherhood, and so on. The text and music become rather patriotic and one has the marching chorus (Example 104).

The music moves without break into scene VI. William and Joan, finished their reveries and back in the present, decide to leave the comfort of the fire and to go skiing. This little final scene is anti-climactic, especially musically. Those responsible for the first performance tacked on a repeat of the marching chorus – a much stronger ending, easy to accomplish because both sections were in C major. The effect was so natural it sounded like the composer's original intention.

In general mood the opera seems to divide itself into two halves: scenes I and II both end with light 'pops' sections and are concerned mainly with cheerful recollections; scenes III and IV are more serious and deal with frustration and the seeking of purpose. A moralistic and almost sermonizing tone pervades the work, however, and all the incidents, light and serious, are part of the message.

The opera begins and ends in C, but D tends to be the main linking tonality throughout (see the accompanying chart; only the main tonalities are indicated). The leitmotifs are less immediately apparent and striking

123 Dramatic cantata and operas

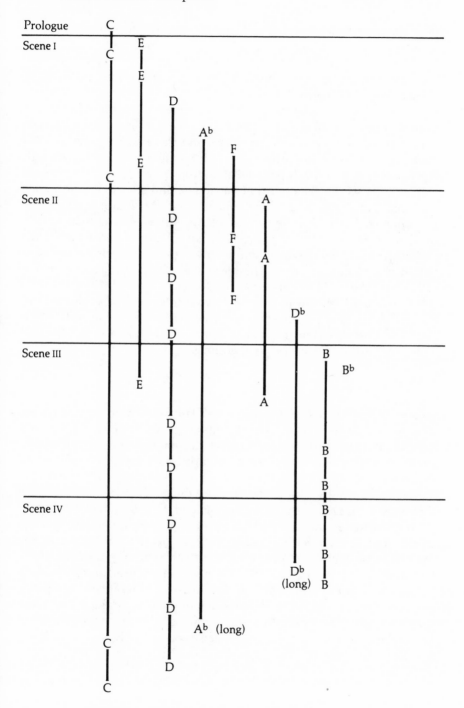

than those in *Brébeuf* or *Deirdre*, and their meaning more difficult to pinpoint. They tend to be used rather sparsely, and many lengthy passages of general arioso and chorus have no leitmotif. Willan employed his leitmotifs here in a more general way and with less frequency than in some of his other works.

There is more chorus work in this short opera than in the full-length *Deirdre*. The chorus frequently comments upon the action and joins in as part of the group (eg the dancing class and the marching chorus). The choruses tend to be short and to the point, homophonic, and with little repetition of text or contrapuntal elaboration.

Agostini's scoring is at all times adequate and sometimes more than that: the 'pops' numbers which conclude scenes I and II and the later marching song are effective because of Agostini's experience in scoring music of that type. A few passages evoking Wagner and Elgar do not realize their implied idiomatic sound with Agostini's scoring and tend to be fairly neutral as a result. The opera was successful at the time and coped with the problems of a new form remarkably well. The music is of a high standard: Willan has written a well-integrated score and has set the text clearly and sensitively. Yet by having 'our say in operatic terms about certain aspects of the contemporary scene' (preface) Coulter and Willan cut their work off from other times.

DEIRDRE

Following the success of *Transit through Fire*, Willan and Coulter were approached by the CBC to write a full-length radio opera. Willan and Coulter felt they must 'choose a subject far removed from the contemporary. We had no wish to compete with ourselves in saying again what we had once said' (preface, *Deirdre of the Sorrows*, Toronto 1944). So they chose the story of Deirdre, part of the two-thousand-year-old Tales of the Red Branch Knights of Ulster, and persuaded the CBC of its suitability for operatic treatment. Coulter added: 'It has long seemed that the hero tales of the Red Branch were as susceptible to operatic treatment as the legends around which Wagner evoked his vast sombrely-coloured phantasmagorias of dramatic sounds.' He noted also: 'In countries such as Canada, still in the process of colonization by immigrants from various stocks of the old world, a national idiom in the arts can hardly be more than emergent. The art of a Canadian remains ... the art of the country of his forebears, and the old world heritage of myth and legend remains his heritage.' The time for operas about Louis Riel or based on Canadian

Indian lore was not yet upon us, yet Coulter (and presumably Willan) felt that a word of explanation might be necessary 'to justify choice of an ancient Gaelic legend as the subject of a Canadian opera' (ibid).

Deirdre of the Sorrows was based on Coulter's radio play *Conochar's Queen*, for which Willan in 1941 wrote music (see chapter 13). Though the story of Deirdre had been retold many times by poets and dramatists (such as Yeats and Synge) Coulter believed this was the first time it was told in operatic form. Some years later Coulter discovered that a libretto titled *Deirdre of the Sorrows*, written by a Dr Crofton for music by Geoffrey Palmer, had been published in Dublin in 1925. (In 1926 Cecil Gray, a former pupil of Willan's, completed a three-act opera called *Deirdre*. Sir Arnold Bax wrote a five-act libretto on the subject, but never composed the music for it.)

Willan said: 'I had already made several sketches for incidental music for *Deirdre* as a stage play, and when the opportunity came to cast it into operatic mould I used several of the incidental themes, and in one case ... I found that a somewhat lengthy passage fitted exactly the same operatic situation, and that the words adjusted themselves with the most complete ease to the music already written' (1965 interview with Ruby Mercer on 'Operatime').

A narrator was required, and so, in the first (1946) radio production, each of the ten scenes was introduced by the bard, who set the locale and supplied whatever other details were necessary. These ten passages, some fairly lengthy, were written in the arioso recitativo style used nearly all the time by the other solo singers. This led to monotony and made a long opera seem even longer. Perhaps the narrative should have been spoken rather than sung; yet one can understand the temptation to follow the ancient practice of using singing story-tellers. For the 1951 radio production, the first passage was sung, the rest spoken.

Willan had always wanted to see the opera staged. Coulter tried to get it staged in Ireland; a proposed performance for the 1948–49 season of the Royal Dublin Operatic Society did not transpire. Coulter tried to obtain a performance in the United States through an appeal to the Irish people there; in a letter to the president of Fordham University in 1947 he wrote: 'We should be happy to give permission for the premier American performance to any musically adequate organization of the American Irish.' This attempt also proved fruitless. In the early 1960s, the Opera School of the University of Toronto aand the Royal Conservatory of Toronto decided to mount a stage production of *Deirdre*. Much revision would be required. Willan said 'Passages of introduction, continuity and identification necessary for radio performance are really superfluous for the stage. The same thing applied to the bard-narrator, so John [Coulter] cut him out. Wherever I was obliged to cut, I naturally had to compose special transitions' (*Opera Canada* 7, 1966). The most obvious difference is the removal of the passages for the bard. However orchestral preludes or interludes had to be composed to allow time for scene changes. The increased amount of orchestral music did provide greater variety and interest.

The opening chorus, quite impressive musically, was cut considerably. In act II the original scene 2 of the radio version was removed, reducing the act to two scenes; Willan wrote sixty-four bars of music for text Coulter added at the beginning of the new scene 2. Act III scene 3 has an orchestral prelude to replace the bard and the orchestral coda at the end is expanded from four to twenty-four bars. At the end of the last scene, the keening of the women and the Druids' chorus take place simultaneously – a condensation which works brilliantly.

The radically revised, second version, called simply *Deirdre*, was made between 1962 and 1964 for production in 1965. The third version, a slight revision of the second, was made during 1965 for production in 1966; this version appears in the published piano-vocal score and is the final, definitive form of the opera. A detailed discussion of the final version follows.

Like the great orchestral preludes to Elgar's *The Dream of Gerontius* and *The Kingdom*, the orchestral introduction to act I of *Deirdre* sets out most of the main leitmotifs, beginning with a unison passage for cellos and basses (Example 105). This motif, which I call 'foreboding,' appears infrequently (it was more extensively used in *Conochar's Queen* and in the 1945 version). It is a type of passage Willan had been fond of using as early as *Cleopatra*, and there are resemblances between it and passages in *Piano Concerto in C Minor*.[2] The orchestra next plays the bard motif (Example 106). It, too, is not used much. (It was used more often in the original version which had an actual singing part for a bard, and first appeared there to accompany the bard's opening words 'Now to the music of plucked strings'). The third leitmotif, Deirdre's (Example 107),

---

2 In a radio address Willan said: 'At that time I had written part of my second Symphony; I broke off to write the music for *Deirdre*, and stopped half-way through the second act in order to write a piano concerto; I then returned to *Deirdre*, finished it, and then I completed my symphony.'

is used more extensively than any other and is subject to ingenious variation – melodic, rhythmic, and harmonic. Following a short passage based on developments of the Deirdre motif, reference is made to two further important leitmotifs, Conochar (Example 108) and tragic fate (Example 109). The other two main leitmotifs which appear soon after the close of the orchestral prelude are Cathva (Example 110) and the prophecy (Example 111). The prophecy motif is the one part of *Deirdre* Willan borrowed from an earlier work – *Prospice* for choir and orchestra, ca 1905–10 (at the words 'Where stands the Arch-Fear in a visible form').

Most of *Deirdre* takes place in Ullah (Ulster), near the town of Avon Macha (Armagh); one scene is set in Alba (Scotland). The time is the early Christian era. In the opening scene Druid priests, led by Cathva (a bass), are engaged in a ceremonial ritual. The short solo and chorus are accompanied throughout by the Cathva motif used as an ostinato. (This impressive brief section was considerably longer in the original version and its truncation here seems unfortunate.)

Upon the scene come Conochar, high king of Ullah (a baritone), his fighters, and Fergus, Conochar's step-father and ex-high king (a bass). Relations between Conochar and Cathva are not cordial, largely because of the Druids' disapproval of Conochar's desire to wed his ward, the foundling girl Deirdre. There is a confrontation, and Cathva, solemnly accompanied by the Cathva, tragic fate, and prophecy motifs, pronounces his curse on Conochar: 'The gods forbid you that one prize your heart desires above all else ... seven years of fret and loneliness ... an empty throne beside you, an empty bridal bed, and at the end flaming desolation that will leave your kingdom nothing but a tragic name.' Conochar scoffs and reaffirms his intention of marrying Deirdre. The scene closes with a vigorous orchestral passage, starting with the Conochar motif, which seems to underscore Conochar's determination as well as his majesty and kingly power. The passage ends quietly, though, with an appearance of the foreboding motif, an indication that all is not going to be well.

Scene 2 is set in a timber house in the woods, where Levercham, Deirdre's nurse (a contralto), and her women are anxiously awaiting Deirdre's return from her day in the woods. The orchestral introduction opens with the Deirdre motif, and shortly afterwards one hears for the first time the extension of the Deirdre motif which, according to the composer, represents Deirdre in her love for Naisi (Example 112). (Perhaps, since Deirdre and Naisi are usually together, Willan thought the extension of the Deirdre motif sufficient for Naisi.) Deirdre eventually returns from the woods, singing a love lilt (Example 113). She confesses to Levercham that she has been with Naisi, son of Usnagh and one of the princes of Ullah (a tenor), and is betrothed to him. Levercham and the women, aware of Conochar's designs and of an ancient prophecy foretelling a tragic fate for Deirdre and the sons of Usnagh, are horrified. The scene ends with a marvellous ensemble in which Deirdre sings ecstatically in the manner of the love-lilt while Levercham and her women sing of their apprehension and grief. This is one of the most moving passages in the opera.

Scene 3 introduces Naisi. It is dawn, and Naisi, with his brothers Ardan and Ainnle, is at a hunting camp near the woods. The orchestral introduction (a revised version of the orchestral passage from *Conochar's Queen*, act I, scene 2) is built around the Deirdre motif and its Deirdre-Naisi extension. Naisi has spent a sleepless night thinking of Deirdre and sings a short aria to that effect. The scene is really an extended aria for Naisi in which, interrupted by comments and protestations from his two brothers, he sings of his love for Deirdre, their chance meeting, and his intention to marry her in spite of Conochar. The music covers a wide range of moods to test the tenor lead's mettle: lyric, tender, impassioned, teasing ('I'll rhyme you a riddle'), conversational, slightly mad, and strongly determined. Ardan says to Naisi 'There's magic on you'; Willan has produced magic in this beautiful music. Based largely on the Deirdre and Deirdre-Naisi motifs, the music of the scene concludes with an orchestral coda based on Conochar's motif, following Naisi's last words, 'I will wed Deirdre ... in spite of Conochar.'

Act II scene 1 is again set in the woods. The orchestral prelude of some forty bars begins with an allusion to the foreboding motif; little else in this prelude relates specifically to the rest of the opera. (The prelude was composed for the 1962–64 revision.) Toward the end of the prelude, just before the voices enter, there is an interesting reversed version of the Deirdre-Naisi motif played on the flute (Example 114). Deirdre and Naisi are together: Naisi is in a happy mood ('Come girl, let you be gay with me'), but Deirdre is apprehensive lest Conochar's men catch them. Deirdre imagines she hears all sorts of sinister noises, and these are echoed in some imaginative touches in Willan's score; Example 115 is indicative. Their opposing moods are not conducive to a long and impassioned love-duet and the composer wisely does not attempt one here. The lovers make plans to flee to Alba, and Deirdre manages just in time to persuade Naisi to leave before Conochar arrives. While Naisi is rapturously singing about 'the long years before us to make our lives together' Willan introduces a curious quotation from his *Piano Concerto* (Example 116). After Naisi has gone, Conochar does indeed arrive, looking for Deirdre. He has brought her a costly gift, but she is in no mood to humour him and, flinging down the gift, recklessly announces her betrothal to Naisi. The scene ends with Conochar, in a frenzied rage, pronouncing 'death to Naisi' and throwing a guard around Deirdre.

Act II scene 2 concerns itself with the escape, largely engineered by Levercham, of Naisi and Deirdre during the night. This scene is the result of much chopping and changing from earlier versions. It is given over mainly to short phrases of conversation, and, as a result, there are few passages of great musical sweep. There is a little musical figure, played by bass instruments, which by fairly consistent use in this scene seems to be raised to the status of a sub-leitmotif, for Conochar's fighters (Example 117). It has previously appeared in the 'trampling feet' example (115). There is a rare appearance of the bard motif, in the orchestral interlude during which Deirdre gathers her belongings for the journey.

The most impressive part of the scene is the last, where Conochar arrives to find Deirdre gone away with Naisi. Having deployed his fighters to block off escape and having sworn to hang the sons of Usnagh, he achieves his grandest moment when he sings, to stark and unforgettable music: 'One day or the next, one year or the next, My word that Deirdre will be bride to me and queen.' Its overpowering effect is impossible to describe. The short orchestral coda ending the scene contains an interesting example of leitmotifs in combination, this time prophecy and Deirdre (Example 118).

The orchestral prelude which opens act III (Example 119) is similar in mood, style, and colour (especially the use of harp) to the great dirge that constitutes the second movement of Elgar's *Symphony No. 2*. In the course of the piece there are passages based on the tragic fate, Deirdre, and Conochar motifs. Scene 1 takes place in Conochar's house. He is brooding, but his mood gradually improves when he hears that Deirdre has been found, with Naisi and his brothers, living in exile in Alba. Conochar is told that these sons of Usnagh are homesick and would gladly return, bringing Deirdre with them, upon receipt of a pardon from Conochar (to be borne by Fergus, whom they would trust). Conochar sends Fergus at once to Alba to bring them back. The scene concludes with one of the two 'detachable' arias in the opera, in which Conochar sings of his satisfaction and joy at the finding of Deirdre ('O little white doe of the woods of Fuah'). This is one of the musical highlights of the opera: it is full of wonderful things too numerous to mention, though one should note Willan's deft touches of orchestration and figuration to accompany Conochar's lines 'I will call in the nimble dancers to the pipes. I will call in the rhyming shannacies.' If the third scene of Act I is Naisi's, this scene is Conochar's. It ends with a reference to the bard motif.

Scene 2 is the only one outside Ullah and is set at the camp of the exiles in Alba. Fergus has arrived with the message from Conochar, and the sons of Usnagh are rejoicing at the thought of returning home, singing their *Song of the Clansmen*: 'After long exile in Alba, oh, it will be grand to go back.' This choral song (Exmple 120) is very attractive music, spritely and cheerful in an otherwise rather gloomy score. This is the only place where the composer allows an Irish or Scotch folk music flavour in the music (in a 1965 interview with Ruby Mercer on 'Operatime' Willan said that he had deliberately left out popular Irish melodies in *Deirdre*, though some of Conochar's melodic lines come close to being pentatonic). The modality of this music clashes somewhat with the chromatic harmonic idiom of the rest of the scene (and of the opera) and it may have been an afterthought. (Willan had not set this text in his original short-score draft; five pages of short score were subsequently inserted in order to include the song.) Following this outburst of joy, Deirdre, who senses treachery in Conochar's offer, tries unsuccessfully to dissuade them from going. She makes Naisi angry with her, and the scene ends with her resigned singing of an expressive lament (the second 'detachable' aria).

Scene 3, in Ullah, takes place around a shed in the woods. Lavercham and her women are inside preparing the shed for visitors, while outside Conochar is deploying his men and setting up his treachery. (A long orchestral prelude, which follows on without a break from the orchestral coda of scene 2, is another added piece for the 1962–64 revision – its musical connection with the rest of the opera is vague.) The scene is short and, like act II scene 2, is largely conversational. It sets the stage for the coming tragedy and the music helps to build a mood of suspense and impending disaster.

Scene 4 follows without a break. Deirdre and Naisi, with the men of clan Usnagh, arrive with Fergus at the shed in the woods. Here they are stopped by Conochar's men, who tell Naisi that only Fergus and Deirdre are to proceed while the others are to remain until summoned. By this ploy Conochar knows he can force the hot-tempered Naisi to strike the first blow and thereby absolve the king of his pledge of safe conduct. This is precisely what happens and Naisi and his brothers are slain in combat. At this point Deirdre kills herself rather than go to Conochar. Conochar comes upon the scene and, shocked to find Deirdre dead, joins the women in a great lament ('Ohone!'). He tries feebly to sing again his aria from scene 1, 'O little white doe of the woods of Fuah,' but is interrupted by the news of rebellion (led by Fergus, who is incensed by Conochar's treachery) and the burning of the palace. To add to Conochar's woes, Cathva and his Druids arrive to wag the finger of judgment; Conochar ends up in a pathetic state ('The pattern is finished in the figured web the gods are weaving. It is the fate that was foretold'). The magnificent ensemble which concludes this final scene has, as its basis, the Druid chorus from the opening scene of the opera ('Blow low, red wind from the east') accompanied by the Cathva motif used ostinato-fashion in the orchestra; over this Cathva sings 'It is the curse of the Gods on Conochar'; and on top of all that the chorus of women is keening a poignant lament, 'Ohone! Ohone!' Cathva has the last word, 'The gods have spoken.' The music comes quickly to a close with an impressive statement by the orchestra's brass instruments of an augmentation of the prophecy motif.

Willan saw his dream of a stage version of *Deirdre* successfully realized. It was first performed in 1965 to two sold-out houses, and a repeat performance was necessary. The next year the Canadian Opera Company included the slightly revised, final version of *Deirdre* in its regular season. The 1965 and 1966 performances received standing ovations. Critical reaction, too, was generally favourable. The pruning and altering of the radio version vastly improved the score dramatically and musically. The radio version had been overly long and somewhat tedious; the tightening necessary to produce the stage versions has resulted in a fine opera.

The pruning was probably harder on the librettist than on the composer; John Coulter noted: 'Economy of words. That is probably the most essential characteristic of good libretto-writing. With the staged *Deirdre* words have been sheered away to an absolute minimum. A massacre! Whatever virtue the longer, earlier version may have had as a piece of writing, as dramatic literature – the shortened stage version has almost none at all. *Deirdre* has lost a lot of the lyric quality of *Deirdre of the Sorrows*, but is a much better ... libretto' (*Opera Canada* souvenir issue 1965–66, 75). Coulter lost a play to gain a libretto. And what a fine libretto it is! Willan lost very little of importance musically and the results were nearly always improvements. The passages of new music were written some twenty years after the original version and when the composer was in his eighties. In all but one or two cases the new music seems to flow from what was written twenty years earlier.

Yet it must be said that the cuts did materially affect the characterization of several of the principal personnages in the opera. In the original scene 1 of act II it is obvious in the conversation between Naisi and Deirdre that they are aware that Conochar knows about them and that they have already carefully planned flight to Alba. In the long conversations between Conochar and Levercham and, more particularly, between Conochar and Deirdre, it is equally clear that Conochar was fully aware that Deirdre was seeing Naisi. Not only that, but he tried at length to reason with Deirdre and to persuade her that her passion for Naisi was a fleeting affair and that she would be more comfortably off with him. Conochar was even prepared to deal leniently with Naisi, and it was only when Deirdre infuriated Conochar by insulting him and flinging down the costly gold torque he had brought her as a present that he said 'I might have spared him [Naisi] ... but your foolhardy talk has clasped the seal to his doom.' In the stage version nearly 200 bars of these conversations are removed, and what is left conveys to the audience a quite different impression; namely that Conochar is unaware of Deirdre's attachment to Naisi and does not find out about it till Deirdre tells him at that particular moment (ie the throwing down of the torque). Conochar immediately condemns Naisi to death (the word 'jeopardy' had been used at this point in the original version). This puts Conochar in a different light and makes him more of a villain and an unsympathetic character than he was in the first version, at the same time making Deirdre even more lily-white by comparison!

The original scene 2 of act II dealt with Levercham's ' crystal ball gazing' into the future, followed by the ploy of Deirdre and Levercham to trick Conochar. They call to Conochar and tell him that Deirdre has changed her mind and that she will go with him the next day (in the mean time plotting to leave with Naisi that night). Conochar is so pleased that he calls off his fighters and says 'No harm will come to Naisi ... I have but little spleen to punish folly for the sake of punishing.' The omission of this scene in the stage version again robs Conochar of some display of humanity and glosses over the extent of Deirdre's scheming.

The original text of act III scene 2 seems to suggest that after seven years Naisi's infatuation with Deirdre has cooled somewhat; this suggestion largely disappears as a result of the revisions. A ten-bar passage near the beginning of scene 4 in the original version had indicated that Naisi would sooner die now 'in a brave fight' than live on and grow old – an insight into his character now lost to the audience as a result of this passage being removed.

The tonal scheme of the published (final) version is not easy to formalize beyond the fact that E minor appears to be the main tonality. Act I starts in E minor and ends in B flat. Act II commences in B minor and concludes in E minor. Act III begins in C minor and ends in E minor. Passages of any length in a single definable tonality are few and far between, tending to act when they do appear as brief anchorages in an otherwise flowing current of constant tonal drift. No diagram of tonalities seems possible, and there is no apparently consistent pattern of relationship between tonalities and corresponding dramatic situations.

Willan liked *Deirdre* best of all his works. Always responsive to good words, he was much affected by the beauty of Coulter's text. He considered the libretto to have a good plot and a text full of imagery, and his musical imagination was obviously stirred by it. (In a radio address Willan stated: 'The words themselves are so elegant and so replete with music that the actual notes for the singers very nearly sang themselves, and I simply wrote them down on paper.') Willan often said that one of the reasons he liked the Anglo-Catholic liturgy was that it was similar to opera, having principals and their attendants, movement, and colour.

Some critics complained about the influence of Wagner on *Deirdre* (though one critic suggested it had many of the finer attributes of the Ring cycle – without the latter's 'dreary length'!). Willan wrote to Coulter in 1947: 'I still think that the Wagnerian Music Dramas are supreme and ideal. Probably I am getting old and crotchety. Opera, to my way of thinking, should be the idealization of some tremendous emotion, or group of emotions, and should utilize in its production all the elements of voice, colour, movement and music.'

In *Deirdre* Willan followed the pattern he had already established and used fairly consistently: keep leitmotifs few in number and use them only when the emotional situation requires it (not every time a name is mentioned!). Willan's leitmotifs for *Deirdre* are not particularly Wagnerian-sounding in themselves; the influence appears in the harmonic background of parts of the score, the continuous music, the arioso-type writing for the solo voices, the comparatively infrequent use of chorus, and the style of some of the orchestration. Yet it would be a mistake to say that *Deirdre* is simply Wagner; rather it takes its place in that noble succession of works, including the operas of Richard Strauss and the oratorios of Elgar, which, though they might exhibit certain stylistic features first discernible in Wagner, also exhibit the musical personalities of their creators.

Deirdre, the first full-length opera to be commissioned and assured of performance in Canada, will occupy a unique and solitary place in Canadian operatic history. The work of two old men, it was not a forward-looking or unusual piece which might have acted as a catalyst to inspire others to develop fresh paths. Stylistically it belongs to the turn of the century, yet it is a great work and a great achievement. An inspired and well-crafted opera, it is a proven success and quite capable of standing on its own merits. When it is performed few people will be concerned that it was not avant-garde at the time of its conception (though one critic thought it was too avant-garde and wrote after the 1946 radio première: 'The music ... consist[ed] largely of recitative accompanied by perpetual dissonances from the orchestra'). Unlike *Transit through Fire*, *Deirdre* is timeless.

10

Works for choir
and orchestra

Most of the dozen or so works Willan wrote for choir and orchestra were inspired by patriotic themes: the sacrifice of war, a coronation, his adopted land, or his mother country. The others include a setting for a poem, a hymn to the sun, a Christmas cantata, and a choral march for his Arts and Letters Club to use at Christmas.

Willan's first completed work for choir and orchestra was probably a setting of Robert Browning's *Prospice*.[1] The appearance of the full-score manuscript and the style of the music suggest it was composed ca 1905–10. No sketches or short score appear to have survived. A pseudonym had been written and erased and replaced by 'Healey Willan,' suggesting that the composer originally prepared the score to enter for a competition.

The setting is encased by an orchestral prelude and postlude in F major. Both prelude and postlude are based on the same music, though the postlude extends the twenty bars of the prelude to thirty-three bars. The orchestra required is standard (2222/4230/timp, cym/strings) save

---

1 Of Willan's half-dozen unfinished works for chorus and orchestra only one, probably begun in England, is of importance – *Requiem*, for SATB soli, double chorus, and orchestra. The introitus, Kyrie eleison, sequentia, and sanctus movements (numbered 1, 2, 6, and 7 respectively) are complete except for the orchestration and were finished between 1914 and 1918; Willan began them perhaps upon the death of his father. There are brief sketches for a prelude, offertorium, and benedictus. The four completed movements contain much fine music and contrast well with one another; upon completion of the orchestration they could be performed in concert as a satisfactory musical entity of about forty minutes' duration (cf Mozart's unfinished *Great Mass in C Minor*).

for the absence of a tuba part. The orchestration, while not indulging in any great splashes of colour or special effects, is well suited to the music and shows that Willan had acquired a fair grasp of orchestral technique. The music for the orchestral prelude (Example 121) and postlude is remarkably diatonic for Willan, showing perhaps Parry's influence.

At the entrance of the choir one hears right away one of the chords which was to remain a Willan favourite, the augmented triad (Example 122). The music moves into F minor shortly afterwards for the next section of text, 'To feel the fog in my throat.' Willan first introduces the theme to which these words will be sung in the orchestra, and the orchestration is interesting (Example 123). This appears to be Willan-the-organist, doubling his tenor-range melody with a sixteen-foot stop and producing a decidedly 'foggy' effect in the process!

At the text 'Where he stands, the Arch-Fear!' is the first appearance, in the trombones, of the musical motif (Example 124) Willan would use again in *Conochar's Queen* and *Deirdre*. The enharmonic choral writing at this point is also striking.

For the middle section the tempo increases to an allegro. An orchestral interlude of some two dozen bars introduces the next part of the text, 'For the journey is done, and the summit attained.' A new theme appears in the orchestra which seems to express the more triumphal mood of this section, and the tonality – which has largely been in F up to this point – changes to A major (Example 125). F major returns for the final section, and the tempo reverts to the slower pace of the opening for the orchestral postlude.

The work is through-composed, with no musical repetition in the choral parts. Musical unity is given to the piece not only by the return of the opening orchestral music at the end but also by the orchestral use of the figures in Examples 121, 124, and 125 throughout the work almost in the manner of leitmotifs.

Willan's chorus and orchestra setting of W.E. Henley's poem *England, My England* (Pro rege nostro) is actually a resetting, with expanded ending, of a song he had composed in 1909. He completed the new score in Canada during the fall of 1914, probably as a result of the patriotic fervour occasioned by the outbreak of war. This is one of Willan's weaker efforts, but it was published in 1914 and reprinted in 1941. The main source of weakness is the rather jingoistic text, which would make all but the most fanatic believer in 'Empire' and 'the white man's burden' blush with embarrassment. With such a text there was only so much Willan could do and yet remain faithful to the spirit of the words. (Elgar had a much better text for his *The Spirit of England*, a more or less contemporaneous work.)

Following is an outline of the structure:

MUSICAL SECTION	VERSE	TONALITY
A and A^1	1 and 2	E flat major
B	3	C major, A major
C	4	G minor
A^2	5	E flat major

The penultimate line of each verse reads 'As (to, were, in) the song on your bugles blown, England,' and the rather haunting musical phrase (Example 126) which Willan uses each time for these words tends to remain in one's memory. The style for the A sections is rather ceremonial (Example 127). Changes of mood in verses 3 and 4 are reflected in the music by means of changes in tonality, tempo, and music style. Several times in the course of the piece a musical phrase (Example 128) appears: a predecessor of the opening of the theme of the finale of Willan's 1944 *Piano Concerto in C Minor*.[2]

Two fine settings of Whitman's *Dirge for Two Veterans* were written in 1914, by Holst and by Willan. Holst's setting was immediately published and has become moderately well known; Willan's has remained unpublished and unperformed, although it is one of his finer efforts. Neither Willan nor Holst could have known the other's music; a comparison is useful. In each, C is the main tonality. Each uses tramping ostinatos and bugle-call motifs in the accompaniment for the middle part of the poem, 'I see a sad procession and I hear the sound of coming full-key'd bugles.' Holst's setting is comparatively compact and written for male choir, brass, and drums; Willan's is more expansive and intended for large mixed choir and full orchestra (though the music remains in short score only). Holst's work takes about six minutes to perform; Willan's would

2 It is noted in chapter 7 that the third movement of the C minor concerto theme had its origins in the unfinished piano concerto in D minor, estimated to have been written ca 1910. Willan's original song-setting, *Pro rege nostro*, was written in 1909, and thus this phrase seems to have been prominent in the composer's musical imagination at that time. A further coincidence is evident when one considers that the reprinted edition of *England, My England* came out in 1941, just before the composer started work on *Piano Concerto in C Minor*!

take about twelve. Holst's writing tends to be less chromatic than Willan's, with some quite diatonic and modal-diatonic passages.

Verses 1 and 2 of Whitman's poem are atmospheric in character ('The last sunbeam ... the moon ascending') and Willan sets the mood by means of a fifteen-bar orchestral introduction, beginning as in Example 129. This mood is continued by the orchestra in its subsequent accompaniment to the chorus for these opening verses. Holst has no orchestral introduction and sets the first two verses for unaccompanied choir.

At verse 3 ('I see a sad procession') the two settings are most similar, with the ostinatos and bugle-call figures. Holst keeps the tramping ostinatos (with periodic bugle-call punctuations) going right to the end of the poem (verse 9), so that verses 3 through 9 are treated as a single musical unit in the same musical style. Willan changes his musical material at verse 6 and seems to take his cue from the words 'And the strong dead-march enwraps me.' The march-theme he introduces here undergirds much of the music for the remainder of the work, progressing through various developments from its initial dirge-like appearance (Example 130) to its final triumphal statement at the beginning of verse 9 (Example 131). Willan's is basically a three-sectioned work while Holst's is two-sectioned.

An earlier sketch (ca 1900) exists of some two dozen bars showing an orchestral introduction along with the first verse of the text with quite different music. The musical potential indicated is small. His 1914 setting is exciting; though beginning sadly as a dirge ought, it ends in a blaze of triumph. The chorus parts are strong, with many passages for massed unison against an intended full orchestra in a style dictating the use of large forces. The accompanying parts are interesting and show considerable possibilities for orchestral colour.

In 1922 Willan composed *Choral March*, scored for male choir (TTBB) and orchestra, for the use of the Arts and Letters Club of Toronto. With a Christmas text by Fred Jacob, this piece was performed for many years at the club's Christmas banquet during the procession into the dining room. The march is in two sections: one with orchestra alone and the other with orchestra and chorus. For the first section Willan used the march he had written the year previous for his incidental music to *Cymbeline*, though without the 'da capo' and transposed up a semitone.

Willan's next completed major choral composition was the Christmas cantata *The Mystery of Bethlehem*, published in 1923. This work is most often sung in churches with only an organ accompaniment, but Willan did provide supplementary parts for oboe, two trumpets, four horns, three trombones, drums, harp, and glockenspiel. There are six movements, and soprano and baritone soloists are required in addition to mixed choir. It was originally intended to be used with pageantry. It is Willan's only completed cantata besides *Cleopatra*. Both works have six movements with the first three movements run together without a break. They are both about a half-hour in length.

The first movement is titled 'The Prophecy,' with text taken from the Great Antiphons of Advent. It is in D major and is scored for soprano solo and chorus. It is perhaps the most mystical sounding of the six movements, and Willan accomplishes this effect by unusual chromatic shifts (see Example 132).

The second movement, 'The Annunciation,' is also in D major. It is in 15/8 time throughout – a most unusual metre (unique in my experience). The movement is basically a baritone solo, using as text the hymn *Ave Maris stella*. Against this an SSA chorus, doubled by harp, sings part of the magnificat. The effect is exquisite. The opening bars of the movement (Example 133) seem to picture the star shining down.

The third movement, 'The Manger,' is perhaps the loveliest. It is based on verses from the hymn *Pange lingua* and is in three sections. The first, in D minor, is a baritone solo and follows on directly from the previous movement. The second, in D major, is purely instrumental and is subtitled 'A Lullaby for Our Lady.' For the third section the tonality shifts to G flat major, and the beautiful 'lullaby' theme is first taken up by the soprano solo (Example 134) and then treated in faux-bourdon by the whole choir. (Willan borrowed this music from his unfinished setting of *Pange lingua*.)

The fourth movement, 'The Shepherds,' is also in three short sections. The text is taken from the Christmas responsories and a well-known Christmas hymn. All sections are in B minor; perhaps the most interesting is the third where there is a complete canon at the second below between the chorus sopranos and the oboe. The opening of the canon is shown in Example 135.

E minor is the tonality of the fifth movement, 'The Magi.' With text taken from the Epiphany responsories and the carol *Congaudeat turba fidelium*, there are again three sections. The opening section (Example 136) is the most arresting, being built over a one-bar ostinato figure in the bass (probably to represent the loping of the camels carrying the Wise Men).

The sixth and last movement, which takes its text from the hymn *Corde natus ex parentis*, is called 'The Fulfilment,' and it returns to the home tonality of D major. The main part of the movement is a fugato based on a flowing subject (Example 137). Preceded by a ten-bar instrumental introduction (based on the fugue-subject) over a dominant pedal, the gentle fugato gives way to a vigorous final section consisting of a joyful paean by full choir, 'O ye heights of heaven adore Him.' The movement ends triumphantly with a great pealing of bells.

Mystery was still in print in 1980. In addition, four of its six movements are published separately. It is one of the finest Christmas cantatas available to modern church choirs of reasonable accomplishment and is one of Willan's most successful larger-scale works.

Hymn to the Sun (finished version) was composed in July 1930. However this text by T. Hood seems to have been on the composer's mind for many years. There is a thirty-three-bar sketch (ca 1900–10) in B flat major, set for TTBB and accompaniment (undesignated); in style it seems to derive from the Parry-Stanford tradition. There is also a thirteen-bar SATB setting in E flat (probably pre-1905) of a portion of the text ('King of the tuneful lyre') written in an 'album' belonging to Gladys Hall. Its rather sentimental chromaticisms (Example 138) suggest the music of Sir Joseph Barnby, composer of *Sweet and Low*; Willan soon stopped using them.

The completed (short-score) 1930 version of *Hymn to the Sun* is set for SATB choir (with some divisi) and orchestra. As in the case of *Dirge*, Willan never did an orchestration; I did one in 1980. 'The composer's indication on the title page is the only evidence that this work is intended to have orchestral scoring' (*HWC* 35). Yet there is a designation 'Hns' (horns) on page 5 of the manuscript, and the short-score version of the accompaniment is orchestral in style and unplayable on any one keyboard instrument without modification.

The music has energy and force. So much of Willan's choral music is gentle and in a slow or moderate tempo; a piece such as this, with a genuine allegro mood throughout, is unusual. The short orchestral introduction begins with an upward rush of semiquavers (as in some unfinished orchestral works of ca 1910 and the finale of *Symphony No. 1*). This leads to a passage (Example 139) which is used several times again in the work as the basis for orchestral interludes. It is taken from the opening bars of an unfinished symphonic poem, *The Call of the Sea*, B88, which Willan had started some twenty years earlier.

That the choral writing is going to be strong is indicated at the very first entrance of the choir (Example 140). Mixed with highly chromatic passages are others more diatonic (such as Example 141) which seem to show the influence of Vaughan Williams in their use of simultaneous streams of triads (the chord marked 'x' exhibits an unusual degree of dissonance for Willan). The power of words to stimulate the composer's imagination is clearly shown in the harmony chosen to accompany the word 'sweets' in Example 142.

About two-thirds of the way through the work the music comes to a halt, pianissimo. However, it soon starts up again with a shortened version of the opening orchestral introduction which leads back into the final section. The main part of this final section is given over to a fugal treatment of a fine subject (Example 143). The tempo has changed from allegro to moderato. This does not slow the pace much, however, since the time signature has also changed from 4/4 to 3/2, and the conductor would now be beating half-notes rather than quarters; thus the momentum keeps on. The fugue, in the home key of E major, builds to a climax. Then a peculiar thing happens: for the last six bars of the work Willan suddenly jumps into C major! What one has here is an example of an 'interlocking tonal structure,'[3] an interlocking E and C structure, with a B structure contained within the latter (see figure).

In 1930 Willan's A Song of Canada (with optional chorus parts) to a text by H.C. Fricker was published. Ten years later Willan prepared a version for chorus and orchestra, receiving some assistance with the orchestration from Godfrey Ridout. It is not an important work, but not a bad one either. It is certainly better than We Sing a Song to Canada (1939) and Centennial Anthem (1967). It has a good strong tune in the tradition of some of the better early twentieth-century British unison hymn-tunes.

In honour of the coronation of King George VI in 1937 Willan wrote A Coronation Ode, an unsophisticated and frankly popular setting of a four-verse poem by Frederick Harris; Marche solennelle (Coronation March), discussed in chapter 8; and the rather important Coronation Te Deum. The proper title of the latter is Te Deum Laudamus with Antiphons for the Coro-

---

3 Graham George writes in Tonality and Musical Structure (London 1969): 'The hypothesis I wish to put forward asserts that the structure of large-scale musical works in the major-minor period, whether or not composed to a text, is essentially tonal, and that, where such a work ends in a key other than that in which it began, it consists of two closed tonal structures interlocking' (28).

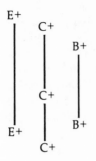

nation of Their Majesties King George VI and Queen Elizabeth. Its use of antiphons is unusual; in the program Willan stated: 'Antiphons are verses sung before and after a psalm, canticle or hymn in order to associate such with some specific occasion.'

Willan had begun to compose a Te Deum in 1935 for the Toronto centennial; however it was not sung on that occasion and he added the antiphons later for the coronation year (the idea came from Sir George Martin, organist of St Paul's Cathedral, London). Willan selected verses from psalms 21, 122, and 125 for the antiphons, beginning with 'The King shall rejoice in Thy strength.' The opening antiphons are sung unaccompanied over a tonic pedal in the orchestra. They are similar in style to *An Apostrophe to the Heavenly Hosts* and *Six Motets*. They are introduced and separated by a unison orchestral figure which gradually lengthens itself out with each subsequent appearance (Example 144). When the Te Deum proper starts, variants of Example 144 appear frequently in the orchestra, used almost in ostinato fashion. In the middle of the work the figure appears even in the vocal parts (Example 145). This motif is similar to the ostinato figure used for the magi in *The Mystery of Bethlehem*. On occasion the chorus splits into double choir and sings antiphonally. Willan uses this device with particularly fine effect to represent the cherubim and seraphim singing 'Holy, Holy, Holy' back and forth to one another.

Coronation Te Deum is written in B flat major and largely remains in that tonality. The harmony is much less chromatic than in many of Willan's other large-scale works up to this point. An unusual change in tonality occurs at about the half-way point, where B flat gives way suddenly to B (Example 146) for fourteen bars and then resumes. The change in tonality corresponds to a change of mood in the text ('We believe that thou shalt come ... We therefore pray thee help.') There is little counterpoint in this piece, the long text being set out in a very straightforward homophonic manner. The work ends as it began with a return of the opening antiphons sung over a tonic pedal. However this time the antiphons are interspersed with trumpet fanfares and the ending of the final section is extended to include a joyous pealing of bells in the orchestra (cf *Marche solennelle*) on the ostinato motif (Example 145).

Public reaction was enthusiastic. First performed at a Promenade Symphony Concert conducted by Reginald Stewart in Toronto on 10 June 1937, the response from the audience of about 7,000 was such that another performance was scheduled for 17 June. There the work had to be repeated after insistent applause from 5,000 people.

Although it was published in piano-vocal score, its special antiphons rendered it inappropriate for regular church use. In 1963 a revised version, *Festival Te Deum* for mixed voices and organ, was published. Willan removed the antiphons and wrote a new opening for organ. An optional ending was inserted part-way through the piece (after the text 'in glory everlasting') for those who wished to use the 'short' Te Deum. The final antiphons were removed, and the original ending was rewritten. The new ending is not as exciting as the original one; however, it may well be more appropriate for general liturgical use. The piano accompaniment is considerably rearranged to make it suitable for organ.

The Trumpet Call was written in 1941 for a 'Salute to Britain' concert held in Massey Hall, Toronto. The poem had been written especially for the occasion by Alfred Noyes. Willan did not receive it till a few weeks before the concert, but was inspired by the words upon receiving them and sat up most of the night composing the music. *The Trumpet Call* is not long or profound, yet it fits the stirring mood of the poem ('Trumpeter, trumpeter, rally us, rally us, Sound the great recall!'). The orchestral introduction for each of the three verses (Example 147) is typical of the style. The music for each verse is similar, though varying considerably in detail of word setting. Thus an interesting part-strophic, part-through-composed result is obtained. Tonality remains centred around C major. This is not a bad occasional piece, and its text – typical Noyes – is certainly better than that of, say, *England, My England*.

In 1953 Willan was asked to write a short homage anthem for the coronation of Queen Elizabeth II. The invitation was the first ever given to a composer from the Commonwealth and, as such, was a great honour not only for Willan but also for Canada. The occasion inspired him to one of his finest efforts. He had wanted to use the final movement, 'Come, Thou Beloved of Christ,' of his newly written *Coronation Suite* (discussed in the next section), but its six-minutes' duration was too long and he was asked to write a shorter piece lasting two to two and a half minutes. *O Lord, Our Governour* was the result.

The anthem is in three short sections, the first and last in D major. The modulation to the middle section (Example 148) is quite spectacular; the director of music for the coronation service, Sir William McKie, asked Willan to reconsider it, but Willan wisely decided to let it stand. The choral parts consist mostly of short phrases, often unaccompanied, separated by short orchestral interludes. Willan designed the music this way in order to fit the disposition of the choir, organ, and orchestra in Westminster Abbey. Antiphonal treatment of choir and instruments allowed both to be used to best advantage without drowning each other. The interludes are usually based on figures derived from the opening bar of the piece (Example 149), thereby giving unity to the overall structure. The choral writing is homophonic throughout, except at the end; here the composer allows himself a little imitative counterpoint in a serenely beautiful 'Amen' (Example 150). Willan's anthem is fully the equal of the other short choral pieces written for the coronation service by his prominent English colleagues.

Coronation Suite, a work for five-part choir and orchestra, was commissioned by the CBC for broadcast on Coronation Day, 2 June. The music was written during the summer and fall of 1952, though the orchestral scoring doubtless carried over into 1953. Willan devised an ingenious five-movement scheme, containing two purely orchestral movements which alternate with two purely choral movements and concluding with choir and orchestra united for the fifth movement. This contrast of performing media was helpful, for there was not much contrast of style between the orchestral movements, or the two choral pieces, or them and the choral-orchestral finale.

The first movement, 'Prelude,' is for orchestra alone and cast in the English ceremonial march form which Willan used for his other orchestral marches. The main section, in D major, is marked 'con spirito' and it cascades along in compound time rather like the equivalent section in Elgar's *Pomp and Circumstance March No. 5*. Bars 4 to 9 (Example 151) give a good idea of the style and musical material of this section, particularly the syncopated repeated-note figure in the tenor register, the bass figure in bar 4, and the highly chromatic – almost Straussian – nature of the writing in general. The expected big tune (Example 152) follows as the next major section. According to custom it is played through once, quietly, and then repeated with fuller orchestration. What is unusual here is that Willan uses the tonic key (D major) for the first play through and only moves to the expected dominant key (A major) for the repetition, thereby producing an almost subject-answer effect. The tune is rambling and seems to lack shape.

The second movement is a setting for unaccompanied SSATB choir of Milton's *Ring out Ye Crystall Sphears*. (Vaughan Williams was setting this text about the same time in the finale of his Christmas cantata, *Hodie*.) These magnificent words inspired Willan to compose a joyous paean, the sheer exuberance of words and music seeming to match the radiance of the young queen about to be crowned. In D major like the first movement, this second movement is through-composed; there are no formal repetitions of music or text, but a unity of style in both pervades the whole piece. Contrast in dynamics and mood is provided by quieter passages in the middle section of the work. The choral writing is massive in style (Example 153). The success of this music depends a great deal on the manner of its performance; Willan marked it simply 'Nobilmente,' and it must be taken at a slow tempo in order to be effective; too brisk a tempo would soon turn it into a meaningless jumble of sounds.

The third movement, purely orchestral, is titled 'Intermezzo.' In style it is like a fanfare or march, and one might have wished that for the sake of contrast Willan had written a truly intermezzo-type piece here. He made a number of changes from the original short score. He had originally introduced the piece by a solo trumpet playing a key phrase from Elgar's *The Spirit of England* (Example 154); unfortunately he substituted a rather trite little fanfare (Example 155) very similar to the one in the 1937 *Marche solennelle*. In example 156 one can observe the consecutive root position fanfare passages similar to those of the latter and the figure in the bass similar to the ostinato figures in *Coronation Te Deum*. (Willan later arranged this intermezzo for organ as *Interlude for a Festival*.)

The fourth movement, 'Come Ready Lyre,' is perhaps the least interesting. Though written with Willan's usual mastery of the choral idiom, it seems a bit pedestrian, with its unrelieved succession of measures in 4/4 metre and the steady plodding of quarter-note movement. It is basically written for SATB choir (and not SSATB as announced on the published score), with occasional divisi in all parts. The words, by Willan's friend James Edward Ward, are similar in content and mood to those of Milton in the second movement, yet they do not seem to have fired the composer's imagination. The piece, marked 'Moderato,' begins and ends in F major, with a short section in D major about two-thirds of the way through. The tempo increases ('animato') at the D major section for the words beginning 'Chant now the paean of desire attain'd,' which, along with the introduction of a few dotted rhythms, helps to sustain interest.

For the last, and finest, movement, choir and orchestra come together for the first time in a setting of 'Come, Thou Beloved of Christ.' The text is compiled from the tract 'Veni sponsa Christi,' Psalm 45, and II John. There are certain similarities of style and turn of phrase with Willan's great festival anthems *Sing We Triumphant Songs* and *Blessed Art Thou, O Lord*. Throughout, various forms of the opening musical phrase are used as accompanimental figures and unifying agents; several of the forms are shown in Example 157.

At the end of the text proper, and before the final alleluias, the blessing is set to a plainsong-like melody treated in a type of composite organum (Example 158) similar to the opening of *Gloria Deo per immensa saecula*. Following the blessing a short fanfare-like passage in the orchestra leads to the final alleluias, for which the music is marked 'Allegro con exultazione.' Exultation it certainly is, bringing the movement and the entire suite to a glorious conclusion.

Coronation Suite is an uneven work. The movements are not equally strong. Many would rank the last movement among the finest things Willan wrote. The second and third movements are also good. The first and fourth movements seem weaker; the musical material is neither memorable nor particularly interesting. However, the stronger movements probably carry the weaker ones.

A Song of Welcome, scored for SATB choir and small orchestra and lasting about six minutes, was composed for the Shakespearean Festival at Stratford, Ontario, in 1955. The text is a four-verse poem by Nathanial A. Benson written for the occasion: 'Homeland, whose song with ours is one. Now Shakespeare's England and his song come home to lasting haven here.' Willan responded by writing one of his most unashamedly Elgarian scores.

The orchestral introduction, after some bars of fanfare over a dominant pedal, states the thematic material (borrowed from his own 1941 song 'If I Were a King'), which will be the source of much of the accompaniment and interlude music in the opening and closing sections (Example 159). The drop of a seventh at the end of the example puts one in mind of the 'In the Name of Jesus Christ' passage in Elgar's *The Kingdom*.

11

Music for plays

An important part of Willan's work as a composer was the writing of incidental music for various dramatic works. During more than half a century he composed and/or arranged music for about thirty such works. His incidental music falls roughly into three genres and periods: music for plays (most between 1919 and 1925), ballad operas (1927 to the early 1930s), and radio plays and pageants (1940 to 1964); in chapters 12 and 13 I will examine the last two periods and in this chapter the music for plays. Willan composed or arranged music for fourteen productions at the Hart House Theatre at the University of Toronto from 1919 to 1925. In addition, he wrote one score before he left England and two others in the mid-1920s.[1]

Willan's first completed incidental score was for *Glastonbury* by W.T. Seward. Composed and first performed in 1912 at the Court Theatre in London, this is apparently the only incidental music finished by Willan before he left England. It is scored for string orchestra and piano and consists of four sizeable movements: 'Prelude,' 'The Abbey Porch,' 'The Assize Court,' and 'Ruins of the Abbey.'

'Prelude' (originally titled 'Overture') is basically a ternary structure, the first section of which is built almost completely upon the motif in Example 160, which appears in nearly every bar, though often transposed and moving through colourful, shifting harmonies with counter-melodies added. A model for this treatment might have been Mendelssohn's

---

1 In October 1936 Willan arranged the music (plainsong and some of his own) for the Toronto première in Massey Hall of T.S. Eliot's *Murder in the Cathedral*. Willan directed the choirs, one male and one mixed.

Fingal's Cave, though there are no direct resemblances save for the ♫♩ rhythm. During the middle section Willan introduces one of the many versions of the Somerset folksong *Seventeen Come Sunday*, the tune that Vaughan Williams made famous in the first movement of his *Folksong Suite* for band (though Willan gives no hint in his manuscript score as to what the tune is).

The remaining movements all have points of interest. Particular mention might be made of the noble dirge (Example 161) in the middle of 'The Assize Court'; ostensibly in E minor, it shows some Phrygian influence as well as colourful chromatic writing (Willan used this music also for the 'Tuba mirum' of his unfinished *Requiem* and in both cases associates it with some aspect of 'judgment').

Willan's next incidental score, *The Chester Mysteries*, marked the beginning of his association with the Hart House Theatre at the University of Toronto. Roy Mitchell, director of the theatre, early in December 1919 requested Willan to provide incidental music for a production of *The Chester Mysteries* scheduled for later in the month. Willan wrote the score in one evening between 9 and midnight and copied parts till 3 am. He rehearsed the music with some of his students at the Toronto conservatory the following noon and then took the whole group to Hart House that evening to an astonished Roy Mitchell for a full rehearsal with the cast. The work was performed for several years at Hart House and also at the Arts and Letters Club and St Joseph's College, Toronto. The composer referred to these performances as 'an emotional experience.'

The music is written for a unison choir of eight mezzo-soprano voices, string quartet, double bass, and harp (ad lib) and consists of five movements: prelude, gloria in excelsis, carol, interlude and adoration, and amen. The purely instrumental movements (1 and 4) are based on the Dorian mode motif of the sixteenth-century French noël which constitutes the third movement (Example 162). Likewise, the second movement, the missa de angelis version of the gloria in excelsis, is basically modal. However, for the adoration section of the fourth movement (Example 163), in which the three kings appear, Willan suddenly switches to a turn-of-the-century ceremonial English idiom! The music for *The Chester Mysteries* is good 'incidental' music but no more; its publication was perhaps the result of the play receiving so many performances.

Music for Ben Johnson's play *The Alchemist* was the first of Willan's five 1920 scores and included an overture and twenty-two musical cues. The small orchestra employed consists of flute, clarinet, and strings. In the music for act III there is a short gavotte written for harpsichord solo, but the harpsichord does not take part in any of the other numbers.

The overture is a tuneful little piece which displays its composer's gift for melody. It is well worth performing on its own; though it ends inconclusively at the 'curtain,' Willan uses the last few bars again as closing music for acts I and V and both times provides conclusive endings. The structure is a C major ternary one, preceded by an andante introduction. The introduction is built up of various transformations of a motif (Example 164) which also plays a prominent part in the rest of the overture and in some of the later musical cues. The main part of the overture (marked 'Con brio') begins with the theme in Example 165. The middle section, in A minor, is built around a passage (Example 166) used later in acts II and III. Following this a new tune appears in A major and, later, F major (see Example 167), after which the opening section is recapitulated in the home key of C major. The motif from the introduction is used in the 'con brio' largely as the basis of the link and transitional passages. In all, this overture is a well-written, well-integrated, and charming piece of music. It is easy for amateur groups to play and requires only a small orchestra.

The twenty-two musical cues which follow the overture are all attractive, but are generally too short to stand on their own. A number are based on material in the overture.

Willan's 1920 music for *The Trojan Women* by Euripides (Gilbert Murray's translation) is scored only for harp, flute, and soprano (solo and chorus) and consists of Cassandra's dance, two choruses, three dirges, and a song. The dance is only seven bars long for harp alone and of little musical interest. The other pieces involve sung texts. The program remarks: 'For those unison passages which are inevitable in the piece, Mr. Healey Willan has composed settings based on the rhythmic principle of plainsong as the first step in a new effort to reconstruct the Greek method of delivering the lines.' (The first attempt to reconstruct Greek drama led to the development ca 1600 of monody and opera.) Here, the score is disappointing. It is in the dirges and the song (each only a few bars in length) that Willan's attempt at a plainsong style is most successful. The two choruses, in contrast, are long and tedious. Melodically and harmonically, passages such as that in Example 168, chorus II, do not remind one much of plainchant. Although a flute is added to the voices and harp for these movements to play interludes and counter-melodies and the composer varies the accompanying harp figurations, the music emerges more dirge-like than the actual dirges and drags on and on. Perhaps these choruses, with their long texts, would have been better left to unison speaking.

In *Love's Labour's Lost*, the third 1920 score, Willan introduces published music by composers other than himself, including madrigals by Palestrina, Gibbons, and W.H. Bell (1903); solo songs by Thomas Arne; and William Byrd's famous 'Earl of Salisbury' pavane. Willan wrote an overture and six short musical cues (many repeated) for the same orchestra as *The Alchemist* (with the addition of a horn). The overture is an unsuccessful reworking of the *Alchemist* overture and suffers from the addition of material which does not blend with the rest of the score. Willan reused some of his *Alchemist* musical cues for acts IV and V. The incidental music to *Love's Labour's Lost* was thrown together in rather a hurry with the composer borrowing liberally from himself and others.

In November 1920 Takeda Izumo's *Matsuo* (The Pine Tree) was performed at the Hart House Theatre with incidental music, scored for celesta (or piano) and strings, by Willan. The music consists of an overture and five musical cues. The 'overture' is just a short prelude of less than forty bars. Willan attempts to introduce a Japanese flavour by two means; a time signature of 7/4 (3/4 + 4/4) (bars of 3/4 and 4/4 do not always regularly alternate as the time signature suggests, and even the odd bar of 2/4 appears) and pentatonic melodies harmonized with open fifths (Example 169). Only one of the musical cues follows the 'Japanese' flavour; the others have a decidedly Wagnerian tinge (see Example 170). One can only wonder how this Japan-Wagner amalgam came off.

Rasmus Montanus, another 1920 incidental score, consists only of two short pieces of spritely trivia.

The first of Willan's 1921 Hart House scores was for Euripides' *Alcestis* (Gilbert Murray's translation). It comprised five unison chorus songs and two songs intended for solo voice. Accompaniment is for harp (or piano). In the chorus songs Willan uses a fairly severe modal style, yet the pieces are short and simple and the vocal lines are melodic and expressive; there is little evidence of the oppressive 'doctrinaire' quality of his earlier Greek setting, *The Trojan Women*, and the results are more musical and successful. The two solo songs use similar musical material, and the second, *There Be Many Shapes of Mystery*, is deeply moving and beautiful (it was published thirty years later in a *School and Community Song Book* under the title *Alcestis*).

Willan's 1921 score for *The Romancers* required only voice, two violins, and cello. There are five pieces of music, the third a rather charming song, *Yes, the Sweet Night Has Come*.

Willan scored *Cymbeline* in 1921 for clarinet, horn, cornet, and strings. A solo voice is needed for the song, *Hark! Hark! the Lark*. Besides the song the music consists of a splendid little march and six short musical cues (one borrowed from *The Alchemist*). The musical material for the march is taken from an unfinished 1912 march in E for piano duet. The song is effectively written, in the style of Arne, and uses thematic material from Willan's 1900 song, *Rondel*.

The 1921 music for Sir James Barrie's *Pantaloon* is one of Willan's most fascinating incidental scores. The music, written for piano alone, shows Willan's tunefulness and imagination at their best. Unfortunately, the score follows the play so closely (like a silent movie pianist) that the music cannot be performed separately. Willan uses several leitmotifs by which, through their various reappearances, transformations, and combinations, he binds the score together. Example 171 illustrates the love motif with variants, Example 172 the dance (mazurka), Example 173 the Pantaloon motif with variants, and Example 174 the combination of the love and Pantaloon motifs.

There is no Wagnerian heavy-handedness here despite the leitmotif approach; Willan's touch is delightfully light, more in the manner of Walton's 1922 *Facade* with its parody of some of the 'light' music of the period. Likewise the chromatic harmony used is not Willan's more usual quasi-lugubrious type but is effervescent, more in the *Rosenkavalier* manner. Much thought and imagination have obviously gone into this score. It is well written and shows a marvellous side of Willan and his music – the cheerful, impish, worldly Willan with his vast storehouse of limericks, anecdotes, and funny stories.

During the 1921–22 season at Hart House Willan played incidental music on the piano for *Georgian Revue – Playbills*. He played Handel's *Overture to Richard I*, but there is no record of what other music he used or composed. The holograph, if there ever was one, has been lost. It is possible that Willan improvised whatever other music was necessary.

Willan's only extant 1922 score is for Shakespeare's *The Tempest*. The main items are merely arrangements of pieces originally written for *The Tempest* by composers such as Purcell, Cooke, and Arne. Willan's original contribution amounts only to a few short cues. The play did not inspire Willan as it did Sibelius in 1926. Willan's score is for string quartet, with three of the numbers having music for two-part chorus as well.

Castles in the Air is Willan's only 1923 score. There are twenty-nine musical cues, but there is no overture and many of the cues are repeats; there are in fact only seventeen pieces of music. Four of the most substantial are taken from the 1920 score for *The Alchemist* and three others are only four- or five-bar parodies of *Three Blind Mice*.

The most interesting new pieces are the three ballet numbers: *Pantomime of the Tin Soldiers*, *Valse (The Twelve Years)*, and *Eastern Dance*. Since this is music for a child's dreams of fairies, wizards, and the like, it is deliberately unsophisticated. Some of *Pantomime* recalls Gilbert and Sullivan – there is even a parody of Mendelssohn's *Wedding March*. *Valse* is in style rather like the typical easy piece written for young children in the first conservatory grade books. *Eastern Dance* has some of the flavour of the Arabian Dance from *Nutcracker Suite*.

Willan arranged music for a pageant, *The Christmas Mysteries*, performed on 22 December 1924 at the Church of St Mary Magdalene, Toronto. (It was subsequently performed there annually for many years.) The score, set for children's voices, SATB choir, and organ, consists entirely of Willan's arrangements of some traditional carols as well as two tunes by Father Leslie Rose. Willan's settings are tasteful, simple, and effective; their appearance of non-sophistication covers considerable art. The score does not contain original pieces by the composer.

Willan's fourteenth and last score for the Hart House Theatre, for Shakespeare's *The Winter's Tale*, was composed in 1925, for the familiar small orchestra of flute, clarinet, and strings. The music is entirely new. The main musical numbers are three songs and four dances. It is difficult to write critically for here one finds Willan at his most tuneful; the music has a great deal of appeal. Yet it is basically eighteenth-century: the three delightful short dances at the end might well have come out of *The Beggar's Opera*. Of the songs, *When Daffodils Begin* deserves particular mention. The score has beautiful music in 'olden style.'

Perhaps ca 1925 Willan wrote music for a play called *Let's Pretend* (HWC 31). There is no date on the manuscript or any record of a performance. The music consists of four choral songs for women's voices: two for SS or SA and two in unison. The accompaniments are neatly written out in piano score by the composer, yet sections are virtually impossible for a pianist to play as written and suggest that Willan had an instrumental ensemble in mind. Unlike most of his incidental scores this one does not have a set of parts (either choral or instrumental); they may have subsequently disappeared. The *Let's Pretend* music is among the most significant incidental scores Willan ever wrote. The four choral songs are all first class and could make an interesting group of pieces for a women's choir to perform. The texts might be considered a bit simplistic, but the play is to some extent a children's play along the lines of Alice in Wonderland. The titles, *Song of the Tree, Leaf Song, Wind Song,* and *Rain Song,* indicate their character, and Willan's music is almost impressionistic.

12

Ballad operas

In the late 1920s and early 1930s Willan composed and/or arranged music for six ballad operas: *The Beggar's Opera, L'Ordre de Bon Temps, Prince Charlie and Flora, The Ayrshire Ploughman, Maureen,* and *Indian Christmas Play* (the last two now lost). J. Murray Gibbon provided librettos (translation or original) for four of these works.

Willan's version of John Gay's *The Beggar's Opera* appeared in 1927. From its first performance in 1728 till the 1880s *The Beggar's Opera* was a popular national classic in England. Following what Edward Dent calls 'a certain eclipse after 1886,' the opera was revived in 1920. A new arrangement of the music by Frederic Austin was published, containing fifty-two numbers (Dent's authoritative edition, containing sixty-nine numbers, appeared in 1954).

The original opera was in three acts, the scheme followed by Austin and Dent, but Willan's version condenses it into two acts and reduces the number of movements to forty. Willan has scored his arrangement for his familiar Hart House-style orchestra of flute, clarinet, and strings. The use of the clarinet and not the oboe is not consistent with 1728 practice! Willan uses the original Pepusch overture for his orchestral version. He wrote a new overture (more correctly a medley of ten tunes selected from the opera) for piano, perhaps to facilitate performance of the whole work with piano alone. Willan's settings are for the most part tasteful and restrained, avoiding unnecessary complexity (though Macheath escapes to strains reminiscent more of Vaughan Williams than of Pepusch). Undoubtedly Willan's version is not as stylistically pure or as historically accurate as Dent's; nevertheless it was an effective piece of work and could still be useful for a two-act production.

L'Ordre de Bon Temps was written for the 1928 Canadian Folk Song and Handicraft Festival in Quebec City and was performed again, in Vancouver, Victoria, and Toronto (Arts and Letters Club), in 1929 and 1930. Willan arranged ten (and in 1930 two more) French-Canadian folksongs for soli, TTBB chorus, flute, oboe, violin, cello, and piano. Although a harpsichord was used at the first performance, the keyboard part is in piano rather than harpsichord idiom.

There was at this time a deliberate attempt to find and to found a 'national' musical literature in Canada and a number of traditional French-Canadian melodies were being collected and/or edited by Marius Barbeau. J. Murray Gibbon translated ten of these for *L'Ordre de Bon Temps*. Willan's settings of these folksongs are among his most imaginative (see chapter 18 on his 1929 volumes of *Chansons canadiennes*). These songs, foreign to his experience, kindled and sparked his imagination.

The published piano-vocal score includes also three short Indian dances, with Indian texts, not contained in the manuscript score. The title page reads: 'L'Ordre de Bon Temps, the name of the society of good cheer founded by Champlain at Port Royal in 1606, tells the story of the life at the garrison during those bitter winters when the Order stood for the best in good living and Poutrincourt's table groaned beneath the luxuries of winter and forest ... These repasts were always attended by ceremonial followed by song, and the guests frequently included Indian chiefs.'

Willan wrote *Prince Charlie and Flora* in 1929 for the Highland Gathering and Scottish Music Festival at Banff. It was first performed at the Banff Springs Hotel 30 August. J. Murray Gibbon was the librettist. Willan set traditional Scottish melodies – seventeen in all, for six voices, flute, violin, cello, and piano. The arrangements display his usual craftsmanship.

The score contains the first version of Willan's exquisite setting in D flat major of the old French carol *Quelle est cette odeur agréable?*, which has become deservedly popular; see also the discussion of *Nativity Play* (1940) in chapter 13, and the section on carols in chapter 22. This setting is for solo voice rather than choir. One notes in the score the close similarity between *Quelle est cette odeur agréable?* and the Scottish drinking song *Fill Ev'ry Glass*. The two songs are placed side by side as Nos. 6 and 7 (Example 175).

Another ballad opera arranged by Willan from traditional Scottish melodies is *The Ayrshire Ploughman*. It consists of fifteen numbers arranged for voices, flute, oboe, and strings and is similar in style to *Prince Charlie and Flora*. The *Ayrshire Ploughman* does not have a full score: Willan must have followed his more usual custom of writing the instrumental parts directly from the piano-vocal manuscript. The librettist remains unknown. Willan's manuscript suggests at least seven characters in the opera.

The work, billed as 'a Romantic Ballad Opera ... incorporating songs of Robert Burns,' was advertised for performance on 29 August 1930 at the Scottish Music Festival at Banff Springs. There was no mention of Willan's name in the advertisements! There must, in fact, be some doubt that it was Willan's version which was actually performed. In later years, Willan tended to be rather tight-lipped about some of his ballad operas.

Two further ballad operas arranged by Willan appear to have been lost: *Maureen* and *Indian Christmas Play*. Bryant (HWC 32) suggests that the libretti were written by J. Murray Gibbon. One wonders whether Willan's arrangement of the Huron Carol (*Jesous Ahatonhia*), which had been published in 1927 and which he would use later in the second score for *Brébeuf*, was part of the music for *Indian Christmas Play*. Perhaps the three Indian dances tacked on to the published score of *L'Ordre de Bon Temps* came from this score. In Willan's *Nativity Play* of 1940, discussed in the next chapter, there is a short passage which would seem to have come from the lost *Indian Christmas Play*.

13

Radio plays
and pageants

In Willan's third and final period of dramatic work (1940–64) he returned to writing original scores. This period saw the composition not only of his two operas (see chapter 9) but also of the large-scale *Brébeuf* pageant, a number of radio plays, and several other pageants. (The unfinished *Pageant of Our Lady* was begun in the 1920s and Willan's latest work on it probably took place in 1936; a similar work, *The Play of Our Lady*, started in the mid-1960s, was left unfinished at the time of his death. Both are discussed at the end of this chapter.)

Nativity Play (1940) was the first work Willan wrote especially for radio. The text was compiled by Andrew Allan from the medieval mystery plays of Chester and York. The music, set for SATB choir, strings, and harp, is made up almost completely of earlier pieces by Willan. It includes a Christmas anthem published in 1907, all of the incidental music for *The Chester Mysteries* of 1919, and some later Christmas publications of ca 1926–35. The setting for SATB and strings of *What Is This Lovely Fragrance?* was published the following year for SATB and organ; he had set this carol before, in his ballad opera *Prince Charlie and Flora* of 1929. Some of the borrowed pieces are left in their original form; others are rearranged. Of the twenty-one numbers (some repeated) only two appear to have been originally composed for the work: 'Nativity Prelude' (which quotes the first line of the Christmas office hymn *Christe Redemptor omnium*) and 'Shepherd's Adoration' (a 'quasi-Sicilienne'). The music (based on the gloria from the missa de angelis) for cues 6 and 8, a passage of twenty-one bars for three violins, is referred to in the script as 'Interlude from Indian Play' (presumably the lost *Indian*

Christmas Play discussed in the previous chapter). The radio play[1] was very impressive: the text was excellent and Willan pulled out some of his finest music to go with it.

In 1941 Willan wrote incidental music for John Coulter's radio play *Conochar's Queen*. The radio play has four acts; the opera *Deirdre* based on it has three. Most of the musical leitmotifs in *Deirdre* (see chapter 9) are present in this score in some form or other. There are only two complete sections of music transferred from *Conochar's Queen* to *Deirdre*, however, the most important being the chorus of Druids from the opening scene.

Only this chorus could be taken successfully for separate performance; the rest of the score consists of musical cues with introductory or background functions, though some are quite lengthy and well developed. Some of the music for acts III and IV is weak, and Willan did not use this music again for *Deirdre*. As in *Pantaloon* (1921), Willan here uses the leitmotif technique for instrumental music to go with the spoken word.

Willan's 'timings' of many sections are pencilled into the score. He prided himself on being 'able to write by the stop-watch,' and he was very conscious of the need to provide music of just the right length to accompany any situation. (This precision was also required in his church music!)

The music for *Conochar's Queen* exists only in piano-vocal score; the play was never performed with Willan's music, and the music was not orchestrated. A radio version of *Conochar's Queen* was broadcast from Belfast in 1934 with music arranged by Peter Montgomery.

While busy with several big scores, notably *Transit through Fire*, *Deirdre*, and *Piano Concerto in C Minor*, Willan found time to write a short piece of incidental music in 1942, *Hymn for Those in the Air*. This piece is set for narrator and orchestra (cf Copland's *A Lincoln Portrait*). The well-known hymn by D.C. Scott is read against an orchestral background which is primarily that – background. The music is rhapsodic, with no discernible form, theme, or thematic development. It is Willan the organist impro-

---

1 Bryant notes (HWC 33) that 1) the first performance was given in 1940 and 2) the full score is dated December 1944; he questions this apparent anomaly. *Nativity Play* was performed annually on the CBC from 1940 to 1945, and a comparison of the recording of the 1943 performance with the 1944 and 1945 scripts shows three additional pieces in the latter, as well as a different magnificat. Willan probably made his 1944 full score to incorporate these additions.

vising: the one unifying structural feature is the constantly descending stepwise bass, as the organist's foot moves gradually down the pedalboard from one note to the next.

One of the largest and most widely mentioned incidental scores by Willan is that for E.J. Pratt's narrative poem *Brébeuf and His Brethren*. The work was originally intended as a pageant for performance at the Martyrs' Shrine in Midland, Ontario, but war intervened and plans for the pageant had to be put aside. The CBC commissioned a shortened version for radio presentation; it was broadcast in 1943. The next year the score was performed in Massey Hall, Toronto, under the title *The Life and Death of Jean de Brébeuf*. The work requires two narrators, mixed choir, and orchestra.

By 1947 Willan had completed a second, expanded version of the music for a pageant at the Brébeuf Festival in Midland. Arrangements fell through, however, and the second version was not heard until 1967, when it was performed with choir and organ under the composer's direction at Timothy Eaton Memorial Church in Toronto. The two versions of the score differ considerably from one another:

NUMBER	VERSION I (1943)	VERSION II (1947)
1	prologue for chorus and orchestra (218 bars)	prologue; same chorus parts but with lengthened orchestral sections; long coda includes all the music of 2, 3, and 8 of version I (309 bars)
2	short orchestral cue	new, longer orchestral cue
3	very short orchestral cue	expanded version of I 11, chorus and orchestra
4	short orchestral cue	new, longer orchestral cue, but making some use of I 4
5	short orchestral cue	new, longer orchestral cue, but making some use of I 4
6	very short orchestral cue	new movement for chorus and orchestra
7	very short orchestral cue	expanded version of I 10, for chorus and orchestra
8	short orchestral cue	interpolation of *Jesous Ahatonhia*
9	movement for chorus and orchestra	(nothing indicated in the score at this point)
10	movement for chorus and orchestra	slightly expanded version of I 9

NUMBER	VERSION I (1943)	VERSION II (1947)
11	movement for chorus and orchestra	new movement: orchestral introduction followed by unaccompanied chorus
12	short orchestral cue	two new orchestral movements of some length (12 and 12A)
13	epilogue; chorus and orchestra (seventy-three bars)	epilogue; chorus and orchestra, expanded to 138 bars

The first movement (prologue) of version II uses the same chorus parts as its counterpart in version I, but the orchestral introduction and coda (as well as an intervening interlude) are considerably lengthened. The orchestral introduction in I is a scant seven bars of music over a tonic pedal, whereas in II it becomes thirty-one bars of orchestral prelude built upon the four main leitmotifs that will appear throughout the score. This prelude opens with the martyrdom motif (Example 176) derived from the opening notes of the plainchant of the Offertory of the Mass of the Communion of Many Martyrs, III. This motif appears only in II. There follows the call-to-service motif (Example 177), a sort of trumpet fanfare suggested by the words 'With sound of bugles ... the saints come' which occur early in the prologue. A few bars later in the prelude another motif appears which might also be labelled 'martyrdom' or 'fate' (Example 178). The prelude concludes with the vow motif, a melodic phrase based on the notes of the first line of the hymn-tune *Beata nobis gaudia* (Example 179 shows this source, followed by the vow motif itself), generally associated with martyrs. Following some alleluias for chorus there is an orchestral interlude, after which the chorus takes up the long text of the prologue proper, beginning with the magnificent phrase 'The winds of God were blowing over France.' The chorus-writing is primarily through-composed in narrative style, the structure of the music being held together by means of a fairly elaborate orchestral part which makes frequent reference to the various leitmotifs.

Number 4 of version I describes the ocean voyage of the missionaries and is interesting because it shows not only Willan's fondness for augmented triads (Example 180) but also his associating them with 'sea' music, as in his unfinished symphonic poem *Seaside Elegiacs* (ca 1910). Other points of musical interest in the score of version I are the use of the opening notes of the plainchant *Dies irae* in number 6 to accompany the fiery death of the Iroquois captive, the beautiful reflective writing in the chorus 'Along an incandescent avenue' (number 9), the lovely movement for women's choir and orchestra in which the missionaries remember sunny summer days in their native France (number 10), and the effective simplicity of the lines of the plainsong hymn *Veni Sancte Spiritus*, set for choir in organum with orchestral interludes (number 11).

Of the new music Willan composed for version II, number 2 has an eighteenth-century horn-call flavour which contrasts rather sharply with the highly chromatic writing of the previous movement; number 8 is an interpolation of Willan's already published (1927) arrangement of Brébeuf's *Huron Carol* (one wonders why it was not included in version I); and number 11 is a setting of *Ave verum corpus* for choir in 'primo prattica' style and preceded by a fugue for string orchestra the subject of which is based on the opening of *Ave verum corpus*. (*Ave verum corpus* was published as a separate motet in 1948 and the fugue, arranged for organ, as part of *Three Pieces for Organ* in 1951.) Number 12 consists of two new and sizeable orchestral movements (12 and 12A). The music of number 12 portrays the Iroquois attack and the capture of Brébeuf, concluding with a 'paganization' of the vow music to accompany Brébeuf's mock baptism in boiling water by his captors. Number 12A is a wild Indian dance based on a theme (Example 181) with a peculiar rhythm of 3 plus 3 plus 3 plus 2. It repeats over and over again like an ostinato, accompanied by an ever increasing orchestral complexity and building to a frenzied conclusion: a most unusual piece for Willan, yet very successful.

The recordings of the CBC performances in 1943 and 1948 of version I impress one above all with how beautifully Willan's music suits the text. Pratt's magnificent poem inspired Willan, who wrote music which sensitively mirrors the underlying moods and actions of the story. Taken separately, little of the music of version I could stand by itself, yet in combination with the libretto it seems unerringly right and appropriate – unselfish greatness on the composer's part. The performance is profoundly moving. Several numbers belonging to version II have been published separately, but, except for the *Jesous Ahatonhia* arrangement, they do not have the same impact when removed from their original surroundings.

In spite of the leitmotif technique, the size of the work, and the highly chromatic writing in the main choruses, the music shows comparatively little influence of Wagner. There is a stylistic unity throughout version I:

the style, while owing perhaps a bit to Delius and to plainchant, is quite typically Willan. Version II is less unified; numbers 2 and 11 do not fit well into the whole.

For version II only the short score is complete. Willan began a full orchestral score but never finished it, probably ceasing work on it when he discovered that the projected performance at Midland was not going to take place.

In 1954, Willan produced music for an Arts and Letters Club production of Lescarbot's play *Theatre of Neptune* (in English translation). This play is set in Port Royal (in 1606), like his 1928 ballad opera *L'Ordre de Bon Temps*. Willan bases the first part of his little overture on the tune of the song *Chantons les louanges* (on a text by Lescarbot) which is the first musical number in *L'Ordre de Bon Temps*. Likewise the influence of this tune is apparent in some of the male chorus *Great God Neptune*, the only other musical number in the score save for a couple of 'themes' of a bar or two each. The second part of the overture is borrowed from the new second movement Willan had originally written for version II of *Brébeuf* (discussed in the previous section), using the opening and closing sections of the latter. In all, the *Neptune* music is rather inconsequential, but this was doubtless intentional. The translator, R. Keith Hicks, gives the clue: 'The reader is entreated not to forget that this is pageant material, and that the original is simple, even naïve in versification and thought: without this reservation most of it becomes merely doggerel.' Sophisticated music would have been out of place here; one wonders why Willan scored it for male choir and *two* pianos when one piano would easily have sufficed.

In 1960 Willan wrote incidental music for a radio adaptation of W.B. Yeats's *The Shadowy Waters*. Consisting of four pieces, the music is written for solo harp to give an authentic Celtic effect. For the first piece (which accompanies the prologue) Willan conveys the atmosphere of 'shadowy waters' by means of a short passacaglia consisting of seven presentations of the three-bar ground bass in E minor, though the last two presentations of the ground are expanded to four bars and five bars respectively. In the fourth variation, the ground bass (in Example 182) is, in fact, the bard motif from *Deirdre*. This is the only time the composer used a ground bass form in his incidental scores. The last piece is a little gem of twenty-five bars in 5/8 time which might be called the 'sleep music.'

The Pageant of Our Lady, set to words by Laurence Housman, for four solo voices, SATB chorus, and instruments, is an unfinished pageant with an aura of mystery about it. The instrumentation is never specified in the forty-six pages of condensed score and seventeen pages of sketches, though in the sketches the composer indicates at one place parts for harp, celesta, pianoforte, and strings, and at another place, parts for flute. An Angelus bell is also required.

Willan completed the opening scene, which has to do with the annunciation and visitation of the Virgin Mary, up to the end of the magnificat. An instrumental prelude (based on the plainsong hymn *Ave Maris stella*) leads directly into the opening choruses, and one is immediately struck by the vigour and sheer happiness of the music. There are few of the constantly shifting Wagnerian chromaticisms typical of so many of Willan's large-scale works; instead the harmony is much more diatonic and the rate of harmonic change much slower. There is also a modal influence, and though the music is no mere copy, the style seems to lean more to Vaughan Williams than to Wagner. Willan seems remarkably free with his handling of diatonic dissonance throughout this scene, as brief extracts (Example 183) illustrate. Here we see the composer experimenting with quartal harmony. Following this is a setting of the magnificat for soprano solo; this involves a slight change of style but not one which clashes too violently with what has gone before. The harmony is a bit more chromatic, but there is still a fair amount of modal influence. The text is beautifully set and would make a fine sacred solo on its own (the version in the sketches does have a conclusive ending: in the condensed score the music carries on without break).

Some disillusionment sets in with the next section, 'The Dance.' Here Willan uses as the opening and closing sections a short piece which had been titled *Solemn Music* in an early score of incidental music (B37). The material is in the style of Purcell, and between its two appearances there is a long middle section in a much later style. The middle section is not very dance-like, but gives the impression of a rather symphonic development of material in 3/4 time. This movement appears to be complete.

The third and last part is, like the first, incomplete. It deals with what amounts to a love scene between Solomon and the Shulamite ('I am black but comely ... stay me with flagons ... Rise up, my love, my fair one ... the voice of the turtle ...'). In the text, this episode becomes mystically interwoven with the nativity scene which follows, but Willan's unfinished score stops before that point. What we have is a rapturous love-duet, complete to its soaring climax, followed by a short chorus. The duet begins in a rather interesting manner (bars 1 and 4–6 are shown in Example 184), reflecting the quartal harmony and dissonance found in the opening movement. However as the music proceeds the style becomes more and more Wagnerian, and the duet becomes a sort of biblical *Tristan und Isolde*. It reaches a magnificent climax and is a fine piece of music drama. One wonders, though, what it is doing in a 'pageant of Our Lady!'

Willan did not complete *The Pageant of Our Lady*, probably because of its irreconcilable stylistic incongruities. The first section, which is so promising, may have been written in the late 1920s, when a number of Willan's famous Christmas pieces (eg *The Three Kings*; *Tyrle, Tyrlow*; *Here Are We in Bethlehem*) were published; a similar atmosphere and style prevails in this movement. The second section clashes stylistically with itself and with what comes before and after. (Willan used here the same piece of borrowed early material as in his 1925 score for *The Winter's Tale*.) The third section clashes stylistically with both previous sections. Willan may have taken it up in 1936; he was quoted as saying he would now have time to finish *The Pageant* since he had just left the conservatory. The Toronto *Globe* spoke of the work as a 'sacred' or 'religious' opera. He had just completed his first symphony and begun his second, and their somewhat Wagner-Strauss idiom must have been in his mind when writing the third section. Perhaps he did not complete *The Pageant* because he found himself unable to return to the mood of the opening section. Something could still be salvaged from the opening music, for it is music in Willan's best Christmas style.

In the years immediately prior to his death Willan was considering music for a similar work, *The Play of Our Lady*, but he managed to compose (in 1964) only one new piece for the score. This piece is a charming little movement for men's voices, recorder, and harp, based on an intertwining of a sixteenth-century French Noël (*Christ Is Born This Day*) and the plainsong hymn *Ave Maris stella*. The text for *The Play of Our Lady* was compiled from medieval sources for radio broadcast and the play was produced after the composer's death; the rest of the music was assembled from earlier Willan works.

14

Chamber music

Sketches of chamber music by Willan are dated as early as 1903; his early (and relatively brief) interest in writing chamber music may well have been stimulated by his admiration for the music of Brahms and by his studies with Evlyn Howard-Jones, an authority on Brahms's piano music. Willan's two major original chamber works – *Trio in B Minor* for violin, cello, and piano and *Sonata No. 1 in E Minor* for violin and piano – were composed by 1916. After 1916 he wrote only the Baroque-style *Sonata No. 2 in E Major* (1923), the unfinished *Sonata No. 3, Poem* (1930), and a few small chamber pieces.

Some early sketches and fragments (ca 1905–10) show Willan's plans for three or four string quartets, a second piano trio, and a piano quartet. These unfinished works show less of the influence of Wagner than of Brahms and the turn-of-the-century English and French schools. Some material was reworked in later pieces, eg *Sonata No. 3* and *Poem*. Willan's first completed chamber work, *Romance in E Flat* for violin and piano, appeared in 1906. It was one of his few pieces of chamber music to be published – a charming 'salon' work of the type made popular by Elgar. It is not profound, but is well written and attractive and never sentimental.

Willan's *Trio in B Minor* for violin, cello, and piano was performed in Toronto in the fall of 1915 with Willan at the piano, Frank Blachford on violin, and Leo Smith on the cello. Bryant gives the completion date as 24 December 1907, but in program notes for a 13 April 1916 performance, Leo Smith said the work was composed between 1909 and 1915; in the 1963 Parker tapes Willan said that he wrote the finale (fourth movement) in England as a separate work and that later Viggo Kihl persuaded him to write the first three movements to make a full-length piano trio.

Unfortunately the score of the first movement has been lost; all that remains are the violin and cello parts. A reconstruction would be next to impossible, since the piano part is the most substantial. No sketches and none of the original manuscript survive. A single sheet of manuscript in Willan's hand would appear to be his attempt to reconstruct the first movement; he gave up after a few bars. The extant scores and parts are in a copyist's hand; the parts are well used and much marked up and contain revisions. The complete *Trio* received at least six performances, the last on 20 November 1941.

From the surviving violin and cello parts it is possible, however, to discern the general structure of the missing first movement. Predictably it turns out to be an introduction and sonata-allegro. The twelve-bar introduction opens with a phrase in the cello part (Example 185) which will appear again in the ensuing allegro. The exposition of the sonata-allegro proper begins with the main subject, in B minor, played once through on the violin and then repeated at the same pitch on the cello (doubled an octave higher on the violin); see Example 186. This tune uses the same rhythmic pattern in nearly every bar (cf the main theme of the finale of Elgar's *Symphony No. 2*). It is followed by a subsidiary motif in F sharp minor, which is treated somewhat canonically. (It is not known if the piano participated in the canon; this would have been possible if it had begun a bar prior to the cello entry – see Example 187.)

The bridge section uses the opening phrase of the introduction in augmentation. The lyrical second subject of the exposition is in D major (Example 188) and is played at a slower tempo. The pace increases again with the arrival of the long development section, which ranges through many tonalities and appears to be based mainly upon figures derived from the first subject. The recapitulation returns to the tonic key, B minor, with an abridged version of the main subject. The canonic subsidiary theme which had appeared in the exposition is omitted. The second subject returns in the expected tonic major (B major), but then jumps unexpectedly into A flat major. Actually this parallels a move from D major to B major at the corresponding point in the exposition, but here the change comes as somewhat of a surprise. A substantial coda, based on both main subjects, brings the movement back to the home tonality and to a conclusion. This movement was a considerable piece of work; the loss of its score and the unlikelihood of its eventual reconstruction are deeply to be regretted.

The second movement, 'Fantasy,' seems to be the precursor of later Willan works, such as the beautiful middle movement of *Symphony No. 1*, which wend their rhapsodic way apparently without benefit of a discernible form or structure. The main unifying feature here is the two-bar accompaniment figure in the piano part, made up of secondary seventh chords over a combined tonic-dominant pedal point (Example 189). This figure is used continuously by the piano as a sort of accompanying ostinato for the first third of the piece, repeating half a dozen times in the tonic key (E major) and then wandering through a maze of other tonalities.

All this time the violin and cello have been weaving rhapsodic melodic lines above the shifting ostinato; these melodic lines, though they have no formal shape, exhibit a unity of style by various means, including a fairly frequent use of the following rhythm: 3/4 ♩♫|♫♩. The music, having started pianissimo, undergoes a gradual crescendo and eventually reaches a forte level. The ostinato in the piano now gives way to arpeggiated left-hand figurations as the music becomes more agitated and pushes on to an impassioned fortissimo climax in C major at the very centre of the movement. The climax dies away, and the final third of the piece returns to the calm of the opening section. However this final section is not a repetition of the first: there are a few appearances of the ostinato figure, but it is not used consistently and some new ones appear. The home tonality of E major returns for the last twenty bars. There is a certain feeling of French influence throughout the movement, of which the passage in Example 190, occurring near the start of the final third of the piece, is the most obvious. This succession of ninth chords, and the free and somewhat impressionistic use of seventh chords elsewhere in the piece, indicate that the developments of Fauré and even Debussy were not lost on the young Willan. A French influence will be seen again in *Sonata No. 1*.

The third movement is one of Willan's very few scherzos. This scherzo is not on the same scale as that of *Symphony No. 2*; nevertheless it is a worthy precursor. Its structure is simply ‖:A:‖B A + Coda. Its introductory eight bars (Example 191) show Willan's fondness for augmented triads. The main motif from which section A is developed is a four-bar phrase (Example 192) which seems to belong hardly to the tonic key of G major but rather to C minor. Later in this section a related motif appears (Example 193). The broken leaps of these motifs – often fourths, fifths, or outlined triads – form the main stylistic feature of the section, and this material shows an affinity with some of the themes in the scherzo in

Symphony No. 2. Other perhaps coincidental resemblances between the two scherzos include the same tonality (G major) and time signature (3/8). Section B commences with a reference to the material of the previous section, following which a new theme is introduced (Example 194). This theme encompasses two tonalities, beginning in E major and finishing in G major. A little later it is repeated, this time starting in G major and finishing in E flat major. The remainder of this section is a development of material from the previous section. The final section is an exact repetition of the first section save for the last few bars (here lengthened out into a coda of nearly fifty bars in the same general style). Willan seems to have understood from the start the light texture and touch required for a true scherzo. There are many examples here of unaccompanied single-line passages, staccato notes, and rests; little musical figures are airily tossed back and forth among the three participating instruments. The composer realized that one must let some daylight into such music.

The structure of the long fourth and final movement is interesting and unusual. It might be explained as a sonata-form movement with a new theme in place of a central development section, but with a large development-section-cum-coda at the end (in which all the preceding materials are mixed up together). A simple diagram would be: introduction, A, B, C, A, B, and development-coda (based on A, B, C, and introduction). The movement is one of Willan's most Brahmsian, as becomes apparent immediately in the slow introduction. This introduction, in the tonic key of B minor, has a ternary structure, beginning and ending with a Brahms-like theme (Example 195). The use of 5/4 metre here is questionable, since the music seems to fall naturally into measures of 4/4 (see brackets over Example 195). In the middle of the introduction is a second theme (Example 196) which not only recalls some of the flavour of Brahms's *Symphony No. 3* but also foreshadows the openings of the themes of sections A and B to follow.

The main movement itself is marked 'allegro feroce,' one of Willan's favourite directions in his early years. Section A starts in the tonic key with a rather 'busy' subject (Example 197) played by the cello. It is then repeated in E minor by the violin, following which the opening portion of the theme is tossed antiphonally among the three instruments until the home tonality of B minor is re-established. A short transitional passage leads directly to section B and its lyrical tune (Example 198). Presented initially by the violin in D major, the tune is repeated by the cello in F major. After an intervening passage of free material this theme is played twice more, once in B major and then back in D major (note the parallelism of tonalities used here between the two pairs of entries). A short episode follows, leading to section C. This third section has a new theme, a four-bar phrase (Example 199) which again is rather in the style of Brahms, exhibiting a distant connection with the material in the introduction to the first movement. Introduced by the piano in D minor and then repeated in F minor, this motif is used as the basis for tonal journeys through C major, E minor, E flat major, and G major. The section concludes with 'dominant preparation' for a return of section A and the home tonality of B minor.

Section A is repeated intact, though the violin and cello parts are interchanged from their original order. The repeat of section B is very much shortened, consisting of a single and incomplete appearance of the lyrical tune, this time in B minor (notice the change of mode from major to minor for this theme).

We then move directly into the long development-coda, based on all the themes. It consists of six parts: 1 / development of the opening portion of the section B theme, starting in C minor; 2 / development of section C material, starting in E minor; 3 / full presentation of section B theme, plus extensions, in B major; 4 / molto allegro – build-up based on material from section A, starting in B major and followed by E major, shifting tonalities, and then C major; 5 / further build-up based on a major-mode treatment of the section C theme, over a dominant pedal; and 6 / largo – a triumphant major-mode presentation of the opening theme of the introduction, followed by a final flourish. In number of bars this development-coda accounts for one-third of the movement. The scheme, though unusual, is quite logical and works very well here.

Trio in B Minor is an important work. Willan's first completed major chamber work, it is in some ways his best. Perhaps only the first movement of *Sonata No. 1 in E Minor* surpasses any of the movements in this piano trio. The structural experiments of the last movement would not be equalled again till those of *Piano Concerto in C Minor* some thirty years later. As with *Cleopatra*, this early work demonstrates that Willan had acquired the ability to handle large-scale forms successfully.

Sonata No. 1 in E Minor for violin and piano was started in October 1915 and completed in February 1916 (though some of the music had its origins some years earlier in England). It marks the apex of Willan's chamber music. (In 1916 he also produced his most famous organ piece, *Introduction, Passacaglia and Fugue in E Flat Minor*.)

Sonata No. 1 is in three movements. The first is particularly powerful and compelling, showing a remarkable amount of French influence (Franck and Fauré) as well as some of Elgar. Cast in sonata form, the movement commences (Example 200) with a nine-bar slow introduction, bars 4 and 5 of which clearly show the French harmonic influence.

The allegro movement proper begins with a thirty-one-bar musical paragraph in E minor, commencing with a powerful 'striding' subject (Ia) characterized by wide leaps; two subsidiary motifs, Ib and Ic, follow; see Examples 201–3. Ia and Ib are in a rather Franckian style and Ic is in the style of Elgar. The music comes to a full stop (with a fermata) at the end of the opening paragraph and starts up again with a bridge passage (Example 204) consisting of rapid piano figurations around a violin motif which is a rhythmic variant of Ib. The tonality shifts into G sharp minor for the second main subject, a rather unusual second tonal area for a piece in E minor (Example 205). The dotted rhythms in this subject (♩♪♪) will play a major part in subsequent development of material. Though commencing in G sharp minor, the subject finally cadences in F sharp minor.

The development of material commences (around letter C, bar 73, in the published score) with the dotted rhythms previously mentioned. Between C and D (bar 105) the momentum and interest of the music flag somewhat, though this certainly makes the sudden bursting in of a freely canonic treatment of subject Ia at D all the more telling. The climax of the development is reached at letters F (bar 137) and G (bar 157), following which the music dies down (largely by means of the reappearance of material from the slow introduction to the movement).

Tonality throughout the development section, after starting off in the general area of F sharp minor, is highly fluid. The first big climax, at F, is in C sharp minor, but this is almost immediately contradicted by a spectacular jump into F minor. The climaxes at F and G are both preceded by forceful build-ups of arresting chromatic progressions: the first based on the dotted figure from subject II (Example 203), and the second on material from subject Ia. The second climax, at G, establishes F major and F minor for eight bars, after which the music drifts through more highly chromatic journeyings back home in E minor at the recapitulation. The recapitulation is fairly conventional, with subject II, commencing in C sharp minor and cadencing in B minor, being a transposed version of its G sharp minor to F sharp minor appearance in the exposition.

The coda starts off, immediately prior to J (bar 259), in a manner similar to that of the development section, but settles in E minor just before K (bar 277) with a thrilling free canonic treatment of Ia with its inversion. This is the basis of a powerful chromatic build-up, which is interrupted momentarily by yet another appearance of material from the opening slow introduction (this time forte instead of piano) and then resumes allegro molto with a final wind-up over a bass ostinato derived from Ia. In all, this movement shows Willan's gifts of melodic invention, his well-integrated use of materials, and his command of colourful and complex chromatic harmony to excellent advantage. In spite of a somewhat sectional style at times and one or two weakish spots, the music sweeps one along with glorious momentum.

The second movement, marked adagio, is in D flat major – an unusual tonality for the middle movement of a sonata in E minor. Its structure is that of a rather free three-refrain modulating rondo (ie a rondo in which not all the refrains appear in the tonic key):

A	B (long)	A'	C (short)	A^2 plus coda
D flat major	D flat major	E major	E major	D flat major
	G flat major		D flat major	
	E major			

After a four-bar introduction (consisting of an unharmonized unison melody in the bass which foreshadows the refrain), the sixteen-bar refrain appears in D flat major (Example 206). There follows an episode, during the first part of which some of the refrain melody is extended and developed over a new accompaniment figure (Example 207). Four bars before C (bar 40) a new theme (Example 208) is introduced in G flat major. This is subsequently answered in its dominant, D flat major, after which it is extended through various tonalities, eventually leading into E major. At this point, when E major is established three bars after D (bar 78), the first half of the refrain reappears. At its initial appearance the refrain melody was played by the violin with the piano accompanying; here the piano plays it while the violin supplies a lyrical counterpoint. The second episode, starting at E (bar 88), grows out of this material and works its way back to the home key of D flat major. The final appearance of the refrain is preceded by the four bars of introduction, though this time the bass melody has harmony above it. The refrain itself, somewhat shortened and altered from its original form, leads directly into a sixteen-bar coda over a tonic pedal. At the very end of the coda, reference is again made to the introduction.

Though this second movement can be considered a three-refrain rondo, the treatment of the form here is rather free. In particular, the episodes do not balance, the first being very long and the second quite short; the material of the second half of the opening refrain, and the new material introduced in episode I, are never recapitulated or put to any further use; and the middle appearance of the refrain is not in the tonic key, but the rather remote key of E major. Willan may well have chosen E major in order to anchor this otherwise D flat major movement more firmly into the E structure of the sonata as a whole. Musically this movement displays a tender lyricism and colourful chromaticism worthy of Fauré.

The third and final movement is a four-refrain rondo:

SECTION	COMMENTS	TONALITY
A	twenty-one-bar refrain: a closed musical paragraph in 6/8 time	E minor to B minor
B	new subject in 9/8 time, followed by an episodical passage based on material from sections A and B	E minor
A	exact repetition of opening twenty-one-bar paragraph	E minor to B minor
C	lyrical theme in 4/8 time, followed by an episodical passage based on section A	E major
A	exact repetition of opening twenty-one-bar paragraph	E minor to B minor
B	repetition of the 9/8 subject, but this time in the major mode rather than the minor mode	E major
A'	very brief reference to the refrain – only the first two bars of it; leads directly into the coda	E minor
coda	based on materials from A and B	E minor, E major

The openings of the three principal themes are illustrated in Examples 209–11. Tonally this rondo is unconventional: all the sections are based in E minor or E major. This is balanced to some extent by the unusual refrain, which modulates to its dominant minor in each of its first three appearances. In addition there are transitional key changes during the course of each section which further compensate for the rather heavy emphasis on the tonic throughout the piece.

The refrain itself is a perky tune which shows some French influence both in its harmonization and its generally light-hearted and airy treatment. The antiphonal arpeggios between piano and violin toward the end of the refrain are reminiscent of Tschaikowsky. The second subject, in 9/8 time, goes equally well in major or minor mode; Willan sets it first in E minor and then, later in the movement, in E major. The lyrical middle theme (C), a ternary paragraph of twenty-four bars, has the flavour at times of an English or Irish folk melody. The echoing of the opening piano phrase by the violin, as seen in the first two bars, occurs several times in the course of this section. After having been repeated three times without variation, the refrain is cut to a mere two bars on its last appearance and then leads directly into a fairly extensive coda.

The coda, based on materials from sections A and B, provides an impressive climax not only for this particular movement but also for the sonata as a whole. After letter H (bar 145) there is a fine build-up (Example 212) over a descending chromatic bass, above which the violin seems to recall the striding opening subject of the first movement.

This sonata is probably the most French-influenced of any of Willan's larger compositions. The influence of Brahms and Wagner, so noticeable in Willan's other chamber and orchestral music of this period, is small here. Willan's models appear, rather, to have been the violin and piano sonatas of Franck and Fauré. Though not the equal of Franck's magnificent *Sonata in A Major, Sonata No. 1* is perhaps the equal of the fine sonatas of Fauré. It is certainly Willan's greatest chamber work.

Sonata No. 2 in E Major for violin and piano is very different from *Sonata No. 1.* It is unique in Willan's chamber music in being modelled deliberately on the Baroque sonata in both form and musical style. (Willan adopted an early-eighteenth-century style in some of his incidental music.) *Sonata No. 2* was written as the result of an invitation from Dr Vogt in 1921 to give a lecture on Baroque violin music at the Toronto conservatory. Willan wrote the sonata, as he says (Parker tapes), 'to get experience of thinking in that particular school'; it was subsequently first performed at the lecture. The work was published in 1923.

Sonata No. 2 is patterned on middle and late Baroque models, particularly those of Corelli and Handel; the completeness and, at times, intricacy of the keyboard part suggest J.S. Bach. There are four movements in a slow-fast-slow-fast relationship, as in a *sonata da chiesa.* However the two quick movements are dance movements (courante and gavotte), such as one might find in a *sonata da camera*. Willan follows the later Baroque procedure of merging the *da chiesa* and the *da camera* varieties in one work. Typical schemes of modulation for the period are followed, and the third movement ends with the standard Phrygian cadence.

The first movement, largo ed espressivo, moves along throughout in the lyrical style of its opening (Example 213). It is in three sections. The first moves from the tonic key of E major to the dominant key of B major, the middle cadences on the mediant minor (G sharp minor), and the final re-establishes E major. The thematic material of all sections is similar, following Baroque practice of developing a single figure, or 'affection,' throughout a movement. The almost continuous octaves in the left-hand keyboard part betray Willan the organist (pedals 16' and 8'). These low octaves are not used in the other movements of the sonata.

The second movement, an allegro, is written in a loose imitative counterpoint (Example 214). It is called a 'courante' and is the first of two instances in this sonata where the composer's understanding of Baroque dances appears incomplete. He writes an allegro in quadruple metre and gives it the title of a dance always written in triple metre! The structure of this second movement is E major binary, though the second part is not repeated. Within the binary structure there is a distinct ternary element, as in the first movement; the only difference in the tonal scheme between the two movements is that the middle section cadences here on the relative minor (C sharp minor) rather than on the mediant minor.

The third movement, adagio (sonore), is very short and, with an inconclusive Phrygian cadence at the end, seems to act as an introduction to the fourth movement. The music is written in a saraband-like slow triple metre, though it is not strictly a saraband and is not called such. The key is C sharp minor.

The fourth and last movement, allegretto, is called a 'gavotte.' Like the second movement it is a binary structure with the second repeat sign omitted and contains a ternary element. Unlike the second movement, this movement cadences on the mediant minor (G sharp minor) at the end of its middle section (following the example of the first movement). Willan's 'gavotte' begins on the first beat of the bar (Example 215) – a real gavotte would have been barred as Example 216. The correct barring would have caused problems later, since the opening sentence is half a bar too long.

Although a deliberate imitation of an earlier style, *Sonata No. 2* is skilfully written.

Sonata No. 3 (in B minor), started in 1922, was apparently not finished – unless Willan was using the word 'sonata' in its older sense (a piece that was played rather than sung). The completed movement is an adagio, yet its title page says simply *Sonata No. 3, Violin and Piano* and gives no indication that it is the slow middle movement of a projected three- or four-movement work. Willan might have been planning a Baroque slow-fast-slow-fast movement structure (like *Sonata No. 2*), which would account for the adagio coming immediately after the title page; it is not at all Baroque in style. Because of its length and completed structure, it is also most unlikely that this adagio was intended to be a slow introduction to a sonata-allegro movement.

The structure is a modified sonata form. The exposition commences with a gentle rocking figure (Example 217) in the piano part, a quasi-sicilienne style that tends to pervade the whole movement. The main theme proper (Example 218) is a delightfully plaintive tune with an almost Russian flavour. The tune is repeated, punctuated by the sicilienne motif, and a bridge section follows. This bridge section is based upon a figure from the main subject and ends in E minor for the entrance of the subsidiary subject (Example 219). There is something of the flavour of Delius in this section. The tonality is very fluid, but finally comes to rest in E major with a codetta-like passage over a combined tonic-dominant pedal.

As is common with slow movements in sonata form, there is no development section but merely a short link-passage back to the recapitulation. This link-passage is in C major: it contains a brief reference to the subsidiary theme and concludes with a quasi-recitativo for the violin. The home tonality of B minor returns with the recapitulation. There the main subject is repeated in its entirety, but the ensuing bridge section is much altered and considerably lengthened, giving the impression of a partial development section of the opening materials. Tonality ranges as far afield as B flat minor and D flat major. The subsidiary theme then makes its reappearance, followed by a short coda based on all previous material. The music seems very reluctant to settle home in B minor until the last three bars! This procedure of omitting the development at its usual place, and then putting a development between subject I and subject II of the recapitulation, was one that Brahms used (eg the finales of symphonies no. 1 and 3).

The origins of the main thematic material can be found in an unfinished sketch (ca 1905–10) for a slow movement in C minor of a string quartet (B110). The later treatment is a considerable improvement. This adagio is an exquisitely beautiful work, quite the equal of *Poem* for strings (with which it shares an inscription from Yeats, 'And evening, full of the linnet's wings'), and deserves to be better known.

Poem (1930) for string quartet was Willan's last significant chamber work. The composer originally intended the piece to be the first of a group of 'Celtic Sketches' for string quartet; hence the quotation from Yeats on the score 'And evening, full of the linnet's wings' (also used in *Sonata No. 3*). The other Celtic sketches did not get written, and the composer changed the title of this piece to *Poem*. The work was rewritten for string orchestra in 1959 (see chapter 8 for a detailed discussion of this music).

Following *Poem* of 1930 only a couple of small and inconsequential chamber pieces came from Willan's pen. Mention might be made, however, of an undated piece for piano quintet, *Grave e lugubre*, a pot-pourri of themes from Grieg, Wagner, Richard Strauss, Beethoven – and Willan. It was a musical joke, probably intended for the Arts and Letters Club (cf his 1948 *Alouette* fantasy for two pianos, discussed in chapter 17).

15

Organ music
1906–1933

Willan's organ music is justly famous. A handful of major works rank with the masterpieces of the recital literature for the instrument. His reputation was established by works written between 1906 and 1918 – including *Epilogue in D Minor* (1908) and, most notably, *Prelude and Fugue in C Minor* (1908) and the awesome *Introduction, Passacaglia and Fugue* (1916). In the late 1920s and early 1930s he wrote several new works and some arrangements – a minor interlude between the towering early accomplishments and the more numerous and occasionally brilliant organ works of his later years, examined in the next chapter.

Willan's first published organ piece, *Fantasia upon the Plainsong Melody 'Ad Coenam Agni,'* dates from 1906. It is still interesting to play today and makes a fine concluding voluntary. The piece is written in three sections. The introductory and rhapsodic first section, marked 'Lento,' treats the opening line of the plainsong (Example 220). The second section, marked 'Allegro moderato,' turns the opening phrase of the plainsong into a march-like theme (Example 221). The third and final section, marked 'Adagio e molto maestoso,' presents the whole plainsong melody in the garb of a majestic processional (Example 222).

Willan makes no attempt to produce a modal, plainsong atmosphere. He treats his plainsong melody strictly as a melodic base for a work written in the idiom of his own time. Yet there is an imagination and breadth of treatment displayed which raises the 'Ad Coenam' fantasia above the ordinary. Once again Willan's first example of writing in a genre has been auspicious.

The St Alban's Pageant of 1908 (in which the composer took part, dressed as a monk!) was the occasion for the composition of Willan's next organ work, *Epilogue in D Minor*. This is one of his finest organ works, far surpassing in vigour and sheer melodic invention many of his late pieces.

Epilogue is cast in sonata-allegro form, and the opening subject is in D minor (Example 223). Here one has the strength and quasi-modality of the finest of Stanford's organ music. This material is developed and extended until the lyrical second subject, in B flat major (Example 224), is reached.

The development section, based mainly on the second subject, shows considerable imagination and covers a wide range of tonalities (E flat major, D minor, D major, C sharp minor, G sharp minor, B major, and E flat major). At one point (see Example 225) the two main subjects (I and II) are presented together. A dominant pedal, over which the opening of the first subject is treated sequentially, leads back to the recapitulation. Here the first subject is presented much as before, but the second subject is transformed from a quiet, lyrical theme in B flat major into a majestic march in D major (Example 226). The latter is a similar treatment to that at the end of the 'Ad Coenam' fantasia. This may be the extroverted music of youth, but it is certainly not immature in the treatment of its material, and the bombast at the end is not offensive. *Epilogue* is still a stirring recital piece.

Also in 1908 Willan composed one of his greatest masterpieces for organ, *Prelude and Fugue in C Minor*. It is also one of his longest organ works, lasting more than eleven minutes.

The prelude is built from two short motifs (x and y: see Example 227). The sheer harmonic colour of this music is quite overpowering, embodying the extension of the Wagner idiom to organ music, as do Bruckner's symphonies to symphonic music. Example 228 shows the powerful chromatic writing. Later (Example 229) the theme is treated canonically. Though the prelude begins and ends in C minor, tonalities progress as far afield as C sharp minor and B minor in the middle section.

The fugue is a double fugue, with two expositions. The majestic subject of exposition I makes prominent use of the first three notes of the principal motif of the prelude. The main tonalities here are C minor and G minor, with one excursion to A flat major. Exposition II has a more florid and chromatic subject. The tonalities here are G minor and D minor, so that exposition II has the effect of being 'in the dominant' of exposition I. The first exposition is written in four-part counterpoint, the second in three-part. Exposition II has a counter-subject also, whereas exposition I does not use one. In the middle and final sections of the fugue, subjects I and II are combined together in three-, four-, and five-part counterpoint. The initial combination of the two subjects and the counter-subject (Example 230) was described by Alan Gray as 'the finest piece of triple counterpoint since Rheinberger.'

Two other features of the fugue should be mentioned: the long dominant pedal leading to the final section in five-part counterpoint, during which tension is carefully built through constantly rising sequential and stretto treatments of the opening phrase of the first subject; and the coda, which presents a massive treatment of material from the prelude (a procedure often favoured by Rheinberger in the fugal movements which conclude many of his organ sonatas).

Prelude and Fugue in C Minor is a towering work: Willan would scale such heights only once again, in his *Introduction, Passacaglia and Fugue*.

In 1909 Willan composed his fine *Prelude and Fugue in B Minor*. This work is conceived on a smaller scale than its great predecessor of 1908, and the fugue is comparatively straightforward and conventional (though not without interest). The noble prelude, however, displays some of the same splendid harmonic imagination as its C minor colleague, as can be seen in Example 231.

During this period Willan wrote six short pieces for organ. They were published individually in 1910; in 1947 they were revised as a set titled *Miniature Suite for Organ*. These little pieces have become quite popular with organists and are cut from the same cloth as the attractive small pieces for piano which the composer was writing ca 1910. *Communion* and *Intermezzo* are the weakest of the set; the former verges on the sentimental, and the latter is rather too reminiscent of Edward MacDowell's *To a Wild Rose*. (Willan admired MacDowell's music and heard the London première of his *Piano Concerto in D Minor*.) *Prelude*, *Trio*, and *Finale* are good and solid pieces. But it is the delightful *Scherzo* in B minor (see Example 232) which is the most imaginative and colourful. It is often performed separately, and in 1943–44 Willan arranged it for string orchestra (though it is difficult to imagine this music without the colour of a horn and some light woodwinds).

It was not until 1916, in Canada, that Willan completed his next (and generally considered his greatest) organ work, *Introduction, Passacaglia and Fugue in E Flat Minor*.

Willan liked to tell two stories about this piece. He claimed that he had attended an organ recital at which Reger's *Passacaglia in D Minor* was played and had been jokingly told by his friend Dalton Baker that only a 'German philosophical mind' could compose such a work; this remark spurred Willan to write his own passacaglia. He later sent Baker a photograph inscribed with the passacaglia theme and the words 'To the cause, from the effect.' He claimed also that he wrote the variations for the passacaglia while riding on the radial (inter-urban tram) between Toronto and the summer cottage he had rented near Jackson's Point on Lake Simcoe – one variation each trip; the passacaglia was composed first, followed by the introduction, and then the fugue.

The introduction is one of the most arresting and dramatic passages in all organ music. It begins (and ends) with a marvellous succession of mystical chords (Example 233). (This progression would seem to have its origin in a passage – Example 234 – from an unfinished orchestral rhapsody of 1911, *From the Highlands*.) This is followed by a passage (Example 235) in dotted rhythm which likewise appears to have originated in early sketches, particularly one for piano and orchestra in A minor (Example 236). Sketches for the arpeggiated animato section of the introduction (as well as for variation X of the passacaglia) are in E minor rather than E flat minor – perhaps the composer initially intended the work to be in E minor, which would have made it much easier to read! However he was learning Rheinberger's *Sonata No. 6 in E Flat Minor* at the time, and this may have influenced his choice of key. The maestoso penultimate section of the introduction, commencing with an abrupt jump into B major, introduces the powerful tubas which Willan found on the magnificent organ at St Paul's, Toronto. Indeed, much of the musical colour of the work was probably stimulated by the composer's experience with this instrument. The final section of the introduction returns to E flat minor and is built around the five mystic opening chords. There is a slight foreshadowing of the passacaglia theme towards the end. The style of the introduction is rhapsodic and improvisational, yet the short, disparate sections seem somehow to blend into a logical and impressive whole.

The passacaglia is built on a ground bass (Example 237). The eighteen variations which follow exhibit a great deal of diversity and contrast. There are few purely contrapuntal variations (I, XI, and XII), and most are made up of imaginative manual figurations over the pedal bass. In this aspect Willan's passacaglia is closer to those of Rheinberger and Reger than to Bach's. Yet, in spite of their diversity, the variations are welded together into a unified work which progresses steadily and inexorably to the mighty climax of the quasi-marcia funebre at variation XVII. There appear to be three main groupings of the variations.

Group 1 includes variations I to V. Here is found the traditional rhythmic crescendo of passacaglias: variation I using predominantly quarter-note movement, II using eighth-note movement, III introducing some triplet eighths, and IV breaking into sixteenth notes. There is also a crescendo of texture and volume to the first climax at V. Of the individual variations in this group, the treatment of the ground bass in canon-at-the-sixth in I and the introduction of the soaring counter-melody in III are notable features. (A precedent for the canon-at-the-sixth treatment of the ground bass occurs near the beginning of the passacaglia-like first movement of *Symphony No. 3* for organ by Louis Vierne.)

Group 2 includes variations VI to X. Here there is another rhythmic crescendo, leading up to the flourishes in thirty-second and sixty-fourth notes of variation X. VI takes the ground up into the top voice and presents it in ornamented form. The hands are spread over three manuals (keyboards) by means of an ingenious and colourful 'thumbed' part for the right hand. The ground returns to the bass in VII and stays there for the subsequent variations of this group. VIII features the antiphonal use of short overlapping figures between two keyboards. X includes arpeggiated chords for a harp stop (here, again, the influence of the big organ at St Paul's is evident). In his own program notes for this work Willan described variations I to VIII as being 'of sombre character' and IX and X as being 'of a scherzo type.'

Group 3 contains XI to XVII. This group commences with a change of metre to 9/8 time for variation XI. The notes of the ground are here divided up between the four voices of the counterpoint. The use of this procedure in a passacaglia may well be original with Willan. XII reverts to the original 3/4 metre and consists of four-voice counterpoint in sixteenth-note motion. The ground bass is slightly ornamented. XIII, XIV, and XV are figural variations which build toward the final climax. This climax occurs at the marcia funebre (Example 238) which constitutes variations XVI and XVII. Here, perhaps, there is a slight influence of Liszt. Note how the ground is broken up and ornamented. The climax has not quite reached its ultimate level at the end of XVII, so Willan extends the variation with an episode. During this episode the climax is attained, after which the music winds down in preparation for XVIII.

Variation XVIII is a 'quasi-chorale' and is not part of any group. The climax of the passacaglia has been reached in XVII, and XVIII serves as a quiet interlude, separating the passacaglia from the fugue. This conception of using the final variation as an interlude seems to be original with Willan. The melody is based upon the ground, which is divided up into small sections and used in imitation in the pedals.

XVI, XVII, and XVIII are 'characteristic' variations. Such types of variation go back to Bach's *Goldberg Variations* and earlier, but Willan's use of them in his passacaglia for organ would seem to be a precedent. (He had also used characteristic variations in *Variations and Epilogue* for two pianos, written in the years immediately previous; see chapter 17.)

The fugue is built on a subject (Example 239) derived from the first half of the passacaglia theme (Example 237). The four-voice exposition in E flat minor is normal except that it cadences rather unexpectedly (but very effectively!) in D flat major. After an episode and an appearance of the subject in G flat major, series of stretti begin. Stretti with entries at the distance of one bar give way to tighter stretti at the half-bar. Momentum gathers as, half-way through the fugue, the predominantly quarter- and eighth-note motion of the opening section is increased to sixteenth-note motion. The sixteenth notes are, in fact, a counter-subject written in invertible counterpoint with the subject. Tension continues to mount as the metre is changed to 3/4 time over a long dominant pedal in E flat major, and the speed increases. At the climax, marked 'Nobilmente,' the music returns to E flat minor with a massive harmonized version of the canon-at-the-sixth which had been the basis of variation I of the passacaglia. Tubas blare a counter-melody, and the work ends in an overwhelming blaze of sound. Willan's control and timing of events in the build-up throughout the fugue, and indeed throughout the whole of this final, stupendous climax, are masterful.

Introduction, Passacaglia and Fugue is a highly original and precedent-setting work. The composer did have models, of course, particularly those of Bach, Rheinberger, and Reger. Some interesting connections can be observed with the fine but virtually unknown *Passacaglia in B Minor* (1899) by John E. West (1863–1928), musical editor of Novello and a friend of Willan. There is a certain similarity (Example 240) in the use of a 'throbbing left hand' in West's variation V and Willan's variation VI. A still more noticeable influence occurs in the final bars of each work (Example 241, West and Willan respectively). West's *Passacaglia* is dedicated to Josef Rheinberger.

Introduction, Passacaglia and Fugue received international recognition. Joseph Bonnet, the famous French organist, declared that Willan's passacaglia was one of the most significant since Bach's and called it 'a rare and admirable composition, conceived in an extraordinarily pure and lofty spirit, built up on solid architectural lines, illuminated by the light of harmonies by turns sumptuous and delicate; this work does the greatest honour to the organ literature of our time' (*Oxford University Press Music Bulletin*, February 1941). Francis Jackson said in a letter to Willan: 'By Jove it wears well – it never fails to thrill me – and the hearers.'

The only other Willan organ work of consequence from this period was the unfinished *Suite for Organ*, ca 1918. The title page of the manuscript lists four projected movements: prelude; barcarolle; (unspecified); and toccata.

The prelude is complete and is a very fine movement in A minor. It is one of Willan's best organ pieces. The title does not give an idea of the scope or the size of the piece, which covers eleven pages of manuscript. Why it was never published remains a mystery; it is exciting and of musical value superior to much later organ music that was published. In design it is similar to some of the early Baroque organ toccatas, with a freely rhapsodic opening section, a fugal middle section, and a final section again in free style.

The seven-bar extract in Example 242 gives an idea of the general style of the rhapsodic opening section. Within it are contained the three main figures (a, b, and c) on which this section is built. Figure a is the flourish with which the movement commences, initially in A minor and then repeated in C sharp minor; b is an example of Willan's colourful progressions of little-related chords, held together by a descending chromatic scale in the upper part (cf the opening of *Cleopatra*); c, which shows some influence of Franck and Rheinberger, is obviously useful for the working of sequential build-ups and developments.

The fugal section, which commences (Example 243) in C major, has one of Willan's most modern subjects. It narrowly misses using all twelve notes; only the F is missing! There is a four-voice exposition, though the part-writing is treated rather freely after the third entry and the fourth entry is incomplete. At the third entry appears a counter-motif, y (Example 244), that is used subsequently. The opening figure of the subject, marked 'x' in Example 245, is also used extensively for the episodes. (Willan's intricate use of the ♫♩ rhythm reminds one of Rheinberger's treatment of the same rhythmic figure in *Sonata No. 6*.)

Following its exposition, the fugue proceeds very freely, with only one full lead of the subject, in E major, in its middle section. There is no final section to the fugue (ie a return to C major) but instead a return to A minor and a repetition of part of the rhapsodic opening section of this prelude (starting with figures *b* and *c*). A coda, based on x from the fugue subject and figure a from the opening section, concludes the piece amid a certain amount of bravura solo pedal-work in true organ toccata style.

The second movement was to have been a 'barcarolle,' but Willan completed only thirty-four bars. Years later he completed the barcarolle and it was published as a separate piece in 1950. It has an overall ternary structure. Section I, in D major (Example 246), is obviously 'light' music, somewhat akin to Elgar's 'salon' style. The music is raised above the commonplace by some interesting harmonic excursions as the section progresses. Section II, in 5/8 metre, is a ternary structure within itself. It commences with a longish melody in F major, beginning as in Example 247.

Bryant suggests (*HWC* 61) that the twenty-bar fragment of an unfinished elegie (B195) might have been intended as the missing third movement. The manuscript is titled 'Elegie (Organ Suite),' and the key, F sharp minor, would have fitted nicely into the tonal scheme of the suite.

The fourth movement was to be a toccata, but none was forthcoming. However a fragment of some three dozen bars for organ titled 'Toccata Rondo' may have been the intended finale. This unfinished toccata rondo is in A major and would thus fit in with the overall tonality of the suite. Assuming that both the elegie and the toccata rondo were intended for use here, the tonal structure would have been prelude in A minor, barcarolle in D major, elegie in F sharp minor, and toccata (rondo) in A major. Such a tonal structure would indeed be logical.

Between 1918 and 1933 Willan produced only three small-scale organ works. After leaving St Paul's in 1921 his interest in composing for recitals appears to have waned. His pieces would now be largely church-oriented.

Willan's first choral prelude was on *Puer nobis nascitur* and was published in 1926. It is constructed along the lines of Bach's *Jesu, Joy*, with an independent figure continuing throughout; against it the individual lines of the hymn-tune (in this case, carol) come in at spaced intervals. In Willan's piece, however, the lines of the tune are presented in canon. Willan later arranged the prelude for unison voices (or flute, or oboe) and strings; he used this setting in his *Nativity Play* (1940) and it was later published separately.

While the choral prelude on *Puer nobis* is quiet and gentle, his second, on *Andernach* (1928), is loud and vigorous. It follows the Pachelbel model (cf Bach's chorale prelude on *Nun Danket*) in which each line of the hymn-tune is preceded by a free fugal exposition on a diminution of that particular line of the tune. Willan treats each line of the tune in canon when it appears (cf *Puer nobis*).

Elegy (1933, published 1949) was written in memory of Lynnwood Farnam, the great Canadian organist. It began as a largo for organ and orchestra, but this version was abandoned after fifty-three bars. *Elegy* is probably Willan's most Elgar-like organ piece, even to its performance direction of 'Nobilmente.'

The unfinished *Suite for Organ* of ca 1918 had ended the first of Willan's two major periods as an organ composer. In many ways it was the better period, both imaginative and daring. He was writing recital pieces,[1] there being hardly a church piece in the group. Between 1948 and 1967 he would write a good deal more music for the organ, but he would never surpass these early works and only rarely come close to them. Had Willan not written any music for the organ after 1918, his reputation would hardly have been less great.

---

1 Fifteen of Willan's some two dozen organ arrangements were published. Four had appeared ca 1907 and eleven appeared ca 1929 in six books of *Organ Gems* edited by Willan. Five were arrangements of Tschaikowsky, four of Mendelssohn ('Songs without Words'), and one of Handel (*Overture to Richard I*, which Willan played frequently). They are all well set out and no more difficult to play than they need to be.

16

Organ music
1948–1967

In the last three decades of his life Willan was a prolific composer for organ. He wrote about 100 chorale preludes and hymn preludes, a number of smaller pieces, and several works of recital proportions – including one in his eighty-fifth year. And over this vast array of organ music – most good, some inspired – stands *Passacaglia and Fugue No. 2* (1959), perhaps rivalling his *Prelude and Fugue in C Minor* (1908) and his *Introduction, Passacaglia and Fugue* (1916).

Epithalamium (1948) ushered in Willan's final period of composition for the organ. Willan composed it for the wedding of Joan, daughter of Mr and Mrs Roland Michener. He based it on the opening few notes of his motet *Rise up, My Love* (Example 248). No mere organ transcription, *Epithalamium* is a substantial organ piece in its own right. Of all Willan's organ works it is the most Delius-like, composed during his brief Delius period of the late 1940s (cf *Teneramente* for piano of 1946 and the carol *A Soft Light*, of 1948). Example 249 shows the Delius influence clearly.

In 1950 Willan began, in his seventieth year, the long series of nearly 100 chorale preludes that he would compose during the last seventeen years of his life. The beginning was auspicious, with *Six Chorale Preludes, Set I*, published by Concordia. It will not be possible to discuss each of Willan's many chorale preludes; however the pieces comprising the first Concordia set, having become very popular and widely used, deserve some comment.

All the preludes in *Set I* follow the same general structural plan, in which the individual phrases of the hymn-tunes are presented unornamented and separated by interludes. In two of the preludes, *Quem pastores* and *Vulpius*, the tune appears in the tenor part; in *Song 13* and *O Wie Selig*, the tune is given out in the top part. The prelude on *Bevan* combines procedures by treating the tune in canon between soprano and tenor, first at the octave and then at the fifth and sixth below.

In most cases the material of prelude and interlude sections of the pieces is related to the opening phrase (and sometimes additional phrases) of the hymn-tune. In the prelude on *Lasst uns alle fröhlich sein*, Willan follows Pachelbel's procedure of having a series of fugal expositions on subjects which are diminutions of the various phrases of the hymn-tune (cf Willan's chorale prelude of 1928 on *Andernach*), each exposition culminating in the phrase of the hymn-tune being given out in long notes (in this case in the pedals). In *Vulpius*, however, probably the most popular piece in the set, the accompanimental material is independent (though the first four notes in the pedals of the opening are indeed the opening ones of the hymn-tune). See Example 250.

The pieces in this set are all mainly diatonic and quite traditional in style, yet a simple beauty and expressiveness raise them above the run-of-the-mill.

Concordia asked Willan for a sequel, and *Six Chorale Preludes, Set II* (1951) was the result. The pieces are of uneven quality and musical interest. Two are first class, but the set as a whole does not equal the first set. The most expressive is *O Traurigkeit* (O Darkest Woe), where Willan manages to project a mood of sadness which is profoundly beautiful; the music, more chromatic than in any prelude from *Set I*, is in the idiom of Wagner and Brahms. The other first-rate piece is the big festive chorale prelude on *Nun Preiset Alle*. This is really a chorale fantasia; in structure it consists of a free development of motifs derived from the chorale, preceded by a seventeen-bar prelude which returns at the end as a postlude. This is brilliant and imaginative writing, and the music sweeps one along without flagging in momentum or interest.

The remaining four pieces do not sustain the same standard. *Mit Fried und Freud* and *Lobt Gott, ihr Christen* are academic and dull; *Christum Wir Sollen loben schon* tends to ramble (though interesting in design, Willan separating the lines of the chorale with interludes based on the plainsong from which the chorale was derived, *A solis ortus ordine*); *Vexilla regis* starts promisingly with some colourful chromatics and some flourishes for both manuals and pedals, but then settles down into a somewhat ponderous and academic style. Though not comparable to Willan's greater organ works, they are still suitable and useful as church voluntaries.

Another result of the success of *Six Chorale Preludes, Set I* was that Willan was approached to write a set for Oxford University Press, 'in opposition to Concordia' (Parker tapes). In response Willan composed his greatest set of hymn preludes, *Five Preludes on Plainsong Melodies* (1951). Willan's life-long love of plainsong inspired him here, and each prelude is a small masterpiece. The preludes were composed in 1950 and given their first performance by Charles Peaker (to whom they are dedicated) at St Paul's, Toronto, on 14 October 1950, as part of a special concert of Willan's music in honour of the composer's seventieth birthday.

Aeterna Christi munera is a vigorous festive piece in which, as in *Lasst uns Alle*, the various lines of the tune are preceded by fugal treatments of their openings. In addition the motif of the opening bars (Example 251) is used from time to time throughout the piece as an accompanying figure, particularly in the pedals.

In *Christe, redemptor omnium* and *Ecce jam noctis*, the phrases of the tunes are separated by interludes: in the former the interlude material is related to the plainsong hymn; in the latter it is independent. In both pieces the actual plainsong phrases are given out 'senza misura' (Example 252) and are not forced into the regular duple or triple metre of the piece as a whole. The coda of *Ecce jam noctis* (Example 253) is a marvellous example of the composer's magic with harmonic colour as he wends his way back from B major to finish in the home tonality of D major; the harmonic underlay can be reduced to five chords (Example 254).

Ave Maris stella is mystical in style. This is accomplished by the use of the Dorian mode and a 'shimmering' high ostinato figuration (Example 255).

Urbs beata Hierusalem is a brilliant processional. The tune is given out in long notes in the tenor, preceded by a prelude based on a figure (x) derived from the opening notes of the hymn-tune (Example 256). The x figure forms the basis of the accompanying material throughout the piece. *Urbs beata* is a thrilling piece for both performer and listener. It was one of the last great organ pieces Willan would compose.

Between 1952 and 1955 Willan composed a number of small organ pieces which are useful as church voluntaries but not of remarkable musical significance. Perhaps the most interesting is the second work in *Three*

Pieces for Organ (1954), titled *Ostinato*, which is based on a six-note melodic figure which repeats over and over in various voices. The piece is written in 5/4 metre, yet the ostinato lasts for six beats and therefore commences at a different place in the bar at each repetition.

In 1956 Willan wrote *Epithalame* (Sortie) for the wedding of Sir William McKie. Cast in the ceremonial march form Willan employed in his orchestral marches (see chapter 8), *Epithalame*, though well written, is not one of his more original efforts.

Later in 1956 Willan completed what really amounts to a small suite for organ, *Rondino, Elegy and Chaconne*. The chaconne was composed in the previous year, Willan having played it from manuscript in recital on 24 October 1955. The outer movements are in B flat major; the middle is in E flat major. These pieces were the composer's contribution to the Novello Organ Music Club, a venture designed by his former employer for the writing and distribution of new organ music. H. Fowle of Novello wrote: 'You have given us something for the average player, which is what we asked you to do ... Unfortunately some of our composers have found that simplicity defeats them ... so that we are very grateful for your work.'

The rondino, in spite of its three-refrain rondo structure, conveys an impression of rambling – perhaps because of the not very memorable nature of the refrain material. Structurally, however, there are two interesting features. The second refrain starts in E flat major rather than in the expected tonic key of B flat major, though it eventually works its way back to B flat major. The second episode starts in A major, moves to C sharp minor, and concludes in B major and minor, rather unusual tonalities for a rondo in B flat major – the final return to the B flat major refrain from these remote tonalities is accomplished with considerable mastery and smoothness (see Example 257).

The elegy was written in memory of the composer's friend at Novello, Harold Brooke. It is a ternary structure, the third section being an abridged and varied repetition of the first. The opening and closing sections have the typically lyric and flowing music in diatonic style Willan wrote so often and so well. The key, E flat major, is one he often used for such expressive musical utterances. The theme (Example 258) bears some similarity to one found in the composer's song of 1911, *Pro rege nostro* (Example 259); there may well have been some nostalgic association here. The middle section of the elegy provides a striking contrast to its diatonic neighbours by indulging in a colourful orgy of chromaticism.

The chaconne consists of twelve continuous variations around a four-bar ground bass (Example 260). Since the piece is not in triple time it is not really a chaconne; 'Variations on a Ground' would have been a more accurate title. The ground remains in the lowest part for ten of the twelve variations, being treated as a tenor part in variations IX and X. Variations VI, VII, and VIII employ the theme in inversion, while XII (in the nature of a coda) shows the ground in augmentation. An unpretentious and work-man-like piece, this chaconne lacks the rhythmic variety and excitement of the composer's two great organ passacaglias.

In 1956 *Ten Hymn Preludes, Set I* was published by C.F. Peters; two further sets were published in 1957 and 1958 respectively, making a total of thirty hymn preludes. Their musical idiom tends to be quite a bit more chromatic than that found in the two sets of Concordia preludes of 1950–51.

Ten Hymn Preludes, Set I exhibits considerable diversity of structure. Three preludes – *Song 22, Capetown,* and *St Columba* – are written in Willan's common scheme of presenting the various lines of the hymn-tune in the tenor part, separated by interludes and preceded by an introduction. In all three the introductory materials bear a slight resemblance to the opening notes of the hymn-tune, while the interludes tend to be free (though continuing in the same general style). The most attractive is *Capetown,* which is cast in the style of a sicilienne (Example 261). *St Columba* is also beautiful, its pentatonic unison opening phrase (Example 262) setting a suitably Scottish atmosphere which is maintained throughout the piece. *Song 22* is perhaps the most chromatic and has a certain kinship of harmonic style with Willan's earlier prelude, *O Traurigkeit.*

In another group of three preludes – *Hyfrydol, Melcombe,* and *Aberystwyth* – the lines of the tune, separated by interludes, are distributed through several voices. Perhaps the most appealing piece is *Melcombe,* in which the composer treats the tune in canon between soprano and tenor at various intervals. *Hyfrydol* makes a fine postlude and could stand comparison with Vaughan Williams's treatment of the same tune. *Aberystwyth* is a sombre little piece, but not without interest.

The prelude on *Richmond* has a less usual structure: introduction, lines 1 and 2 of the tune, interlude, lines 3 and 4 of the tune, and coda. In addition the notes of the tune are hidden within a florid soprano part, and it is unlikely the hearer would recognize that the prelude was based on *Richmond* at all. As a result the piece tends to go on in similar style from beginning to end without conveying any particular focus.

The prelude on Tallis's *St Flavian* is a full-blown chorale partita, consisting of an elaborate harmonization of the tune in chorale-style (even though it is not a German chorale), followed by five variations. The piece is a good exercise in the general style of Bach, but displays comparatively little of Willan's own musical personality; Bach could probably write Bach better!

Perhaps the least successful prelude is that on *Old 100th*. Here the writing is rather academic and ponderous, with a corresponding tendency toward dullness. The four lines of the tune, given out in chorale-like harmony, are each preceded by a free fugal exposition on a diminution of that particular line. Each section ends with a long fermata (pause), and the overall effect suffers from too much stopping and starting. The tune in augmentation in the pedals under the first exposition looks fine on paper, but does not really help to relieve the dullness.

The most ambitious prelude is that on the Easter hymn *O filii et filiae*. This is a free fantasia and a semi-virtuoso piece, containing some display passages for the pedals. It is dedicated to Francis Jackson. Though not as great a work as *Urbs beata Hierusalem*, it nevertheless exhibits some of the same dash and imaginative harmonic colour. It would certainly make the best recital piece of any in the set. Example 263 shows some of its harmonic colour.

The works in *Ten Hymn Preludes, Set II* (1957) display a diversity of structure. Three – *Wareham*, *Martydom*, and *St Philip* – again follow Willan's common scheme of presenting the lines of the hymn-tune in the tenor, separated by interludes and preceded by an introduction; all are serviceable, but not exceptional. The preludes on *Tallis' Ordinal* and *Old 124th* present the lines of their hymn-tunes in the bass (pedal) part, with three-part free counterpoint above; the style is somewhat academic. *This Endris Nyght* and *Old 104th* (along with *O filii et filiae*) are unique in Willan's hymn and chorale prelude output in that they treat their tunes twice in the course of a single piece. Both are quite attractive. The prelude on *Bristol* is also cast in a structure unique for Willan: most of the prelude is a free fantasia connected to the tune so loosely that the connection is not apparent to the listener; the tune itself does not appear until the end as a sort of coda to the free fantasia.

The finest pieces are those on *Ebenezer* and *Deo gratias*. The form of the *Ebenezer* prelude is, again, somewhat unusual for Willan, being basically a fugue on a subject freely derived from the first line of the hymn-tune. The fugue proceeds normally except that, in place of the expected reappearance of the fugue-subject in the tonic key at the end, Willan presents the whole of the *Ebenezer* hymn-tune. The tune is given out one line at a time with rich accompanying harmonies, separated with rather Brahms-ian interludes (see Example 264). The *Deo gratias* prelude is probably the best of the set. In it Willan rekindles some of the old fire that was evident in *Aeterna Christi munera* and *Urbs beata Hierusalem*. In structure it is similar to *Aeterna Christi*, with the lines of the tune given out in full harmony over a moving bass, separated by interludes. In style it is akin to *Urbs beata* with its colourful and effective mixture of modalism and chromaticism. Example 265 shows a typical passage.

Ten *Hymn Preludes, Set III* (1958) contains several excellent treatments. The most striking is probably that on *Windsor*. Here one finds combined some of the poignant chromaticism of *O Traurigkeit* and some of the mystical beauty of *Ecce jam noctis*. A mystical chord progression (Example 266), or some form of it, is found in the introduction and all the interludes, acting as a unifying element. Example 267 shows some of the colourful rhapsodic writing found in this piece. The prelude on *Newbury* is very expressive. This lovely piece shows Willan at his most romantic and lyric (See Example 268), and its introduction and interludes exhibit some kinship with Delius and with Willan's own *Piano Concerto*. *Tunbridge* is another beautiful prelude.

The other pieces are less successful; some start well but become less interesting as they proceed. The setting of *Iste confessor*, though conservative, does catch one's attention and makes a fine postlude. The weakest prelude is that on *St Venantius*: cast in the form of a trio, the upper part so disguises the notes of the tune as to render it unrecognizable. Furthermore, the disguise is not sufficiently memorable as music to be of much interest.

In all, there is much that is worthwhile in *Ten Hymn Preludes*, sets I, II, and III. Charles Peaker wrote: 'These 30 preludes ... are very welcome, since they deal with tunes we know rather than German chorales which, alas, have for the most part been forgotten in our churches today' (*CMJ* 4, winter 1960, 63). Some are of sufficient musical interest to allow them to take a place on recital programs.

Postlude in E Minor (1957) is a fine piece, composed in the form of a pre-lude-fugue-postlude (a repeat of the prelude) in one continuous move-ment. In it Willan uses many of his old and proven tricks. The opening bar of the initial three-bar phrase (Example 269) – which forms the main thematic substance from which the prelude section is developed – is a harmonic progression which was conspicuous in the introduction of

Introduction, Passacaglia and Fugue. The flourishes, duplets-mixed-with-triplets-mixed-with-dotted-rhythms, left-hand counter-melodies in octaves, and other familiar signposts are all here. The fugal middle section has several points of interest, not the least of which is the somewhat unconventional answer the composer provides for his modulating subject (see Example 270: subject and answer, respectively). Someone more conventional would probably have used the answer in Example 271 in order to avoid answering the leap of a minor sixth with a tri-tone.

Postlude in D Major (1957) is a much slighter work than the E minor postlude. It is written in free ternary form. The composer himself remarked upon a certain resemblance between this piece and a minuet by Boëllman. It is a tuneful trifle.

A number of people have written favourably of *A Fugal Trilogy* (1958), but I consider the work rather run-of-the-mill and unimaginative. It consists of *Chorale and Fugue, Aria and Fugue*, and *Elegy and Fugue*. The three fugues are all rather academic in style, lacking the sweep of the great organ fugues of Willan's early period. They do, however, display Willan's unerring craftsmanship and show that, like Bach or Handel, he could toss off a fugue at the proverbial drop of a hat. The fugue subjects are based on the motifs of their respective introductory movements. Of the introductory movements, *Chorale* shows a good grasp of Bach's style but contains little of Willan; *Aria* has the quiet beauty of many such Willan movements (often, like this one, in D major); and *Elegy* is of little musical interest melodically and rhythmically, despite its 5/4 metre and some modal-chromatic harmony.

Five Pieces for Organ (1958) is also of limited interest. The short *Fanfare* has some arresting moments, but employs the same formulas which the composer had used for his coronation works of 1937 and 1953. *Prelude and Fughetta* and *Intermezzo* are easy pieces which make good church voluntaries. *Scherzo* displays a certain impishness in its opening (Example 272); its contrasting 'trio' section (Example 273) merely gives us some more of Willan's usual lyrical middle-section writing. There is nothing wrong with this music, but Willan has taken us there so many times before.

The most spectacular piece is *Finale Jubilante*. With ternary structure, it has vigorous opening and closing sections in A major, between which a somewhat pensive and severe episode, starting in F sharp minor and moving to C sharp minor, is placed (we are spared another 'lyrical trio'). The title is probably taken from a piece, by Willan's friend John E. West (1863–1928), which Willan used frequently as a 'chaser' for his organ recitals. Charles Peaker observed that *Finale Jubilante* would make a good 'pontifical postlude' (*CMJ* 4, winter 1960, 62). Yet the piece shows the composer repeating himself not only in style but now also in substance, as a comparison of some of its opening bars (Example 274) with those of *Epithalame* (1956; Example 275) will illustrate.

In 1959 Willan composed the greatest of his later works for organ, *Passacaglia and Fugue No. 2 in E Minor*. That a composer close to eighty years of age could have produced such a powerful work is remarkable. He was encouraged to do so by Walter Hinrichsen of C.F. Peters. Hinrichsen was concerned about Willan's spending so much of his time writing short hymn preludes and encouraged him to write a biggish work for a change.

Unlike *Introduction, Passacaglia and Fugue*, *Passacaglia and Fugue No. 2* has no lengthy introduction. It has only seven introductory bars which consist of a rhapsodic treatment of the first half of the passacaglia theme. The opening bars are almost identical with the beginning of Willan's motet of 1937, *Who Is She That Ascendeth*. The work does contain one device which had remained a favourite one: the use of a succession of a half-dozen chords, mostly minor and of a striking chromatic relationship to one another, as a musical motif (Example 276); the chord progression returns at the end of the piece in the coda of the fugue.

The passacaglia itself is smaller than its predecessor, having only twelve variations as compared with eighteen. The passacaglia theme is shown in Example 277. The opening phrase is identical to that of the theme of Reger's *Passacaglia in D Minor* (Example 278). A comparison of Willan's passacaglia themes of 1916 and 1959 reveals some similarities, particularly in the use of the raised fourth of the scale in the middle and towards the end of the theme, and also in the use of a syncopated semitone rise ♩♩♩ at the end. The 1959 theme is perhaps a little less interesting rhythmically, not having the dotted patterns ♩♪|♩ which add rhythmic interest to the 1916 theme. There is less differentiation and contrast between the variations in the second passacaglia than in the first. The 1916 is colourful, imaginative, and highly emotional; the 1959 is more serene and contemplative, youthful exuberance being replaced by the mellowness of old age.

Variations I to X of Passacaglia No. 2 form really a single, continuous unit, being a rhythmic crescendo beginning with eighth-note motion, moving into triplet eighths, and eventually settling into sixteenth-note movement. The rhythmic crescendo is, of course, a procedure found in most passacaglias. Variation I commences in a very similar manner to that of Rheinberger's great passacaglia in the same key (from *Sonata No. 8*); indeed the first half-dozen variations proceed in a quite Rheinbergerian manner.

Variations I to VII consist of flowing counterpoint in a three- and four-part texture. In IV the passacaglia theme is presented in canon-at-the-octave between the upper and lower voices at one bar's distance (cf Willan's first passacaglia, where the ground bass is shown in canon-at-the-sixth). In V the theme is put in the tenor part and treated like a faux-bourdon. The theme returns to the pedal (bass) part at VI, where it remains (except for one excursion to the treble at IX). His ground bass theme always appears in its original form and is never subject to decoration or variation (unlike Passacaglia No. 1).

Variations VIII to X are of a more figural nature, again reflecting the influence of Reger's *Passacaglia in D Minor*. X is extended by an episode which continues to build to the major climax of this passacaglia – the same procedure used at the end of variation XVII of the 1916 passacaglia.

Variations XI and XII, in E minor and E major respectively, form a small group on their own, a sort of quiet interlude between the climax of the work after variation X and the start of the fugue (cf the effect of the 'quasi-chorale' final variation in the earlier passacaglia, even to the change to the major mode!).

The fugue is a complex piece of writing. Its procedure is almost identical with that Willan used for his *Prelude and Fugue in C Minor* of 1908; both are double fugues with two expositions. In the first exposition of the 1959 fugue, subject I (a modulating subject derived from the passacaglia theme) is given out in all four voices in normal fashion; following an episode, there is an additional lead in the bass. A second episode leads to the second exposition. Here subject II, a florid affair reminiscent of the second subject of the 1908 fugue but not as good, is presented in a three-voice exposition without pedal (again as in the earlier fugue). The answer (in B minor) is given first, followed by the subject (in E minor) and then the answer again (in B minor) – the reverse of the usual procedure. This second exposition also uses a counter-subject, of which more later. The third entry in the second exposition is incomplete and leads directly into the third episode and the middle section of the fugue. Here, starting in F sharp minor, various combinations of themes take place: answer I with subject II, answer II with counter-subject, and subject I with countersuject. All through this section the climax has been building and, after a long dominant pedal, it finally arrives with the return of the home tonality of E minor and subject I, subject II, and the counter-subject all gloriously combined in triple counterpoint. This is followed by incomplete two- and three-part stretti (using massive harmony), and the fugue concludes with a reference to the chord progression heard in the introduction. The combination of the three subjects is shown in Example 279. This fugue does not quite scale the heights of its 1908 model, but it comes astonishingly close to doing so.

Willan wrote to Paul Murray, on 13 February 1962: 'I think No. 1 is more interesting and varied, but I think the fugue in No. 2 is a better piece of workmanship.' Though *Passacaglia and Fugue No. 2* is not very original (being written in conservative style and indebted to Willan's earlier works – as well as those of Rheinberger and Reger) it is unquestionably a good and successful 'piece of workmanship.'

In 1960 Willan's *36 Short Preludes on Well-Known Hymns* for organ appeared (in three books of twelve preludes each). Willan had already written nearly sixty pieces in this form and now, in his eightieth year, thirty-six further examples appeared! These preludes maintain a high level of craftsmanship and interest throughout.

All the pieces are comparatively short and easy; an experienced organist could read them at sight and play them without practice. It is not easy to write simple music which is worthwhile. The composer observed: 'I have evolved and used the following scheme: a short introduction, a reharmonization or a resetting of the tune, followed by an improvisation in conclusion. Such a pattern could also be useful for teaching purposes.' Achieving variety while using the same general form thirty-six times is remarkable. As models for improvisation of composition in traditional idioms these pieces serve very well. Those who heard Willan improvise after service at St Mary Magdalene's will recognize the same deft hand in the improvisations of these preludes and postludes.

A few of special interest might be mentioned. In book I *Darwell* is a postlude with an effectiveness far exceeding its difficulty. In book II the prelude on *Bangor* is particularly expressive, while that on *Irish* sets an Irish atmosphere by certain turns of melody and harmony, particularly in the introduction and in the coda. In book III the level seems to drop off somewhat, though this may be at least partly due to the poor quality of some of the tunes Willan had to set. (Gladys Willan wrote to a friend: 'Healey has been working very hard on some hymn tunes ... sent him to turn into choral preludes, 36 in all; the hardest part has been that he doesn't like most of the tunes! But it will mean a substantial cheque for advance royalties on receipt of the Mss.') For the setting of *All Saints New*, the composer seems unable to transcend the banality of the tune; likewise his setting of *Eventide* comes in a poor second to Parry's. Fine tunes such as *Bedford* and *Southwell* inspire him to better efforts.

Willan wrote one more work of recital proportions, *Andante, Fugue and Chorale*, published in 1965. As in Franck's *Prelude, Fugue and Variation*, the three pieces run together as one continuous work. All sections make use of the same motif (Example 280). Found at the beginning of the andante, as the first four notes of the subject of the fugue, and in the interludes in the chorale, it acts as a unifying agent. The andante is rather beautiful, invoking a mystical atmosphere and occasionally recalling the slow movement of *Symphony No. 2*. The fugue is somewhat dull, a good specimen of an 'examination fugue.' The chorale is rather novel (though models occur in one or two of Bach's chorale preludes): the lines of the chorale, presented in block harmony, are separated by rhapsodic recitative-like passages. In his eighty-fifth year, the composer tried a structure he had never before used! Though the model may be Bach, the semi-modal musical style with arabesques is reminiscent of Vaughan Williams (eg *The Lark Ascending*). *Andante, Fugue and Chorale* is of uneven interest.

Willan's last organ piece, and the last musical work he prepared for publication, was a prelude on the hymn-tune *Slane*, reflecting the words 'At the close of the day.' Its appearance in 1967, just months before the composer's death, seems particularly appropriate; one is reminded of Bach, blind and dying, dictating his last chorale prelude, *Before Thy Throne I Stand*. Both pieces exhibit a similar mood of serenity.

17

Piano music

Willan studied piano at St Saviour's School and pursued advanced studies ca 1900 with Evlyn Howard-Jones. At the age of twenty he had ambitions to be a concert pianist, particularly for the music of Brahms. An arm injury in childhood eventually limited his progress as a pianist; nevertheless he remained a fine and sensitive player throughout his life. He held the instrument in high regard, but wrote comparatively little for it, and that chiefly for young pianists. At least some of Willan's children's pieces can stand on the same level as their counterparts written by, say, Kabalevsky. There is only one completed major work: *Variations and Epilogue* for two pianos (written 1913–15).

Four Holiday Pieces for Children were composed in 1908. These are charming and well written, being cut from the same cloth as the six short pieces for organ which he wrote about the same time. In numbers 1 and 3 Willan skilfuly avoids a too 'four-square' effect by the use of seven- and five-bar phrases. Numbers 1, 2, and 3 were published, with minor modifications, in 1909 as *Three Easy Pieces* (*HWC* incorrectly lists these as additional pieces).

Valse in A Major for piano duet was composed in August 1911 or 1912. Musically this valse is more for adults than for children and is not easy to play. Though the thematic material employed might suggest light salon music, it is written on a somewhat higher plane. Here one has no mere 'tune plus oom-pah,' but instead a well put together piece with a good deal of running counterpoint and even some thematic development. It is salon music of a very sophisticated type, somewhat in the manner of the valse from Rachmaninoff's *Suite No. 2* for two pianos (1901). The structure is a free ternary one.

The waltz-accompaniment pattern used under the main theme suggests the dual tonality of A major and C sharp minor (Example 281). The main theme of part 1 exhibits a certain Lydian-mode atmosphere (Example 282). The other big waltz theme occurs in part 2 (Example 283). With a duration of six and a half minutes, *Valse* is a substantial piece of writing; that it has remained unknown and unpublished is to be regretted.

Variations and Epilogue on an Original Theme for two pianos was written between 1913 and 1915. *Passacaglia in E Flat Minor* for organ was completed in 1916. One can observe similarities in figuration between some of the variations in both works. Whereas the organ variations have been frequently played, the variations for two pianos have been rarely performed and remain unpublished. Willan said: 'I always wish I could get it published ... I think it's really a good work' (Parker tapes). Among the models for *Variations and Epilogue* must loom the variations by Brahms on themes by Handel, Paganini, and Haydn. A number of variations use Brahms-like figurations. As with some of Brahms's piano music, so here one sometimes feels the music is more difficult to play than it needs to be. Perhaps this is one of the reasons that *Variations and Epilogue* has not been performed more frequently.

The thirteen variations contrast well with one another, are grouped logically for climax as well as contrast, and show considerable imagination and originality. There are several 'characteristic' variations in which the theme is turned into a chorale, a nocturne, and a polonaise.

The theme (Example 284) is sixteen bars long, in style rather like a modal folk tune. The unexpected harmonies in bars 8 and 9 might at first appear to be stylistically inconsistent with what had gone before; such was my own initial impression. Longer acquaintance with the music has now convinced me that Willan has, by what happens in these bars, neatly avoided the four-square and strengthened the overall shape of his tune.

Variation I is written in relatively simple style, all in the treble register. The unison theme in piano II is set against three-voice quaver motion in piano I. In variation II the theme appears in piano I, harmonized in three-part semi-imitative counterpoint. Piano II takes over the continuous quavers of piano I from the previous variation, but only in two voices and using the lower register. Variation III (Example 285) is written in a more complex style, the connection with the theme being much less apparent. Variation IV is a free treatment of the tune, allegro molto, extending over thirty-seven bars. There is a continuous tonic pedal in the bass. In variation V the theme is in the tenor register, against Brahms-like double thirds (Example 286). Variations I to V form a group of increasing complexity and speed.

Variation VI is in A major! In 'quasi-chorale' style, the tune remains at the original pitch (ie starting on the note E), but is harmonized as being in A major (see Example 287). Variation VII is back in E minor, with a change to 9/8 metre. It consists of continuous quaver motion in octaves, ingeniously split up between the two keyboards. Variation VIII has a change of mode to E major, and the theme is treated in the style of a nocturne. There is some very strange notation for piano I, producing on paper too many beats per bar (see Example 288). Variation IX goes back to the E minor tonality and 9/8 metre of variation VII. The harmony is quite chromatic in the figurations in the piano I part, against which piano II moves in continuous octave quavers. Variation X returns to the major mode of variation VIII. The tune is in the bass, while the cross-phrases in the upper part produce a hemiola-like effect (Example 289). Variation XI is a free fantasia in E major, developing fragments derived from the theme. Variation XII moves to C major, with a combination of 3/4 and 9/8 metres. An ornamented version of the theme in the tenor register (see Example 290) is left at its original pitch (ie starting on the note E) but harmonized in C major (cf variation VI). Variation XIII returns to E minor, and the tune is turned into a polonaise.

The epilogue is a free fantasia of about 100 bars in E minor and E major. It consists of a free development of motifs derived from the theme (cf Beethoven's *32 Variations in C Minor*). This section contains also quite a bit of bravura passage-work for the pianists. In 1943 Willan composed a four-voice fugue of 116 bars to be inserted into the middle of the epilogue, making the total length of this final movement well over 200 bars; the fugue subject (Example 291) is based on the first three bars of the original theme. The fugue exposition is strict, but the part-writing becomes freer in the middle section and includes some homophonic passages (cf Beethoven, Franck, Brahms). The exposition is written in quadruple invertible counterpoint, though unintentionally. The composer later said (Parker tapes): 'It's really quite a contrapuntal feat, but ... in this case it was an absolute fluke.' The middle section contains leads of the subject in A minor and C major. The fugue is not self-contained, however, but is designed to lead directly into the second half of the original epilogue following its return to E minor in its final section.

There appears to be an 'extra' variation written on a separate sheet of paper. It is not part of the regular score; in it a somewhat altered outline of the tune is harmonized in an exceedingly chromatic manner. Maybe Willan decided it was too extreme to use in this context.

Willan's next original writing for piano probably occurred in *Course of Graded Studies for the Pianoforte*, which he edited and arranged and which was published in 1924. There are quite a number of anonymous short, easy studies in the first four books, some or all of which may have been written by Willan himself. A more substantial piece, the three-page étude on arpeggiando chords in book 5, is acknowledged by Willan as his own.

In 1927 Willan's *Intermezzo* for piano was published under the pseudonym of Raymond Clare. The reason for the nom de plume becomes quite obvious upon looking at the music, for it is frankly 'cocktail piano' of the twenties! (Willan used the same pseudonym in 1924 for the publication of a song, *O Love of Mine*.)

All Willan's original piano music during the 1930s was designed for young piano students. In 1930 *Three Character Sketches of Old London* was published. It contains pieces of moderate difficulty for the intermediate grade student and continues the general style of the *Four Holiday Pieces* (1908). In the first sketch, *The Policeman*, one can see the composer trying to avoid the four-square by using – as he did in 1908 – five-bar phrases. An examination of the phrase structure of the third sketch, *The Whistling Errand Boy*, again shows the composer attempting to avoid the commonplace, as the number of bars in each phrase shows: 5 + 5 + (4 + 3) + (3 + 2) + (3 + 2) + 3 + 5 + 6. The virtual absence of four- and eight-bar units is noticeable. In structure the first sketch resembles a small, three-refrain monothematic rondo; the second and third sketches have a ternary basis. *Three Character Sketches* contains tuneful and engaging pieces; the waltz-like second sketch, *Flower Girl*, is particularly attractive, even though it comes closer to 'salon music' than its companions.

Four unpublished miniatures, titled simply *For Jamie*, *For Mary*, *For Micky*, and *For Madge*, make an attractive set of easy pieces which are fun to play and by no means trivial. They appear to have been written at different periods, presumably for some of Willan's students. *For Micky* is dated 1934 and *For Madge* would seem to belong to the same period. The other two, by musical style and manuscript appearance, would seem to date from ca 1900–10.

The remaining Willan piano music for students consists of two pieces for the Grade III Toronto conservatory examination books, *Alla Marcia* and *Tempo di Menuetto,* and a collection of short pieces, for the composer's first grandson, entitled *Peter's Book* (published 1936). *Alla Marcia* and *Tempo di Menuetto* are in the style of Bach's *Anna Magdalena Book.* The seven pieces in *Peter's Book* are in a more modern idiom, though they are all in C major and intended for beginners. The two most original, *Peter's Donkey Jenny* and *Peter Enjoys a Swing,* have had a fairly wide currency in the Toronto conservatory piano grade books.

Willan's last solo piano piece of any importance was written in 1946. Its original title has been erased from the manuscript, and the composer's signature is nowhere to be seen. The only title remaining is the performance direction, *Teneramente.* This expressive little piece in E major has two main sections. The first is a sicilienne very much in the style of Delius (Example 292); the only other piece of music I know which succeeds in imitating Delius's style to such perfection is Percy Whitlock's *Carol* for organ, written in homage to Delius – Willan had owned a copy since 1936. The second main section is composed in a more usual Willan style.

In 1948 Willan wrote another of his musical jokes, a variation-fantasia for two pianos on the French-Canadian tune *Alouette,* for the fourteenth annual spring revue of the Arts and Letters Club. The *Alouette* tune is given several treatments, including being made into a funeral march and then being presented in the style of a passage from Chopin's *Scherzo in C Sharp Minor.* Willan introduces fragments of other pieces: *Rule Britannia, There's No Place like Home, Comin' through the Rye, The Campbells Are Coming,* and the openings of Tschaikowsky's *Piano Concerto No. 1* and Schumann's *Piano Concerto in A Minor.* Thematic combinations also take place, eg Schumann with *There's No Place like Home* and even *Rule Britannia* with *Alouette!*

18

Solo songs

Willan was prolific in song-writing. He wrote or arranged more than 200 secular songs, of which about 110 are original works and 70 are settings of traditional songs. (To this could be added the songs – original or arranged – in his ballad operas and incidental scores.) Unfortunately this area of Willan's work is comparatively little known or appreciated. It was a source of some disappointment to the composer in his later years that his many art-songs for voice and piano had not made a greater mark; only about 30 of the 110 original songs were ever published. A small number of singers had championed them (eg George Lambert, distinguished voice teacher at the Toronto conservatory), but the circulation was not wide and most of the published songs eventually went out of print. Of the original songs for voice and piano, 14 are lost. The manuscripts of a number were probably given to friends and then disappeared.

Two-thirds (seventy-six) of the art-songs were written before Willan moved to Canada, with fifty-three of these between 1899 and 1905. Song-writing was Willan's first major preoccupation as a young composer. Later high points were the two collections *Healey Willan Song Album No. 1* (1925) and *No. 2* (1926) and the beautiful love songs of 1941. In the late 1920s he concentrated on arranging, producing most of his seventy settings,[1] as well as his ballad operas.

The years 1899 to 1901 produced fourteen songs, of which five have been lost. Of the remaining nine, three were composed in January 1899 and show a high level of accomplishment. These songs, *Sonnet, Farewell,* and

1 For four songs set to sacred texts, see chapter 22.

Serenade (all with words by Thomas Hood), are quite English in character, following in the song-writing tradition of Parry and Stanford: there is little sign of Willan's later complex Wagnerian chromaticism and the harmony is relatively diatonic.

Sonnet starts out quite innocently (Example 293), almost in the style of Thomas Arne. Some rather spectacular key shifts (notably to B flat major and D flat major) in the middle of the song add a more modern touch. Already one can observe the smoothly flowing, highly vocal melodic lines characteristic of all the composer's music for voices. His gifts for pleasing melody and for the sensitive setting of a text are also in evidence. *Farewell* is more adventurous in its use of sudden shifts in tonality; see Example 294. *Serenade* is rich in accompaniment figuration. This imagination in the invention and use of accompaniment motifs would be another feature of Willan's original songs and his arrangements. In this case the figures are taken from the piano's introductory bars (Example 295). The mastery of the medium these songs show is remarkable – particularly for an eighteen-year-old. They are interesting and pleasing for both performer and audience and mark out a style for song-writing which Willan would not alter much during the next half-century.

In January 1900, Willan composed a little song called *Rondel*. This is the best of the surviving songs of that year and has the same innocent charm as *Sonnet*. It is an early example of the type of semi-strophic form that Willan would use quite often, with the music for each verse commencing in the same way but then breaking off into something new as the verse proceeds. On 12 October 1900 Willan wrote himself a twentieth-birthday present, *Birthday Song*, with words by Tennyson. It is one of his more maudlin efforts! Three days later he set another Tennyson text, *Tears, Idle Tears*, again with somewhat less than satisfactory results.

To Daffodils and *To Electra* (both 1901) are to words by Robert Herrick and both are good. In *To Daffodils* Willan uses the inversion of his semi-stophic plan (see *Rondel*), for here he makes the final phrases of music for each verse correspond, while the music for the beginning and middle parts of the verses is different. *To Electra* (only sixteen bars long) was the composer's first song to be published. Willan wrote it for his pupil Miss Lillian Toulmin (possibly others of these early songs had a similar genesis). The opening (Example 296) suggests an almost 'salon' style.

Three 1902 songs were published: *To Blossoms*, *Dedication*, and *Absence*. *To Blossoms*, with words again by Herrick, is completely through-composed (save for a short two-bar melodic phrase in the middle of verse 1 which turns up again in verse 3) and is Willan's first surviving successful attempt at that type of song-structure. Musical unity is achieved through the fairly consistent use of accompaniment figures derived from the introduction (see Example 297). The highly chromatic ending in A minor to accompany the final words, 'glide into the grave,' is particularly effective. *Dedication* and *Absence* are among the first of Willan's settings of the poems of Owen Meredith (pseudonym for the Earl of Lytton), whose work Willan admired during the first decade of the century. They are both good songs, though the harmonies may be a bit 'sweet' for some tastes. *Absence* has an interesting structure; through-composed, it derives its musical unity not from the frequent use of an independent accompaniment figure but rather from a melodic leitmotif taken from the opening two bars of the vocal part (Example 298). This melodic motif is then used periodically in the piano part, but never again in the vocal part!

Several unpublished songs from 1902 are of interest. *The Night Has a Thousand Eyes* is the only original song for voice and piano by Willan to have an instrumental obligato part – in this case for a cello. *To The Genius of Eternal Slumber* sets the text as a recitative accompanied for the most part by sustained, low-register chords of a highly chromatic nature. *Love and a Day*, to another Meredith text, is an attractive little song, even if the piano owes a little to Dvořák's *Songs My Mother Taught Me*.

Willan wrote ten songs in 1903. Only one, Shakespeare's *O Mistress Mine*, was published. It is one of Willan's most tuneful songs; its strophic structure and change of musical style part-way through each verse fit Shakespeare's words very well. Willan composed a song to Heine's *E'en as a Lovely Flower* (*Du bist, wie eine Blume*). The short song *Under the Hill* is an exquisite little gem, again in strophic form. As in previous cases where Willan has treated his texts strophically (ie the same melody for each verse) he here varies the accompaniment for the second of the two verses.

The Tourney (1904) was a setting of Tennyson. For the three verses Willan uses a modified strophic plan. The first verse is set to a tune of a somewhat modal type, as if to mirror the atmosphere of a narrative song sung by a minstrel (Example 299). For the second verse Willan starts out as before, but he changes the tune as he goes on in order to follow more clearly the meaning of the text (at that point a description of the actual tournament). The final verse is Edith's, in which she crowns Sir Ralph the victor. For this the music changes to the major mode and a new theme (Example 300); note that the accompaniment is made up of quasi-horn-calls to create the mood of chivalry, knighthood, and so on. Willan uses the same four-bar phrase of music for the end of each verse as a sort of musical refrain. The absence of sentimentality in words and music helps to make *The Tourney* one of Willan's most impressive songs of this period.

Summer Night (1904) is perhaps the finest of Willan's Meredith songs. It has a full and constantly varied piano part – one of the more interesting piano accompaniments to play. It tends to avoid the super-tonic sevenths and dominant thirteenths which make some of the other Willan songs of this period sound rather popularly oriented.

Two 1904 settings of Heine, the semi-strophic *Dimly Sinks the Summer Evening* and the through-composed *Night Lies on the Silent Highways*, are very beautiful and, appropriately, show some influence of German Lieder and very little influence of the English drawing-room.

Willan composed also in 1904 three outstanding but unpublished settings of Robert Herrick under the general title *To Music*. This work is a small song cycle and was so named by the composer. In the first song, also called *To Music*, and in the second, *To Music – To Becalm His Fever*, the harmony has become noticeably more chromatic than in Willan's earlier songs. The harmony in the third song, *To Music – To Becalm a Sweet Sick Youth*, reverts to a more diatonic type. All three are basically through-composed. In the latter part of the third song Willan creates a cyclic element musically by bringing back variants of some of the motifs from the first song. This short song cycle represents the high point in Willan's song-writing to that date.

In 1905 Willan composed eight songs. Only one, *At Dawn*, was published. The new Meredith pieces, *Two Songs from 'Marah,'* are of little importance – the second is not even completed. Two songs to Heine poems, *Where E'er My Bitter Teardrops Fall* and *Soft and Gently through My Soul*, are beautiful in their artless simplicity. *A Violet* is one of the composer's lighter songs and one of the few intended to be sung at more than a slow or moderate tempo (the direction here is allegretto). There are some remarkable sudden shifts of key in the latter part of the song (E flat major, B flat major, E major, E flat major, A major, B flat major, and E flat major) which are all the more remarkable because of the light and effortless way they are handled.

Up to this time Willan had written fifty-three original songs, about half of his life's output in this area. Thereafter he would on occasion write a song or group of songs, but never again would there be the concentrated production of 1899 to 1905. The first significant period in

Willan's compositional career was largely one of song-writing; in this medium he first achieved musical maturity and excellence.

Willan's compositional interests and abilities were broadening and along with a decline in song-writing came the composition in 1906 and 1907 of his first important organ and chamber works and works intended for or with orchestra (eg *Cleopatra*).

The years 1906 and 1907 produced only four songs. One was published: *O Death! Thou Art the Cooling Night*, the last of the six songs Willan wrote on texts by Heine. It is a good song, with a mild Wagner-Strauss influence. The most interesting of the unpublished songs, *One of These Days, My Lady Whispereth* (author unknown), commences in a fairly simple and leisurely manner, but increases in speed and complexity as it proceeds, finally arriving at a dramatic climax (Example 301) which is uncommon in Willan's songs and seems to cry out for orchestral rather than piano accompaniment. Towards the end of the song (Example 302) there is a startling use of a whole-tone scale, as if to obliterate tonality as death obliterates life.

Love's Springtime (1908 or 1909) is a good song, written in semi-strophic style (similar music for verses 1 and 2, different music for verses 3 and 4).

Also in this period Willan wrote and later grouped together *Three Songs* by Margaret E. Arkoll. All three are chromatic; the cross-fertilization of Willan's 'English' style of song-writing with Wagnerian harmony now seems comfortably accomplished. The new elements are handled smoothly and with assurance. *Red Rose of Love* is the most concentrated and compact of *Three Songs*, containing a wide range of expression within its two dozen bars. *Rest* is a gentle lullaby which nevertheless manages to pass through a number of diverse tonalities within nineteen bars. The passage in Example 303 is typical. Its main accompanimental motif (overlapping phrases of descending sixths) is taken from 'Great Silence Is O'er Everything,' the fourth movement of *Cleopatra*. In both instances Willan associates this motif with quietness and repose. *To You* is through-composed like the others. The cadence at the conclusion of the voice part (Example 304) is unusual. *Three Songs* can be an effective concert group.

Of six undated songs tentatively ascribed to 1908–9, three have incomplete accompaniments. Of the others, *Sunset in the Desert* shows a very clear influence of Delius (Example 305) for the first time in Willan's songs; *Mine and Mine Only* is one of the composer's comparatively few dramatic songs; and *Love Me Not, Dearest* is very beautiful, through-composed, but maintaining the style of the opening throughout (there is a counter-melody to the voice part always present in either the bass or tenor registers of the accompaniment; see Example 306).

Cavalier Song (published 1910) is one of Willan's few in allegro tempo and is longish, with three verses and refrain. The three verses are set to different music, but the refrains are set to the same music. *Cavalier Song* follows in the tradition of Stanford's *Cavalier Songs* (1880) and *Songs of the Sea* (1904).

Pro rege nostro (written 1911) seems to require more than solo voice with piano to achieve its fullest effect. In 1914 Willan expanded the song into a work for chorus and orchestra, *England, My England* (see chapter 10).

Willan composed six songs – all first class – between May and September 1912. *Eve* and *Dreams* show him comfortably settled in his highly chromatic idiom and using it with naturalness and imagination to evoke impressions and moods. *Wind at Midnight* is his most vigorous song to date; it rushes head-long from beginning to end and is quite exciting. As in many of Willan's songs, the mood is established in the opening bars of the piano part with a figure (Example 307) which will appear frequently in the accompaniment. This song is almost symphonic in style and, though the piano part – while not easy – is quite playable, one feels that an orchestra would be more appropriate for this colourful and dramatic music. The three short verses of *Requiem* show how Willan, in his strophic songs, modifies the tune to suit different word accentuations and moods. The three versions of the melody are given in Example 308; as in this instance, the piano accompaniment is usually varied from verse to verse as well. In *Dawn* the 'impressionistic' tendencies exhibited in *Eve* and *Dreams* are taken much further. The influence of French impressionism is clearly seen in the opening bars of the song (Example 309). The piano part seems to cry for orchestral colour here! For a song ostensibly in B minor the ending of *Dawn* (Example 310) is highly unusual.

In the summer of 1913 Willan went to Canada to live, leaving behind, except for two brief lapses, the English drawing-room style. On 13 December 1913 he completed his first song in Canada, *Shamrocks* (on a poem by Rosa Mulholland). It was published separately and in *Healey Willan Song Album No. 2* (1926). (The manuscripts for many of the twelve songs in the two song albums have been lost, and their dates of composition are not known.) *Shamrocks* is one of Willan's most beautiful and popular songs. It is an early example of his interest in Irish poetry and literature. It is a modified-strophic structure, the vocal part being supported by an ostinato-like accompaniment figure which adapts itself easily to frequent changes in metre from 5/4 to 4/4 to 3/4 (Example 311).

The dramatic sweep and quasi-symphonic style of Willan's 1914 *Prospice* (to Browning's text) had some antecedents, eg *Wind at Midnight* (1912), but *Prospice* has a drive and a force of passion which takes it beyond the earlier pieces. Willan had already set this poem for choir and orchestra (see chapter 10). The choral-orchestral and solo settings bear little resemblance to one another except that both are in F and the song uses one theme from the earlier choral setting, though in 9/8 instead of 3/4 metre (Example 312). In *Prospice* we see a dramatic abandon; in *The Wind on the Wold* (1914) there is an abandon of exultation and the sheer joy of living. These two songs are among Willan's finest and would be exciting in concert performance. *Music, When Soft Voices Die* (also 1914) is in a gentler, earlier style – more akin to the *To Music* cycle of 1904. It appeared in *Song Album No. 1* (1925).

One of Willan's most popular songs, *Drake's Drum*, was composed in 1919, the first of five songs and two partsongs Willan wrote to texts by the Irish-Canadian poet Norah M. Holland. It was published separately and in *Song Album No. 1*. *Drake's Drum* is a stirring, extroverted piece in the grand tradition of Stanford's *The Revenge*, *Songs of the Fleet*, and so on. The drum is represented periodically throughout the song by the figure in Example 313. The music has a ternary structure – unusual in Willan songs – in which verses 1 and 4 of the poem are set to similar music, while 2 and 3 are through-composed and explore other tonalities. In 1920 Willan set Holland's *O Littlest Hands and Dearest*. He completed this gentle lullaby 3 August about three weeks after the birth of his daughter, Mary.

During the early 1920s Willan wrote two songs in the current 'popular' style: *O Love of Mine* (published 1924) and *Harvest Moon*. He used the nom de plume Raymond Clare and wrote the lyrics under the pseudonym H.E. Leigh (Healey). The texts come close to doggerel; however both text and music are a fair imitation of the current drawing-room style.

Healey Willan Song Album No. 1 appeared in 1925 and contained six songs. *Drake's Drum* has been discussed. *Sea-Song*, also on a text by Holland, is much more introspective and does not yield up its treasures easily. Treasures it does have, however, and it works its own way slowly but inexorably to a fine climax near the end. The opening bars for the piano, somewhat reminiscent of a plainsong Amen, show an interesting case of syncopated mirroring (see Example 314). This figure is used again toward the end of this long, through-composed song.

Sonnet, to a poem by Elizabeth Barrett Browning, is a serious and brooding piece in F minor. The mood brightens somewhat in the middle section, and the tonality moves to B major (as distant from F minor as it is possible to go!). The gloom of F minor returns for the final section. Does such a poem, so compact and full of mystical meaning, lose rather than gain in musical setting? This song would seem to require serious and dedicated artists performing to a serious and dedicated audience.

Robert Bridges's *Since Thou, O Fondest and Truest* was also issued separately. The structure is similar to *Drake's Drum*, ie ternary-like with similar music for verses 1 and 4 and different settings for 2 and 3. The musical style is basically diatonic, rather unusual in Willan's songs of this period. The melodic line is simple, and yet it exhibits remarkably flexible constructions of phrase and subtle touches of word accentuation which conceal much art in seeming simplicity (Example 315).

Willan once said a song should be considered a 'tone poem for voice and piano,' and *Sonnet – To Sleep*, with words by Keats, is surely an example of what he had in mind. The compass of the voice part is quite narrow, and the voice seems to be semi-chanting the text. Around this waft appropriate atmospheric sounds from the piano. Although the music settles down in D flat major after a few bars and returns to D flat at the ending after the expected tonal excursions in the middle, the opening bars of the song are deliberately vague tonally. When the music finally eases itself into D flat major at bar 7 the effect is quite magical; one truly experiences the sensation of the coming of sleep as the 'soft embalmer' (Example 316). Several commentators have called *To Sleep* one of the finest examples of Willan's genius as an art-song composer.

In his setting of another of Holland's poems, *To Ireland's Dead*, Willan is in one of his 'nobilmente' moods and the musical result is more English than Irish. The voice enters with a musical phrase (Example 317) identical to one from the middle section of *England, My England* (Example 318)! The mystical middle section (Example 319) of the song contains some remarkable false-relations.

Healey Willan Song Album No. 2 (1926) has six songs. *Shamrocks* (1913) and *Music, When Soft Voices Die* (1914) have been discussed above.

The Cashel of Munster is written almost entirely in modal style and is the first of the few secular songs by Willan of this type. Much of the vocal line (see Example 320) is reminiscent of folksong, which gives a more

Irish flavour to the music than earlier Willan settings of Irish texts. The song is structured on a ternary basis, with similar music for verses 1 and 3 and different music for 2.

The Lake Isle of Innisfree (Yeats) displays a very effective use of simple musical means: a declamatory, almost chant-like vocal line supported by a comparatively sparse accompaniment. The piano's opening bars (Example 321), featuring a rising fifth (x) and a 'snap' of thirty-second notes (y), provide the basis of much of its part. The rising fifth is also a prominent feature in the vocal line. This through-composed setting contains the words 'And evening full of the linnet's wings,' which Willan wrote over two of his chamber works, Poem and Sonata No. 3 (see chapter 14); a musical quotation from Sonata No. 3 appears in the piano part of the song at this point. In To an Isle in the Water (also Yeats) the style is quite diatonic and there is a folksong flavour to much of the vocal line. The accompaniment is largely built on secondary sevenths (Example 322). The clash between the C sharp and the D in the first chord produces a degree of dissonance unusual for Willan.

A Fairy Tale, to Holland's six-verse narrative ballad, has the same tune for each verse, but Willan varies the melody each time in a most subtle manner to accommodate changes in emphasis in the text (see Example 323). The ballad is carried along by a vigorous accompaniment derived from the figure in Example 324. It is one of Willan's most exciting and appealing songs.

Willan arranged some seventy traditional songs, most during the years 1927 to 1929 (when he was also arranging the music for his ballad operas; see chapter 12).

In 1928, thirty-five Willan arrangements were published in Songs of the British Isles: volume 1 for men's voices, volume 2 for women's. In 1929, twenty-four arrangements of Chansons canadiennes were published in two volumes. These two two-volume sets contain the bulk of Willan's song arrangements. His arrangements are always tasteful and appropriate, displaying a high degree of craftsmanship even in the simpler ones. Very often they show considerable imagination, especially in the invention and development of accompaniment figures for piano. In Chansons canadiennes the accompaniments are always interesting; the imagination shown is comparable to that in Benjamin Britten's folksong settings. Perhaps some arrangements are a bit over-elaborate for some tastes, but this does not diminish their artistry.

Among the post-1930 arrangements, the most significant is an incredibly beautiful setting of Brigg Fair (published 1935). It is doubtful if

Delius himself could have produced a more exquisite setting for voice and piano.

Willan's last burst of song-writing came in 1941 when he produced six final examples of his art. They might be called 'Six Songs of Love,' for they are products of his 'summer of '41.' One seems to have here a last (musical) fling by the sixty-year-old composer, setting love-poems with all the fervour of a young man.

The forty-one-year gap between *Rondel* of 1900 and *Come, O Come My Life's Delight* of 1941 is not mirrored in the music. *My Love in Her Attire*, a little song of twenty bars, was revised in 1944, at which time Willan wrote 'With thought as is becoming to my dear' at the head of the manuscript and replaced the original single opening chord on the piano with a short musical quotation from his *Piano Concerto* of the same year (Example 325). *If I Were King* is the longest, more ceremonial and vigorous than its neighbours. The main accompaniment motif would be used again in 1955 in *A Song of Welcome* (see chapter 10). The other three songs are quite short. *When I Am Dying* has an interesting tonal scheme: B flat minor, B major, B flat minor, B major, and B flat minor. The first two lines of the poem are 'When I am dying, Lean over me tenderly.' The change of tonality from B flat minor to B major at the word 'tenderly' (Example 326), following five bars of dirge, is one of Willan's magical moments. *O My Fairest* is a particularly lovely song and contains musical quotations from other Willan works, notably *Symphony No. 2* (which Willan was sketching at the time). *Ah, My Beloved* is the most chromatic of the group, certainly in the vocal line.

Willan once stated his credo as a song composer: 'Song should be idealized speech. A melody, in the ordinary acceptance of the word meaning a tune, is not the most appropriate form for a song, but the natural accent of the words should be given their normal accent in the voice part somewhat after the manner of recitative, while the accompaniment furnishes an emotional or atmospheric background. A more suitable title would be "Tone poem for voice and piano."' This attitude seems to apply more to the later songs (eg *To Sleep*) than to the earlier ones, since many of the latter (eg *Sonnet, Rondel, O Mistress Mine*) have good tunes for the singer. Perhaps one reason Willan's songs have not proven popular with singers is that the parts for the voice are often less interesting musically than those for the piano. Also, the vocal range is generally restricted and the tessitura low; transposing the songs will not always solve the problems.

Willan prided himself on his literary taste and made much of how he responded musically to 'good words.' In a radio-talk ('Matters Musical' no. 3)[2] he said, 'To my way of thinking the words of a song are the most important part of it.' In some of the earlier songs the poetry was not always of a high order; even his great favourite, Meredith, was not a heavyweight. However, Heine, Herrick, Shakespeare, Keats, Shelley, and Yeats are also represented.

A remarkable variety is displayed in the art-songs; no two are closely alike. The composer had a seemingly inexhaustible imagination for creating distinctive accompaniments for piano and a great sensitivity to the words of the poems. There is a wide range of variation employed within the two basic types of song structure, through-composed and strophic. Often the two are mixed in various ways. Purely strophic songs are rare in Willan's work; usually the melody is subtly altered to accommodate the change in emphasis, meaning, and word accentuation of each new stanza; if the vocal line remains unaltered, the accompaniment is usually varied. A favourite procedure is to start off each verse in a similar manner and then move on to new material, or vice versa. ABA (or song-form) structures occur infrequently, and Willan's experiments with the setting of songs completely in recitative were terminated after the two attempts in 1902–3.

The increasing chromaticism of Willan's songs becomes apparent. The earliest songs are relatively diatonic in the English tradition of Parry and earlier composers. The Brahms-like chromaticism of Stanford, the influence of the nineteenth-century German Lieder, and the harmonic idiom of Wagner and Strauss gradually become more noticeable. Before 1913 Willan tended to maintain two distinct styles in his song-writing: the main one incorporating the influences listed above, and the other maintaining more of an English drawing-room style. The latter seemed to disappear after the composer moved to Canada (Raymond Clare excepted!). Towards the end of his song-writing career Willan appeared to back off a little from the ultra-chromatic style of his middle period; this can be seen in many of the songs in *Song Album No. 2* and in the songs of 1941.

2 In the same talk he gave some tongue-in-cheek advice to potential song writers: 'Select fine words, add music which will if possible enhance their value, get a singer ... to sing it for you, and then honestly ask yourself if you ever want to hear it again. If you really do want to hear it again, try it out on your friends; if they can stand it, try it on the public; if the public applaud, examine it very carefully – there may be something wrong with it. Then send it to a publisher and be prepared for the worst.'

19

Partsongs

Willan wrote fifty short secular works for choir with – or without – piano accompaniment. Thirty-three are original pieces – thirty were published in his lifetime and two in 1979. Seventeen are arrangements – fourteen published. He also composed or arranged music of this type for use in larger works and left four unfinished pieces.

Willan wrote nine partsongs between 1906 and 1912. Eight were published at the time. The beginning of this activity coincides with the decline in the number of solo songs Willan was composing and his increased activity in other fields.

Two partsongs were written in 1906: *Come, Shepherd Swains* and *My Little Pretty One*. *Come, Shepherd Swains* is set to a madrigal text and the music itself is rather madrigal-like. The music, in A minor, is remarkably diatonic for Willan in this period. Touches of chromaticism are used only for word-paintings of wailings and other sad thoughts (Example 327). The musical structure is ABCA, giving a ternary feeling. The tempo is slow, and the general mood is sad. *My Little Pretty One* is not at all madrigal-like, though the words come from the seventeenth century. The mood is light and the tempo quick. The harmony is well sprinkled with late Victorian sentimental chromaticisms (see Example 328). The form is ternary, with an exact repetition of the opening words and music at the end. There are a few bars of imitative counterpoint in the middle section; otherwise the style throughout is largely homophonic.

We Must Not Part was composed in 1907. Again the words are from the early seventeenth century. The music is quite diatonic; its structure is rather interesting:

Music	A B	C D	A' D'
Text	a b	c d	e d e
Tonality	E major	E minor	E major

A and B sections are homophonic, whereas C and D use some imitative counterpoint. Section D' is a full four-voice exposition on the subject shown in Example 329. This might seem a rather intricate plan for a simple partsong, but it emphasizes and exalts the positive message contained in the final lines of the poem, 'True love ... by which alone a power is given to live on earth as they in heaven.' Again Willan's sensitivity in the setting of words is evident. The music is impressive and foreshadows Willan's familiar motet style of later years.

Gently Touch the Warbling Lyre (1908) is to words by Oliver Goldsmith. The musical style (Example 330) reflects the more recent lyrics. The composer seems to have discovered the Elgarian sequence!

The two partsongs of 1909, Chloe, That Dear Bewitching Prude and Had I a Cave are very different from one another. Chloe is fast and light, in diatonic style, full of fun and good humour. Had I a Cave, to a poem by Robert Burns, is serious, and the composer seems to have gone on a binge of chromaticism (see Example 331) – like some latter-day Gesualdo – in order to represent the howling winds! Maybe the wind does howl slowly in semitones, yet the passage does not convey the total impression of the text (wildness, roaring waves, and so on); it seems to lack vigour and movement. It also seems rather odd to suggest piano e diminuendo over the word 'roar!'

Come, O Come My Life's Delight and Fain Would I Change That Note (both 1911) are to early seventeenth-century texts. Come, O Come is Willan's first published example of true five-part writing for voices throughout a whole work, in this case SSATB. Though this piece is mostly homophonic in style, the composer writes flowing and melodic parts for all his voices. Fain Would I Change is written for the usual four-part (SATB) choir. Its complexity is rhythmic, with duplets, triplets, syncopations, and incomplete quadruplets often found mixed together simultaneously in the four voices. Bar 4 (Example 332) provides a good example of this.

Sweet Are the Charms of Her I Love (1912) is set in bar form, AAB, unusual for Willan; his unerring sense of fitness when setting a text made it a logical choice. Verses 1 and 2 deal with love from a personal point of view and the same music is appropriate for both. Verse 3 considers love in a broader and more universal sense; different music is needed. *Sweet Are the Charms* is one of Willan's most tuneful and appealing works of this type, yet it was not published till 1979. It was the last partsong Willan wrote in England.

Willan returned to writing partsongs in 1927[1] and wrote at least a dozen between then and 1931. In 1927 he composed *Angel Spirits of Sleep* for women's voices and piano, one of his most beautiful pieces. The vocal lines flow in compound time (Example 333) in a similar manner to those in the 'Annunciation' and 'Fulfilment' movements of his 1923 Christmas cantata *The Mystery of Bethlehem* (see chapter 10). Another partsong for women's voices and piano, *Spring*, appeared in 1928. It is the last of the poems of Norah Holland set to music by the composer.

In 1929 Willan wrote two partsongs for Harold Brooke: *Weep You No More Sad Fountains* and *In Youth Is Pleasure*. The former was composed at Brighton, England, during a visit by the composer. It is a strophic piece, with both verses of the anonymous seventeenth-century poem being set to almost identical music. Yet this is one of Willan's most 'advanced' partsongs, a fact indicated in the very first bar with the E flat major tonality, briefly established by the opening chord, immediately contradicted by the G flat in the second chord (Example 334). There is no time-signature; and the rhythm of the piece is quite free, pulsing in measures of quintuple, quadruple, triple, and even duple metre, depending upon the flow of the text. This type of rhythm comes from Willan's motet style, though the motets generally tend to be written in a fairly diatonic idiom.

---

1 Shortly after his election as president of the Arts and Letters Club in 1922 Willan set its constitution to music. The result is hilarious. The text is solemnly proclaimed in an antiphonal manner by a cantor (who sings in pseudo-plainsong) and a four-part male chorus (TTBB). The chorus periodically interjects irreverent comments which, according to the composer, 'exemplified the feelings of certain members.' The composer threw in snatches of Wagner's *Die Meistersinger* during the statement concerning the powers of the president, Gounod's *Funeral March of a Marionette* at the reference to the duties of the vice-president (reflecting, according to the composer, the 'heavy, limpey walk' of the incumbent), *Nobody Knows the Trouble I've Seen* to accompany the duties of the treasurer, *We Won't Go Home until Morning, Nun Danket Alle Gott, Dresden Amen*, and *Dies irae*. An extended plagal cadence for the frequently recurring words 'the executive committee' becomes a leitmotif for the whole piece. This may not be one's usual idea of a partsong, but it is a fine example of the composer's humour and his skill in expressing it musically. Willan used to tell his composition students that a properly trained composer ought to be able to set the telephone book to music if necessary.

Here the harmony is more adventurously chromatic, with passages (such as Example 335) which approach the boundaries reached by Delius. *In Youth Is Pleasure* is a very conservative, almost madrigal-like piece, as if Willan were deliberately imitating the seventeenth-century ayre. It was published in 1930; *Weep You No More* was not published till 1979. The former was 'safe' and marketable in 1930; the latter was probably felt to be too 'advanced' and difficult (and is by far the more interesting of the two).

A Clear Midnight was written in 1930 for a large choir (Westminster Choir of Ithaca, New York), and there is much divisi within the SATB sections. At the end a double chorus is called for, with further divisi within each of the two SATB groups. (However chorus I here is really only a semi-chorus, since the score directs that there be only one voice to a part.) The text is from Walt Whitman. The mystical opening (Example 336) is particularly impressive. There are some colourful cadences in the middle part of the work (see Example 337). The music builds to a fine climax for double chorus, at the end of which the opening line of text and music is repeated. The inconclusive cadence (VII^7 to IV^6, 'perdendosi') is somewhat strange from a musical point of view, but it faithfully mirrors the last words of the text, 'flight into the worldless.' *A Clear Midnight* is slow and mystical.

Sigh No More Ladies (also 1930) is, to quote the composer's performance directive, 'light and naive.' The two verses are set strophically though the 'hey nonny's' are somewhat expanded the second time. The melody is rather like an English folksong, and the whole piece is a remarkably natural-sounding exercise in quintuple metre (see Example 338). The music is effectively written for unaccompanied four-part women's choir.

Sweet Echo (1931), a setting for unaccompanied SATB choir of a song from Milton's masque *Comus*, is one of Willan's least successful partsongs. The music is cast in the style of his liturgical motets and masses and seems out of place; it also tends toward dullness – there is no imitative counterpoint and the melodic line seems to lack direction, covering the same limited compass of notes over and over again.

Eternity (1931) is also set for unaccompanied mixed choir. With words by Herrick, this is one of the composer's most impressive partsongs. The music is in two main sections. Section 1 (largo) is mainly homophonic and contains some very colourful chord changes (cf *Gloria Deo per immensa saecula*). Example 339 illustrates this. Section 2 (nobilmente) is fugal, in five-part counterpoint. A homophonic coda, marked 'con exultazione,' brings the work to a glorious conclusion. This coda is similar in style and effect to the 'con exultazione' section at the end of Willan's Christmas motet of 1928, *The Three Kings*.

Two little partsongs for ladies' choir (SA) and piano, *When Belinda Plays* and *Clown Song*, were also published in 1931. They are comparatively lightweight; the former is lyrical and flowing, the latter vigorous and rhythmic. One can imagine these strophic songs being popular with school choirs, as they have much in common with the Martin Shaw–Arthur Somervell type of British school or music festival song of the time. The same is true for another partsong for ladies' voices from 1931, *To Violets*, though it is somewhat more substantial. The work is through-composed, and the writing for the three voices (SSA) is quite sophisticated. The opening two bars for the piano (Example 340) suggest this is not going to be run-of-the-mill. The left-hand motif carries on, in various forms, throughout much of the accompaniment. The sudden change to the minor mode at the end of the song is startling but effective; it is, of course, dictated by an equally sudden change of mood in the last line of the poem. The final cadence is also not, by any means, conventional (see Example 341).

The remaining 1931 partsong is a through-composed setting of Walter Scott's *Border Ballad* for four-part unaccompanied male quartet (or chorus). The style is straightforward and remarkably diatonic. There are few distinguishing features in the music, excepting perhaps the use of a double metre (3/4 2/4); see Example 342.

We Sing a Song to Canada was written in 1939. Set to an impossible text full of sentimental and patriotic platitudes ('There is no fairer country,' etc), the music is really only a longish hymn-tune with refrain. The music is stronger than the text and possesses some of that unsophisticated yet stirring quality of congregational song.

Willan's next original partsongs appeared in the early 1950s. Two partsongs for three-part women's voices (SSA) and piano were completed in 1950 and 1951: *On May Morning* and *To Daffodils*. The manuscripts suggest they were begun much earlier. Stylistically either one could have been written by 1905! *On May Morning*, a setting of a poem by Milton, is rather similar in style to *Spring* (1928). *To Daffodils* has a text by Herrick which Willan set as a solo song in 1901. Though there is no musical connection between the two settings, the type of harmony Willan uses in this partsong is similar to that he might have used in the early years of the century.

Say Not the Struggle Naught Availeth, for unaccompanied four-part male choir, was written in memory of Nicholas Ignatieff, warden of Hart

House, University of Toronto. Willan wrote to Mrs Ignatieff, 'I wish it were more worthy of a man for whom I had so great an admiration.' The piece is adequate but not great Willan.

In 1952 Willan wrote and saw published two partsong arrangements of chansons canadiennes, for mixed choir and two pianos. *Sainte Marguerite* is a rearrangement of his 1937 setting for women's voices.[2] It contains some charming canonic effects, and towards the end there is a fine example of the composer's skill in varying the harmony under a four-fold repetition of a melodic phrase (Example 343). *Le Navire de Bayonne* is a considerably expanded setting of another *Chansons canadiennes* arrangement. The earlier version had the three verses sung strophically to the same music; here Willan treats the three verses differently (though the tune remains the same). Likewise the very active accompaniment changes from verse to verse, though it takes its point of departure from that which had been used in the solo song (Example 344). The accompaniments for *Sainte Marguerite* and *Le Navire* are set out for two pianos. In fact, two pianos are not necessary, and the parts can be played on one piano, four hands.

Willan's last partsongs date from 1957: *Three Songs to Music* for SATB choir and piano. The three short pieces, all to poems by Herrick, were commissioned by the University of Toronto Faculty of Music Alumni Association. In *An Hymn to the Muses*, choir and piano perform antiphonally, playing with variations and extensions of the opening phrase (Example 345) of the choir. What Willan does with this simple material is remarkable. One of the charming features of the music is the cadencing of the choral sections on the weak beats of the bar (Example 346). *To Music* is a resetting of the composer's solo song of 1904 on the same text. The partsong is no mere four-part harmonization of the original song melody, however, and considerable revisions were made to the music. *To Be Merry* features some antiphony between male and female voices (see Example 347). With *To Music* acting as the slow, lyrical movement between the vigorous and gay outer movements, *Three Songs to Music* can make an effective concert group. The pieces have a vigour and spontaneity which make them a worthy conclusion to a half-century of partsong composition.

2 Willan's partsong arrangements for women's voices and piano of five chansons canadiennes were published in 1937. They were resettings of five solo songs from volume 2 of *Chansons canadiennes* (1929), discussed in chapter 18.

20

Music for
the liturgy

Willan composed seven settings for the complete communion service and three settings for parts of the service; a series of missae breves for St Mary Magdalene's; four other masses, including two to Latin texts; and more than fifty canticle settings, both plainsong with faux-bourdons (to be considered generically) and full-anthem type.

COMMUNION SETTINGS

The Anglican communion service is virtually a setting for choir and organ of an English translation of the ordinary of the mass in the Catholic church – Kyrie eleison (Lord have mercy), gloria in excelsis (Glory be to God on high), credo (I believe in one God), sanctus (Holy, holy, holy), benedictus (Blessed is He that cometh), and Agnus Dei (O Lamb of God). In the Anglican service the Kyrie is replaced by a response to the Commandments and the order then is response, credo, sanctus, benedictus, Agnus Dei, and gloria in excelsis. The Anglican communion service is often a musical work of considerable dimension, in several movements. Before he left England Willan composed two settings of the complete communion service (1906 and 1910) and three settings for parts of the service; in Canada he composed five full settings (1928, 1929, and three in 1954–5) as well as editing a sixteenth-century communion service.

Willan's first communion setting was *Sanctus, Benedictus and Agnus Die in E Flat* for SSA and organ. It is not a complete communion office, there being no response, credo, or gloria. Published in 1900 (though perhaps written in 1899), it was the composer's second publication, and he spoke of it with some affection as late as 1963 (Parker tapes). He wrote it while organist at St Saviour's Church, St Albans, where there was a special women's choir to sing the various saints' days' services. The music shows the gift for effective vocal melody typical of the composer. The sanctus is a fine piece of writing and begins with the theme in the organ part (Example 348). This motif, with the triplet figure which would be characteristic of Willan, appears in another movement; it thus becomes a unifying element. (Willan did not employ this device in his subsequent settings of the communion office.) The sanctus (Example 349) shows also that the young Willan was conversant with the chromatic harmonic colourings of Dvořák and Grieg. The benedictus is perhaps a bit too indebted to Mendelssohn, though it ends strongly with the 'Hosanna.' The Agnus Dei is quite beautiful but is rather too secular in style; it would have been better suited to an art-song.

Willan's first published full communion service is *Office of Holy Communion in G*, composed in 1906 and dedicated to the choir of Christ Church, Wanstead, where he had been organist and choirmaster from 1900 to 1903. The credo commences with an organ passage, typical of several passages in the piece, which shows Willan still using the style of chromaticism found in much late Victorian church music (Example 350). However there are many passages of strong harmonic and melodic interest in the credo, as well as imaginative settings of particular texts (Example 351). The sanctus shows the neo-modalism that was beginning to appear in the music of Stanford and Vaughan Williams (Example 352). The Agnus Dei, like its predecessor in Willan's earlier setting, is rather worldly in style, especially during the opening tenor solo (Example 353). The final movement, the gloria in excelsis, receives by contrast a vigorous Stanford-like treatment (Example 354). The gloria, like the sanctus, is first class.

Another full setting, *Office for the Holy Communion in C and E Flat*, appeared in 1910. The responses at the beginning anticipate Willan's motet style (Example 355). This music is meant to be sung unaccompanied and exhibits a distinctly modal atmosphere (in spite of being written ostensibly in C major). The credo is a fine piece, containing some colourful and interesting chromatic harmony in the robust style of Stanford. At several points the influence that Wagnerian harmony was beginning to have on the composer can be seen (Example 356). The setting of 'And the third day He rose' to rising imitative entries over a dominant pedal foreshadows completely the credo in the composer's later and better-known *Communion Service in E Flat* ('Missa de Sancto Albano')!

The sanctus is a marvel of mystical harmonies, of which short extracts can give only an imperfect glimpse. The organ opening (Example 357) hints that what is to come will not be commonplace. Later, after three indescribable 'Holy's,' one finds the passage in Example 358. The mysticism of the first part of the sanctus is then brought to a positive reality in a vigorous fugato in C major on the words 'Heaven and earth are full of Thy glory.' The benedictus is expressively set for bass and tenor soloists in a passage which anticipates the exquisite 'Lo, He lies' movement from *The Mystery of Bethlehem* (see Example 134). The Agnus Dei, unlike its somewhat operatic predecessors, possesses a dark, almost Sibelian intensity (Example 359). The gloria in excelsis maintains the consistently high standards set by the previous movements.

In toto, this *Office for the Holy Communion* of 1910 is a work of imagination, inspiration, and craftsmanship which the composer would not surpass in his later communion settings. Doubtless, passages in it might have stretched the boundaries set by the general series within which it was published by Novello: 'parochial and general use ... easy execution ... well within the capabilities of an ordinary choir.' Perhaps because of this stretching the work is of more than ordinary interest.

Sanctus in C Minor and *Benedictus in E Major* were completed in 1912 and remain in manuscript. *Sanctus* is mystical in style, with some striking chromatic changes. The double-pedal part for the organ at the opening is unusual.

Sixteen years intervened before Willan again turned to setting the communion service. In 1928 there appeared *Missa de Sancta Maria Magdelena* (a communion service in D) for unison voices and organ. The vocal line, while not plainchant, is certainly influenced by it. There is a modalism at times in the organ accompaniment which is obviously derived from the same influence (Example 360). It is a full setting with English words (though there is also an optional Kyrie eleison for the response to the Commandments) and has become one of the most widely used of all settings. It has been reprinted in several hymnbooks, and in 1965 a special version was published for Roman Catholic use. The original 1928 publication continued to sell well also: 1,804 copies were sold in 1955 and 1,212 copies in 1957. It is easy without being trite – a difficult thing to accomplish – and well within the grasp of any amateur church choir of modest resources.

Easy Communion Service in E Flat, subtitled 'Missa de Sancto Albano,' appeared in 1929. It accomplishes the same purpose as the 1928 *Missa de Sancta Maria Magdalena*, only this time for SATB choir and organ. The Nicene Creed is a long text, and settings of it – especially those attempting simplicity – can soon tend toward tediousness. Here Willan's setting is exciting, and the organ blazes forth with great splashes of modally influenced harmonic colour. The mystical music accompanying the incarnation, crucifixion, and burial is striking (see Example 361).

Willan's edition, with organ accompaniments, of *Office of Holy Communion Set to Music by John Merbecke* (ca 1550) first appeared in 1934, and a revised edition came out in 1959. It has achieved a very wide circulation, appearing in many hymnbooks as well as being published separately. Most churches in Canada know Merbecke through Willan's settings, and the same is true for many American churches. Willan's expertise in devising suitable organ accompaniments for plainsong melodies will be remarked upon again in connection with the plainsong canticles.

Late in life (1954–5) Willan wrote three more communion settings: two in D major for unison voices and organ and one for Lutheran use. They are competently written and vocally effective, but do not add anything to the picture as it had emerged by 1928–9.

MISSAE BREVES

Between 1928 and 1962 Willan wrote fourteen missae breves, all for his own use at St Mary Magdalene's. They consist of settings of the movements with comparatively short texts, namely the Kyrie eleison, the sanctus, the benedictus, and the Agnus Dei. Willan uses the Kyrie rather than the response to the Commandments; the long texts – the gloria and the credo – are not set.[1] Willan's settings are for four-part (occasionally five-part) choir. They are really quite small works with vocal scores no

1 In Lutheran usage a missa brevis consists of the Kyrie eleison and the gloria only (eg the missae breves of J.S. Bach). In Roman Catholic usage the term refers to works in which all the movements were set, but those with long texts expeditiously (eg some of the masses of Haydn and Mozart).

larger or longer than those of most full anthems. Nevertheless they form an important segment of Willan's sacred music and share a place with the motets at the apex of his unaccompanied writing. They are less well known than the motets because their regular use is restricted to a small number of churches.

Willan's first three missae breves were published in 1932, but he had used them at St Mary Magdalene's for several years prior. No. 1 was completed in October 1928. An unfinished missa brevis in D, composed in November 1928, is called 'No. 3' on the manuscript but bears no resemblance to the published No. 3. Bryant suggests (HWC) that the missae breves published as No. 2 and No. 3 were composed before November 1928.

Missa brevis No. 1 in E flat is one of Willan's most attractive masses. The music is very diatonic, though with some hints of modality. Chromaticism is completely eschewed, as if it would introduce a worldly and profane element into the purity of the music (cf Palestrina). Willan's writing here is a happy juxtaposition of homophonic and contrapuntal styles. There is no direct thematic connection between the movements, but there is a unity of style. An ABA structure is used for those movements with a three-fold text (Kyrie and Agnus Dei). The Kyrie is actually a paraphrase of the Kyrie of the plainsong mass of the angels (missa de angelis). Its opening (Example 362) is typical of the smooth vocal writing found throughout the work.

Missa brevis No. 2 in F minor is penitential in mood and is suggested for use in Advent and Lent. Mostly homophonic in style and more modal than No. 1, it is obviously plainsong-influenced not only in the severity of the music but also in the free metre employed. Musically this mass tends a little towards the monotonous.

Missa brevis No. 3 in F major is more akin to No. 1 in style, though it is not quite as tuneful. The sanctus and benedictus are written in 5/4 time, and this quintuple metre seems particularly suitable for certain phrases of the text (see Example 363).

In 1934 *Missa brevis No. 4* in E major was published. It has become one of the composer's most popular masses, probably because its music is based on the well-known tune of the Christmas sequence *Corde natus* (commonly sung as the hymn *Of the Father's Love Begotten*). Willan bases the Kyrie, 'Christe,' sanctus, benedictus, and 'Hosanna' on motifs derived from successive lines of the hymn-tune (Examples 364–8). For the Agnus Dei he uses the complete tune as a cantus firmus.

Missa brevis No. 5 in F sharp minor (1935) is the first of the few that Willan would write for five-part (SSATB) choir. The massive Kyrie eleison is particularly impressive (see Example 369). The remaining movements do not quite match its level. Willan achieves some variety of texture by introducing three-part passages for women's voices alone (SSA) in the benedictus and Agnus Dei, along with some four-part (SATB) writing in the sanctus and Agnus Dei.

Missa brevis No. 6 in F minor (1935) is based upon Bach chorales. Willan chose appropriate chorales to adapt (eg *Heilig, heilig* for the sanctus and *O Lamm Gottes* for the Agnus Dei). The benedictus is not set as a separate movement here but is contained within the sanctus.

In 1936 the seventh of the missae breves, *Missa brevis 'O Westron Wynde,'* was published. It is based on an early sixteenth-century English secular song. The song concerns the coming of spring, and Willan was inspired to compose this mass as a result of seeing the first violet peeking through the snow in spring. (The early Tudor composer John Taverner had also written a mass based on this tune.) Unlike in the earlier *Corde natus* mass, where all the lines of the borrowed tune were used, Willan here appears to use only the first and third lines of *Westron Wynde* as source; there is, however, a slight hint of the second line of the tune in the second Kyrie eleison (Example 370). As in *Missa brevis No. 6* the benedictus is not set as a separate movement but is contained within the sanctus. The mass has a setting of the gloria in excelsis in plainsong with faux-bourdons printed at the end. The latter bears no relationship to the *Westron Wynde* song and is in mode VIII (whereas *Westron Wynde* is in mode II).

Missa brevis No. 8 in D minor (Missa SS Philippi et Jacobi), published in 1939, was written for the birthday of the composer's mother, 1 May, the feast of saints Philip and James. This is one of Willan's most immediately appealing masses: the Kyrie is composed in a moving elegiac style, while the 'Heaven and earth' and 'Hosanna' are among his most uplifting settings of those texts. This mass also contains settings of the nine-fold Kyrie, responses,[2] and the gloria in excelsis, all in a somewhat plainsong-influenced Tudor style.

Missa brevis No. 9 in A minor ('Missa Sancti Michaelis') appeared in 1947. St Michael was the patron saint of the sisters working in the parish of the Church of St Mary Magdalene, and this mass was always sung on St Michael's day. Like its two immediate predecessors this mass is written in a Tudor-influenced style. The Agnus Dei is its most attractive movement.

---

2 The ordinary Anglican communion order uses a response to the Commandments in place of the Kyrie. Willan provided his missae breves No. 8, 13, and 14 with responses as alternatives.

In 1948 Willan wrote one of his more important works in this genre, *Missa brevis No. 10* in C minor and major. Composed for the feast of the dedication (anniversary) of the Church of St Mary Magdalene, this mass was conceived on a somewhat more extended scale than its predecessors. Willan manages to break away to some extent from the heavy Tudor influence of the three previous masses and to return to his more usual motet style. Though the work is written predominantly in the minor mode, the composer uses the major mode very effectively for certain sections: notably the sanctus, the 'Hosanna' of the benedictus, and the 'Grant us Thy peace' at the end of the Agnus Dei. Passages such as Example 371 add a certain spice to the music. This is the first missa brevis since No. 5 to make extensive use of five-part writing.

Missa brevis No. 11 in G minor and major ('Missa Sancti Johannis Baptistae'), published in 1953, is another impressive example. In fact, it is probably the most elaborate of all Willan's missae breves. Written for five-part choir, it exploits various textures: the Kyrie contrasts SSA against full choir; the benedictus is scored for SSA only, followed by a five-part 'Hosanna'; the Agnus Dei is chiefly in four parts (SATB). The sanctus exploits the antiphonal possibilities inherent in the text with answering phrases by four-part women's and four-part men's voices (Example 372) – a passage unique in Willan's missae breves. As with No. 10, some sections are in the minor mode while others are in the major. Another unique feature is that one of the movements, the benedictus, is set in a different key (E major).

Missa brevis No. 12 in D major (1956) is – like No. 4 – based on a plainsong Christmas hymn, *Christe Redemptor omnium*. This mass bears some resemblance in its thematic material to the unfinished missa brevis in D of 1928; Willan may have taken this as a point of departure. Unlike in No. 4 Willan here uses only the first two lines of the hymn-tune: the Kyrie (Example 373) and the sanctus (Example 374) being based on the first line, and the 'Christe' (Example 375) and Agnus Dei (Example 376) being based on the second line. The benedictus is not founded on any portion of the hymn-tune. Though *Missa brevis No. 12* is appropriate for a number of occasions in the church year, it is particularly so for Christmas. Like *Corde natus*, it is one of Willan's most immediately attractive masses.

In 1961, for Francis Jackson, Willan added a gloria and a credo for *Missa brevis No. 12* to make it a complete unaccompanied mass. The result was not very satisfactory, the credo especially tending to be long and dull (Jackson's opinion also). Neither piece shows any connection with the *Christe Redemptor omnium* tune, and both remain unpublished.

In his eightieth year (1960), Willan composed *Missa brevis No. 13* in G minor ('Holy Cross'). This work reverts to the simpler and less extended style of his earlier missae breves and, like No. 2, is intended for use in Lent and other penitential seasons. Though quite suitable for liturgical use, it is not one of the more interesting examples musically.

Composed in 1962 and published in 1963, Willan's last mass was *Missa brevis No. 14* ('St Alphege'). (Albert Mahon, Willan's cantor for many years at St Mary Magdalene's, had been a chorister in the Church of St Alphege, Suffolk. Willan, wishing to honour Mahon, couldn't call the mass 'St Albert,' so he called it 'St Alphege' instead!) Like No. 10, 11, and 12, it is written on a comparatively extended scale. It shows that the octogenerian composer could still write expressive music even if the style were somewhat academic. The sanctus and benedictus are particularly interesting. Willan appends a fugue in E minor for organ at the end for use as an offertory or postlude (this is the fugue that he 'extemporized' in *Man of Music*). The opening notes of the Kyrie (Example 377) and the fugue-subject (Example 378) are the same.

OTHER MASSES

Willan composed four other masses – two to Latin texts (1927 and 1930), one highly mystical mass for the Royal School of Church Music (1935), and a setting (1954) of the Lutheran text.

Mass of St Peter for unison voices and organ was written in 1927. It has a Latin text throughout (except for the Greek Kyrie) and was dedicated to Dalton Baker. It is quite diatonic in style, with surprisingly little modal influence. There is a motivic connection between most of the movements (Examples 379–83) derived from the opening Kyrie. Musically, however, this mass is not as interesting as his 1928 communion setting, *Missa de Sancta Maria Magdalena*, discussed in the first section of this chapter. The longer movements of *Mass of St Peter* (the gloria and the credo – particularly the latter) seem to ramble on interminably, and the whole work tends to be monotonous.

Of more interest is Willan's other Latin mass, *Mass of St Theresa*. Set for unison voices and organ, and published in 1930, this work had been requested by Frederick Harris, who wanted a mass setting for convents in Canada. It is a charming setting, full of gentle, artless beauty – as if the composer were directly inspired by the thought of St Theresa ('Little Flower') herself. The style is mainly diatonic, with little modality except in the credo. Some passages (such as Example 384) are almost carol-like.

The addition of an English text might have made *Mass of St Theresa* more extensively known and used; this could yet be done.

In 1935, *Mass of St Hugh* for treble voices and organ was published. It was requested for the Royal School of Church Music in England by Sir Sydney Hugh Nicholson. (Since Willan could not call the mass 'St Sydney,' he called it 'St Hugh.') Though written for unison voices (with occasional divisi) and organ, the general style is similar to that of Willan's unaccompanied motets and missae breves of the same period, and the impression created by it is thus rather different from *Mass of St Peter* and *Mass of St Theresa*. Its musical idiom is quite modal, and a mystical atmosphere pervades all the movements (though to a lesser extent in the gloria). In fact, this is among the most 'otherworldly' church music Willan ever wrote. Brief musical examples cannot convey the overall impression.

From 1950 onwards Willan enjoyed some association with the Lutheran church in the United States through Concordia Publishing house. In 1954 the students of Concordia Seminary commissioned him to write a mass for them, and *Missa brevis in G* for male voices (TTBB) was the result. The work is well written for men's voices and would be interesting for a male choir to sing. True, some of the writing is rather academic, but there are places – such as the opening of the sanctus, or the 'Grant us thy peace' at the end of the Agnus Dei – where the old magic shines through. The ending of the Agnus Dei is too long to illustrate here, but the opening of the sanctus can be shown (Example 385).

CANTICLES

Canticle texts have a special place in the liturgy of the Church of England. The Te Deum ('We praise Thee, O God'), benedictus ('Blessed be the Lord God of Israel'), Jubilate Deo ('O be joyful in the Lord'), and benedicite ('O ye works of the Lord') all belong to the Anglican morning service (matins). The Benedictus Es ('Blessed art Thou, O Lord') is also sanctioned as a morning canticle in some branches of Anglicanism. The magnificat ('My soul doth magnify the Lord') and the nunc dimittis ('Lord, now lettest thy servant depart in peace') are the main canticles for the Anglican evening service (evensong).

Willan made more than fifty canticle settings, of two types: plainsong settings with faux-bourdons, and full-anthem-type settings.

Plainsong settings
Willan wrote thirty-eight plainsong settings; most were of the evening canticles (magnificat and/or nunc dimittis – they were most often set

together as a pair), though four morning canticles were also set in this manner. Eight plainsong settings are arrangements of works by other composers (Viadana being the most frequent); the remaining thirty are by Willan. All thirty-eight were composed after he went to St Mary Magdalene's in 1921 and were part of the plainsong tradition he built there. Most were published (between 1928 and 1958).

The plainsong canticles of Willan follow a basic pattern. The verses of the text are set to one of the eight Gregorian psalm-tones (in one instance the Tonus Peregrinus was used). Each psalm-tone has a varying number of 'endings' (or cadences), each producing a sub-category. Thus there is a wide variety available for the choice of tone and ending in which to put a particular text. Though traditional plainsong is monophonic music (ie a single melodic line without accompanying parts), Willan added organ accompaniments to the plainsong verses. These accompaniments provided a great deal of subtle variety, since even if two magnificats were set to the same psalm-tone and used the same ending they could be made different from one another by means of differing accompaniments. Willan's plainsong accompaniments for organ are a model for all time; their tasteful simplicity and their stylistic integration with the plainsong would be difficult to surpass.

The main source of variety, however, occurs with the faux-bourdons. Faux-bourdons are polyphonic settings of some of the verses of the text for unaccompanied choir (usually SATB, though Willan also wrote some for SSA, TTB, and TTBB). There have been many meanings associated with the French term faux-bourdon ('faburden' in English, 'falso bordone' in Italian) over the ages, and the one in most common use today refers to a piece of part-music, usually a hymn-tune, in which the melody is placed in the tenor (Willan wrote about forty of these). In the sixteenth century, however, the term began to be used for harmonization of psalm-tones and other liturgical recitations (eg magnificats) on alternate verses. These plainsong faux-bourdons were either strict or free, the strict ones having the actual plainsong in one of the voices and the free ones not having the plainsong. Likewise, the faux-bourdons set for certain verses of a particular psalm, canticle, etc could use the same (or similar) music each time, or they could use different music. In his plainsong canticles Willan makes use of all the options, but tends to favour the free to the strict faux-boudon. He tends also to favour a scheme where faux-bourdons are employed for every third verse. The extract in Example 386, showing the first three verses of his setting of *Magnificat on Tone VII* (1928), will give the reader a general idea of the procedure. In the first half of the faux-bourdon, the soprano outlines the main notes of the first part of the chant. The last five notes in the tenor part at the end of the faux-bourdon are those of the 'ending' of the chant. This might be considered a 'partially strict' faux-bourdon.

It is neither possible nor necessary to examine here Willan's thirty-eight plainsong canticles individually, since they all fit within the general framework of the above explanation and the differences of procedure among them are minor. Some of the faux-bourdons are more elaborate and polyphonic than the example shown, but in general there is no appreciable change in style between the earlier and later publications.

Full-anthem-type setting

Willan completed fourteen canticle settings of the full-anthem type. Eight appeared 1906–18, two in the mid-1930s, and the others between 1949 and 1957. From a purely musical point of view Willan's full-anthem-type settings of the canticles are the more interesting, since they involve a much greater amount of actual original musical composition than do the plainsong settings. With the exception of the nunc dimittis settings (the texts of which are very short), they are quite large works, the equivalent of long anthems. As a result they represent a sizeable segment of Willan's original sacred composition. They include six settings of the magnificat and nunc dimittis, four settings of the Te Deum, two settings of the Jubilate Deo, and one each of the benedictus and the Benedictus Es. It will be noted that, as with the plainsong canticles, settings of the magnificat and nunc dimittis are the most frequent.

Magnificat and Nunc dimittis in B Flat (1906) is a splendid work. The influence of Brahms and Stanford is apparent (see Example 387). The opening motif in Example 387 appears periodically throughout the organ part of the magnificat, as well as forming the basis of the subject of a short fugato for choir near the end during the Gloria Patri (Example 388). Example 389 shows a striking bit of colour. The nunc dimittis uses a rhythmic variant (Example 390) of the main motif of the magnificat. Here, as is traditional when a magnificat and nunc dimittis are set together as a pair, the same Gloria Patri is used for both (cf the 'Hosanna' after the sanctus and the benedictus in the mass).

Later in 1906 Willan composed *Magnificat and Nunc dimittis in A Minor*. As with the earlier example in B flat, this uses the opening bars of the organ part (Example 391) as the source of the main accompanimental motifs to be employed throughout the piece. This is a somewhat more expansive setting than its predecessor, and makes use of antiphonal passages between four-part men's voices and four-part women's voices. A solo quartet is used in addition to the full choir. Again there are some Brahms-like sections. The Gloria Patri is unusually long, concluding with a fairly full fugue which changes mode from A minor to A major part-way through. The final cadence (Example 392) is a striking example of the use of the comparatively rare minor triad on the subtonic.

In his later settings of the evening canticles Willan would never surpass these remarkable first two examples from 1906. (Strangely, he appeared toward the end of his life to hold a low opinion of them.) They are works which display an almost symphonic approach with their broad lines, vigour, colour, and craftsmanship and are obviously the product of a lively musical imagination. They deserve to be reassessed.

Te Deum in B Flat (composed in 1906, published in 1909) does not maintain the standard of the other two canticles. The first half displays some vigour and momentum, but is occasionally marred by the appearance of some of the rather maudlin harmonic and melodic clichés of the popular second-rate church music of the time. The second half makes considerable use of solo voices, and interest seems to flag. A return to the style of the opening for the final section rejuvenates things.

In 1912 Willan composed *Te Deum in E Flat*. It is better than the first Te Deum and not marred by the lapses of taste found in the latter. Like its predecessor, it starts off strongly, and the first section contains some arresting passages, such as that in Example 393. There is a lengthy baritone solo in the middle section, during which musical reference is made several times to the 'Dresden Amen.' The final section, though solid, does not quite sustain the interest generated by the opening section, and the concluding bars seem rather weak.

Magnificat and Nunc dimittis in E Flat (also 1912) carries on in the style of its predecessor in B flat of 1906. It shows that the composer had learned from Delius and Wagner since his 1906 settings (see Example 394). Willan's 1912 Te Deum, magnificat, and nunc dimittis are all in E flat; there is a motivic connection between them – as can be observed by comparing the choir entrances for each (see Examples 395–7).

Ca 1914, in Canada, Willan wrote *Jubilate Deo in E Flat*, which was unpublished and has unfortunately been lost. An unfinished *Benedictus in E Flat*, probably also from this period, has thematic resemblances to *Te Deum in E Flat*. Perhaps Willan planned a full set of morning canticles – Te Deum, benedictus, and Jubilate Deo – in E flat.

Benedictus in B Flat of 1917 is fairly long (running to fifteen pages of vocal score) and is perhaps too long. With little change of style throughout, there is too much of the same thing for too long; Willan himself suggested a possible cut on page 5 of the score. Yet there are strong passages in this piece, some suggestive of Stanford (Example 398). There are other passages (Example 399) where Willan's striking sense of harmonic colour to mirror a particular text is evident. The work was dedicated to Dr Miles Farrow and the choir of the Cathedral of St John the Divine in New York.

In 1918, *Jubilate in B Flat* appeared. It uses the same Gloria Patri as *Benedictus in B Flat* of 1917; perhaps Willan originally viewed these two morning settings as a pair (cf also *Te Deum in B Flat* of 1906). *Jubilate* is more successful than the earlier benedictus in the same key not only because it is shorter but also because there is more contrast (eg the soprano solo in the middle section). The Gloria Patri at the end seems to bear little musical relationship to the rest of the piece. However, if it had already been heard in the service during the benedictus, it would not be so much of a musical non sequitur at the end of the jubilate. The work was inscribed to T. Tertius Noble at St Thomas' Church, New York.

From Willan's middle period of church music there are only two full settings of canticles: *Benedictus Es in E Flat* of 1935 and *Coronation Te Deum* of 1937 (see chapter 10). By this time Willan was primarily interested in plainsong canticle settings rather than those of the full-anthem type. *Benedictus Es in E Flat* was written at the request of H.W. Gray and Co for the Episcopalian church in the United States (which had recently sanctioned the use of the Benedictus Es as a morning canticle and thus needed settings). Each of the six verses of the canticle begins with the words 'Blessed art Thou,' so Willan follows here the modified strophic procedure found so often in his songs, namely of beginning each verse of the text with similar music and then breaking off into something new. Tonality changes from verse to verse as well (E flat major, G minor, E flat major, C sharp minor, F minor, and E flat major). The music is comparatively simple in style, largely diatonic, and almost march-like. One is reminded of the Eric Thiman type of English anthem (Example 400). However, the sudden jump into C sharp minor at the words 'beholdest the depths' is anything but commonplace (Example 401).

Willan composed his last full settings of canticles between 1949 and 1957. By this time he appeared to have little interest in this type of setting and tended to look with scorn on his early works in this form.

The settings of the magnificat and nunc dimittis in D (1949) and E flat (1955) tend to be rather bland and contain instances (see Example 402) of the melodic tautology that sometimes makes Willan's later church music dull.

Magnificat and Nunc dimittis in A, written at the request of Francis Jackson for the 1957 Festival of the Three Northern Choirs (York, Durham, and Ripon cathedrals), is the most impressive of the late canticle settings; Jackson remarked upon its 'singability' and its 'subtle chromaticisms.' The magnificat maintains a good momentum, and the nunc dimittis is expressively set.

The good things of the last work aside, these final canticles do not add anything to what had already been accomplished.

21

Motets and anthems

Willan composed thirty-three motets, thirty-eight anthems, and thirty-two hymn anthems – a total of more than one hundred works – between 1898 and 1967. In addition there are seven unfinished works and eight arrangements in these categories. As a group the motets and anthems are probably Willan's most frequently performed and widely known works, and I shall examine them in considerable detail; for the hymn anthems I shall look at the general nature of Willan's treatment of the genre.

MOTETS

For Willan a motet was a relatively short piece of part-music for unaccompanied choir on a sacred text. Willan's motet style emerged in his *Six Motets* (1924) and is discussed along with that collection. Other groups of motets include the eleven liturgical motets (1928–37) and the seven motets he wrote for Concordia Publishing (1949–51).

Willan's first motet, *How They So Softly Rest*, set for eight-part choir, was written in 1917 for the Mendelssohn Choir of Toronto in memory of the members killed in the war. This motet is one of Willan's best. With its contrast of male and female choirs and its requirements for a very soft yet full and rich sound, this work needs a fairly large performing group. The low writing for the basses and the thick chords with many doublings recall the church music of composers such as Gretchaninoff, Tschaikowsky, and Rachmaninoff; Willan was fond of Russian choral music and used to perform it with his choirs. The sudden jump into E major from A flat major at the words 'Until the Angel calls them,' followed by the quiet, sleight-of-hand slipping back into A flat at the very end of the motet, is quite electrifying. The writing in general, however, is remarkably diatonic for Willan at this period.

Six Motets, published in 1924, is Willan's first collection of real 'church' motets; here one meets Willan's motet style for the first time. It has certain distinctive characteristics. The music is conceived for unaccompanied voices. There is frequently a modal flavour to the harmony (often the result of the interweaving of· modally conceived individual voice parts). Willan often writes successions of secondary sevenths which use all inversions freely and which follow one another in modal as well as tonal relationships. These are frequently coupled with a rather free use of passing-type $^6_4$s (triads in second inversion).

The general motet style is more diatonic than one finds in much of Willan's other music. The Wagnerian chromaticism and the higher chromatic discords (ninths, thirteenths, etc) so prominent in the composer's instrumental and dramatic music are largely absent; what chromaticism there is is often modally derived. The free rhythm of plainsong is frequently reflected, with measures of differing lengths following one another naturally according to the flow of the words. (The influence of plainsong is of course implicit in the references to modality above.) There are smoothly flowing melodic lines in all parts, producing a texture which is usually neither strictly homophonic nor strictly contrapuntal but an amalgam of both. The melodies themselves tend to avoid cadencing leading note to tonic, preferring the plainsong-influenced supertonic to tonic. The influence of Tudor motets is evident not only in the modality but also in the careful and effective way that the cadences are written and placed. An element of mysticism which one feels upon hearing the music but cannot explain is often present.

On the whole, the six motets of 1924 tend to be simpler in style than the later motets. *Hail, Gladdening Light* is the most complex. The opening (Example 403) is typical of Willan's diatonic style. The use of the mediant chord in the second bar gives a slightly modal tinge to this otherwise B flat major passage. More obvious modal influences are apparent at the final cadence of the work. *O How Glorious* (for All Saints' Day) is simplicity itself, yet the music glows with a mystical intensity and beauty which no short extract can illustrate adequately. The final bars of *Very Bread, Good Shepherd Tend Us* show not only a considerable modal influence again but also Willan's unerring feeling for cadence (Example 404). *O Sacred Feast* exhibits a few of the secondary sevenths that will increasingly become part of the style (see example 405). *O How Sweet* and *Let Us*

Worship achieve the same mystical glow as *O How Glorious*, and by the simplest means. *Let Us Worship* shows Willan's practice of writing works for his own practical needs: 'I wrote that particularly because it's one of the very few motets in which the idea of sheep or shepherds come in, so we always sing it on Good Shepherd Sunday' (Parker tapes).

The six motets can all be managed by small choirs of modest resources (with the possible exception of *Hail, Gladdening Light*) and this, together with the pure and devotional character of the music, has made them justly popular and widely used.

Willan's next motet, *O Trinity, Most Blessed Light*, his longest up to that time, was published in 1925. The extract from it (Example 406) is a good example of the composer's use of sevenths and other diatonic discords; it also shows one of Willan's common treatments of the $^6_4$ and one of his colourful cadences. This motet is conceived in long phrases and sections and requires a sensitive performance with the points of climax constantly in mind to bring it off. The great opening-up on a C major chord at the end of page 5 in the score, coming as it does after a long period of building, can be quite stunning.

Between 1928 and 1937 a series of eleven liturgical motets appeared. All the texts were taken from various liturgies, particularly the Sarum. They are motets first and foremost, and, even though their texts come from liturgies, their usage is not restricted. They are not a fixed part in the Anglican service in the same manner as, say, the canticles.

The first four liturgical motets appeared in 1928. *Preserve Us O Lord* provides a good example of the influence of the free rhythm of plainsong noted earlier. The soprano part from the opening section of the motet will illustrate this (see Example 407); there are no firm bar-lines except the double bar at the end of the section. In between there are simply a few wavy or dotted lines which indicate sub-groupings of varying lengths. Regular metrical accentuations in the music are avoided in order to enhance the natural flow and rhythm of the words. (This system of notation is used in most of the liturgical motets.) Later in this motet a passage occurs which shows Willan's free use of $^6_4$s, this time three consecutively (Example 408). *O King All Glorious* contains an interesting example of imitation by inversion (see Example 409). *I Beheld Her* and *Fair in Face* are for the Blessed Virgin Mary, with texts taken from an eighth-century *Office of Our Lady*. They are both very beautiful, the subject inspiring the composer as in his Latin *Mass of St Theresa* of 1930. Short extracts cannot convey their exquisite loveliness. The three bars which conclude the first section of *I Beheld Her* show a number of interesting things within a short space; perhaps the essence of Willan's motet style is distilled here: the $^6_4$ s, the sevenths, the unashamed consecutive fifths, the smoothness of the voice parts, and the lovely cadence on the mediant (Example 410).

Three liturgical motets appeared in 1929: *Rise up, My Love*; *O King of Glory*; and *Lo, in the Time Appointed*. *Rise up, My Love* is perhaps Willan's most popular motet. The text, from Song of Solomon, is mystically connected with Easter; it is also suitable for the feasts of Our Lady. The style is similar to that found in the last two motets of the previous year and, indeed, these three motets are often performed as a group in concerts. Again, a short musical extract cannot do justice to the beauty of this piece. (In 1948 Willan based his organ work *Epithalamium* on this motet.) *O King of Glory* (for Ascension-tide) is conceived on a larger scale than its predecessors in the series and concludes with a section of jubilant alleluias. *Lo, in the Time Appointed* (for Advent) is also a large motet. It is the most fugal of the liturgical motets, containing three full fugue expositions. The opening exposition provides an example of answer by stretto at one bar (Example 411).

The remaining four motets appeared individually at two-year intervals. The funeral motet, *O King to Whom All Things Do Live*, was composed in 1931 for the dedication of a memorial to Lynnwood Farnam in Christ Church Cathedral, Montreal. The motet is simpler in style than its two immediate predecessors, and shorter. It contains a passage (Example 412) which clearly shows the use of modally influenced chromaticism in Willan's motets. Though the motet is in F minor, the use of G flats and E flats clearly derives from the Phrygian mode.

Behold, the Tabernacle of God was written in 1933 for the one-hundredth anniversary of the Church of St James, Chicago (the organist of which was Leo Sowerby). This is considered one of Willan's greatest motets; many marvellous things are compacted into a small space, and the piece does not render up all its secrets on first hearing. Though nominally set in G minor, *Behold* is more chromatic than its predecessors, the passage in Example 413 being an extreme case. The writing, diatonic and chromatic, has still a somewhat modal flavour. It is some of the most mystical music the composer ever wrote. The wonderful opening bars (Example 414) give notice that something unusual has begun. The prominent use of A flat, E natural, and F natural gives evidence of the influence of the Phrygian and Dorian modes.

Hodie, Christus natus est is a Christmas motet, the first Willan motet with a Latin as well as an English text, and was composed in 1935. The most vigorous of all the motets with its fast one-in-a-bar pulse, it is almost like a choral scherzo in its expression of the sheer joy of Christmas. The use of an ostinato figure in the upper voices against the principal melody in the lower voices (see Example 415) reflects the influence of Russian church music (eg Rachmaninoff). Toward the end there is some composite organum (Example 416). This is one of the more popular Willan motets, though not easy for the average church choir.

The eleventh liturgical motet, *Who Is She That Ascendeth*, was composed in 1937. The text is taken from the antiphons of the Assumption of the Virgin Mary. Quite unlike any of the composer's previous motets (though in *Behold, the Tabernacle of God* some preliminary signs are evident), this is the most modern-sounding and advanced piece of church music Willan ever wrote. It is also the most mystical. Except that it begins and ends in D, it is almost atonal. Extreme chromaticism is frequent (Example 417). The influence of later Vaughan Williams can be seen. The only thing that does not quite work is the rather abrupt switch to D major at the very end. It might have been better if Willan had not worried about trying to return to the tonality of the opening. Indeed several of Willan's motets published in 1928 had already followed the procedure of beginning and ending in different tonalities.

In 1935, Willan's two short motets for women's voices (ssa), *O Saving Victim* and *Look Down, O Lord*, were published. They are Willan's only motets for women's voices. Their style is quite conservative when compared with his later liturgical motets.

The motet *Ave verum corpus* (1943) was Willan's third setting of the text (the other two being anthem-settings of 1909 and 1922; see the next section). Written as part of his incidental music to the pageant *Brébeuf and His Brethren* (see chapter 13), it is a fine exercise in writing in sixteenth-century style and quite suitable for *Brébeuf*. As a separate piece, however (it was published in 1948), it represents a retrogression from Willan's earlier motets. In any case, William Byrd did it better!

In 1938 Willan edited and adapted five motets by early composers (including one by King John IV of Portugal), and in 1945 he adapted two Latin motets by sixteenth-century composers to English words.

In 1949 Willan embarked on a series of original motets; this set of seven works was published between 1950 and 1952 by Concordia. In comparison with the motets of the 1920s and 1930s, these show very little modal flavour; the writing is diatonic and there is little use of harmonic colour. Likewise the influence of the Tudor polyphony has largely disappeared and is replaced by a rather academic type of counterpoint which seems to be of the eighteenth century. Finally, the free-flowing rhythm derived from plainsong has all but vanished, and a much more metrical musical style is substituted.

I Will Lay Me down in Peace is the most beautiful of the seven. Written in 1949 in a very simple style, it nevertheless manages to recapture some of the atmosphere of, say, *Fair in Face* (see Example 418). *Christ Our Passover* (1950) abounds with examples of academic counterpoint: the passage in Example 419 is typical. The remaining five motets were composed in 1951. Willan was too good a musician and craftsman to write a 'bad' piece of music, but he could on occasion write music which was bland and unexciting: *Grant Us Thy Light* is certainly an example of this! Only *The Spirit of the Lord* (for Whitsunday) comes close to the level of his earlier motets.

In 1950 Willan composed his longest and greatest motet, *Gloria Deo per immensa saecula*. Willan's friend Drummond Wolff had commented on the apparent inability of modern composers to write choral music in five real parts; Willan proceeded to write *Gloria Deo*, set for SSATB choir.

Gloria Deo consists of three sections: the first, in A major and using the first line of the text, is developed from the theme in Example 420. This theme obviously has its origins in plainsong and is subsequently presented in a type of composite organum. The second section, though shifting through many tonalities, is mainly centred in F sharp minor. Freely polyphonic in style, it uses lines 2 and 3 of the text. It contains also many colourful harmonic progressions, as in the last few bars (Example 421). The final section, using lines 4 and 5 of the text, is a complete five-voice fugue in A major on the subject shown in Example 422. The fugue builds to a magnificent climax, at which point its subject is combined (see Example 423) with the theme of the first section. The striking modulation from A major to F major (and then back again) at the very end is truly electrifying.

This motet, because of its sheer size, difficulty, and magnificence, is not standard church service fare; yet it stands as one of its composer's greatest utterances in the realm of sacred music.

Willan's last published separate motet was *Great Is the Lord*, written in 1952 for the centenary of the Anglican Synod of Toronto. It is cut from the same cloth as *Gloria Deo*, only on a smaller scale, and it makes a solid ending to a noble series of motets. Like Willan's first motet (*How They So*

Softly Rest), it was written with a large or massed choir in mind. The three dozen intervening motets were composed for the average small church choir.

ANTHEMS

Before he left England, Willan composed six complete anthems. The first was written ca 1898, and the three best in 1906 and 1907.

Willan's first anthem, *All Hail! All Hail!*, dates from ca 1898 when he was organist of St Saviour's Church, St Albans. The piece is dedicated to the bishop of Colchester, who said to him, 'Don't try to make your music sound religious, it will merely become sentimental; do the best music you can in the best way, and it will automatically become religious' ('Matters Musical' no. 10). Unfortunately, Willan seems to have ignored the bishop's words, and the anthem wallows in the sentimental triteness of the popular church music of its time (Example 424). Perhaps it was this anthem that led the good bishop to offer his advice!

Willan reached his stride in 1906 and 1907 with two Christmas anthems and one harvest anthem. *There Were Shepherds Abiding* (1906) is a big anthem: the first half is almost a small dramatic scene as the story of the encounter of the shepherds with the angel is related in recitative, arioso, and short choral outbursts; the second half is a choral fugue on the text 'This is He Whom seers in old time.' Willan used this text again for the last movement of his Christmas cantata *The Mystery of Bethlehem* of 1923 (see chapter 10); in both cases he wrote fugues. The anthem received its first performance on 24 December 1906 in Worcester Cathedral (H.H. Woodward, precentor); the young composer's work must have been held in high esteem.

While All Things Were in Quiet Silence (1907) follows a similar pattern, the first part being a setting of a biblical prose text and the second a setting of words from a hymn. The piece opens with a mystical succession of four chords (Example 425) which appear again several times throughout the work. The reiteration of a few mystical chords became a favourite device with Willan (eg in his two symphonies). Another accompaniment motif is used in this opening section (see Example 426). Later the two are combined (Example 427). The second part sets three verses of a hymn and could be a model for the composer's later hymn anthems: organ introduction; verse 1 set as a solo; verse 2 (in this case a repeat of the words of verse 1) set in faux-bourdon; organ interlude; verse 3 set in unison for massed choir against a thick, independent organ accompaniment; and coda.

Equally impressive (and more popular) is another 1907 anthem, *I Looked, and Behold, a White Cloud*. This harvest anthem remains in the active repertory. Its form is that of recitative and chorus. The work begins with a mystical succession of chords. The chord succession appears again later, in a transposed version, to accompany the recitative 'And another angel came out of the temple, crying with a loud voice unto him that sat upon the cloud.' The hauntingly beautiful chorus that follows is built on a long, lyrical theme, the first part of which is shown in Example 428. A short recitative, followed by an exquisite choral amen, brings the work to a close. Willan would never surpass these magnificent anthems of 1906 and 1907.

Hail, True Body was published in 1909. It is the earliest of Willan's three settings of the fourteenth-century Latin hymn *Ave verum corpus*. (The 1922 setting is discussed below in this section, that of 1943 in the previous section.) Calling for tenor solo, choir, and organ, it tends a bit towards a sweet and sentimental style (somewhat like the Agnus Dei movements of Willan's first two settings of the office of holy communion). The piece is redeemed by the very beautiful choral amen with which it concludes (Example 429).

The last anthem Willan wrote in England was another one for harvest, *Give Ear Ye Heavens*. It is one of his very few unpublished anthems. It is a long and rather sprawling work, and though there are many points of interest, the structure needs tightening and some non sequiturs need to be removed. The style is almost symphonic at times, causing the score to appear to be in the nature of a condensed version of a work for chorus and orchestra.

During Willan's first thirty-five years in Canada (1913–48) he composed only five anthems – two at St Paul's and three (plus one unfinished) at St Mary Magdalene's. His composing for the latter church (from 1921 on) was centred almost completely upon missae breves, motets, and plainsong canticles (motets rather than anthems were used there).

In the Name of God We Will Set up Our Banners was written in 1917 for the depositing of military colours in St Paul's. Appropriately Willan uses variants of the first line of the melody of the plainsong hymn *Vexilla regis* (The Banners of Our King) as a recurring motif throughout the anthem; it first appears in the opening phrase sung by the chorus sopranos (Example 430). Later in the work Willan develops the *Vexilla regis* motif in the organ part as a means of modulation (Example 431). This anthem is one of Willan's best. Thirty years later he made a version of it for choir and orchestra.

O Strength and Stay (1918) is much smaller. Composed for soprano or tenor solo, choir, and organ, it is really a sacred song in three verses for soloist and organ. The choir joins the soloist in verse 3, but the choral parts are of secondary importance and could be omitted without loss. In 1933 the music appeared, to a different text, *O Perfect Love*, as a sacred solo song.

In 1922 Willan wrote his second setting of *Ave verum corpus*. This is not published, and the surviving holograph is incomplete (there is no organ part shown). Like his first setting, of 1909, this is for solo voice with SATB choir and is rather sweet and sentimental; it is hard to believe it was written as late as 1922.

In 1940, *Sing Alleluia forth* and *Christ Hath a Garden* were published. *Sing Alleluia forth*, with its strong modality and its relentless drive, reflects the influence of Vaughan Williams. This can be seen in the two extracts in Example 432. *Christ Hath a Garden* is, by contrast, quiet and gentle (there is only one loud passage in the middle of the anthem). The main melody (Example 433) has the quality of a simple folksong.

With requests from publishers and commissions for great occasions, the period from 1949 to 1953 saw Willan produce six anthems, among which were some of his greatest.

Like as a Hart started off the series, in 1949. It was Willan's first piece to be published by Concordia and marked the beginning of a long series of choral and organ works for that firm. The anthem is quite short and exhibits a simple beauty. It does, however, give indications that the composer was going to repeat himself at times. The opening (Example 434) is almost identical with the music for verse 3 of *England, My England* (Pro rege nostro); compare also the elegy from *Rondino, Elegy and Chaconne* for organ (1956).

Sing We Triumphant Songs of Praise (1950) is suitable for Ascension-tide or festival use and was written for a choir festival at St George's Cathedral, Kingston. It is structured in three sections, the first section (in D major) consisting of choir and organ making vigorous and triumphant sounds in antiphonal fashion. The contrasting middle section (in B flat major) is built on a lyrical theme, given out first by the sopranos and then treated in faux-bourdon by the choir. The final section returns to the music and tonality of the first. In the final section lines from a verse of a hymn (sung by one choir) are interspersed with alleluias (sung by another choir); however the music is so written that a single choir can easily move back and forth from one part to the other and thus perform the whole thing.

Blessed Art Thou, O Lord (1951) is even more impressive. It was written for the centenary of Trinity College, Toronto. The work is one of Willan's longest anthems, and comprises several sections. The opening bar of the organ part presents the motif from which much of the accompaniment will be derived (see Example 435). It thus gives unity to this otherwise through-composed structure. (It is also similar to the accompaniment figure in *O Lord, Our Governour*; see Example 149.) The majestic opening section eventually gives way to a quiet passage in D major. Here again Willan gives out the melody in the soprano and then repeats it in faux-bourdon. The melody is one of the most beautiful in all Willan's sacred music, as its opening phrases (Example 436) illustrate.

The faux-bourdon over, a recitative-like passage for unison altos, tenors, and basses (a procedure much used by S.S. Wesley) follows. It is encased by organ interludes (Example 437) somewhat reminiscent of the slow movement of *Piano Concerto in C Minor*. B flat major is then re-established for the next section, a series of antiphonal phrases for choir versus organ in the manner of the opening of *Sing We Triumphant Songs*. The final section, in G minor, is a setting out in long notes for massed unison choir of the plainsong hymn-tune *Urbs beata Hierusalem*. Against the unison voices the organ thunders a massive accompaniment. The style of this final section is similar to that of the organ prelude on *Urbs beata* which the composer was writing about the same time (see chapter 16).

Events of 1953 stirred Willan to a peak, and he produced three of his greatest anthems. For the coronation of Queen Elizabeth II he wrote *O Lord, Our Governour* for choir and orchestra (see chapter 10), which can be performed as an anthem for choir and organ. The last movement, 'Come, Thou Beloved of Christ,' of Willan's 1953 *Coronation Suite* for choir and organ (discussed in chapter 10) is also suitable as an anthem.

For the 1953 St Cecilia's Day Festival Service in London, Willan composed *A Prayer of Rejoicing*. It is one of his finest efforts, much longer than *O Lord, Our Governour* and written on a more expansive scale. It would sound well as a work for chorus and orchestra. As with a number of his best anthems, the opening phrase of the organ part serves in various treatments as an accompaniment and unifying figure throughout the work (Example 438). The opening section, in B flat major, starts simply, but becomes more colourful harmonically as it proceeds. It concludes with a particularly impressive series of tonal shifts (see Example 439). The extract shows an instance of Willan's use of his accompaniment motif in various circumstances (see the phrase marked by an arrow).

A quieter and slower middle section in D major follows. Like the opening section it begins simply and then becomes more adventurous as it proceeds. It contains some remarkably Wagnerian passages (as in Example 440) unusual in Willan's sacred music.

The big concluding section consists of a fugue on the subject shown in Example 441. It is preceded by a long dominant pedal, treated in a manner which brings to mind illustrious similar passages in Parry (eg *Blest Pair of Sirens*) and Stanford (eg *Coronation Gloria*). The fugue, though perhaps not as impressive as the one which concludes *Gloria Deo per immensa saecula*, is nevertheless exciting, building by means of partial stretti to a climax consisting of a magnificent melisma for sopranos on the word 'Alleluia.' This climactic melisma is comparable to a similar one toward the end of Parry's motet *My Soul, There Is a Country*.

Only a few of the twenty-odd anthems written after 1953 warrant special mention; most give the impression of having been 'made, not begotten.' Those of the big 'festival anthem' type, such as *O Sing unto the Lord*, generally do not show the musical imagination found in the composer's earlier examples of this type.

Ye Shall Know That the Lord Will Come (1957) is a surprising work; it does not give up its treasures easily. The old composer still had some tricks up his sleeve. The rather strange-sounding organ introduction will, in fact, provide the basis for much of the music in the first main section of the anthem. The passage in Example 442 illustrates the colourful manner in which Willan sets his text. The first section, though ending triumphantly in D major, has been mainly in D minor. The short middle sections use the tonalities of A major, G flat major, and B major. The A major section moves forward 'with increasing animation and texture' over an ostinato figure (Example 443) which seems to come from the composer's piano concerto. The final section returns to D major and consists of a free fugal treatment of a short, almost carol-like subject (Example 444). The style is somewhat similar to that of the final movement, also fugal and in compound metre, of *The Mystery of Bethlehem* (see chapter 10). One does not feel the composer is repeating himself, however, since the contexts are quite different. This anthem, particularly suitable for Advent, is worthy of serious attention.

Of the smaller late anthems two stand out slightly above their neighbours. *Rejoice, O Jerusalem* (for Palm Sunday) contains some of Willan's striking shifts of tonality, where the word 'light' is mentioned. It also contains an expressive melismatic choral recitative (Example 445) of a type unique in Willan's anthems. *Behold, the Lamb of God* (for Passion-tide), though the smallest of the set, is one of the most expressive. The music has a poignancy which recalls the composer's organ prelude of 1951 on *O Traurigkeit*.

Of the several unfinished anthems by Willan, two are of considerable importance. The largest is an incomplete setting of about 300 bars for STB soli, SATB chorus, and organ of the long hymn by Fortunatus, *Sing My Tongue the Glorious Battle*. The work is divided into two parts, part I being complete and part II remaining unfinished. The manuscript is untitled; Willan may have intended the work as a Passion-tide cantata. Part I treats the first five verses of the hymn. Willan makes no attempt to use the plainsong melody associated with the words (Pange lingua), and the style is remarkably diatonic. That this music must date from a reasonably early time is suggested by the fact that much of it was used in other works. For instance, the main accompaniment theme is identical to the theme Willan used for the orchestral prelude and postlude in his *Prospice* (see Example 121). The second half of part I became the third movement of *The Mystery of Bethlehem* (1923). Only the faux-bourdon at the end of that movement is not found in *Sing My Tongue*; otherwise the music is identical. Part II of *Sing My Tongue* does not seem to have become the basis for other works. It was left unfinished after only four of the six verses of the text had been set. The musical style is somewhat more chromatic here than in part I, and the writing for the organ is quite orchestral in nature.

The other important unfinished anthem is also perhaps the most nearly complete. Composed in 1924 and of 223 bars in length, *In the Heavenly Kingdom* is subtitled *Motet for Chorus and Organ*. But it not only requires a regular SATB choir with organ, it also calls for a second choir to act as both an SSA mystic choir (cf *An Apostrophe to the Heavenly Hosts*, discussed in chapter 22) and a unison SATB choir. Mendelssohn had used the term 'motet' for choral compositions with instrumental accompaniment, and Willan probably used it thus here. Some of the music for *In the Heavenly Kingdom* is derived from the Rouen church melody *Coelites plaudant* (Example 446). The opening unison of the chorus (Example 447) would seem to outline the Rouen melody. Furthermore, the first five notes are used as the main accompaniment motif in the organ part throughout the work. In the final section a second choir sings the complete Rouen church melody (spread out in long notes) in unison against an independent, flowing four-part texture sung by the main choir.

In the Heavenly Kingdom as it stands is written in three sections. The first section is in C major and set for SATB choir to the 'In the Heavenly Kingdom' text. In the second section, commencing 'Light perpetual shall shine,' the tonality ranges widely. It is here also that the mystic choir of women's voices is added, punctuating the phrases sung by the main choir with distant alleluias. In the third section the music returns to C major for the appearance of the Rouen church melody. At the end of the third section the composer reintroduces material from the opening of the first section, and this gives all the appearances of being the beginning of a coda. At this point the manuscript ends. *In the Heavenly Kingdom* would thus seem to be in a state of near completion. (The work was completed by me, was subsequently published, in 1979, and received its première performance in 1980.) It is one of Willan's most interesting larger sacred works.

HYMN ANTHEMS

The hymn anthem occupies a sort of middle ground between a fully original composition and an arrangement. The text and tune of a hymn are set out in the form of an anthem for choir and organ. The tune associated with the words is almost always written by someone else. Only four of Willan's hymn anthems are not based on tunes from other sources: in *Guide Me O Thou Great Jehovah* and *From the Eastern Mountains*, the hymn-tunes are Willan's own (*St Osmund* and *Montes orientis* respectively); in *Before the Ending of the Day* and *Let All the World in Every Corner Sing*, the tunes are probably Willan's, though they do not exist separately as hymn-tunes. The composer has to compose an organ introduction and organ interludes for the work. In addition he has to bring his imagination to bear in putting forth the tune in various ways (eg faux-bourdon).

Of Willan's thirty-two hymn anthems all but one were written between 1950 and 1966. They all tend to be conservative and straightforward in musical style and aimed toward choirs of modest accomplishment. 'They seem to fill a certain purpose in the U.S. where choir work is generally speaking on a lower grade than in England but where organists' playing is on the whole much better,' Willan wrote to Fred Emerson in 1964. They do not contain many examples of the flashes of inspiration that raised much of Willan's other sacred music above the commonplace. I will extract and list the various methods and plans Willan used in writing his hymn anthems and mention specific examples of each.

1 *Tonality*. In his first three hymn anthems Willan followed the practice of changing tonality for the middle verse(s). The new key was either the submediant or the dominant. For example, the tonal scheme for his first hymn anthem, *Before the Ending of the Day*, written in 1937, has E flat major C major, and E flat major. However, starting with his fourth hymn anthem, *Lift up Your Heads*, and continuing, except for *Before Jehovah's Awful Throne* (*Old 100th*) of 1960, to his last, Willan did not bother with tonal change and kept to the same key throughout. One would think he would have made more frequent use of key change, one of the most powerful means of producing variety in tonal music. Regretfully one might well conclude that these hymn anthems were for Willan increasingly a matter of 'dollar fodder' and that he expended a minimum of labour on them.

2 *General plan*. The hymn anthem would commence with an introduction for the organ. This introduction might be based on the opening notes of the tune (eg *Sing to the Lord of Harvest*) or it might employ an independent figure (eg *Father of Heaven*). Between verses the organ would also play interludes, often based on the introductory material. Most hymn anthems would have three or four verses of text set out in various ways.

3 *The opening verse*. In his earlier hymn anthems Willan liked to give the tune to the sopranos alone (or soprano solo) for the first verse (eg *Round Me Falls the Night*). Later he preferred to set the first verse for SATB choir (eg *O What Their Joy*). The latter procedure applies to the majority of the hymn anthems. There are also two cases in which the first verse is set for full unison (eg *Rejoice Ye Pure in Heart*) and one case where the first verse is given to unison men (*Let All Mortal Flesh*).

4 *The middle verse(s)*. Here one finds the greatest variety of treatment. If an anthem has begun with an SATB first verse (the most frequent procedure), the middle verse(s) would usually be either for unison soprano (eg *Rise, Crowned with Light*) or, less often, for unison men (eg *Lord of All Hopefulness*). If the anthem had begun with a unison opening verse, the chances are good that the middle verse(s) would have an SATB treatment. (Very often this procedure followed an SATB opening verse as well.)

Willan employed many approaches for treating middle verses in SATB: faux-bourdon – the most common procedure (eg *O Trinity of Blessed Light*);

tune divided up among the four parts (eg *Hosanna to the Living Lord*);

straight SATB (eg *Ye Watchers and Ye Holy Ones*);

tune in the bass (eg *Strengthen for Service*);
tune in the alto (eg *Old Hundredth*);
partial faux-bourdon (eg *O Strength and Stay*).
Other treatments for middle verses include tune plus descant (*Rejoice, O Land*) and SAT, with the tune in the tenor (*Now Thank We All Our God*).

5 *The final verse*. By far the most common occurence here is for the final verse to be given out by the full choir in unison against a free organ accompaniment (eg *Christ Whose Glory Fills the Skies*). A variant of this is to have the final verse set partially in massed unison and partially in SATB (eg *Father of Heaven, Whose Love Profound*). Other procedures are rare. There is one interesting case of SATB plus descant, in *Rise, Crowned with Light*. (Willan did not often write descants because he thought them to be too high and to sound 'screamy.') *Round Me Falls the Night* uses a partial faux-bourdon. *Lord of All Hopefulness* has an SATB final verse in which half the tune appears in the bass part and half of it in the soprano.

6 *Layout*. Nearly all Willan's hymn anthems are written for SATB choir and organ. There are, however, two works for SS and organ (*Fairest Lord Jesus* and *Jesus Good above All Others*) and one for SSA and organ (*Let All the World in Every Corner Sing*).

Willan's reputation as a composer would probably not have suffered at all if he had not written these hymn anthems. Nevertheless they do exhibit a certain variety of treatment and provide models for other composers to study. Likewise it cannot be denied that hymn anthems serve a useful function, not only by providing easy anthem material for choirs of modest resources but also by familiarizing congregations with good hymn-tunes which they might not otherwise know. About half of Willan's hymn anthems are treatments of fine tunes which would not be generally familiar to most congregations.

22

Other sacred music

In this chapter I shall examine some of Willan's carols, *An Apostrophe to the Heavenly Hosts* (1921), and, briefly, his other sacred works, including his sacred songs, his hymn-tunes, his music for children and for junior choir, and his work as editor, arranger, and/or composer for various collections of sacred music.

CAROLS

Willan wrote thirteen original carols and about one hundred arrangements. Of the original pieces, ten are published separately while two are found in the two-volume *We Praise Thee*, one of Willan's junior choir books. Of the arrangements, seventeen are separate pieces while the others are found in various collections edited by Willan: *Red Carol Book* (containing forty), *Children's Favourite Carols* (sixteen), *Carols for the Seasons* (twenty-two – not all for Christmas), and *We Praise Thee*. The original carols will now be considered, along with a few of the more important arrangements.

Perhaps the earliest original carol by Willan is an unpublished and undated setting for SATB and string quartet of *Welcome Yule*. There is no full score, just a condensed score and a set of parts. The appearance of the condensed score would suggest that the composer originally had more than string quartet in mind, very possibly orchestra. The instrumental writing is somewhat dissonant at times, especially for Willan, and a passage such as that in Example 448 is similar to those found in the opening section of the unfinished *Pageant of Our Lady* (see chapter 13). The superimposed fourths and the clashing chord-streams are similar in both works and strongly suggest later Vaughan Williams (or Karg-Elert in his more impressionistic organ pieces). *Welcome Yule* is a sprightly, attractive piece which goes by very quickly. The choir parts are not difficult. The relatively complex accompaniment may have prevented the work's publication.

Willan's arrangements of *The First Nowell* (1926) and *Jesous Ahatonhia* (1927) have become popular and widely used. The former is notable for its descant refrain, while the latter did much to popularize Brébeuf's lovely Huron carol.

Willan's first published original carols, *The Three Kings, Regina coeli letare*, and *Tyrle, Tyrlow*, appeared in 1928. *The Three Kings* (a setting of a poem by Laurence Housman) is for unaccompanied six-part choir (SSATBB). It has become one of Willan's most popular works; one needs a good choir to perform it properly. The first part consists of an effective quasi-antiphonal use of the TBB voices with the SSA ones. Later in the work the six voices come together to build one of the most impressive climaxes in all Willan's vocal music. No single short extract can convey the wonder of this piece. Arrangements for women's voices and for men's voices were made by J. Running and published nearly forty years after the original version. Willan was not too enthusiastic about the men's arrangement: 'I also feel disposed to add that the arrangement was made without my knowledge, and if sung by men's voices only I think that the effect of the alternation between high and low voices in the original will be seriously impaired' (letter ca 1966). Willan had been paid £5 by the publisher for the outright purchase of the piece in 1928.

The other two 1928 carols are written for four-part (SSAA) unaccompanied women's choir. They contrast well: *Regina coeli* is in slow, devotional style, and *Tyrle, Tyrlow* fast and light. The musical idiom of *Regina coeli* is similar to that of the motets Willan was writing at the time, particularly *I Beheld Her* and *Rise up, My Love*. The form is part through-composed and part strophic, with the three verses set to different music but having the refrain 'Regina coeli letare' set to the same music (cf some of Willan's songs: eg *The Cavalier Song*). The final cadence (Example 449) is exquisite. *Tyrle, Tyrlow* uses almost the opposite form: the verses are set to similar music, but they all have long, melismatic cadences which are ingeniously different from one another. The result is a charming piece of music which conceals a great deal of art and imagination. The main theme (Example 450) is simple but attractive, and the final cadence (Example 451) is delightfully unusual. The piece is a gem!

Just before Christmas 1929 Willan composed another of his famous unaccompanied Christmas pieces, *Here Are We in Bethlehem*. Written for SATB, it was published in 1930. The four verses, by Rev F.J. Moore, are set to a free-flowing, almost plainsong-like melody. There is a plaintive quality of great beauty in this piece, a fine example of which is shown in the final cadence (Example 452).

Willan's next significant Christmas piece is *What Is This Lovely Fragrance?* Although this is technically an arrangement, it is of such beauty that it deserves mention. In 1929 Willan made an arrangement of the tune and text for solo voice and small orchestra for his ballad opera *Prince Charlie and Flora* (see chapter 12). In 1940, he wrote a version for SATB and string orchestra as part of the music for his *Nativity Play* (see chapter 13). Finally came the 1941 published version for SATB and organ, which is a rearrangement of the 1940 setting. The first two verses are set for unison voice(s), below which the organ provides beautiful, flowing harmonies (Example 453, from verse 2). The third verse is set for SATB, with some unaccompanied passages. The tune itself, an old French carol (see Example 175), is lovely to start with, but Willan's setting makes it even lovelier.

Seven years elapsed before Willan completed another Christmas work. In 1948 he composed *A Soft Light from a Stable Door*, a short carol set for solo voice and wordless SATB choir. Here the choir performs almost the function of an organ, providing an introduction and an accompaniment (all humming) for the soloist. Indeed the piece could probably be performed quite satisfactorily with solo voice and organ. Except for the undulating introduction, which is completely diatonic and which comes back at the end of the piece, the writing is more chromatic than one usually finds in Willan's Christmas music. There are passages (such as that in Example 454) which recall the style of Delius. (For the Delius influence cf also *Teneramente* for piano, 1946.) *A Soft Light* is one of Willan's most atmospheric pieces and is really quite beautiful. It was not published till 1979.

In 1949 Willan's set of *Three Christmas Carols* was published. One of these carols is an arrangement and the other two are original works. The arrangement is of the traditional accumulative carol *The Twelve Days of Christmas*, set for SSATB unaccompanied. This has become immensely popular, though it is by no means easy to perform. The first sopranos are the only ones to sing the words, the other voices providing a humming background. But what a background it is! Willan's imagination never seems to run out of different things to do under the constantly repeating tune and the ever-lengthening refrains. He spaces his voice entries so that the musical texture gradually 'accumulates' as well: day 1 is for first sopranos alone; day 2 adds the second sopranos and day 3 the altos; days 4 to 7 proceed in three-part SSA texture; days 8 and 9 add the tenors, producing a four-part texture; day 10 adds the basses to make the complete five-part ensemble. One might wonder at Willan's long delay till the entries of the men's voices, but it must be kept in mind that the accumulative refrains are becoming quite long by day 8 and thus, in fact, men are singing for 71 of the 112 bars of the piece. The two original works are *Make Me Merry* and *Welcome Yule*. (*Welcome Yule* was initially composed ten years earlier, in less elaborate form, for the Arts and Letters Club of Toronto.) In both pieces Willan manages to make his music sound like that of traditional carols even though the works are original (see Example 455).

In 1950, Willan's *A Christmas Lullaby* was published. Scored for tenor (or baritone) solo and unaccompanied three-part women's choir (SSA), this is another of the composer's 'atmosphere' pieces (cf *A Soft Light*). *A Christmas Lullaby* achieves its effect by having the women's chorus sing the words 'Sleep, baby' over and over to an ostinato figure (see Example 456). The ostinato is subject to minor modifications as the piece progresses, but remains much the same. Against this ostinato the soloist sings the text to a melodic line which, for the most part, is rather chant-like. The total effect is hypnotic.

Sun of Righteousness, a setting of Ralph Crane's well-known seventeenth-century poem *All This Night Shrill Chanticleer*, was composed in 1952. Requiring an unaccompanied six-part chorus (SSAATB), it is written in a somewhat 'massive' style similar to that in the two unaccompanied movements of *Coronation Suite*, which Willan was composing about the same time (see chapter 10). He employs here something of the accumulative effect that was seen in *The Twelve Days of Christmas*: verse 1 is set for SSAA alone; verse 2 is set for SSAAT, but with the tune in the tenor part; verse 3 adds the basses for the first time, with the tune going back into the top part.

Willan's last original Christmas piece, *Christmas Praise*, was published in 1957. This charming little work, set for unison voices and/or SATB voices with organ, is rather like plainsong in style (indeed, the music for 'Gloria in Excelsis Deo' at the end of each verse is quoted from the missa de angelis).

AN APOSTROPHE TO THE HEAVENLY HOSTS

This 1921 work is universally acknowledged as one of its composer's greatest creations and is widely performed. Large choral forces are desirable, since the score calls for eight-part double choir and two small 'mystic' choirs. The work is unaccompanied, though the choral writing has been described as 'symphonic.'

The text was compiled from eastern liturgies by H.G. Hiscocks (rector at St Mary Magdalene's) and Dixon P. Wagner. There is also a verse from a hymn by Athelstan Riley. The words are splendidly mystical, beginning 'Invoking the thrice threefold company of the Heavenly Hosts, sing we' and then continuing about the 'six-winged Seraphim,' 'many-eyed Cherubim,' 'Dominions, Princedoms, Powers,' and so on. It is interesting to compare *Apostrophe* (1921) with Holst's *The Hymn of Jesus* (1917) – the latter on a similarly mystical text from the apocryphal Acts of St John. The overlay of mysticism, the use of distant choruses, and the influence of plainsong (Holst actually quotes two plainsong hymns) are common features of both works. Holst's work requires a large orchestra, whereas Willan's is written for voices only.

Apostrophe was composed in 1921 for the Mendelssohn Choir of Toronto. The conductor, Dr Fricker, had set 17 August as the deadline for the completion of the music. Early in July Fricker told Willan that there had been a mistake and that 17 July was the deadline! Willan had to disappear from his office for a few days and compose furiously. At first inspiration did not come. Then Willan asked himself, 'What would I want to hear if I were in the hall listening to these words?' At that point he began to write, and the whole gigantic work was finished in about three days!

The music appears to divide into four main sections, each concluding with an amen. Section I is perhaps the most mystical-sounding, and Willan makes prominent use of the augmented triad for his mystical effects (see Example 457). (A similar passage occurs for the words 'many-eyed Cherubim.') Though this section (and indeed the whole piece) is written largely in E flat major, a pronounced plainsong-derived modal effect is produced by the use of the flattened seventh and by frequent cadences on the mediant. The free use of $^6_4$s (already noted in Willan's motet style) is also in evidence and here helps to create the mystical atmosphere. In Example 458 can be seen a cadence on a mediant $^6_4$. The thick, massive texture of this extract, with its many doublings, is reminiscent of the Russian choral church music Willan admired so much. That is but one technique of choral scoring used by Willan in this work: others are the antiphonal use of the two main choirs, the selection of voice parts from both choirs to be mixed together in various ways, and the interplay between the main choir(s) and the mystic choir(s).[1] He manipulates the colours of his large palette of choral forces in an almost symphonic manner. Section I finishes with the first appearance of mystic chorus I, singing amen.

Section II, commencing 'Ye who perform the one eternal will,' is the shortest. The tonality begins to shift around more quickly and to move farther afield. Keys touched upon include C major, E flat minor, D flat major, and B flat minor. The section cadences on the mediant of the home key, at which point both mystic choirs appear with their amens.

Section III, beginning with the words 'Ye ministering Angels,' remains in E flat major for a time. Then, after yet another cadence on the mediant, it moves into an arresting series of sudden changes of tonality in antiphonal fashion:

CHOIR I	CHOIR II
C major, A major	(tacet)
(tacet)	G flat major
G flat (F sharp) minor, E minor	(tacet)
(tacet)	E major, E flat major

The choirs then join together and build to the main climax of the piece so far (fortissimo at the words 'Holy Immortal') with another cadence on the mediant of E flat major. As at the end of the previous sections, the mystic choirs sing their amens, pianissimo.

A great climax has been reached, and one wonders what the composer is going to do now. What he does is unexpected and yet absolutely right; he introduces the majestic and well-known hymn-tune *Lasst uns Erfreuen*, set to the words 'Ye watchers and ye holy ones' (Example 459). This begins the fourth and final section. Commencing in the tonic key of E flat major, section IV treats the first four lines of the hymn in a straight-

---

1 Willan intended the mystic choruses to be placed at some distance from the main body of singers. However, at the famous performance at the St Cecilia's Day Festival in London in 1952 all voices were placed in one large group by the conductor, and Willan was pleasantly surprised at the result.

forward fashion. Lines 5 and 6 are treated canonically between the two antiphonal main choirs. The alleluias follow, and these are treated quite freely and expansively. The tempo increases as the drive toward the final climax begins. Suddenly there is a spectacular tonal shift to D flat major, followed by another to E major, during which the tempo is accelerating more and more. The music makes its way back to a dominant pedal in E flat major, and this leads to a great climax, 'con exaltazione.' The work could have finished there; however Willan adds a further twenty-two bars during which the music winds down to pianissimo, and the mystical atmosphere of the opening is re-established.

A full understanding and appreciation of *Apostrophe* probably requires, like most great works, some study of (or participation in) the music itself and its relationship to the text. Nevertheless, also like most great works, it makes an immediate and thrilling impact and can stir even an audience unfamiliar with it.

OTHER SACRED MUSIC

Sacred songs
Willan wrote four solo songs on sacred texts. The first, *O Perfect Love*, published in 1933, is the music of the anthem *O Strength and Stay* (1918) set to a different text of the same poetic metre.

Three sacred songs were published in 1938 as *Three Songs of Devotion*. All three are through-composed, and the structure of the first, *My Lord, My Life, My Love*, is particularly interesting:

Introduction	F minor	
Verse 1	F minor	
Verse 2	C minor to E flat major	All follow on as one large unit.
Verse 3	C minor to D flat major	
Interlude		
Verse 4	F minor	
Verse 5	F minor, F major	These run together as one unit.
Short coda	F major	

The second song, *Come Thou, O Come*, is set to words selected from a ninth-century Latin hymn. This song is perhaps the most sacred in style of the three and even has an optional chorus part for its ending. This ending consists of fourteen bars of tonic pedal, over which Willan writes music which has a spiritual affinity with passages in Brahms's *German Requiem* (Example 460). The third song, *Eternal Love*, is yet another wedding hymn. It requires no special comment except that it is a much better wedding solo than most one hears.

Original hymn-tunes

In addition to making arrangements of about sixty existing hymn-tunes and to writing faux-bourdons (ie putting the tune in the tenor part) for some fifty others, Willan composed about thirty original hymn-tunes. Of the original pieces none has really become popular with congregations. The writing of a great congregational hymn-tune is very difficult: it must be tuneful and easily remembered without being banal or cliché-ridden; it must have a strong rhythm and sweep which, at the same time, must fit the word-accentuation of the text; it must not be overly complex, and yet it must not be trite.

If none of Willan's original hymn-tunes is a 'hit,' a number are very fine. At least three have achieved some currency in various hymnals: *St Basil*, *St Osmund*, and *Stella orientis*. *St Basil*, written for *St Basil's Hymnal* of 1918, is Willan's first surviving original hymn-tune and one of his best. Unfortunately, with texts for which *St Basil* would be suitable most congregations prefer to sing the well-known Welsh tune, *St Denio*. *St Osmund* is probably Willan's greatest congregational hymn-tune, possessing a majesty and a degree of memorableness which ensures its success with many congregations. Its rather odd metre, 8 7, 8 7, 4 7, is not overly provided for with good tunes, and *St Osmund* therefore has less competition than does *St Basil*. The same is the case with *Stella orientis*, with its fairly rare triple-rhythmed 11. 10. 11. 10. metre. *Stella orientis* is always associated with the hymn *Brightest and Best Are the Sons of the Morning*, and there is no better tune for these words than Willan's. Both *St Osmund* and *Stella orientis* come from a collection called *Five Hymn Tunes*, published in 1927.

Many of Willan's other hymn-tunes are of a high musical quality and would be quite suitable for choir use, but they are musically too sophisticated to be successful with most church congregations.

Music for children and junior choir

In his later years Willan made some significant contributions to the repertoire of the junior choir with the publication of the two volumes titled *We Praise Thee* in 1953 and 1962. These two volumes contain fifty anthems for the church year, set for unison treble, or SS or SSA and organ. Some of the pieces are Willan's arrangements of carols and chorales, and a few are plainsong settings with SSA faux-bourdons, but the majority are original compositions. A number of the pieces in both volumes were also published separately.

The aim of *We Praise Thee* is well stated in E.W. Klammer's introduction to volume I: 'Within recent years the junior choir, or children's choir, has become firmly established as one of the important musical organizations of many churches ... One of the problems confronting most directors of junior and children's choirs has been the lack of sufficient material of real musical interest based on worthy texts that juniors can understand. *We Praise Thee* was designed to meet that need.' Volume I was one of the first such books in the field, and many of us recall what a boon it was to organists with junior choirs. It set a standard of taste and excellence for subsequent collections. The musical settings contain nothing strange or startling; Willan uses much the same conservative, simple, and basically diatonic idiom that one finds in the hymn anthems of the period. Like the hymn anthems, they provide a solid repertoire of suitable material to fill a particular need.

Other works for junior choir are *The Story of Bethlehem* and *The Twelve Sayings of Jesus*. *The Story of Bethlehem*, composed in 1955, is a little Christmas cantata in which the account from St Luke is set for unison voices ('quasi-recitative') and organ, followed by a chorus for SSA and organ ('Glory to God in the highest'). The thematic material of the organ part is taken mainly from Luther's chorale *Vom Himmel Hoch*. *The Twelve Sayings of Jesus*, published in 1958, is a collection of twelve short pieces for unison or SA choir with keyboard accompaniment. These are perhaps the least interesting of Willan's pieces for junior choir, many of them being too short to be of much practical use as separate anthems.

Willan was the sole music editor of *The Hymn Book for Children*, published in 1962. Its 110 tunes were all chosen and arranged by him with an eye to their suitability for young children in Sunday school; the melodies have a small vocal compass and use mainly conjunct movement. Intended for unison singing with piano accompaniment, the keyboard parts of the hymns have been simplified so that they can be played with ease by the average church pianist. Ten of the tunes are the composer's own. His tunes for children are all simple and singable; sentimentality is successfully avoided, but triteness does sometimes creep in. The best of these tunes is probably *Montes orientis*.

Collections and editions

Among the small liturgical pieces by Willan, the collections of introits and graduals are widely used. The first collection, *Introits*, was published in 1950. It contains twelve introits, written for the various festivals of the church year. The structure of each is the same – antiphon, set for unaccompanied SATB; psalm verse and Gloria Patri, set in plainchant with organ accompaniment; and antiphon repeated – producing an overall ternary form. The texts were from the Anglican liturgy. In 1957 *Introits for the Church Year* was published, with texts taken from the Lutheran liturgy. There were twenty-two introits in the collection; Willan added another twelve for an edition in 1964. The structures are identical with that for the Anglican introits. In 1960 there appeared *Graduals for the Church Year* (thirty-seven graduals, again with words from the Lutheran liturgy). Like the introits, the graduals are short. They follow one of two general structures: 1 / gradual, set for SATB unaccompanied, and alleluia, set for SATB unaccompanied; or 2 / gradual, set for SATB unaccompanied, and tract, set in plainchant with organ accompaniment. The settings employing the tract would be used in penitential seasons.

Similar collections of short liturgical pieces include *The Responsaries for the Offices of Tenebrae* (1956), *The Great O Antiphons of Advent* (1958), and *The Responsaries for the Church Year* (1964). The nine tenebrae responses are set in simple motet style for SATB, as are the twelve O antiphons. *The Responsaries for the Church Year* has some sections for SATB and some for plainchant with organ. The pieces for tenebrae are written in a severe, sixteenth-century style. The music of the other collections is less severe and archaic, but still quite conservative.

A large undertaking of Willan's in his last years was the production of the 1963 *Canadian Psalter, Plainsong Edition*. This was a project very dear to his heart, and as editor he was able to bring to bear a lifetime's experience with plainsong. The psalter includes all the offices in the prayerbook, as well as all the psalms; in Willan's own words, 'It has everything there' (Parker tapes). His preface is excellent, the explanations being clear and concise. His *Accompaniments to the Canadian Psalter, Plainsong Edition* stands as a model of tasteful plainsong accompaniment.

Willan's lifelong work with plainchant bore further fruit in *The Propers of the Year*. This was an adaptation of the plainsong of the Roman rite to the English text of the Anglican rite for use in services at St Mary Magdalene's. Introits, communions, graduals, alleluias, tracts, offertories, sequences, and antiphons were adapted to cover all the principal feasts of the church year.

23

Conclusion

Willan employed somewhat different musical styles for his instrumental and dramatic works on the one hand, and for his sacred choral music on the other. This difference is not as apparent in the early works, but by the time one arrives at the period of the symphonies and operas and compares the musical style of these with the motets and missae breves of the same time, the cleavage becomes much more obvious.

In this chapter we shall consider Willan's secular musical style, his sacred musical style, and some final reflections – by Willan and about him.

WILLAN'S SECULAR STYLE

Early influences
Parry, Stanford, Rheinberger, Tschaikowsky, and Brahms; followed shortly by Wagner, Strauss, Elgar, and César Franck; and followed again by Delius, Holst, and Vaughan Williams are the main sources of Willan's secular musical style. The influence of plainsong and the later Renaissance is more noticeable in his sacred music, though it may partially account for the irregular phrase lengths and free harmonic relationships found in some of his secular music as well. There is also an occasional influence of the late Baroque: J.S. Bach in the diatonic counterpoint found in some of the organ chorale preludes, Corelli and Handel in *Sonata No. 2*, and Thomas Arne and his colleagues in some of the songs and such works as the incidental music to *The Winter's Tale*.

Willan's harmony in the very early works at least sometimes shows a diatonicism which was typical of Parry. The opening of Willan's choral-orchestral setting of *Prospice* is a very clear example of this, as well as of other features of Parry's style, such as the solid, steady rhythm and the use of notes and chords of anticipation (see Example 121). The opening of Parry's song *To Althea* (Example 461) is also typical of many passages in Willan's music, even up to some of the later small organ pieces.

From Stanford Willan received many things, some of which apply more to his sacred music. Of the things which apply here, the most important is probably the free use of diatonic and chromatic chords of the seventh. The openings of Stanford's partsong *The Bluebird* (Example 462) and Willan's partsong *Eternity* (Example 463) exhibit a certain kinship. Willan's use of chromatic sevenths would have a basis in passages such as that from Stanford's *Songs of the Fleet* shown in Example 464. From the same Stanford work, the free use of a diatonic eleventh chord – a mediant eleventh in first inversion (see Example 465) – is typical of the sort of chord progression Willan would occasionally favour.

Brahms's influence is most apparent in Willan's early chamber music (much of which was left unfinished), but surfaces now and again in middle and late works as well. The finale of *Trio in B Minor* is one of Willan's most Brahmsian movements (see chapter 14). The finale was the first movement of this trio to be written (ca 1909); the rest of the movements were added later. Among the unfinished early chamber works, the first movements of *String Quartet in E Minor* (existing also in versions for piano solo and piano trio) and *Piano Quartet in A Minor* also show a heavy Brahms influence, as do some other fragments for violin and piano. Several of the variations in Willan's greatest piano work, *Variations and Epilogue* for two pianos, written 1913–15, exhibit a kinship in style and figuration with some of the Brahms sets of piano variations (see chapter 17). As late as 1957, in the hymn prelude on *Ebenezer*, one still finds some Brahms in evidence (see Example 264). Many of the places in Willan's work where the influence of Brahms is particularly noticeable involve pieces either for keyboard or where a keyboard instrument is part of the ensemble. As a young man, Willan made a considerable study of Brahms's piano music with Evlyn Howard-Jones, and at one time entertained thoughts of becoming a concert pianist specializing in Brahms.

The influence of Rheinberger is sometimes evident in Willan's organ works. Willan knew and admired Rheinberger's organ music and played a number of that composer's organ sonatas as well as the first organ concerto. The first half-dozen variations of Willan's *Passacaglia No. 2* for organ are perhaps the lengthiest and most obvious reflection of Rheinberger's style (cf Rheinberger's own passacaglia from his *Sonata No. 8*). Another Rheinberger comparison is sometimes made with Willan's *Pre-*

lude and Fugue in C Minor for organ of 1908. Alan Gray stated that the fugue contained 'the finest piece of triple counterpoint since Rheinberger' (see Example 230). Willan's harmonic imagination in the prelude far exceeds Rheinberger's, however.

In the early years of this century, Willan came under the spell of Wagner, and this composer probably had a greater influence than any other on Willan. Traces of Wagnerian harmony in his work appear as early as some songs of ca 1904, but his first substantial Wagnerian work was the dramatic cantata *Cleopatra*, of 1907. In the latter the leitmotif-technique is used throughout. This Wagnerian technique, though discernible in the instrumental works as well, would be most obvious in *Transit through Fire*, *Deirdre*, and, to a lesser extent, *Brébeuf*. Examples of Wagnerian harmony in Willan's scores are legion, some cropping up in the most unlikely cases (such as the incidental music of 1920 for the play *Matsuo*: see Example 170). Many of his unfinished symphonic fragments of ca 1910 show an influence of the orchestral style of both Wagner and Richard Strauss.

The French composers, particularly César Franck, also had a hand in the formation of Willan's style. Willan did not play much French organ music, except for a few small pieces by Guilmant and the odd movement from a Widor symphony, and no Franck appeared on his recital lists. But Franck was the representative in France of the Liszt-Wagner chromatic idiom. The most striking examples of French – and particularly Franck's – influence in Willan's work occur in his two most important chamber works, *Trio in B Minor* and *Sonata No. 1*. The slow movement of the trio has a French feel to it (a succession of major ninths in a very chromatic relationship; see Example 190). The introduction to the first movement of *Sonata No. 1* is another example of a similar flavour; the main theme of the first movement and its first subsidiary motif are in a very Franckian style (see Examples 200–2). The rondo-refrain of the finale of the same work is perhaps more like Fauré than Franck, but French nevertheless (Example 209). *Sonata No. 1*, owing a fair amount to Franck and Fauré, owes proportionately less to Brahms or Wagner.

The influence of French impressionism is to be seen in several of Willan's songs of 1912: the opening of *Dawn* seems to show the hand of Debussy quite clearly with the stream of parallel sevenths and the generally impressionistic style (see Example 309). Thus the main period of French influence on his music was the early 1910s. After that it disappears from prominence, its residue melting almost imperceptibly into the general musical base from which he drew his style.

Harmony
By the time Willan came to Canada his secular harmonic idiom had
largely settled (a few additions as a result of the influence of such composers as Delius and Vaughan Williams came later). Some trademarks
can be easily singled out:

1 *Sudden shifts of tonality.* This tendency is evident as early as the song
Farewell composed in January 1899. The unexpected shifts from D major
to E flat major (Example 294) and from A flat major to F sharp minor
illustrate this clearly. The song *Rest* of ca 1908–9 abounds in further
examples (Example 303). The alternation of the tonalities of B flat minor
with B major in one of Willan's last songs, *When I Am Dying*, is another
interesting case (see Example 326). Godfrey Ridout observes that Willan
'frequently displays the Lisztian drop from a major key to the major key
a minor third below, or conversely from a minor to a minor a major third
below' (*CMJ* 3, 1959).

2 *Augmented triads, freely approached and quitted, sometimes with a seventh added.* One of Willan's earliest and most effective uses of the chord
occurs at the entrance of the chorus in *Prospice*, at the words 'Fear
death?' (Example 122). Willan seems to associate this chord with, among
other things, the sea, making prominent use of it in the unfinished symphonic poem of ca 1910, *Seaside Elegies*, and much later (1943), in the
passage describing the ocean voyage of the missionaries in *Brébeuf*
(Example 180). The tragic fate motif in *Deirdre* would seem to be a series
of augmented triads, each decorated with an appogiatura (Example 109).

3 *A succession of slow-moving, 'mystical' chords, usually minor triads of a
striking chromatic relationship to one another.* The introductions to both
organ passacaglias come immediately to mind, but Willan was already
using the device by 1907 (see the opening of *Cleopatra*, Example 85, and
also the opening of *While All Things Were in Quiet Silence*, Example 425).
This would remain a favourite procedure throughout his life, not only as
a way of beginning a composition, but also as a unifying element by
means of its periodic recurrence throughout a work. The two symphonies provide excellent examples of the latter use (see Examples 2 and 13).

4 *The chord of the minor thirteenth.* Willan's use of seventh and eleventh
chords, largely derived from Stanford, has already been noted; likewise,
the use of chords of the ninth after the French manner, to which must
now be added ninth chords according to Wagner's usage. Willan also
had a fondness for some particular uses of the chord of the thirteenth; it
was usually the minor thirteenth that he used, very often with the minor

ninth included. He rarely used major thirteenths. The openings of *Intro-duction, Passacaglia and Fugue* of 1916 (Example 235) and *Postlude in E Minor* of ca 1957 (Example 269) are perhaps the most obvious examples of this typical Willan usage of the minor thirteenth (here, in both cases, over a tonic pedal). Early examples are to be found in the sketches of several unfinished chamber and symphonic works from his English days.

5 *Augmented sixth chords.* Willan favoured the French variety, some-times with the minor third or its enharmonic equivalent, the augmented second, as in the famous 'Tristan' chord. Occasionally these became quite complex, especially (as in Example 466, from the score of 1921 for *Panta-loon*) if they involve an added ninth, inversion, and enharmonic notation all at the same time! Example 466 turns out to be the first inversion of a French sixth on E (or F flat) with a major ninth added; Enharmonic equivalents are shown in brackets in the solutions in Example 467.

6 *Series of chords with roots separated by the interval of a third.* This is generally considered characteristic of Liszt and Wagner, though Brahms also used it; the practice goes back to at least Schubert. A very obvious early case (1907) occurs in the love-duet in Willan's *Cleopatra* (Example 468). This is simply an example of major chords with roots a major third apart. The opening of the second movement of *Symphony No. 2* shows a series of minor chords with roots separated by major thirds (see Example 469). A mixture of major third and minor third root separations occurs in a passage from *Symphony No. 1* (Example 2).

7 *Scale-wise descending basses.* Example 470 (from *Epithalamium* for organ) shows this clearly.

A good example of Willan's harmony in terms of the resources dis-cussed so far occurs at the opening of the first movement of *Symphony No. 2*. Some of this music is quoted in Example 12. An analysis of bars 2 to 5 of this passage is given:

BAR	BEAT	KEY	CHORD
2	1	C minor	Third inversion of a tonic seventh
	2	C minor	Root position seventh on the raised submediant
	3	C minor	French sixth without a third
3	1	C minor	Dominant seventh with a flattened fifth
	2	C minor	French sixth on the flattened dominant
	3	C minor	Third inversion of a dominant thirteenth
4	1	C minor	Mediant seventh

BAR	BEAT	KEY	CHORD
	2	D flat major	Dominant ninth (transition to D flat)
	3	{ D flat major { C minor	First inversion tonic triad of D flat, quitted as Neapolitan sixth in C (pivot chord for modulation)
5	1	C minor	Third inversion of a dominant seventh
	2	C minor	German sixth on the flattened dominant (F sharp in bass = G flat)
	3	C minor	Second inversion of tonic triad

Later influences

The influence of Delius turns up occasionally in Willan's music. As early as ca 1908 there is evidence of this in the song *Sunset in the Desert* (Example 305) and later, in 1922, in the subsidiary subject of the one-movement *Sonata No. 3* (Example 219). But it was during the 1940s that Willan seemed to go through his 'Delius period,' and this is noticeable in four works in particular: *Brébeuf* (chapter 13), *Teneramente* for piano (Example 292), *Epithalamium* for organ (Example 249), and *A Soft Light*, carol for choir (Example 454).

Brébeuf was the least Wagnerian of Willan's dramatic works in which he employed the leitmotif technique. Nevertheless it would not be correct to imply that the influence of Delius is more than in the background here. Such is not the case with the other three pieces listed above, however, where Willan is so close to the Delius style that one wonders if they were not intended as 'homage to Delius' in the manner of Percy Whitlock's *Carol* for organ (a copy of which Willan owned). Unfortunately most of the Delius-influenced pieces were not published, with the result that this factor in Willan's work is not widely known.

Another harmonic influence is that of Vaughan Williams and the neo-modal school. In spite of his long association with plainchant, there is comparatively little purely modal writing in Willan's secular music. One of the earliest evidences of modal influence in his work is the main subject of *Epilogue* of 1908 for organ, with its prominent flat seventh (Example 223). This is modality as Stanford might use it. The influence of Vaughan Williams comes later with such things as the bard's motif from *Deirdre* (Example 106). The strange succession of chords that make up this motif have a relationship to one another derived from a mixture of modal sources – a more subtle and sophisticated use of neo-modalism such as is found in the mature works of Vaughan Williams. At least two more of the leitmotifs in *Deirdre*, Conochar and Cathca, are obviously modally inspired. Perhaps Willan's closest approach to Vaughan Williams occurs in the opening scene of the unfinished *Pageant for Our Lady* where, in the orchestral parts, one finds not only modality but also examples of superimposed diatonic dissonance in the style of Vaughan Williams's later works (Example 183).

So far this consideration of influences on Willan's secular style has centred on matters largely pertaining to harmony, either tonally or modally based. A few words about some other aspects now follow, particularly regarding melody, rhythm, form and orchestration.

Melody

Willan was a naturally gifted melodist; he loved 'tune.' Though not all his works are equally interesting from a melodic point of view, the best usually contain fine melodic motifs and phrases. Quite often, especially in the later symphonic and organ works, he puts the tune in the middle voice (eg the opening horn solo in the slow movement of *Symphony No. 2*, or the tenor melodies of many of the organ chorale preludes). This placing probably stems from his early attraction to the piano music of Brahms, in which he especially liked Brahms's habit of hiding the tune in a middle part. The frequent appearance of the device of faux-bourdon in Willan's vocal music is perhaps another manifestation of this.

The main thrust of Elgar's effect on Willan was melodic. Most of the 'big tunes' he composed tend to reflect the warmth and nobility of Elgar. His orchestral and band marches follow Elgar's lead in their melodic material, as well as in their general structure. The 'noble' moments in the symphonies, the piano concerto, and in some sections of the operas have an obvious affinity with Elgar. *A Song of Welcome*, composed in 1955 for chorus and orchestra, is his most blatantly Elgarian work (see Example 159) and one of his less important; another very Elgarian piece is *Elegy* for organ of 1933. In most other cases he keeps the Elgar influence sufficiently under control so that the music is still identifiable as Willan!

Willan's instrumental melodies are often vocally inspired, making use of much conjunct motion. Of many examples, the 'trio' tune of *Marche solennelle* of 1937 (Example 65) might be cited. Leaps there are too, but in many cases Willan 'cushions' the leap somewhat by the use of a note of anticipation. Sometimes the anticipations are eighth-notes, as in Example 48, from *Piano Concerto*; sometimes sixteenth-notes, as in Example 471, from *Symphony No. 1*.

Downward and upward appoggiaturas, changing notes, unaccented and accented passing notes, subsidiary harmony notes, suspensions, ornamental resolution, and so on are all of frequent occurrence in Willan's instrumental and vocal melodic lines and specific examples are hardly necessary here. His propensity for 'constant chromatic passing tones' was remarked upon in a review of *Coronation Suite* by Henry Cowell (*Musical Quarterly* 40, Jan 1954, 59).

One of the distinguishing features of much of Willan's melodic writing is the constant intermingling of duplets and triplets. Bruckner, of course, had his favourite pattern of ♩♩♫ . The triplet within duple measure was favoured by Brahms and Elgar, but the many juxtapositions of these time-units in Willan's music probably stem from Wagner. For an example of the straight 'Elgarian' triplets, the reader is referred to Example 163. For a somewhat more sophisticated mingling of melodic duplets, triplets, syncopations, and so on, the illustrations of the reminiscence motif and its transformations as used in *Transit through Fire* (Example 95) provide a good example. A complex juxtaposition and mixture in all parts of duplets, triplets, syncopations, and incomplete quadruplets is found in the early (1911) partsong, *Fain Would I Change That Note* (Example 332). A rhythmic variation of the triplet ♫♩, much used by Elgar, also appears in Willan. One instance occurs at the change of key (Example 148) in *O Lord, Our Governour*.

Willan was not a 'four-square' melodist but tended rather to irregular phrase lengths. This characteristic appeared as early as *Four Holiday Pieces for Children* for piano, composed in 1908. Sometimes this irregular grouping was more subtle, as in the finale of *Piano Concerto* (Example 50). This theme, a regular sixteen bars in length, might be mathematically subdivided into four four-bar units, but musically the phrasing is much less clear-cut and is constantly changing in a most interesting fashion; it is a truly great tune. At times, however, this non-metrical phrase-structure did not 'come off' and produced a tune which seemed to ramble and to lack shape (eg the 'trio' tune of the march prelude from *Coronation Suite*; see Example 152).

Willan sometimes indulged in unaccompanied melody. One of his favourite procedures was to have this occur in the bass register. The opening of the orchestral introduction to *Deirdre* (Example 105) comes to mind, but this was a late instance. The openings of the final scene of *Cleopatra* (1907) and of the music for act IV of *Glastonbury* (1912) show that this was a common device in Willan's orchestral music from many years back.

Counterpoint

Willan's counterpoint tends to fall into three categories: free modal counterpoint, diatonic counterpoint in a somewhat Bachian style, and what John Beckwith has referred to as 'post-Mendelssohn chromatic counterpoint' (*Musical Times* 3, no. 1534, Dec 1970). Extended passages of modally derived counterpoint are not common in his secular music. Diatonic, 'Bachian' counterpoint occurs chiefly in some later works, particularly in a number of the chorale preludes for organ, eg the chorale partita on *St Flavian* found in the first set of hymn preludes published in 1956. Chromatic counterpoint is the more usual type to be found in Willan's secular works. One of the earliest and best examples is found in *Prelude and Fugue in C Minor* for organ of 1908 (see Examples 228–30).

Rhythm
Like his counterpoint, Willan's rhythm is of several types. On the one hand there is the plainsong-influenced free rhythm found in many of his sacred choral works. Akin to this is the free 'speech rhythm' of the vocal line in his operas and many of his songs. On the other hand there are the more metrical rhythms found in most of his instrumental works. One of the clearest examples of use of a free speech rhythm in his songs is found in his setting of Keat's sonnet *To Sleep*, during which the voice seems to be almost semi-chanting the text. Even when writing a comparatively metrical strophic song, Willan's great care for the proper setting of words would usually lead him to make minor rhythmic alterations in the vocal melody for each verse in order to accommodate subtle shifts of accent and emphasis in the text (eg the song *Requiem*: see Example 308). The arioso-like vocal lines in the operas provide further examples of his rhythmic freedom when setting words (see, from *Deirdre*, Example 115).

In his instrumental works Willan's metrical rhythms tend to remain steady and regular. Occasionally this leads to monotony, as in the case of 'Come Ready Lyre' from *Coronation Suite*, with its unrelieved succession of measures in 4/4 time and steady plodding of quarter-note movement. Sometimes Willan is quite enterprising and successful in the employment of unusual metres for pieces, or sections of pieces: the 15/8 metre used for the second movement of *The Mystery of Bethlehem* (see Example 133) is perhaps the finest example. There are a number of pieces written in 5/4 time, one of the first being the introduction to the finale of *Trio in B Minor* (ca 1909), and one of the last being the elegy in *Fugal Trilogy* for organ (1958). An early unfinished sketch of an adagio for string quartet reveals him contemplating a movement in 7/8 time. Once in a while he indulged in the mixing of metres within a passage: the effective juxtapositions of bars of 4/4 and 5/4 time in the main theme of the intermezzo in *Coronation Suite* is an example, as is the main subject of the first movement of *Symphony No. 2* (Example 14).

The use of cross-rhythm and syncopation is fairly common with Willan. Cross-rhythm sometimes takes the form of the melody being treated in this manner over a steady, rhythmic bass. The mazurka from the score to *Pantaloon* (Example 172) provides a simple example. Another would be the hemiola-like effect in variation X of *Variations and Epilogue* for two pianos (1915) (see Example 289). A much more complex situation is illustrated by the opening of the first movement of *Coronation Suite* (Example 151); here there is some syncopation in the bass as well, with a rhythmic ostinato in the tenor. An example of particular interest occurs in the second piece in *Three Pieces for Organ* (1954), in which an ostinato figure of six beats' duration is superimposed upon a regular 5/4 metre, thereby causing the ostinato to commence at a different place in the bar with each repetition. (Stravinsky had employed a similar device in his *Symphony of Psalms*; this is perhaps the closest Willan ever came to that composer!) Willan occasionally uses different time signatures simultaneously in different parts. An example of this is the combination of 3/4 and 9/8 metres in variation XII of *Variations and Epilogue* (Example 290).

Sometimes one hears Willan's music described as being rhythmically dull. This may be the case with a few run-of-the-mill pieces he churned out in his later years, but it is certainly not the case with his best works. No one who has been swept along by the scherzo movement in *Symphony No. 2*, for example, can say that he was rhythmically uninspired. The subtleties of his free-rhythm vocal works may escape some listeners initially but are bound to become more apparent as appreciation deepens.

Musical form

Musical form was always a major concern of Willan. In one of his 'Matters Musical' radio talks in 1938 he said:

It has always been my contention that a work, in order to live, must first of all possess a sound architectural form ... Just as the eye rebels at the sight of an irregular building, so does the ear rebel at an illogically constructed movement, be the rhythm never so arresting or the melodies never so enchanting. The symphonies of Tschaikowsky are great examples of logically built-up movement, and I have a shrewd idea that it is not only their vital rhythm and haunting melodies which make them so popular, but the regular return of the various parts which make up a perfectly balanced whole and give the hearer a sense of completeness and satisfaction.

Willan's first major area of compositional endeavour was the art-song, which was thus his first major encounter with the problems of finding and writing suitable musical forms. In song-writing one can, to some extent, take one's form from the words. Nevertheless, Willan did use a number of different types of structure in his songs (above, 213). None was particularly new – nearly all can be found in the songs of Parry and Stanford. The individuality of Willan's songs lies in other aspects.

Willan's earliest *completed* examples of sonata-form movements are *Epilogue* of 1908–9 for organ and the first movements of *Trio in B Minor* and *Sonata No. 1*. Later examples are found in some movements in the first and second symphonies and the piano concerto. (The later sonata-form movements tend to exhibit a greater degree of unity and integration than the earlier ones, which tend to be more sectional.) A comparison of the first movement of *Sonata No. 1* (ca 1916) and the first movement of *Symphony No. 2* (1948) shows this clearly.

Some of Willan's sonata-form movements are adventurous in the choice of key for their second tonal areas. The first movement of *Sonata No. 1 in E minor* uses an unusual G sharp minor-F sharp minor combination for its second tonal area. Other exceptional cases occur in the first movements of the symphonies and the piano concerto, where the first two tonal areas are, respectively, D minor and E major, C minor and E minor, C minor and E major-C sharp minor. Willan is here following the lead of other late Romantic composers (eg Mahler and Elgar). Others of his sonata-form movements use more 'regular' (in the classical sense) keys for their second tonal areas.

Many of Willan's unfinished sketches of symphonic and chamber works dating from his early period seem to stop after the exposition, giving rise to the suspicion that the young composer had difficulty with development of material and could not proceed with the 'development' sections. If it was a problem, it was one he would overcome. The development section of his first completed piece in sonata form, *Epilogue in D Minor*, 'shows considerable imagination and covers a wide range of tonalities (E flat major, D minor, D major, C sharp minor, G sharp minor, B major, and E flat major). At one point (see Example 225) the two main subjects (I and II) are presented together. A dominant pedal, over which the opening of the first subject is treated sequentially, leads back to the recapitulation' (above, 178). The words 'treated sequentially' are significant. Especially in his later works one of Willan's favourite devices was the sequential development of motifs over constantly shifting chromatic harmony, laced with appoggiaturas. The extract in Example 472, from *Symphony No. 1*, is typical.

Within his overall sonata structures (symphonies, sonatas, etc) Willan did engage in a number of structural experiments. The finale of *Trio in B*

Minor might be diagrammed as introduction, A, B, C, A, B, and development-coda (based on A, B, C, and introduction) – a sort of sonata-form movement with a new theme in place of a central development section, but with a large development-section-cum-coda at the end. In the one-movement *Sonata No. 3*, also in B minor, one sees the following structure: A, B, short link, A plus development, B, and coda (on A, B). This placing of the development between subject I and subject II in the recapitulation did have precedents in the finales of the first and third symphonies of Brahms. The first movement of Willan's *Symphony No. 2* is unusual in that, though ostensibly in sonata form, the various short motifs which appear in the exposition seem to coalesce into one big tune at the midpoint of the development section, as if Willan were giving us the fragments first and then the whole (a reverse procedure similar to one followed by Sibelius in the first movement of his second symphony). But perhaps Willan's most ambitious structural experiment is found in his piano concerto, where the key of the first movement, C minor, is not re-established till the end of the concerto, and the finale thus commences in a key other than that in which it ends (in fact the finale is a three-refrain rondo, with each refrain in a different key!). See chapters 7 and 14 for a fuller discussion of these works.

Motto themes are used in the two symphonies and in the piano concerto. In both symphonies the mottos consist of a short series of striking chords. In the piano concerto, the motto is a melodic figure of four notes (Example 40). All three works are linked together by the periodic recurrence in all of them of what I call the 'Willan motto' (Examples 10, 25, and 44).

Willan uses rondo form within his sonata structures comparatively rarely, but on the three occasions he does use it he subjects the form to some interesting irregularities. Of the three rondos in question, two are of the three-refrain variety – both of the 'modulating' type. The slow movement of *Sonata No. 1 in E Minor* is in D flat major (an unusual key in itself for a sonata in E minor), and the three refrains are presented in D flat major, E major, and D flat major respectively. The finale of *Piano Concerto* goes even farther (as mentioned above) by having each of its three refrains in a different key: E flat major, B major, and C major. The finale of *Sonata No. 1* is a four-refrain rondo, and every one of its eight sections begins in the home tonality of E!

In the beautiful slow movements of *Piano Trio* and *Symphony No. 1* the form is rhapsodic and improvisational. A similar approach in *Hymn for Those in the Air* is less satisfying.

Willan early excelled in the fugue: his fugues for organ of 1908 and 1909 stand among his finest works. His secure command of contrapuntal technique certainly gave him an edge, yet his best fugues are no mere dry specimens from academia, and he is able to breathe life and excitement into the form. He wrote quite a number of fugues – both instrumental and choral – in addition to many fugal passages in larger works. Only in some of the organ fugues composed in the last decade of his life does he tend to revert to a rather dry 'examination fugue' style. His contrapuntal tours de force are the pieces of triple counterpoint found in the fugues of *Prelude and Fugue in C Minor* (1908) and *Passacaglia and Fugue No. 2* (1959), the almost continuous stretto of the fugue in *Introduction, Passacaglia and Fugue* (1916), and the quadruple counterpoint in the fugue he added (1943) to his *Variations and Epilogue* of 1915.

Willan's earlier fugues use non-modulating subjects, whereas the later ones tended to favour modulating subjects. The fugues of Bach are basic to all fugue-writing since his time, and Willan had something of Bach's fluency and musicality in his fugues. The influence of Rheinberger is also present, particularly in the double fugues (C minor of 1908 and E minor of 1959), which seem to take their cue from the finale of Rheinberger's *Sonata No. 7* (which Willan often played). The impressive return of the material of the prelude at the end of *Prelude and Fugue in C Minor* is another Rheinberger trait.

An interesting off-shoot of Willan's fugue-writing is his rather novel idea of presenting some of his lyrical 'middle subjects' in non-fugal pieces in a subject-answer relationship, putting the repetition of the tune into the dominant rather than repeating it in the same key. He did this several times in his late works, as in the 'trio' tune of the first movement of *Coronation Suite*. The movement is an orchestral march, one of a half-dozen he wrote. In all these he followed Elgar's model:

march: in a tonic key;
lyrical 'trio': in a related key;
march: in tonic key;
coda: consisting of a grandioso treatment of the trio theme, followed by a brief concluding reference to the march theme, all in the tonic key.

The only exception is *Élégie héroïque* for band which, though a march, follows the highly unusual procedure of having all first three sections in one key (D flat major), followed by coda in B flat major! (Even Elgar sometimes deviated from his general pattern, as in *Pomp and Circumstance March No. 2*.)

Willan's treatment of other forms, such as the various types of chorale prelude, follows fairly traditional lines, and there are few structural surprises.

Willan's use of the leitmotif-technique in his dramatic works has been considered at some length in chapter 9. In summary, he used his leitmotifs in the manner more of Elgar (*Gerontius, The Apostles, The Kingdom*) than of Wagner. He used only a small number (maybe a half-dozen) per work and introduced them only when he felt the emotional situation required it. Another influence in this regard was Debussy's opera *Pelléas et Mélisande*, a work Willan admired. Its influence on *Deirdre* has perhaps been underestimated in the face of the more readily obvious influences of Wagner.

Willan employed the leitmotif-technique in at least two of his incidental scores: *Pantaloon* (1921) and *Brébeuf* (1943). In neither case is the music Wagnerian in essence; he could divorce the leitmotif-technique from a Wagnerian musical style if he so wished.

On occasion one can observe him associating certain melodic phrases or harmonic progressions with specific things and using them for that purpose in several different works. His use in a number of instances of augmented triads to suggest the sea, as well as the various appearances of the Willan motto, have been noted. Further examples are the music representing judgment in *Glastonbury* and again in *Requiem* (see Example 161); the repose accompaniment motif used in *Cleopatra* and again in *Rest*; and the short musical phrase in two works associated with Yeats's phrase 'And evening, full of the linnet's wings' (*Sonata No. 3* and *Poem*; see chapter 14).

Orchestration

Opinions differ widely on Willan's orchestrations. Godfrey Ridout has written (*CMJ* 3, 1959): 'The orchestra appears to inhibit him, and he tends, often, to apply his organ and choral technique to his orchestration, which leads to a certain opaqueness in the texture; or he will borrow orchestral devices, those he knows to be safe, from other composers ... In the opera *Deirdre* there is a monotony of orchestral colour attributable to his reluctance to give the strings, especially the double basses, a rest.' Ridout admits that Willan's music is difficult to orchestrate because of its texture, with real counterpoint in place of orchestrally conceived figurations. 'Effective orchestration is often the result of skilful cheating, and, Willan won't cheat.' Ridout made a perceptive remark to me: 'Healey Willan had the knack of making a large orchestra sound small.'

Some conductors of performances of Willan's symphonies have expressed themselves more favourably. Reginald Stewart, who conducted the première of *Symphony No. 1* in 1936, wrote in 1960: 'Healey made believe that he needed guidance in finding the most effective registers and in achieving the proper balance between single instruments and groups. Actually, he knew it all and there was nothing one could suggest which could in any way affect his *innate instinct* for the right orchestration.' 'Innate instinct' applies to much that he achieved outside the narrow aspect of orchestration.

Walter Susskind, who conducted one of the most brilliant performances of *Symphony No. 2*, said of the work, 'The orchestration is colourful and it's meaty ... [with] appealing use of the woodwind instruments in little phrases coming after passages for full orchestra ... It has original rhythmic patterns, especially in the scherzo movement ... It is a most satisfying work, one into which one can sink one's teeth!' (*Toronto Star* 1 March 1958).

For his incidental music to plays, pageants, and so on, Willan used various ensemble combinations. His standard Hart House orchestra seemed to consist of flute, clarinet, and strings, with possibly a horn or some other instrument. Two of the most important and successful of his incidental scores, *Nativity Play* and *Brébeuf*, use chorus with orchestra (strings and harp only for the former, and a small orchestra consisting of 1121/2321/ timp, perc/strings for the latter). His scoring in both is more than adequate. The interplay between voices and orchestra and the music itself and the manner in which it is presented within the context of the play produce a highly satisfying musical experience. Innate instinct proved itself entirely suitable here.

Of the works written for large orchestras, such as the two symphonies, the piano concerto, *Deirdre*, the orchestral marches, and certain works for chorus and orchestra, perhaps the most successful from the point of view of orchestration is *Symphony No. 2*. By 1948 Willan had learned to keep his flutes up high in orchestral tuttis, where they would do some good; he produces a fuller and richer sound and yet allows daylight into his orchestral textures. And, as Susskind pointed out, there is a colourful use of wind instruments, especially in the scherzo. One would have difficulty imagining *Symphony No. 2* scored in any other way than it is, for then it simply wouldn't sound like Willan (according to Ridout Willan received guidance in his final orchestration of this work from Ettore Mazzoleni).

The piano concerto must also be considered a successful orchestral work. Here Willan has found an excellent balance between piano and orchestra; the piano solo has a full share of bravura, yet the orchestral part is far from being a mere perfunctory accompaniment. There are many colourful orchestral passages in this concerto, some tender and lyrical, others forceful and arresting. The combination works well. Willan once said that he did not entirely like the commercial recording (CBC, and later RCA Victor), since the solo piano was too prominent and much of the beauty and interest of the orchestral part was not fully audible.

Both Franck and Bruckner have been castigated for 'scoring like organists' (they were the first great composers since Bach who were organists by profession). What is so sinful about scoring like an organist? Some of Willan's colourful and distinctive use of orchestral brass in his symphonies may have its origins in his experience with the many chorus and solo reed stops on the big organ at St Paul's. Surely the criterion for any orchestral scoring must be simply 'Does it work?' The symphonies of Bruckner and Franck are firmly planted now in the general symphonic repertoire; they obviously 'work.' At its best, Willan's orchestration also works, certainly for his own music. Brahms's orchestration was criticized for being 'grey' and lacking the splashes of colour found in Tschaikowsky and others, yet his scoring grows out of, and is appropriate to, his own musical style. Cannot the same be said for Willan?

WILLAN'S SACRED STYLE

Influences
Willan's sacred style has its roots mainly in plainsong, late-Renaissance polyphony, Russian church music, and the church pieces of Parry and Stanford.

Stanford is earliest in evidence in Willan's church music, and aspects of his influence continued to affect his writing all through his life. Stanford had revitalized English church music and had introduced into his service settings and anthems some of the principles of thematic development used by the great German symphonists. In his famous Te Deum in B flat from *Morning Service in B flat*, composed in 1879, he builds the whole fabric from the short germinal motif announced at the beginning of the piece. Willan held 'Stanford in B flat' in great respect and, in a speech ca 1940, said it was 'a splendid piece of pioneer work ... All modern writers are indebted to it ... Stanford uses the organ in many passages as an antiphonal effect to the voices. Thus we get the effect of two ff's, but neither interfere with the other, rather they enhance the other ... If the organ was used with the same volume with the voices they would undoubtedly be completely smothered ... In many places the bass voices of the choir do not sing the actual pedal bass of the composition. How wise!' How much Willan had learned from these observations can be seen in many of his anthems, a particularly fine example being *Blessed Art Thou, O Lord* of 1951 (see chapter 21). The musical style of Stanford – and to some extent of Brahms – is apparent in Willan's church music as early as 1906 in *Magnificat and Nunc dimittis in B Flat* and its sister-work in A minor (see chapter 20).

When the emphasis shifted after 1920 from communion, canticle, and anthem settings for choir and organ to unaccompanied motets and missae breves, along with plainsong canticles, the influence of Stanford followed. In 1907 Stanford had written his *Evening Service on Gregorian Tones, Opus 98*, and this provided the inspiration for the nearly three dozen settings of the magnificat and nunc dimittis in plainsong with faux-bourdons that Willan would make. (His choir at St Mary Magdalene's used to sing Stanford's *Magnificat on Tone II with Faux-bourdons*.) Stanford's motets also had some influence on Willan's. The extracts from Stanford's motet *Justorum animae* (Example 473) have considerable affinity with the middle section ('Sit tibi nate decus et imperium') of *Gloria Deo per immensa saecula*. The sudden shift in tonality in the first example from G major to B major (ie major keys a major third apart) should be noted and compared with Willan's harmonic procedures discussed earlier in this chapter.

A final example of the influence of Stanford is in the endings of Stanford's *Bluebird* (Example 474) and Willan's *A Soft Light* (Example 475); both pieces finish inconclusively on a supertonic seventh, producing a highly unusual and 'magical' effect.

Parry's influence is not as extensive as Stanford's though his *Seven Chorale Preludes*, Sets I and II, may well have influenced the style and structures of many Willan chorale preludes. Probably the most spectacular Parry-like passages occur in the large anthem *A Prayer of Rejoicing* (1953). The long dominant pedal preceding the final fugue recalls the one in Parry's *Blest Pair of Sirens* (or in Stanford's *Coronation Gloria*), and the climactic soprano melisma at the end is comparable to the one that forms the climax of Parry's motet *My Soul, There Is a Country*. *A Prayer of Rejoicing* is one of the few sacred works of Willan which contain some remarkably Wagnerian passages.

The influence of Russian church music becomes evident by 1917 with the motet *How They So Softly Rest*, in which the low writing for the basses and the thick chords with many doublings recall the choral works of

Gretchaninoff, Tschaikowsky, and Rachmaninoff. Similar techniques appear in *An Apostrophe to the Heavenly Hosts* (1921). Willan was fond of the Russian church composers and performed a considerable quantity of their music with his choirs.

Another influence that becomes apparent in *Apostrophe* is that of Holst. The overlay of mysticism in text and music and the influence of plainsong, which are prominent in Holst's *The Hymn of Jesus*, composed in 1917, are present here. The use of ostinati is another Holst trademark and could well have sparked Willan's use of it, as in the fifth movement of the Christmas cantata, *The Mystery of Bethlehem* (1923), or in *Coronation Te Deum* (1937), both discussed in chapter 10.

The influence of Vaughan Williams has already been noted in connection with the opening of *Pageant for Our Lady*. Further examples are to be found in some of Willan's small sacred pieces, perhaps the two most notable being his first setting of the carol *Welcome Yule* (ca 1925–30?) and the anthem of ca 1940, *Sing Alleluia forth*; see Examples 448 and 432. The *Welcome Yule* quotation shows Willan experimenting with Vaughan Williams's 'tri-planar harmony' (to use Tovey's expression), with independent chord-streams sounding at different registers. The quotations in *Sing Alleluia forth* are typical of Vaughan Williams's brand of vocal part-writing and neo-modalism respectively.

Willan's motet style
Perhaps Willan's most characteristic sacred music is found in the unaccompanied motets, missae breves, and faux-bourdons which he wrote for his choir at St Mary Magdalene's after 1921. Here the influence of plainsong and late-Renaissance polyphony is most apparent and here, according to a number of commentators, Willan achieved his greatest originality. The music is composed in his motet style, which first crystallized in *Six Motets* (1924); see chapter 21.

Whenever Willan is writing a motet on the Blessed Virgin Mary there is a noticeable 'style within a style'; while written within the general motet style, they exhibit a tenderness, beauty, and feeling which set them apart from Willan's other motets and his masses.

Willan probably reached his farthest boundary of 'modernism' in the last of the Blessed Virgin Mary motets, *Who Is She That Ascendeth*, composed in 1937. As well as being the most mystical of Willan's motets, it is the only one where the realms of atonality are approached.

In some of Willan's later motets and anthems organum-like passages appear (eg *Gloria Deo per immensa saecula* and the 'Come, Thou Beloved of Christ' movement of *Coronation Suite*). Willan was fond of organum and said of it: 'This style of writing under certain given circumstances can be inexpressibly and most mystically effective. The effect of the Sequence for the Feast of Pentecost, "Veni Sancti Spiritu," sung alternately by cantor and choir in organum, as it used to be sung in Westminster Cathedral under the late Sir Richard Terry, was one of the most moving things I have ever heard. I have since adopted this principle of singing many of the sequences in St. Mary Magdalene's.'

Conclusion: three periods of sacred composition
In conclusion, there would appear to be three periods in Willan's sacred compositions. The first period runs from ca 1900 to ca 1920. During this time Willan composed communion service settings, canticles, and anthems – all for choir and organ. With the exception of *How They So Softly Rest*, there are virtually no unaccompanied works. The musical style was less sharply separated from Willan's secular writing than would be the case later. Brahms, Stanford, some Elgar, a little Wagner, and an occasional hint of modality, plus Willan's own musical personality, were the sources of this music. And it is good music too! In later years Willan quite unjustly disparaged these works, simply because his views on church music had altered radically in the intervening years. Yet it becomes more and more apparent that much of his most imaginative writing took place prior to 1920, and the church music is no exception!

The second period begins ca 1921, when Willan went to St Mary Magdalene's. When it ends is difficult to say, but one might suggest 1949. During this time, with a few exceptions, the writing is for unaccompanied choir. Nearly all the motets and missae breves belong to this period, as do many of the plainsong canticles with faux-bourdon, and it was during this time that Willan's characteristic motet style, so different from his secular style, developed. The writing of anthems virtually ceased (except for two composed ca 1940), chiefly because Willan did not use anthems at St Mary Magdalene's, only motets. The four mass settings written between 1927 and 1930 – three for unison voices and organ, and one for SATB and organ – are other exceptions to the unaccompanied rule and tend to carry on stylistically from the first period.

The third and final period begins ca 1950, coinciding with the composer's retirement as professor of music at the University of Toronto. This was the period of the flood of commissions, as publishers, now aware of the commercial value of his reputation, sought him out. He was requested to write anthems again, large numbers of them. At the start, a few of these anthems were of very high calibre, containing some of his best work (eg *Blessed Art Thou, O Lord; O Lord, Our Governour*; and *A Prayer of Rejoicing*), but in time they tended to become more run-of-the-mill royalty-fodder. A few more motets were composed in 1950 and 1951, including the fine *Great Is the Lord* and the masterpiece *Gloria Deo per immensa saecula*. After 1951 the composition of church motets comes to an end, though the last five missae breves were written between 1953 and 1963. This third period saw also the production of some thirty hymn anthems, a form which had not interested Willan very much previously but which was at that time in great demand and commercially profitable.

In general it could be said that Willan's final period of church music, save for some notable exceptions in the early 1950s, represents a regression of style and quality. The imagination and colour of the first period, and the purity and mysticism of the second, largely fade, to be replaced with a rather academic and very traditional type of writing, solid in craftsmanship and always respectable, but rarely of unusual interest.

SOME FINAL REFLECTIONS

Willan on composing
'I regard myself as a musician who rather likes to compose – and has a good time doing it.' So Willan described himself in 1946 at the time of the radio première of *Deirdre*. It is a typical English understatement. An examination of his enormous output reveals that, far from just dabbling, he was, to use István Anhalt's apt phrase, 'a dynamo of productivity.' He thrived on work.

He wrote quickly. His very facility carried its own dangers; in his later years, he did not always worry as much as he should have about the intrinsic value or originality of the musical ideas with which he was working, or about repeating himself.

He could spend much time in revision: 'A long time ago I wrote a madrigal in ten minutes and having written it, I examined it carefully and spent about three or four hours revising it ... When people heard it they liked it because it was so spontaneous! ... As a rule the idea comes quickly ... and then you make notes on it – just jot notes down – and then you may spend hours revising it, as I have often done' (Parker tapes).

Once he had completed a composition, he said, he had little further interest in it; it had to sink or swim on its own merit: 'I'm not a publicity hound at all, and I never pushed anything: if they wanted to play them, well that was that; but if they didn't I never bothered about their being done.' No composer could be totally uninterested in the fate of his creations. Nevertheless Willan (unlike some of his less reticent and more blatantly ambitious colleagues) was too much of a gentleman to pester conductors and hound performers to play his music.

Willan on plagiarism

A number of critics profess to hear echoes of Franck, Tschaikowsky, Rachmaninoff, Wagner, Strauss, Elgar, and others in Willan's secular music. They seem on occasion to come close to accusing him of plagiarism. Willan had very definite views on the subject, and loved to quote George Macdonald's little verse:

Under the sun
  There's nothing new;
Poem or pun
Under the sun
Said Solomon,
  And he said true.
Under the sun
  There's nothing new.

In a radio talk ('Matters Musical' no. 5) on the matter of plagiarism, Willan said: 'We must be careful to distinguish between piracy and the logical extension of ideas.' He added:

Difficulties begin when we have to determine whether two melodic phrases or two harmonic progressions written by two composers are conscious or unconscious plagiarism. I am disposed to think that 90 per cent of them belong to the unconscious class – in fact I think that it is remarkable that there is so little. In a modern dictionary we can find thousands of words all made up of various combinations of twenty-six letters. Music, with its thousands of compositions, is all made up of twelve sounds repeated at various pitches ... From the very beginnings of art there have been resemblances without end, chiefly because music – like ladies' hats and motorcars – has always been a slave to fashion and style.

It is apparent he did not consider 'unconscious' plagiarism a serious sin and viewed similarities between works written in the same style as quite normal.

He was particularly contemptuous of those persons who delight in searching for such things: 'Should a composer use three or four notes which remind a hearer of something else, he is immediately pounced upon and denounced as a plagiarist; and the person who does the denouncing thinks that he has shown a somewhat remarkable intelligence and a very erudite knowledge of music' (ibid). He added: 'May I suggest to my hearers that, when they are next struck by similarities, they examine both sides very carefully from the angle of melody, harmony and rhythm before passing judgement, for unless these three are involved, the accusation of plagiarism is – in the judgment of a musician – very likely to fall to the ground.'

Willan and modern music
Although Willan did not concern himself with popular music, he could imitate the style for fun (eg his songs and piano pieces published under the nom de plume Raymond Clare) or for a definite purpose (eg the *University Football Song* and *Lambeth Walk* sequences in *Transit through Fire*). Concerning jazz, he once said, 'I do recognize jazz, and when played by a good jazz orchestra – and not too loudly – I can hear a definite charm of rhythm and colour, even if the subject matter is somewhat banal' ('Matters Musical' no. 1).

Willan did not object to his students using a more contemporary idiom than his own, and said even that twelve-tone music is fine if it is the natural idiom for the composer using it. As he grew older, Willan felt himself more and more alienated from what he called 'modern' music: 'I don't like the way tradition is being swept aside. Real growth is a matter of evolution. Now we tend to tear down what already exists, rather than building upon it. The result is the disappearance of beautiful things ... The trend of the day seems to be contentment with that which is not beautiful' (*Globe and Mail Magazine* 24 December 1966).

Willan's four musical periods
If Willan's sacred music can be divided into three periods, for his output as a whole a division into four periods is more appropriate. The first period would still end ca 1920 and would include the majority of Willan's art-songs; his most significant chamber works; his early organ masterpieces; his finest piano work, *Variations and Epilogue*; a number of partsongs; full settings of the Anglican liturgy and anthems with organ accompaniment; and some works for choir and orchestra, including the dramatic cantata, *Cleopatra*.

The second period, from 1921 to ca 1935, sees a shift away from accompanied vocal music to unaccompanied, and the development of the motet style in his sacred choral works (motets, missae breves, and plain-song canticles with faux-bourdon). Yet it would be a mistake to conclude that this was an exclusively 'church' period, since it was also the time he wrote most of his incidental scores for plays, as well as all his ballad operas. Likewise the production of secular art-songs and partsongs continued, though at a slower pace. The composition of organ music was reduced to a trickle, however.

The première in 1936 of *Symphony No. 1* marks the beginning of his third period, running till 1948 or 1949. During these years Willan wrote his major symphonic and dramatic works: the two symphonies, the two operas, and the piano concerto. Yet, this is not an exclusively secular period, since all through it Willan was continuing to write his motet-style church music. In addition there were more songs, partsongs, and incidental scores (eg *Brébeuf*). However, there was no organ music, except for one unpublished piece in 1948, and no chamber or piano music of importance.

The fourth and last period begins ca 1950, with his retirement as professor of music. No large-scale works appear, with the possible exceptions of *Coronation Suite* for choir and orchestra and *Passacaglia and Fugue No. 2* for organ. However it was a time of immense productivity in smaller forms. Organ pieces and anthems with organ accompaniment return to favour, and in large quantities. It was also the period of the hymn anthems and other ecclesiastical *gebrauchmusik*. There were, in addition, some orchestral marches, but no major symphonic works. Songs, chamber music, and piano music were categories largely ignored, though there were a few partsongs. Stylistically the music of this fourth period looks backward, quite often to the first period. One finds Willan tending to repeat himself as he strives to keep up with the requests of anxious publishers. However, this last period did produce a few works which can stand with his best.

Conclusion

In a speech to the Canadian Club in Toronto in 1958, Willan put forth his musical credo:

The process of creation, in its largest sense, is at once a reduction and an enlargement. Disorder, cacaphony, chaos, if you like, must be reduced, tempered, by the discipline of form into order, in my case, musical order. Along with the reduction of the range and variety of sounds available to the composer is necessary the awareness of beauty, the wonder and awesome grandeur of what God Himself hath wrought. This awareness of beauty, the sudden recognition that one has somehow enlarged, that one's spirit has soared, is perhaps what the word inspiration attempts to convey. For more than three quarters of a century I have lived and written by the precept that one must know and abide by the rules of whatever one is doing. Judicious breakage is allowable but only when buttressed by reason. I believe, I think I may say, with passion, in the necessity for orderliness in music, for what musicians call form. Without order, anarchy erupts. Without form, one's ears are assaulted with hideous, meaningless blaring. What is there in atonal confusion to lift the heart with thankfulness, with vigour, with nobility of purpose, and with love? If there are other sentiments worth arousing, I confess they have escaped me.

Unfortunately Willan implied that atonal music was without form (a statement both inaccurate and likely to raise the hackles of some of his younger colleagues). Yet, that aside, this statement expressed Willan's outlook and approach quite elegantly.

Most of the characteristics of his musical style were formed at the end of the nineteenth century. He was content with this situation. He was one of the last Romantics, and not only in his music. His mysticism had its roots in the Romantics' fond yearning for the Middle Ages.

His music was deliberately conservative, though his avant-garde detractors might have used stronger adjectives such as reactionary. Yet, as late as 1946, he said: 'One always writes as a contemporary. If one has anything to say in music, it will be written out of his day – in my case, today, the present time.' He went on to add, 'It will be written out of the way you feel musically, in your environment' (CBC press release, 6 April 1946). Apparently he was not conscious of any discrepancy between his musical environment and his musical feelings.

Willan's approach evoked a warm response. His large orchestral works were always popular with the audience, the composer almost invariably receiving an ovation after performances of them. It is apparent that the *people* liked his music. They could immediately identify with it, doubtless in part because of its tunefulness. Willan himself was a great lover of 'tune' and possessed a considerable melodic gift. He once said, 'Is it not true that if we are questioned about a sonata, or a symphony, or in fact a work of any dimension, we immediately try to identify it by a tune? – at least I do! ... And I am sufficiently old-fashioned to admit unblushingly that where there is absence of tune, I very soon get hopelessly bored.'

Another reason for the popular appeal of Willan's instrumental music was its readily apparent warmth and humanity. That this was intended is again borne out by his own words: 'The scientific or mathematical approach [to music] bores me to sobs – it is like poring over a skeleton and ignoring all the life and warmth of human existence.' All this was clear to John Beckwith when he wrote, 'Willan's style is often called "academic": the term would hardly apply to these instrumental pieces or to the operas, where the unbridled expressiveness often reaches orgiastic proportions' (*Arts in Canada* 1958, 4). Even Henry Cowell, who considered Willan's work 'conventional,' admitted that 'its conventionality consists not in dryness ... [but] in its rather exaggerated, late 19th-century effusiveness' (*Musical Quarterly* 40, Jan 1954, 59).

Willan had the misfortune (for a person of his naturally conservative leanings) to live during a major revolution in music. He did not jump on the bandwagon and chose to continue in his own path. For this he was of course condemned by the progressives. Obviously his music was not representative of its time in his later years, but then neither was that of Bach or Rachmaninoff. Bach is, of course, a law unto himself; Rachmaninoff might be a better parallel here, for, however much the pundits might sniff, Rachmaninoff's music is good music – well written and expressive – which has held its place in the repertoire quite firmly. Willan's music is good music too, also well written and expressive.

No one now, when enjoying one of the 1770 *Overtures* by William Boyce, worries that the music was written forty or fifty years after similar stylistic developments elsewhere. Likewise it is unlikely that anyone listening to Willan's music a century from now is going to be concerned with its degree of modernity at the time of its composition. Fashions come and go – we are now rediscovering the recently out-of-fashion minor Romantics such as Hummel and Spohr and the 'conservatives' of their time such as Rheinberger and Reinecke. Some of Willan's sacred music, like that of S.S. Wesley a century before, will probably be assured a permanent place in the repertoire of English-speaking churches, and it is unlikely that all his organ music will be forgotten. If his orchestral and dramatic music fades from view it would be unfortunate, but if it does, its eclipse, I am convinced, will be temporary, for good music is usually rediscovered.

A note on the musical examples

This section contains the musical examples referred to by number in the text. I acknowledge with thanks the permissions granted by the publishers listed below to quote brief examples from works by Willan for which they hold copyright (all rights reserved). My thanks also to Michael H. Willan, executor of Willan's estate, for his kind permission to reproduce examples from Willan's works not mentioned in this list. These examples include the quotations from works which remain in manuscript as well as from those, formerly published, with copyrights that have reverted to the estate.

Associated Music Publishers, Inc
Royce Hall Suite (67–71)
Belwin-Mills (H.W. Gray division)
Hail, Gladdening Light (403), *In the Name of God* (430, 431), *Magnificat and Nunc dimittis in D* (402), *Missa brevis No. 10* (371), *Missa brevis No. 12* (373–76), *Mystery of Bethlehem* (132–7), *O Sacred Feast* (405), *Very God, Good Shepherd* (404)
Berandol Music Ltd
A Christmas Lullaby (456), *Coronation Suite* (151–8), *Deirdre* (105–20), *Epithalame* (275), *Five Pieces for Organ* (272–4), *Make We Merry* (455), *Marche solenelle (Coronation March)* (62–5), *Marching Tune* (66), *Missa brevis No. 14* (377, 378), *Overture to an Unwritten Comedy* (72–6), *Piano Concerto in C minor* (35–56), *Poem* (77–9), *Sonata No. 1 in E Minor* (200–12), *Symphony No. 1 in D Minor* (1–11, 471, 472), *Symphony No. 2 in C Minor* (12–37, 469), *Three Songs to Music* (345–7), *Welcome Yule* (455)
Bosworth and Co Ltd
Sonata No. 2 in E Major (213–16)
C.F. Peters Corporation
Andante, Fugue and Chorale (280), *Missa de Sancto Albano* (361), *Passacaglia and*

Fugue No. 2 (276, 277, 279), *Ten Hymn Preludes*, Sets I, II, and III (261–8), *Ye Shall Know That the Lord Will Come* (442–4)
C.F. Peters Corporation, sole agents for Hinrichsen Edition Ltd, London
Postlude in E Minor (269, 270)
Carl Fischer, Inc
  Behold, the Tabernacle of God (413, 414), *Hodie, Christus natus est* (415, 416), *Missa brevis No. 1* (362), *Missa brevis No. 4* (364–8), *Missa brevis No. 5* (369), *O King, to Whom All Things* (412)
Concordia Publishing House
  Chorale Prelude on 'Vulpius' (250), *Christ Our Passover* (419), *I Will Lay Me Down in Peace* (418), *Like as a Hart* (434), *Missa brevis in G* (385), *Rejoice, O Jerusalem* (445)
Frederick Harris Music Co Ltd
  An Apostrophe to the Heavenly Host (457–9), *Chester Mysteries* (162, 163), *Christ Hath a Garden* (433), *Coronation Te Deum* (144–6), *England, My England* (126–8), *Healey Willan Song Album* (311, 313–24), *Mass of St Theresa* (384), *Le Navire de Bayonne* (344), *Regina coeli* (449), *Sainte Marguerite* (343), *Sigh No More, Ladies* (338), *Sing Alleluia forth* (432), *Three Songs of Devotion* (460), *To Violets* (340, 341), *Tyrle, Tyrlow* (450, 451)
G. Schirmer, Inc
  Introduction, Passacaglia and Fugue (233, 236–41)
G.V. Thompson, Ltd
  A Soft Light (454, 475), *Blessed Art Thou* (435–7), *Come Shepherd Swains* (327), *Fain Would I Change* (332), *Five Plainsong Preludes* (251–6), *Gently Touch* (330), *In the Heavenly Kingdom* (446, 447), *Missa brevis No. 3* (363), *Missa brevis No. 7* (370), *The Trumpet Call* (147), *Weep You No More* (334, 335), *What Is This Lovely Fragrance?* (453), *Who Is She That Ascendeth* (417)
Leslie Music Supply
  Gloria Deo per immensa saecula (420–3)
Oxford University Press, London
  Angel Spirits of Sleep (333), *Eternity* (339, 463), *Missa de Sancta Maria Magdalena* (360)
Oxford University Press, New York
  Here Are We in Bethlehem (452), *I Beheld Her* (410), *Lo, in the Time Appointed* (411), *Magnificat on Tone VII* (386), *O King All Glorious* (409), *Preserve Us, O Lord* (407, 408)
Stainer and Bell Ltd (also Galaxy Music Corporation)
  The Bluebird (Stanford) (462, 474), *Songs of the Fleet* (Stanford) (464, 465)
Waterloo Music Co Ltd
  To Blossoms (297), *To Electra* (296), *The Tourney* (299, 300)

10

11

Lento

Allegro

15

extension of **x**

(inversion)

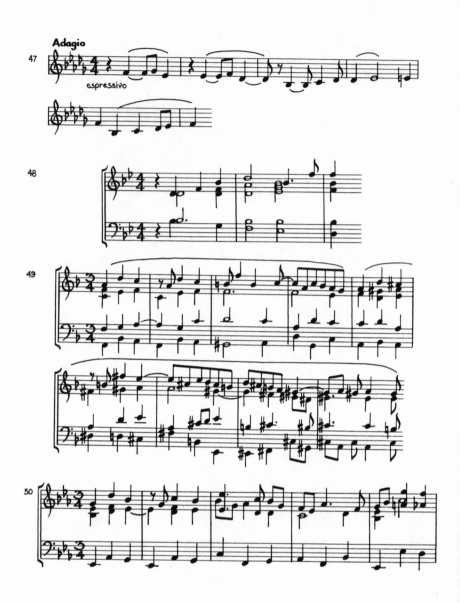

You— maid-ens, now pi-ty the— sor-row-ful moan I make.

Molto maestoso

80

81

82

83
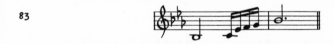

84

Con—quer-or___ of the peo-pled world.___ Rul—er of

When bat-tle's done and the reek——ing plain___

land in East and West. Ev'n E————gypt

crim-sons the sky from East to West.———— O E——gypt

89

Largo e mesto

90 Now all is fin-ished, all is done; my world is dead. And

he whose glo———ry shamed the sun Lies shamed in—stead.

Lento

91

Adagio

92

S
A

Two suns have gone a-way to sleep; ———— they bid the

T
B

they bid the

last— long night pre-pare their py—ra—mid.

S
A

T
B

93

OR

Marziale

But we are march-ing march-ing and we who are march-ing to-day

Lento

117

118

Lento e lugubre

119

Bassoon

120

In the song___ on your bug-les blown, Eng-land.

What have I done for you,___ Eng—land, my Eng—land?

Andante
pp
133

molto legato

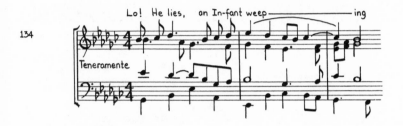

134

Lo! He lies, an In-fant weep————ing

Teneramente

135

Shep-herds in the field a—bid—ing, watch—ing o'er your flocks by night

S
A

Oboe

Bass

Andante maestoso

136 From___ the East there came Sa—ges to Beth-le-hem

Andante

137 This is He__ Whom seers of old time chanted of__ with one_____ ac-cord

138 **Allegretto con espressione**

Allegro

139

140

(Sopranos & tenors)

f Giv — er of glow —————— ing light.

(Altos & basses)

141

No more thy clouds——— of

hours give up their sweets_____ to meet thee

142

148

poco largamente   a tempo

149

150

Con spirito

151

Maestoso

152

Make up full con-sort of th'An—gel—————ic sym-phon-y

Trumpet _pp_

(Spir-it of Eng——land, go be-fore us.)

Trumpets

Grace be with you, mer — cy and peace

Andante maestoso

162

Largo e nobilmente

163

Andante

164

165

166

167

168

(Flute)

(Voice)

my heart,   my heart   cri————eth O

Lord   Zeus   on   high.

169

Moderato

Largo

"Love Theme" with variants

172

180

181

Lento

182

183

184

I am black but I am come-ly—

Largo e pesante

185

Allegro moderato ed energico

sul G

sul D

186

Allegro molto

mf

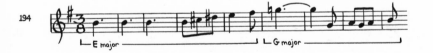

E major ——————————— G major ———————————

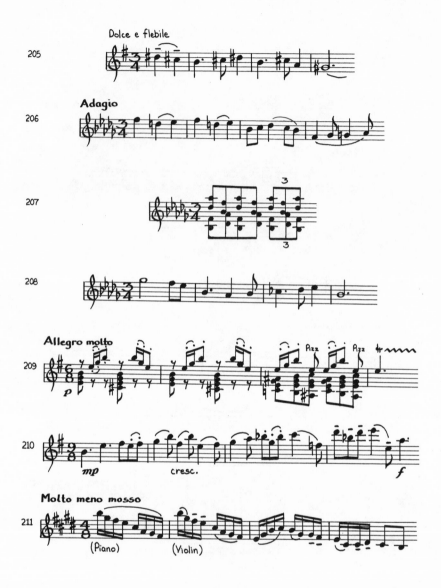

226

227

228

229

Largo

232

233

Lento

234

Maestoso

235

Piano

Adagio

236

Organ

ped.

Andante moderato

237

245

Allegretto grazioso

246

247

248

(Rise___ up my love___)

Molto maestoso

ped.

senza misura

Chri—ste Re— demp——tor— om—ni——um

ped.

ped.

254

Andante mistico

255

A — ve _____ ma — ris _____ stel-la

ped.

Molto maestoso e marcato

256

257

Ev-er the faith en-dures, Eng-land, my Eng-land.

Placido

Con spirito

ped.

Molto sostenuto e teneramente

268

Moderato e con spirito

269

270

271

Solenne

Teneramente

292

Lento

293

Love, see thy lo-ver hum-bled at thy feet. Not in ser-vil-it—y but hom-age sweet.

294

cut—lass and lance trum———pets swell

Lento

I dare not ask— a kiss

Not— in my life, but

Allegro con molto spirito

Ralph would fight in E-dith's sight, for Ralph was E-dith's lo—ver

Andante con espressione

306

mp Love me not, dear—est, for___ the smile

Allegro feroce

307

Molto moderato

308

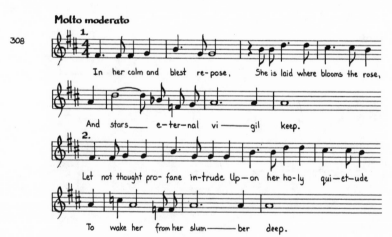

1.

In her calm and blest re-pose, She is laid where blooms the rose,

And stars___ e-ter-nal vi———gil keep.

2.

Let not thought pro-fane in-trude Up—on her ho-ly qui-et-ude

To wake her from her slum———ber deep.

Speak low, soft-ly whis-per, hush! Light-ly tread lest you should crush

The pe—tals of her flower of sleep.

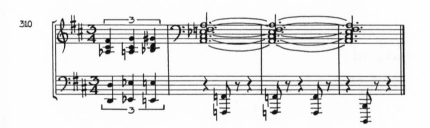

Andante mistico

311

I wear___ a sham-rock in my heart,___ Three in one

312

To feel the fog___ in my throat, The mist___ in my face

Lento lugubre

313   314

Nobilmente

315

Since thou, O fond—est and tru-est, Hast lov'd me best___ and long-est___

Lento

316

317
318

Ev—er the faith en-dures

Ah, gold—en youths! who

319

Your sun-lit sails flash for a mo-ment's space____

mistico

arpeggiando

320

I would wed you, dear, with-out gold____ or gems, or cour-ted Kine,

332

333

An—gel spir-its of sleep,   White—robed with sil—ver hair

334

Weep_ you no_   more_

335

Heav'n——ly   eyes_____

soft——ly   now,__   soft——ly   his__   sleep

Lento This is thy hour O Soul, thy free flight in-to the world-less

(night)_____ , sleep_____ , death__

(♪=192) Sigh no more, la——dies, Sigh no more, Men were de-ceiv-ers ev-er

Sigh no more, la–dies, Sigh no more, Men were de-ceiv— ers ev-er

sea____ of vast_____ E—— ter— ni—ty

Allegro

344

345

Hon-our to you who sit.

346

Near to the well of wit,___ and drink your fill of it!

347

Let's now take our time,   While we're in our prime.

Let's now take our time,   While we're in our

Andante

348

349

Allegro maestoso

350

Andante

351

Who for us men and for our sal—va—tion came down from heaven.

Quasi adagio

352

357

358

359

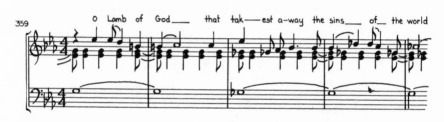

360

367

Bles —sed is— He

368

Ho —— san-na in the high ———— est

369

Ky—ri—e ———————— e—le———i—son ——————

Ky—ri—e

Ky—ri—e

Ky—ri—e—

370

West-ron winde when will thou blow? The small rain down doth rayne.

Oh! if my love were in my arms, Or I in my bed a——gayne

Ky—ri—e e-le——i—son

Chris-te e-le———i—son

Ho ———————— ly—

O Lamb of God that ta——kest a—way

385   Ho—ly,   Ho———ly,   Ho—ly,   Lord God___   of   Sa—ba—oth

Magnificat

386

My soul doth mag-ni-fy the Lord: and my spirit hath rejoiced in God my sav-iour

For he hath re-gard-ed: the   lowliness   of   his hand-maid-en

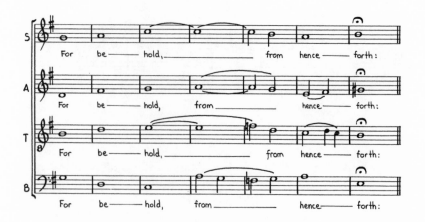

For be — hold, _____ from hence — forth:
For be — hold, from _____ hence — forth:
For be — hold, _____ from hence — forth:
For be — hold, from _____ hence — forth:

all gen-er-a — tions shall call__ me bless _____ ed
all__ gen — er — a — tions shall call _____ me bless — ed
all gen-er-a — tions shall__ call me bless — ed
all gen-er — a — tions shall call me__ bless _____ ed

As it was in the be—gin—ning

As it was in the be-gin—ning,——— is now

me,—— and Ho———ly——y   Ho——y   ly——y

Lord, now let-test Thou thy ser—vant de—part in peace

392

393

394

395

We praise Thee ____ O God ____ we ack—

396

My soul doth mag—ni—fy the Lord, and my

397

Lord,__ now let—test Thou thy ser—vant de—

of the High——est   for____ thou shalt go__

398

To give light to them that sit in dark—ness and in the sha——dow of death.

399

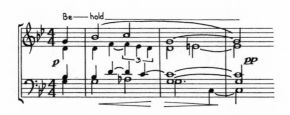

414

415

Allegro

416

Glo—ri—a in ex—cel———sis De—o

428 Lift up your eyes, and look up-on the fields; for they are white ev-en un-to har-vest

429 A——men, A——men A——men.

430 In the Name of our God

431 solo

432

433 Christ hath a gar-den walled a—round, A Pa-ra-dise of fruit—ful ground

Like as the hart de——sir—eth the wa-ter-brooks

434

Ev——er the faith en-dures, Eng—land, my Eng—land

Maestoso

435

441 And all her streets shall say,___ Al___le—lu—ia

The peo——ple that walk——eth in dark————ness have

442 seen a great light.

443

444 Christ is born, go forth to meet him

445 recit. senza misura

Re—joice____ O Je—ru—sa—lem be—hold___ thy King com-eth

446

447

In— the heav'n—ly king—dom— the souls of the saint

448

sf   *sf*   *sf*   *sf*

449

le—ta——re

f   *3*   roll. molto e dim.

3   *pp*

A

le—ta——re

450

Tyr—le, tur—low, tyr—le tyr—low

469

470

471

472

coll 8ve

a — ni—mae in ma———nu De————i sunt

473

(Jus-tor-um an-i-mae)

474

ppp The lake lay blue be—low the hill

blue

(Gᵇ major)   (quasi niente)   II⁷

475

pp   estinto

(Eᵇ major)   II⁴₃

A note on sources

Because this is the first book to be written about Willan and his complete works, a problem arises when one comes to providing a bibliography of any significance. Admittedly there are many short newspaper and magazine articles, and brief entries in numerous reference works (most listed in *HWC*, 147–51, along with additional items noted in the 1982 supplement to *HWC*), but the list of major contributions to the literature on Willan is rather short.

Probably the most important biographical article is that by Godfrey Ridout in *CMJ* (3, no 3, 1959, 4–14). Other contributions of substance include entries in several reference works:

Bradley, Ian, in *Twentieth Century Canadian Composers* Agincourt, Ont, 1977, 1–15
Bryant, Giles, in *Contemporary Canadian Composers* Toronto 1975, 238–42
– in *Encyclopedia of Music in Canada* Toronto 1981, 999–1002
– in *The New Grove Dictionary* London 1980, vol 20, 428–30
McCready, Louise, in *Famous Musicians* Toronto 1957, 103–34
Proctor, George, in *Canadian Music of the Twentieth Century* Toronto 1980 (many references)

Several theses deal at length with Willan's choral and organ works:

Campbell-Yukl, Joylin 'Healey Willan: The Independent Organ Works' PhD thesis, University of Missouri, 1976
Hamelin, Keith 'Healey Willan: His Use of Plainsong' master's thesis, University of Toronto, 1979
Lehl, Allan 'The Choral Style of Healey Willan' master's essay, Eastman School of Music, University of Rochester, 1957

Marwick, William 'The Sacred Choral Music of Healey Willan' EdD thesis, Michigan State University, 1970

Massingham, Robert 'The Organ Works of Healey Willan' MM thesis, North Texas State University, 1967

Renwick, William 'The Contrapuntal Style of Healey Willan' MMus thesis, University of British Columbia, 1982

Telschow, Frederick 'The Sacred Music of Healey Willan' DMA thesis, Eastman School of Music, University of Rochester, 1970

Wagner, Edward 'Healey Willan at St Mary Magdalene's' MDiv essay, Yale Institute of Sacred Music, Yale Divinity School, 1979

Wagner, Jacob 'Healey Willan, His Life and Organ Literature' MSM thesis, Union Theological Seminary, New York, 1957

Various biographical materials are located at the National Library of Canada (Music Division) in Ottawa, in particular:

tapes and transcriptions of interviews with Willan conducted by Lister Sinclair, Rev Gilbert Parker, Horace Lapp, Godfrey Ridout, and Alec Wyton and of various Willan tributes broadcast over the CBC, and a tape of George Maybee's interview of Norah Michener regarding Willan;

many dozens of personal letters to and from Willan, some dating back to 1901;

brief unpublished essays about Willan collected at the time of his eightieth birthday (1960) from some of his colleagues and friends, including those by D. Baker, H. Ball, R. Blais, W. Bowles, J. Bradley, Father Brain, J. Cook, J. Coulter, F. Ferguson, R. Godden, A. Gough, E. Humphreys, T. Hyland, E. MacMillan, W. MacNutt, B. McCool, W. McKie, C. Peaker, and K. Scott;

other miscellaneous materials (newspaper reports, etc), including Willan's scrap-book.

Special mention should be made of the special spring (1979) issue – a Healey Willan booklet written and compiled by Margaret Drynan – of the Royal Canadian College of Organists' *Quarterly*.

Index

Major works by Willan are listed under 'Willan, Healey: MUSIC.' His small pieces can be located in discussions of the appropriate genres (eg anthems, canticle settings, chorale preludes), which are indexed under the same entry.

Healey Willan
LIFE AND MUSIC

F.R.C. CLARKE

In the summer of 1913 Healey Willan, a thirty-three-year-old organist-choirmaster with a wife and three sons to support, left England for Toronto. Though he had already gained considerable attention as a composer of secular and sacred works, the Church of England, which was for him a lifelong musical and spiritual home, could not provide an adequate income to support a growing family. He reluctantly accepted the post of head of the theory department at the Toronto Conservatory of Music.

Toronto seemed unpromising: 'Yonge Street then was about as interesting as an English village street,' he later recalled. 'It seemed like the last place in the world for the development of music.' But for more than half a century Willan was to play a major role in the development of music in Toronto and in Canada as a whole. In his teaching, at the conservatory and later at the University of Toronto, and in his work as organist-choirmaster at St Paul's, Bloor Street, and then for 47 years at his beloved St Mary Magdalene's, he inspired several generations of young singers, musicians, and composers. Opinions vary as to his abilities as a teacher, but the impact of his colourful and warm personality is legendary.

In England and in Canada he composed some 800 works. Inspired by his love of plainchant and Tudor music, he produced a vast range of liturgical and non-liturgical sacred music. His tastes were formed, as he readily admitted, by the English choir school and concert hall, and he owed much to Elgar, Stanford, and Parry – as well as to Wagner, Richard Strauss, Brahms, and Tschaikowsky. Yet he developed his own distinctive style in his operas, symphonies, and songs, and in his organ, piano, chamber, and band music.

Dr Clarke considers the entire range of Willan's compositions, analysing in detail his major works and bringing to light the unexpected